CARRY THAT WEIGHT

A Secret History of the Beatles

Also by Geoffrey Giuliano

Lennon in America

Dark Horse: The Life and Art of George Harrison

The Lost Beatles Interviews

The Lost Lennon Interviews

The Illustrated John Lennon

The Illustrated George Harrison

Not Fade Away: The Rolling Stones Collection

Blackbird: The Unauthorized Biography of Paul McCartney

The Beatles: A Celebration

John Lennon: My Brother
(with Julia Baird)

The Beatles Album: 30 Years of Music and Memorabilia

Glass Onion: The Beatles in Their Own Words
(with Vrnda Devi)

Behind Blue Eyes: The Life of Pete Townshend

Rod Stewart: Vagabond Heart, The Unauthorized Biography

The Illustrated Paul McCartney

The Illustrated Elvis Presley

The Illustrated Jimi Hendrix

The Illustrated Eric Clapton

Things We Said Today: Conversations with the Beatles
(with Vrnda Devi)

Two of Us: John Lennon and Paul McCartney
Behind the Myth

Gloria: The Autobiography of Gloria Hunniford

Paint It Black: The Murder of Brian Jones

GEOFFREY GIULIANO

CARRY THAT WEIGHT

A Secret History of the Beatles

SIDGWICK & JACKSON

First published 2003 by Sidgwick & Jackson
an imprint of Pan Macmillan Ltd
Pan Macmillan, 20 New Wharf Road, London NI 9RR
Basingstoke and Oxford
Associated companies throughout the world
www.panmacmillan.com

ISBN 0 283 07360 8 (hb)
0 283 07361 6 (tpb)

1 3 5 7 9 8 6 4 2

A CIP catalogue record for this book is available from the British Library.

Typeset by SetSystems Ltd, Saffron Walden, Essex
Printed and bound in Great Britain by
Mackays of Chatham plc, Chatham, Kent

"God bless the mad ones, the ones who are mad to live, mad to talk, mad to be saved, desirous of everything at the same time, the ones who never yawn or say a commonplace thing, but burn, burn, burn."

Jack Kerouac

This book is dedicated to my wife Vrnda Devi for thirty-two years of unceasing love, devotion, and friendship well above and beyond the call. I love you. To my spiritual master His Divine Grace A. C. Bhaktivedanta Swami Prabhupada whose gentle, insightful teachings pilot my life and inspire my eternal hopes and dreams. To Patrick Hayes for his profound friendship out of the blue. To Peter Max, the greatest living artist on earth and a true visionary. To the Moody Blues for their awe-inspiring music. That they should soon be inducted into the Rock'n'Roll Hall of Fame is undeniable. To everyone working together as one to someday see a drugless, vegetarian world. To my loving daughter Avalon, for the many months of great personal self-sacrifice she spent in the realization of this book. To my talented young friend Erek, thank you. Also Deborah Lynn Black, my accomplished colleague and friend of twenty years. Thank you for your loyalty, patience and creativity. To my agent and mate Robert Smith, a pop publishing pundit! Finally to Sriman George Harrison for his unflinching dedication to his unique lifelong vision of truth and his gentle, compassionate heart for the suffering humanity he saw around him. That he is now in a far better, more graceful place is beyond doubt to anyone who knew and loved him. Hare Om Tat Sat.

Contents

INTRODUCTION

Rishikesh Rising

There is a rare film of a long-ago afternoon in February 1968 preserved by an Italian television crew who, along with the rest of the world's media, descended on the Maharishi Mahesh Yogi's enclave in Rishikesh for a glimpse of the Beatles as aspiring mystics. Even today it is an enticing image. Here are John, Paul, George, Ringo, Mike Love, Donovan, Mia Farrow with her sister Prudence and brother Johnny, and the Beatle wives singing sweetly to the jangling of acoustic guitars, "She'll Be Coming Round The Mountain", "When The Saints Go Marching In" – fronted by George Harrison and Mia Farrow – "You Are My Sunshine", "Jingle Bells", as well as a ragged rendition of the Hare Krishna mantra.

The Maharishi urged everyone, "Fathom the infinity, dive into the Ganges. Fathom the infinity!"

To which George replied, "Hey, I guess we don't merely just exist after all!"

I played it back in my head in the early summer of 2000 as I struggled along in the stifling midday sun past the sparkling Ganges, past the thatched huts of a small group of ash-covered, dope-smoking *babas*, and finally the monsoon-carved, boulder-strewn left turn that took me to the Maharishi's padlocked front door.

Over the years I've spent a lot of time in Rishikesh, first drawn there in the early 1990s by images I saw as a kid flickering across my family's old black and white TV, of George, John and their friends walking peacefully along brick walkways lined with painted stones, deep inside the Maharishi's secret Shangri-la. Driving along the road from Hardwar (the nearest train stop from Delhi) I might have missed it, but even without being told I *knew* somehow that this was the place. Although the area has been built up over succeeding decades, Rishikesh is still a quaint village highlighted by an astounding black-topped suspension bridge, Ram Jhula, that connects the seeker to the opposite side of the Ganges. It is only just wide enough for two or three people to walk across shoulder to shoulder. After a sharp right turn, you are on the home stretch to Maharishi Central, *circa* 1968, the place where the Beatles were inspired to write some of their most compelling and spiritual music. Look hard enough and you will find photos of all of the Beatles, arriving as I did, on that gently swaying bridge.

If nothing else, the wide, swirling Ganges and the cloud-covered blue mountain range are enough to touch the hardest hearts. In this still magical valley there are dozens of tiny temples from which, by four thirty in the morning, you can hear the echoes of blowing conches, the chanting of the Hindu faithful, smell the pungent aroma of *doop* (north Indian hand-rolled incense) and smouldering cow-dung fires. Rishikesh overwhelms the senses and, within moments of arrival, transmits an immediate peace. After a few days the restless mind reads that as boredom but it soon turns into something deeper, richer and much harder to define.

Almost as soon as the Beatles had left, in the late spring of 1968, the Maharishi ordered the heavy iron front gates locked. No one, except local caretakers, some Indian followers and those foreigners bearing a signed letter from the master, was allowed entrance.

As I fell into none of these categories on my first trip to Rishikesh in 1998 I was turned away in brusque Hindi by the guard. Still, I was determined to see inside the place in hopes it might somehow have remained frozen in time. After some debate, my wife Vrnda and I decided that if we got up early enough, around five or six, we might sneak in.

Not expecting intruders at such an early hour the guard was sound asleep, his rifle tucked under his chin in the small booth at the outside perimeter. We walked silently through the ten-acre estate, with its own functioning post office, a large multi-storey dormitory and several dilapidated stone cottages, then decided to sneak out through a second gate at the opposite end of the property. There we met a good-natured wide-awake guard, who advised us politely not to go out that way as there were man-eating tigers, spitting cobras, and several wild elephants in the jungle beyond. Not to mention the three-hundred-foot drop directly into the rock-strewn river below.

Several months later I took my twenty-four-year-old son Devin, along with Sanjay Khemani, a family friend from Delhi, and a couple of mischievous Indian boys inside at dusk. This time there was no guard, no guns and even, no gate. Apparently the decades-long policy of guarding the birthplace of the Beatles' *White Album* and the spiritual revolution of the sixties had been abandoned.

As we ventured inside the basement of a large dormitory, an old man rushed over from one of the cottages and warned us to come out immediately: the tigers often came at dusk to feast on young deer in the ravaged rooms that had once hosted the élite of the pop world. We didn't have to be told twice. We made our way to the famous house where the master had met privately with the Beatles to discuss the inscrutable Truth he had offered the war-weary world of the late 1960s. It was not at all the "million-dollar staccato house" to which John Lennon had referred impishly in his quasi-musical litany to the Maharishi but, rather, a simple stone and wood house with several large windows that allowed us to see inside. There was a moderately large living room, a kitchen, and perhaps two bedrooms at the back. Legend has it there is a cave underneath the house where the Maharishi performed deep meditation. What struck me was how often writers like myself, without any first-hand knowledge, exaggerated John's description that this house was some kind of mansion with a helipad.

The Maharishi's elaborate chair – *asana* – with carved lion's feet stood empty on a veranda facing the compound, broken, weather-beaten, and perhaps not used since the Beatles had sat round him and strummed their acoustic guitars.

The next morning I came back alone, excited and almost able to feel the imprint of the Beatles and co. from some thirty years before. This time I met an old *sannyasi* (renunciant), His Holiness Ravindra

Damodara Swami, a god-brother of the Maharishi. He remembered well the Beatles' brief, but very public time there, and dancing with Mia Farrow during an impromptu acoustic concert by Donovan, the Beatles and Mike Love on the roof of the dining hall. He also recalled the day a helicopter took John Lennon and the guru for a ride over the Rishikesh valley. Intrigued, I questioned him further but he only smiled and offered me a tattered notebook he took from a trunk. It contained some seventy pages of scrawled Hindi which had evidently been a monk's diary.

"You write book about Beatles and Guru Maharaja then you must read this, my writing from that time. Everything is here. You please take, sir!" he ventured. He asked me to return it after I had read it. He then walked me down the curving lane to the front gates and the Ganges, pointing out along the way four pebble-covered stone domes, which he said the Maharishi had built for the Beatles to use for advanced meditation. Inside, the little buildings were about ten feet round at the base with a small area for resting, reading or eating, and a little wooden ladder to a platform on which they would presumably have sat in the lotus position to ascend into the lofty Godhead from which we all spring. They were never used.

In many ways the Maharishi's Rishikesh estate is a kind of cultural time-warp. The events that took place there so long ago have somehow imprinted themselves on its fibre. Pilgrimage is an ancient and important element of human history and my trek to Rishikesh informed and inspired this book. There, among the old stones, rusted signs, tigers and solitary *sadhus*, many of my views on the Beatles' real import in our cultural history were crystallized. In the exotic, perfumed Himalayan foothills I was surrounded by the ghosts of John Lennon and his cohorts and simultaneously exorcized any doubts I might have had about going forward with this potentially risky book.

Here, in a visionary flash, John and Paul were sitting on the stone steps of the former's bungalow composing the gentle 'I Will' while Ringo smoked a cigarette at their feet. As Donovan and George played love songs in the sunny grounds, the Beatle wives chatted in a circle with the children of the ashram staff.

Overwhelmed by the enduring magic that hovered among the

broken buildings I left my companions to stand alone on the edge of the mountain about which Donovan had once sung: "First there is a mountain, then there is no mountain, then there is," and made a kind of silent pact with the history before me. For everything that this place – and, indeed, the Beatles – had given me I would write without reservation or restraint. Two years later, I am in a cramped mobile home in a northern Florida campground and you are at the other end of this collection of words, which spilled out in my search for the Beatles' secret history. Whether or not I got it right now seems entirely up to you.

Geoffrey Giuliano (Jagannatha Dasa)
8 December 2002, Alachua, Florida

ONE

Will I Wait A Lonely Lifetime

Liverpool and Hamburg

1940–61

"After I stopped living at Penny Lane, I moved in with my auntie who lived in the suburbs in a nice semi-detached place with a small garden and doctors, lawyers and that ilk living around – not the poor slummy kind of image that was projected in all the Beatles stories. In the class system, it was about half a class higher than Paul, George and Ringo, who lived in government subsidized housing. We owned our house and had a garden. They didn't have anything like that."

John Lennon

"I was always very well-mannered and polite. My dad brought me up to always tip my cap to my elders and I used to do it until I was about fourteen and I didn't wear a cap any more."

Paul McCartney

After leaving Liverpool's Bluecoat Orphanage at fifteen, where he and his brothers resided since their father's death, Alfred Lennon drifted through a succession of dead-end jobs and ended up as a porter at a smart Merseyside hotel. It was around this time that he first became acquainted with the teenaged Julia Stanley. "It was a beautiful meeting," remembered Alfred. "A mate and I were sitting in Sefton Park where he was attempting to show me how to pick up girls. I'd recently bought myself a cigarette holder and a new bowler hat to boot, just to try and impress the ladies! There was this little girl we had our eye on.

As I walked past, she said, 'You look silly.' 'Well,' I replied, 'you look lovely,' and sat down beside her . . . Anyway, she said, if I really wanted to sit beside her, I would have to take that silly hat off. So I got up and flung it in the lake."

It was, as they say, the beginning of a momentous relationship, if not one that the clannish Stanley family would easily embrace. As Julia's sister Mimi Smith remembered, "He was really quite good looking, I'll admit. But we all knew he would be of no real use to anyone."

Young love, however, overruled common sense, and on 3 December 1938 the couple married at the Mount Pleasant register office in Liverpool. Alfred recalled the grand occasion: "One day, Julia said to me, 'Let's go get married.' I said, 'If we are, then we've got to do it properly.' She said, 'I bet you won't.' So damned if I didn't, just for a lark. It was all a big laugh, really, getting married."

They spent their honeymoon at the cinema and afterwards each went home to their respective families. The next day, Alfred packed up his few belongings and signed on for a three-month tour of duty aboard a passenger liner bound for the West Indies. Julia, somewhat constrained by the circumstances in which she now found herself, had little to do but wait for his return. Over the next year or so Alfred breezed back into her life from time to time, each time settling in for a week or two with the Stanleys. After one such visit, Julia discovered she was pregnant. Typically, Alfred Lennon was nowhere to be found. A few months later, she packed a suitcase and checked into the maternity hospital in Oxford Street. Just after seven o'clock the next morning, on 9 October 1940, John Winston Lennon was born, and placed under Julia's bed in case the hospital was struck by one of the bombs that regularly rained on Liverpool. Mimi rushed home through the war-torn streets to pass on the good news to the rest of the family. By this time, their widowed father had moved into a modest three-bedroom terrace house at 9 Newcastle Road in the Penny Lane district. It became John Lennon's first home.

Charlie Lennon, Alfred's youngest brother, remembered visiting young John there once while Alfred and Julia were still together. "I was on leave from the army when Alf happened to be ashore. He asked me if I'd mind coming up to Newcastle Road to help him with a bit of inside painting he wanted to do. Afterwards, we went out for a drink together and he confided his feelings about Julia and John. He told me he felt very guilty about being away so much, but that on several occasions the ship's captain had threatened to clap him in irons if he attempted to leave the ship. Every now and again he'd ring up Mimi from Southampton just to see how they were getting on. She'd tell him not to worry, as they were all okay and being well looked after by the Stanleys. Anyway, my second day at the house, little John and I took a stroll to the shops just for something to do. I bought him a red tin bus, and while I was chatting with the young lady behind the counter, John suddenly stormed outside with a huge toy Donald Duck tucked precariously under his arm. Well, after I finally collared the little bugger, we both went back inside and I ended up paying for both his presents! But it was all right by me, of course. He was a lovely little boy. All in all, I only ever saw John a few times as a lad. I know he certainly didn't visit our home. It was never 'Oh, I'm going to see my gran,' or anything like that. His mother absolutely never came near our side of the family, as she had been that hurt by Alf."

In early 1942, Julia received word that Alfred had left his ship in America, thus effectively closing the door on their relationship, and decided it was time to move on. Years later, though, John said he had the impression that Julia and Alfred enjoyed some happy times together: "She always used to tell me about them larking around and laughing. I think Alf must have been very popular with his shipmates as he used to send us concert programmes with his name down for singing things like 'Begin The Beguine'."

The next chapter in Julia's life began when she got together with John Albert Dykins. Some say they met at a dance, and others that they bumped into each other while Julia was working part-time in Penny Lane as a waitress. Whatever the truth, the couple fell in love, sparking great controversy in Julia's family.

John's maternal cousin, Dr Leila Harvey, explains, "From the little I have been able to gather, Mimi, and to a significantly lesser extent, Pop [Julia's father], had some very grave reservations regarding John

Dykins' basic suitability as a partner for Julia. The general consensus was that Bobby [Julia's nickname for her new lover] might have been from a lower class than they." Anyway, Julia was still legally married to Alfred. The couple threw caution to the winds and promptly moved into a tiny flat in Gateacre with five-year-old John. Mimi then took it upon herself to intervene in what she supposed were her nephew's best interests. One day she stormed in and demanded John be handed over to her: she felt Julia was no longer fit to look after him. It was her contention that in view of her sister's recent so-called "indiscretion" involving the out-of-wedlock birth of a daughter Victoria Elizabeth it would be wrong to keep John, especially when Mimi, she said, could offer him a well-ordered, financially secure environment. Dykins overruled Mimi's objections: he informed her that as John was Julia's child, she could keep him if she wanted. And, of course, she did. Julia Baird, John's younger half-sister,* insisted it broke Julia's heart to consider giving John up. After all, within five years, circumstance had robbed Julia of her husband and her infant daughter, Victoria, who had been put up for adoption via the Salvation Army, and was now threatening to snatch her son.

Soon, however, Mimi reappeared with a social worker, vowing not to leave the house without John. "They're not properly married," Mimi declared. "Therefore, John should come and live with me, at least until Julia gets her life together."

"I'm afraid that doesn't really make any difference as far as we're concerned, Mrs Smith," said the young woman. "The boy, after all, is her son."

Julia must have been thrilled to have the full force of the law on her side, but this was short-lived. A routine inspection of the flat revealed that John didn't have his own sleeping quarters: Julia tucked him in beside her at night. He would have to live elsewhere until a separate bedroom could be arranged. This time Julia had no choice but to agree, and so John was packed off to Mimi's.

As a child John was surrounded by a clan of five women he termed his "Amazon aunties". He called the experience his "early

* Julia went on to have two daughters with Dykins, Julia and Jacqui.

feminist education". "It was scary because there was nobody I could relate to," he remembered later. "Neither my aunties, friends, nor anybody could ever see what I did. It was very, very frightening, and many times the only contact I had was reading about people like Oscar Wilde, Dylan Thomas or Van Gogh in all those old books Mimi had. They talked about the suffering they went through because of their visions. They were tortured by society for trying to express themselves. All I ever saw was loneliness."

A precocious child with a talent for drawing and writing, by the age of seven he was penning his own little books. One of them, *Sport Speed and Illustrated* by J. W. Lennon, contained a witty collection of poems, caricatures and short stories that demonstrated his keen sense of the absurd. In 1986 Paul McCartney recalled the literary Lennon: "Inside the house he'd often be busy at the typewriter writing in his famous *In His Own Write* style. I never actually knew anyone who personally owned a typewriter before!"

At the age of twelve John left Dovedale Primary for Quarry Bank Grammar School, a mile down the road from Mimi's. He was soon restless and bored with his studies: "People like me are aware of their so-called genius even as a kid. Didn't they see I was cleverer than anyone else in the school and that the teachers were stupid too? I used to say to me auntie, 'You throw my bloody poetry out and you'll regret it when I'm famous,' and she threw it out! I never forgave her for not treating me like a genius when I was a child. Why didn't they train me? Why did they keep forcing me to be a cowboy like the rest of them? I was different, I was always different. Why didn't anyone notice me?"

By the mid-fifties, Julia's passion for American rock music had transmitted itself to John, and she purchased his first guitar, which he soon learned to play. In early 1957, at fifteen, he formed a skiffle group with his friend Pete Shotton. Initially called the Blackjacks, they later renamed the group the Quarry Men. It wasn't long before Lennon was cutting the image of the rabble-rousing Teddy Boy, decked out in drainpipe trousers, sparkly white jacket and slick, pompadour coiffure. Rock had become the outlet for the young man's inner demons and profound insecurity.

Lennon's half-sisters, Julia and her younger sister Jacqui, were never really aware that the young man who came to stay at weekends, amusing them with his cartoons, caricatures and sketches, was a budding superstar. But the family's rented home, at 1 Blomfield Road, just fifteen minutes from Mimi's, was John's musical training ground and his mother, who could not only sing and dance but also play the ukelele, the banjo and juggle, was his mentor. Julia Baird recalls her mother and John jiving about the house to Elvis's "Hound Dog", and that she and Jacqui were often chased out of the bath so that their brother could rehearse in the cramped, but acoustically superior, bathroom with his fledgling band.

The first time the girls saw their brother perform was at the 1956 Empire Day celebrations on Rosebury Street. "As we struggled through the rowdy crowd," says Baird, "John suddenly caught sight of us and summarily hauled us on to the makeshift stage [on an old lorry parked sideways along the middle of the street] so we could watch the fun reasonably unscathed."

"I remember the first guitar I ever saw," recalled John, in an interview conducted for *Rolling Stone* in 1970, "it belonged to a Liverpool guy in a cowboy suit with a western hat, and a big dobro. They were real cowboys all right, and they took it seriously. Don't forget, there had been cowboys long before there was ever rock'n'roll." Be that as it may, young John was a confirmed, die-hard, rock'n'roll convert, from the very first Elvis record Julia ever played. And it wasn't just the King who succeeded in quickening John and Julia's pulse either, but also the legendary Buddy Holly.

"'That'll Be The Day' was the very first tune I ever learned to play," said John. "Julia taught me on the banjo and patiently sat with me until I worked out all the chords. I remember her slowing down the record while I attempted to scribble out the lyrics. First hearing Buddy absolutely knocked me for a loop. To think, it was me own mother who was turning me into it all!"

According to Mimi, Lennon's first real interest in playing any sort of musical instrument came about differently: "As far as I know, the only musical encouragement John ever had was from a bus conductor on the way from Liverpool to my sister's in Scotland. He happened to have an old mouth-organ my husband had given him, and was trying to play it all the way there. Which, of course, drove all the other passengers mad, I'm sure. This conductor was apparently very taken with John, and when they finally arrived in Edinburgh, told him if he came down to the station the next morning he would give him a really good harmonica. Of course, John kept everyone up half the night going on about it. Early that next morning, John was down there first thing. I believe he must have been around ten at the time. That poor conductor had no idea what he started!"

Mimi, who had watched her nephew, with his friends George and Paul, dash in from riding his bike to write songs together, never really accepted his career choice. "I just couldn't understand it," she once commented. "Here was a nicely spoken boy, attending church three times on Sunday of his own free will, in the church choir, suddenly taking to twanging a guitar. I told him it was distracting him from his studies as an art student. Nothing would have convinced me John would ever make his fortune with that boy at the front door [Paul McCartney]. But in the end I had to concede that music was far more important to him than the career as an artist, illustrator, or even school teacher I'd mapped out for him."

"Well, Mimi reacts like all mothers," Lennon has said. " 'What are you doing with that long hair and what's all this I read about in the press?' She'll never change."

The fact was that while Mimi was all business, Julia was quite simply fun. When Mimi pooh-poohed John's music, Julia encouraged it. When John took to wearing tight clothes Mimi was outraged but Julia was thrilled. Still, for all her gaiety, there were dark corners in Julia's life.

In the mid 1980s John's paternal uncle Charlie introduced me to Taffey Williams and Eddie Balour, two old drinking buddies, who both had a tale to tell about the pretty, leggy former cinema usherette and her lifestyle before she hooked up with Dykins. Her name was Julia "Judy" Lennon. "She always wore those seamed stockings and very high black heels," Taffey told this author. "She had a nice figure, and bright red hair. She was a good-looker, and funny. Judy was a laugh. She drank like a lady, I remember, and made love like one as well. I didn't always pay her. At least after a while. But in the beginning it was purely business. She didn't come cheap either. Lots of blokes were after her all the time. It was more the fun in her we liked, I suppose. The sex was sort of a bonus. She was the kind of woman men liked. Certainly no one ever thought of her as any kind of criminal! First you had a good old knees-up with her in the pub then you went to her room and did what you had to. To give such a beautiful lady a few quid was all right. It wasn't any sort of big business for her or anything. I think she just used the money for makeup, hair things, all that kind of kit."

There is no question that Julia Lennon was a party girl. She played the banjo in pubs, entertained the neighbourhood children in her home, and was close to her four sisters. Most of the time she was also flat broke. Seemingly happy with her simple Liverpool life, she had to depend on handouts from her father and what she could earn as an usherette. By all accounts, she was an intelligent, independent woman – independent enough to do what she wanted when she wanted, and if that stretched society's post-war mores so be it. Judy was her own woman in whose short life she had many men but only two extended, loving relationships, one with Alfred Lennon and one with Bobby "Twitchy" Dykins.

Eddie Balour also insisted he'd "had it off with old Judy". He was then a merchant seaman on shore leave due to a hip injury. "The way Judy saw it, there was nothing wrong with a little fun for money. Liverpool was full of girls like her. Though she never walked down Lime Street like the others. That was the difference, you see, she wasn't really a pro. She was too good for that, just a fun-loving girl short on cash. If a mate could help her out, why not? I still think of her often. Poor Judy."

Pauline Lennon, John's stepmother after Alfred remarried late in life, told me privately, and also stated publicly in her little-known book *Daddy Come Home*, that John was aware of his mother's early extracurricular income. In fact, on the occasion she and Alfred visited John at his Tittenhurst Park estate in Ascot in 1969 John referred to his mother as a "fucking whore", "a slut", "a cocksucker" and "an old slagger".

"Whoever told him such things about his mother, I have no idea," Pauline said, in a transatlantic telephone interview. "But it's true he said them. Perhaps he just made it up in his mind. It hurt Freddie [Alfred] very much to hear it, I can tell you, because even though their marriage was by all accounts a failure, he loved her very much until the day he died."

Although John was always Julia's strongest supporter in the face of the criticism that often rained down on her from other family members, privately he was affected by her overt sexuality and sometimes over-the-top behaviour. But his sketchy relationship with her wasn't the only emotional bump in the road for the sensitive young man.

Over the years this author became close to several members of John Lennon's extended Liverpool family, especially his younger half-sister Julia Baird. However, one of the most engaging characters I met while making my way through a cadre of nieces, nephews, aunts, uncles, old friends and neighbours was Norman Birch, his maternal uncle who lived in a house Lennon bought in the mid-sixties. I spent days sitting in the cluttered front parlour, hearing about John, "the naughty little boy with gooseberry eyes". Birch told me that John was sexually molested from an early age by George Smith, the gentleman dairy-farmer uncle with whom he lived, Mimi's husband. George "got up to *all sorts* with young John". When I asked Birch what he meant he demurred at first, saying everyone involved was now long dead so there was no point in bringing up such unpleasant memories. I countered that John was an important figure to the world, and only a small part of his history belonged now to the surviving family. To understand the music you *had* to understand the man, and a series of sexual assaults by the only father figure he'd known must have had an important influence on the composer's complex character.

"Yes . . ." he said, his teacup rattling as he spoke in a near whisper about the "things" George had done to John. I didn't have the heart to press him for details, but he swore to me it was true and that Mimi had been aware of it at some point. This, he ventured, was one of the reasons she was always so hard on John – as if somehow she blamed him for it. It is fairly common knowledge that John occasionally indulged in homosexual encounters, which might have been inspired by Uncle George's visits to his bedroom. "It didn't happen often," Birch told me, "and George wouldn't dare stay long for fear of Mimi. Long enough, though . . ."

"How do you know about it?" I asked.

"John told me . . . once," he replied. "He begged me not to tell as he was a bit older by then and George had died. And I never did, not even to my wife Harrie."

Whether or not George ever laid a finger on the little boy no one can now know for certain. But what I heard and, more importantly, *felt* in that tiny front room just off Penny Lane had the ring of truth or, at least, the *possibility*. Only a mind filled with such dark secrets, fantasies and fears could have been so expressive, original, forward-thinking and often black as John's was. In any case, what would Norman Birch, by then well into his seventies, have had to gain by lying to me or anyone else?

Reflecting on Birch's unproven allegations, I think Lennon was certainly a tortured soul. There are many examples in his lyrics of his inner frustration and even paranoia. In "Yer Blues" he sings, "I'm lonely, wanna die." In "Mother", from the *Plastic Ono* album he shouts, "Mother, you had me, but I never had you. I needed you, you didn't need me." And on and on.

The Second World War was in its third year when James Paul McCartney was born on 18 June 1942. Although money was often scarce, cotton salesman Jim McCartney was determined to give his two boys Paul and Michael a good upbringing. Jim's motto was "toleration and moderation", and this later showed itself in Paul's gentle lyrics, which tempered his partner's biting edge. As *Mersey Beat* editor Bill Harry confirmed, "I'm sure it was his father's influence that was behind Paul always liking ballads and soft songs and numbers from musicals."

At grammar school Paul was voted head boy of his form several times, which brought him extra privileges. His fellow students at the Liverpool Institute remembered him as an exceptional class organizer, a skill he would exploit as a Beatle. "If anyone was my big inspiration it was my dad," he has said. "I used to like the radio a lot. Fred Astaire I loved! From a very early age I was interested in singing tunes. Dad used to play a lot of music and even had his own group called Jim Mac's Band, so I suppose I was quite influenced by him. He had to give it up eventually because he got false teeth and couldn't play the trumpet properly any more."

Paul took up the trumpet at thirteen and quickly discovered he could pick out tunes by ear. His musical tastes included an eclectic mix from Pat Boone to Ray Charles. When Lonnie Donegan spearheaded Britain's skiffle craze in the mid-fifties, Paul was hooked: "You only had to know a couple of chords. Somebody had to get a washboard to do the rhythm so you'd have to go to your mum and say, 'Have you got a washboard?' "

From the humble McCartney house – now a full blown tourist attraction – on Forthlin Road in Allerton, Liverpool, the two almost equally talented brothers both pursued careers in entertainment. But talent isn't always enough. From their childhood Mike always seemed to draw the short straw, due in part to his accommodating nature and unswerving sense of loyalty. It was Mike who, more often than not, took the heat for Paul's childhood misadventures – like the time the boys burned down their auntie Jin's garage – and acted as intermediary between his brother and their father. As Mike pointed out about Paul, "He was the first boy, the best-looking one, the one who got all the girls and then all the fame."

Still, the brothers were close. They especially admired the Everly Brothers and listened to virtually every word and nuance of their songs until they could do a near-perfect impression. "Paul imitated Little Richard," added Mike, "and was one of the few white people Richard has acknowledged as being a good interpreter of him."

Ironically, despite his reputation as the "most outgoing Beatle", James Paul McCartney has always kept his emotions in tight check, even to the point of controversy. Many suggest that this characteristic stems from his mother's abrupt death from breast cancer when he was just fourteen. When Jim McCartney told his two boys of their mother's death on 31 October 1956 the first words that flew out of

Paul's mouth were: "What are we going to do without her money?" As he sang in "Yesterday": "I said something wrong now I long for yesterday." That night he cried himself to sleep, praying for a miracle to bring his mother back. Two days later, he acquired the new love of his life: his cheap Rosetti Lucky Seven six-string acoustic guitar. Brother Mike's now familiar observation, "Lose a mother, find a guitar," spoke volumes.

The early loss of his mother has always shaped his relationships with women. Like Mary, his mother, a selfless, hard-working nurse and midwife, the women who mattered to him were strong and independent, like actress Jane Asher and photographer Linda Eastman. When it came to marriage, however, what he wanted – *demanded* – of a wife was the traditional role of homemaker and mother, which he had lost so early in life.

Of all the Beatles, George Harrison hailed from the most conventional and stable family. Born on 24 February 1943, he was the well-behaved son of a bus driver and the youngest of four children; the others were Peter, Harry and Louise. "George and his brother Pete," said their mother Louise, "were always together. As a tot George would often look at photographs of his brother and think it was him. He never played about the streets as a child. He used to like swimming and always found something constructive to do in his spare time."

Unlike John and Paul, George didn't demonstrate a serious interest in music until he reached his mid-teens. When Louise, a ballroom-dancing teacher and lover of big bands, spotted that her son's notebook was filled with sketches of guitars she promptly bought him a cheap acoustic from the father of one of his classmates. Young George put it away in a cupboard for some three months. Then he began to practise, sometimes through the night, until he mastered the chords. Eventually he formed his first band, the Rebels, with brother Peter.

When George realized he needed a better guitar he took a job as a delivery-boy to pay back his mother for the thirty-pound, solid wide-body acoustic with white inlaid trim – which soon came to a tragic end when a friend accidentally pushed a chair into it. Although Harrison had it repaired it was never the same again. He really wanted an electric guitar but his father was none too keen on him buying it on credit.

George was determined, though, and approached his brother Harry. "He persuaded me to go to Hessy's, where all the groups bought their instruments," says Harry. "There he showed me the guitar he wanted. It was a hundred and twenty pounds. George fiddled with it, trying to look like an expert, but no sound came out. So the salesman pushed a button on the amplifier and suddenly there was a tremendous blast and all the instruments on the opposite wall crashed to the floor. After that, I just had to let poor George have his guitar!"

The Harrison brothers weren't the only ones to encourage George's dream. Mrs Harrison also took an active role in supporting her son's budding career. She allowed the boys to rehearse in her living room and told the other parents not to worry because the four occasionally missed school. She supported their trip to Hamburg, even though George was deported because legally he was too young to play in a bar. She was the world's first Beatle fan and never lost her enthusiasm for the group. She even took calmly Paul's 1967 announcement that they had used LSD. In front of television cameras she said that she trusted George not to do anything to harm himself. If he took drugs then drugs were okay because he knew what he was doing.

Sister Louise followed in her mother's footsteps. Despite the eleven-year age difference between them she shared a particularly close bond with him: "I love all three brothers very much but I suppose because I had now reached the mature age of eleven I felt a greater sense of protectiveness towards George. The four of us grew up in a strong and secure, good-natured family atmosphere. Mum and Dad nurtured us in a way that helped us to grow into self-confident individuals with great compassion."

When Louise moved to the USA and married an engineer in the mining town of Benton, Illinois, George and his brother Peter visited for almost three weeks during September 1963. Louise, an ardent Beatles supporter, was instrumental in getting their early records played on American radio. During his visit, George and she hitchhiked to the town of West Frankfort to persuade radio station WFRX to play "She Loves You". It is said he even composed the melody to "Day Tripper" at his sister's 1940s bungalow.*

But something even more significant happened on that visit: Louise arranged for George to play with a local country-rock band, the Four Vests, so he'd have some fellow musicians to hang out with. She had given the band several Beatles records so they could learn the music before he arrived. A gig held at the Eldorado VFW Hall was the first appearance by a Beatle in the USA, some six months before their *Ed Sullivan Show* appearance. George was introduced grandly as the "Elvis of England".

It was Richard Starkey's affable and easy-going nature that got him through a bleak childhood in the impoverished Dingle section of Liverpool. Born on 7 July 1940, he was an only child whose parents divorced when he was three. He spent three years confined to hospitals (first at the age of six when he suffered a burst appendix, and at thirteen he caught pleurisy and spent two years in a children's sanatorium). "I wish I had brothers and sisters," he once lamented to his barmaid mother Elsie. "There's nobody to talk to when it's raining." Later he regarded the Beatles as "the brothers I never had".

His neighbour and distant relative Nellie Coutts, dubbed "Auntie Nellie with the Wooden Belly" by the local kids, recalled that Ritchie was musically inclined from an early age. "In Liverpool they used to have the annual Orange Day Parade," explained Nellie. "When Orange Day came along the Starkeys all paraded. Their homes were decorated and they all marched in the band. I remember seeing Ritchie playing a little tin drum marching along as pretty as you please. He also played the accordion. In Liverpool it was generally

* In 1996 she turned it into a bed-and-breakfast called A Hard Day's Night. This upset George so much that even on his deathbed he had to be convinced to see his sister. He apparently felt that Louise was cashing in unfairly on the Beatles' name. She insists the story is nonsense.

passed down from father to son but Ritchie was a member of the accordion band at the Orange Hall. He learned there."

He took up the drums when he joined a hospital-ward percussion band. His kindly stepfather Harry Graves, known to sing for his supper in a pub or two, encouraged young Ritchie's blossoming interest in music and bought him his first drum kit.

Well into the 1960s Elsie was still looking out for her son. She confided to close friends, "Ritchie gives me an allowance and I put ten pounds away each week for him in case he's ever down on his luck."

The seed that would soon blossom into the songwriting collective known as Lennon–McCartney was sown when they greeted each other in passing outside a local suburban chippy late in the spring of 1957. Then a couple of weeks later, Paul recalled seeing John climbing aboard the number 86 bus bound for town. Their official first meeting took place at St Peter's parish church Garden Fête in blustery Woolton village on 6 July 1957, some time in the early afternoon where John and his ragtag skiffle group, the Quarry Men, were busking on a makeshift stage to the delight of the hamlet's rocking youth.

In October 1986, McCartney granted me a rare interview in response to my questions regarding his first meeting with Lennon. "As it turned out, John and I were mates with a fellow from Woolton, Ivan Vaughan," he said casually. "One summer's day, he invited me to come along to a fête in Woolton. John was about sixteen, so I was maybe fourteen or fifteen. I remember coming across the field hearing all this great music, which turned out to be from the Quarry Men's Tannoy system. I thought, Oh great, I'll go listen to the band, because I was very much into music. Later I met the lads in the church hall. They were having a beer, I think. The line-up of the band was Len Garry, Pete Shotton, Colin Hanton on drums, Eric Griffiths on guitar, and Nigel Whalley who acted as their manager.

"We all used to think John was pretty cool. He was a bit older and would do a little more greased-back hair and things than we were allowed. He had nice big sideboards and with his drake he looked a bit of a Ted. That particular day I happened to pick up a guitar that was lying around and started to play 'Twenty Flight Rock'. I knew a lot of the words, which was very good currency in those days."

Lennon's recollection of their historic meeting was one of grudging respect. "He could obviously play," he later admitted. "I thought to myself, He's every bit as good as me. I'd been the kingpin up to then. It went through my head that I'd have to keep him in line if I let him join. But he was good, so he was worth having."

The young Paul revelled in his role as John's on-stage foil and steady street-corner accomplice. What they really needed now, however, was a solid lead guitar on which to hang their funky back-street sound. Paul remembered the events leading up to their settling on George: "He was always my little mate. Nonetheless, he could really play guitar, particularly this piece called 'Raunchy', which we all used to love. If anyone could do something like that it was generally enough to get them in the group. I knew George long before any of the others as they were all from Woolton, and we hung out with the Allerton set. We both learned guitar from the same book, and despite his tender years, we were chums."

Lennon, who was now attending Liverpool College of Art, was sceptical about admitting such a baby into the group. How would it look for someone as talented and popular as he to be consorting with someone so young and undistinguished as George? In the end, however, the young man's exceptional skill coupled with Paul's insistence that he be brought on board overcame John's reservations.

The Quarry Men's first recording session, in the summer of 1958, was viewed by the lads as something of a lark. The band, which included pianist John "Duff" Lowe, arrived at the home of one Percy Phillips, a retired railwayman, to lay down a demo in his makeshift studio, which was at 53 Kensington, Liverpool. Duff recalled the afternoon in a rare 1993 interview. "I can't really remember who organized it. I've a feeling it was John who'd heard of this little recording studio in Kensington. It was a Saturday afternoon and we waited in an anteroom. It was someone's lounge, I think, whilst somebody was finishing off. Then we ran through two numbers, 'That'll Be The Day' and 'In Spite Of All Danger'." The latter, a one-off McCartney–Harrison collaboration, was a spirited late-fifties "doo-wop", which held the distinction of being the first original song recorded by three members of the band that became the Beatles.

According to Duff, the session left much to be desired: "The guy did a soundcheck, such as it was, as there was only one microphone hanging in the middle of the room. Then he said, 'Right, lads, you can go on tape and I'll do the record off the tape, or you can go straight on to record. It's an extra half-crown if you want to go on tape.' We said, 'Oh, we can't afford that; we'll go straight to record.' 'In Spite Of All Danger' was getting a bit long and he started to wave his hands to bring us to a finish, as we were getting pretty near the hole in the middle of the record. It was just a shellac demo: the more you played it, the worse the quality was. Paul wrote on the label, 'That'll Be The Day' (Holly–Petty) and 'In Spite Of All Danger' (McCartney–Harrison)'."

The summer was momentous, for Lennon at least, for another reason. His mother Julia died on 15 July 1958, when she was hit by the car of an off-duty policeman. She had just visited Aunt Mimi at Menlove Avenue and was waiting for a bus home. Seventeen-year-old Lennon was shattered. "We were sitting waiting for her to come home," he remembered. "Twitchy and me was wondering why she was so late. The copper came to the door to tell us. It was just like it's supposed to be, you know, the way it is in the films, asking if I was her son and all that. Then he told us, and we both went white. It was the worst thing that could happen to me. We'd caught up so much in just a few years. We could, at last, communicate. We got on. She was great. I thought, Fuck! Fuck it! Fuck it! That's really fucked everything. I've no responsibility to anyone now!'

The shocking loss of their mothers created a bond between Lennon and McCartney. "John was devastated," McCartney said later. "He loved his mum more than anything, but at that age, you're not allowed to be devastated, particularly not teenage boys. You just shrug it off. I know he had private tears. It's not that either of us were remotely hard-hearted about it, it shattered us, but we knew that you had to get on with your life. We were like wounded animals and, just by looking at each other, we knew the pain that we were feeling."

Before the Quarry Men made their first real splash at the Cavern on Mathew Street in the city centre, their initial home was the Casbah coffee club. It was run by Mona Best, mother of future drummer Pete, in the basement of the family's fourteen-room Victorian house in the affluent West Derby area of Liverpool. Mrs Best recalled: "I used to have them coming in and out of my house as if it were a railway station, so I thought we've got a nice cellar, maybe the gang would all like to go down there. I've never seen a club with such atmosphere. It was all volunteers that helped get the club together. They put in a lot of hours, including John Lennon."

Pete remembered how, on 29 August 1959, Lennon's band officially christened the Casbah: "We needed a group to open on the Saturday. I knew George because there was another club down the road called the Lowlands and he used to play there with Ken Brown. Ken said the group had broken up but George said, 'I know a couple of guys who say they've played in a band before. If they're interested in coming down would you let them open?' Mum said, 'Yes, let's see them.' It turned out to be John and Paul. But there was no drummer. It was John, George, Paul, Ken Brown, and they played under the name the Quarry Men."

What stood them apart was their refusal to play the usual hit-parade fare, preferring the American rock icons Chuck Berry, Carl Perkins and Gene Vincent. "They had great charisma," said Pete. "The way they stood, the things they did, made them stand out from the rest of the groups."

Mrs Best initially frowned upon this motley bunch with unkempt hair and grubby clothes. Her relationship with John Lennon, in particular, was uneasy: the Quarry Men's leader openly criticized the pseudo-Beatnik climate that Mona was trying to cultivate in the Casbah. According to John, the crowd that hung out at the club was merely posturing at intellectualism; the Casbah was a teen-dance hangout, nothing more. Also, he jeered at Mona's attempts to promote the handsome Pete as a musical James Dean. Once John recited a poem on stage that denounced both the club and Mrs Best's machinations on behalf of her son. All this, however, didn't stop him hanging out there himself, "raiding the stores", as Best put it, "putting his head down for the night and listening to records. At the time John was still at art college so he was a typical Bohemian. He'd come in with his black jacket and chukka boots. He never used to wear his glasses. He painted several murals on the ceiling. They were his usual potbellies and caricatures, but the Casbah had to be dark so one day he said, 'I'll just paint the ceiling black,' and they all went. Paul was a little more sedate: he'd wear jeans, an off-white shirt and a cashmere jacket. That's the way they knocked around. They were always laughing and joking. There was nothing serious about them. Somebody would crack a joke and they wouldn't work for two hours. They were scruffy, but don't get the impression they were tramps."

The Quarry Men continued to rock the Casbah, eventually with the much older drummer Tommy Moore and going for better gigs with better pay. Ever intent on cultivating their blossoming image, they tried several new names over the following year, including the Beatles, the Silver Beats, the Silver Beetles, the Silver Beatles. By August 1960, they settled on the Beatles. Earlier that year, in January, John invited his art-school friend, Stuart Sutcliffe, to join the band. John and Stu's connection had been both immediate and profound. The cultured Stu opened up to John a world of Kierkegaard and Nietzsche, whose philosophies the two constantly debated. In turn, Stu was fascinated by John's fiery, take-no-prisoners attitude. While Stu painted intimate portraits of him, John wrote his friend long, thoughtful letters and reams of abstract poetry. For the first time he could let down his guard and pour out his deepest feelings. But although he was a talented painter and designer, Stu made no pretence at being any sort of musician and was obliged to learn the bass as he went along.

By now the Beatles were becoming quite successful – for a local band – and if John wasn't playing somewhere, he was either rehearsing or at art college. Once in awhile, though, he would pop in at his Aunt

Harrie's for a quick meal and to see his sisters, who were now living there, or maybe even chat with a girlfriend on his auntie's phone. This, however, sometimes required a degree of subterfuge on John's part. Harrie, apparently, didn't approve of people using the phone for what she called "non-essential" purposes. If John wanted to assure himself of absolute privacy he had to crawl out of the front window and sit in the bushes.

Later, he started bringing over a girl called Cynthia Powell, from the Wirral. They had met at art college in a lettering class and soon become an item. Lennon insisted she bleach her hair out of reverence for his own personal sex symbol, Brigitte Bardot.

"Unfortunately for Cyn," said Paul, "she just happened to come along at the time everyone was trying to turn their girlfriend into a 'bargain-basement' Bardot. You see, we all happened to be at an age when a ravishing sex goddess taking off her clothes was the fantasy for us boys. We were all smitten. So the girls had to be blonde, look rather like Brigitte, and preferably pout a lot. John and I used to have these secret talks where we intimated we would be quite happy for our girlfriends to become Liverpool's answer to Bardot. My girl was called Dot and, of course, John was going steady with Cynthia. So, eventually, we both got them to go blonde and wear miniskirts. It's terrible, really, but that's the way it is."

Julia Baird remembered, "Both Jacqui and I grew up with Cynthia around. She and John first courted at our house, the Cottage, and always seemed very much at home. Often visiting Saturday afternoons, they would sit quietly holding hands on the settee, while we all gathered round to watch the telly. Sometimes we'd be sent out of the room by Harrie so that the two of them could be alone. This, of course, always engendered a lot of good-natured oohs and aahs from us, as we sauntered into the kitchen to wait impatiently until they wanted tea. Then, at least, we were allowed in to serve them. Which also carried the added bonus of giving us both an opportunity to see what they were up to.

"Cynthia was very good for my brother. She loved him desperately and only wanted the best for him. Anyone could see how terribly in love they were. I've always felt it was a great pity they eventually parted so unhappily. Seeing them there together at Harrie's, no one could have guessed how terribly cruel their ultimate fate would be. Back then, they were both the absolute picture of teenage love."

By the end of 1959, Lennon moved into a dingy flat with Sutcliffe, at Hillary Mansions, Gambier Terrace, near Liverpool cathedral. Mimi, of course, hated this idea, and did her utmost to convince him to return to her home – to no avail. However, John continued to visit her at least once a week to get his laundry done and have a good, home-cooked meal. A local newspaper, looking for a good story, concocted a piece on John's flat entitled "The Beatnick Horror of Northern England".

Stu's influence on Lennon was a double-edged sword. As a talented artist, he encouraged John to explore his own ability as a painter, yet his presence in the group engendered controversy. McCartney explained: "I had problems with Stu, I'll admit. It's a regret now as he died, but sometimes you can't help it if you run up against controversy. The main thing was he couldn't really play the bass very well in the beginning, so when we did photos and things it was a bit embarrassing. We had to ask him to turn away from the camera, because if people saw his fingers they'd realize he wasn't in the same key as the rest of us. I was probably overly fussy, but I thought, Well, this isn't really a very good thing for an aspiring group. We obviously have a weak link here. He was a lovely guy and a great painter, but he was the one I used to have all the ding-dongs with."

By April 1960, as the Silver Beatles, the boys snagged seven gigs backing balladeer Johnny Gentle on a ballroom tour of Scotland. Although they were encouraged by a taste of real work, they came home as broke as ever. "Someone actually asked for my autograph," Paul wrote to his dad from Inverness. "I signed for them too, three times!"

Their initial trek to Germany in August 1960 came about more as a result of a lack of alternatives than of any great success in England. They were under the impression that they'd been booked at Hamburg's popular Kaiserkeller, by small-time Liverpool promoter Allan Williams, but later discovered they were to appear as the new house band at the seedy Indra in the red-light district on the Reeperbahn in the notorious St Pauli district.

Meanwhile, Pete Best had formed his own band, the Blackjacks, and was playing on a spanking new drum kit Mona had purchased for him. When Tommy Moore quit the Beatles in June 1960, he left an opening for a drummer. Best auditioned on 12 August and four days later he was on his way to Hamburg. "I didn't think we were going anywhere," he conceded, "but it was a chance to break into the business. The German audiences were wild and that's when the charisma really started. I don't think in their wisdom they thought they'd ever become megastars either." He fondly remembered donning a stage costume of a leather jacket and pink hat. "We loved Gene Vincent. That was where the leather came from. You could buy it very cheaply in Germany. Vincent had a fantastic band called the Blue Caps. In the film *The Girl Can't Help It* Gene and the Blue Caps wore these flat pink hats. So for the first time we went on stage in leather jackets, flat pink hats and cowboy boots."

Living in close quarters with the others in cold, dingy rooms at the Indra gave Best time to observe the mercurial, complex Lennon. "There were two sides to John. He would spend an awful lot of time by himself writing very lengthy letters, and he'd talk about Cynthia and his family. But Mimi he wouldn't open up about at all . . . Some might say he was callous or crazy. But I think that was just his way of handling people, to make sure they didn't get too close. Once he was by himself, or in the company of friends, he was a very different John Lennon."

In Germany Lennon, alone among the Beatles, hiked to the post office every week to send home almost his entire earnings to be sure that Cynthia had what she needed. As for his own expenses, he'd often hire himself out as a guitarist to one of the local strippers to earn a few extra marks. Best remembers him as outwardly aggressive, but soft when it came to Cyn. "There would be moments in Hamburg when John used to settle down and we really talked. Sometimes the two of us would go out and down a couple of beers together and chat about our hopes for the future. He used to tell me how hard it was being away from her and how they planned to settle down and seriously begin raising a family just as soon as the Beatles began to pay off. There were definitely two distinct sides to John. One was the outrageous guy on stage who continually lost his temper, took the mickey out of people, and generally acted the goat. The other side of John, which, of course, the public didn't often see, was really very gentle and tender. And never more than when he was speaking of his Cindy."

For the Beatles, life on the Reeperbahn was an eye-opening experience. They could drink for free throughout their raucous sets but soon that didn't deliver quite the kick they needed to keep going during their eight-hour musical shifts. They then turned to an array of amphetamines, such as black beauties, "prellies" (Preludin) and black bombers to rocket them into high gear and keep them there. Sex, too, became an enjoyable diversion and they took full advantage of their freedom. George Harrison lost his virginity in St Pauli.

In Allan Williams's 1975 memoir, *The Man Who Gave The Beatles Away*, he proclaimed that one of the Beatles, whom he couldn't name at the time for legal reasons, used regularly to date the buxom, leggy transvestites of Hamburg's red-light district. Lennon later noted that Williams's memoir was by far the most accurate account of that time in the Beatles' lives. Horst Fascher, a bouncer in one of the clubs, also corroborated his story: "There was a transvestite who regularly used to give John blow-jobs. When he found out she was a man, he was merely amused."

That alluring "lady boy" was in fact an AWOL American GI who went by the street name of Jacki Heart. He lived in one of the seedy flats above a club near the Indra and according to what he told this author during a 1991 interview was "really in love with John for a time". To Lennon, of course, it was merely sex, but Heart told me he had deep feelings for the inwardly sensitive Beatle. "He never did anything fem," he said, "he was all man and merely allowed me to go down on him. There was never any possibility of anything else. He said he thought of me as a woman with 'a twist'. When it was over, more times than not, he would pick up his bottle of Scotch, slap me on the backside and lumber back down the stairs without saying a word. He sometimes even seemed a little embarrassed by his sexuality. But I didn't care, John was beautiful, both as lover and a person.

When I would see him in the clubs he would ignore me. He once warned me that the others must never know. So he was obviously very much in the closet, which was fine. As for me in those days, I defy anyone to have ever known my secret."

By his own admission, John was always a hitter, striking out at both boys and girls from an early age. Likewise, he was often deliberately hurtful and verbally aggressive to those he felt were in a weaker position within his orbit. It is now known that in addition to several early sexual episodes with local girls, including a neighbour Barbara Baker and schoolmate Thelma Pickles, from around the age of twelve, Lennon also experimented with one or two older boys while visiting his aunt Mater in Edinburgh.

John confessed this in a private conversation in mid-September 1979 with Lenono – an abbreviation of Lennon and Ono, used for their business in New York – staff member George Speerin. "John knew I was gay, and told me he'd had a number of experiences himself both as a kid and an adult," Speerin confided to me in the winter of 1984. "He said his first encounter was with an older boy who spent the day playing soccer and carousing with John, and then forced him to orally copulate the young man in an old milk van in a parking lot. He said he was embarrassed by the incident, and other than Yoko had never told anyone. I am sure he was telling me because he knew I was having a tough time back then, and wanted to try and reach out to me as if to say, 'Hey, I know what you are going through, man.' John was always a very kind, compassionate human being, at least to me. He also told me that while he had gone on to have several homoerotic experiences and even one brief relationship in Germany, many years previous, he didn't consider himself either gay or straight. 'Sex is sex,' he told me. 'The expressions are almost irrelevant. I had needs and I fulfilled them. That's all there is to it.'"

Still, if Lennon was gender blind when it came to sex, he certainly didn't allow others the same latitude. "John was always on at anyone he thought might be gay," said his uncle Charlie Lennon. "I didn't see him that much as an adult, but I remember he was always going on in a joking way about 'poofters, fags, and queens' in conversation."

As long as Lennon maintained that gays were different from himself no one would discover his humiliating secret.

Had all been well between Klaus Voormann and Astrid Kirchherr, Hamburg would have been an entirely different experience for the young Beatles. Klaus, a seventeen-year-old studying illustration at the Meister Schule, found himself outside the Kaiserkeller one evening in October 1960 following an argument with his girlfriend Astrid which left their steady two-year relationship seriously in doubt. It was the sound of Rory Storm and the Hurricanes, at the time sporting drummer Ringo Starr, that drew him in at 36 Grosse Freiheit. Just finishing up their set, Rory left the stage and the sound of feedback ushered in the next group in line, the Beatles, whose current list of covers was stretched to the limit with having to extend the likes of Ray Charles' "What'd I Say" and Chuck Berry's "Johnny B. Goode" into fifteen minute musical marathons. Returning to the Kaiserkeller a few days later, Klaus summoned the courage to approach the group, and after showing Lennon a record sleeve he'd created for the German release of the Ventures' "Walk Don't Run" he was immediately directed to Stuart Sutcliffe, whom Lennon dubbed "the artist in the group". Astrid and a friend, Jurgen Vollmer, attended the next excursion. "They looked like their audience, very rough and tough rockers," said Jurgen, "but there was something different about them, for they were basically not rockers. They just had to put up that act in order to please their audience, and, of course, their music was sensational."

During the between-song conversations Sutcliffe was quietly captured by the blonde photographer. "I couldn't see Stu's eyes behind those glasses, but I knew, somehow I just knew, he was looking at me," said Astrid. "At this first moment, I also knew that one day there would be something real between us." Kirchherr invited the Beatles out for a photo session the next day at the city funfair, and the group enthusiastically obliged, assuming "typical Dean poses", as Stu termed them. "The image of James Dean was certainly there," said Jurgen. "With Stuart, the mystery was behind the sunglasses."

Few know that Sutcliffe was given the occasional singing role in the Beatles, with his rendition of "Love Me Tender" drawing particular attention. "Everybody says I sing it better than Elvis," Stuart proudly pronounced.

His love affair with Astrid grew over the coming weeks, but seeing as her relationship with Klaus was still up in the air, they proceeded with caution. "I haven't slept with Astrid yet, in case you think this is just an erotic affair," Stuart assured his mother in mid-November 1960.

With the pair spending more and more time with each other and Sutcliffe distancing himself from the band, Astrid was already proposing marriage by late November. That same month George was deported for being under-age, and Paul and Pete were arrested for setting fire to a peeling tapestry hanging from the wall of the Bambi-Filmkunsttheatre. They were never charged – but were deported anyway. John headed back to Liverpool on 10 December but Stuart stayed in Hamburg until January and the Beatles were forced to look for a replacement bassist. Even an impassioned letter from George failed to convince Stu to return home earlier. It was soon after his return that Stu, John and Pete got involved in a scuffle outside Lathom Hall in Liverpool. While Lennon's guitar-playing would now be affected by the damage done to his hand, the fight left Sutcliffe gravely injured. "I got knocked unconscious," he told his mother, "my glasses are nonexistent. I couldn't even pick up the pieces, but John got one of the thugs, and he broke his wrist giving him what he'd given me."

In June 1961, during their second trip to Hamburg, Tony Sheridan, a popular transplanted English club singer, invited the Beatles to play with him on a Polydor recording session produced by well-known German orchestra leader Bert Kaempfert. Although the Beatles had recorded before, this was their first truly "professional" session. On the morning of 22 June they climbed into a taxi, followed by another piled high with their gear, and made their way through Hamburg's sleepy side-streets to a school on the outskirts of the city. They set up on the tiny stage in the gymnasium, and recorded eight tunes, six backing Tony and two others, "My Bonnie" and "Cry For A Shadow".

The latter, a parody of the Shadows' "Frightened City", was

written under the working title "Beatle Bop". It earned a pair of lofty distinctions: it was the only song ever written by Lennon–Harrison, and it was the Beatles' first original song to appear on record.

John and Paul returned to Liverpool on 2 July, and were playing the Cavern on the fourteenth, Holyoake Hall, near Penny Lane, on the fifteenth, Blair Hall in Walton on the sixteenth, and back to the Cavern for a lunchtime session on the seventeenth. That night they roared off to the Litherland town hall. Thereafter, they maintained a gut-wrenching schedule of virtually non-stop performances throughout the North for the remainder of the year.

They were now down to four members. Sutcliffe soon became a member of the Beatles in name only, his mind constantly elsewhere. He was more concerned with returning to his true passion, and began taking sculpture classes at Hamburg's State School of Art. At the Top Ten Club in Hamburg in June 1961, Stu played his final gig with the Beatles, performing "Love Me Tender" for the last time. As a parting gesture, he gave Paul his Hofner President bass. McCartney, never an admirer of Sutcliffe's abilities on the guitar, had already begun taking over bass duties.

John Lennon's solidly working-class Beatle cohorts were impressed by their leader's middle-class relatives, who included a teacher, a dentist and an uncle who worked for the BBC. Among this circle was his kindly maternal aunt Mater who lived in Edinburgh. She made it a practice to give her many nieces and nephews a hundred pounds on their twenty-first birthday. John reached that milestone in October 1961, and casually pulled out his cheque to show it to a flabbergasted Paul, who was then earning about ten pounds a week from gigging. Over hamburgers Lennon suggested, "Hey, what do you say we hitchhike to Spain?" The pair cancelled the group's upcoming bookings and left town. But the adventurers never made it. "It was supposed to be Spain but we never got past Paris," Paul said. "We suddenly thought, we can't get to Spain on a hundred quid! We soon realized we needed a gimmick to get people to stop so we both wore bowler hats in addition to our leather jackets. We thought that might take the edge off the kind of hoody look we had then. I guess people would just think, Whoa, look, there's a couple of daft kids in bowler hats there. They don't really look like a threat."

According to Lennon, however, they took a train most of the way to Paris. There, they checked into a modest hotel and found the famed cafés and bars along the avenue des Anglais much to their liking. "We got a bit drunk on the French beer," McCartney conceded. "We had been drinking the British stuff and we thought we could handle it, but this foreign stuff really went to our heads. It was all so adventurous. I had never done anything like that. I'd hardly been out of Liverpool before! I'd been to Pwllheli, Skegness and Leamington Spa but that had been the whole of my travels. It was very exciting to get off on your own with a mate. John was a great guy because he was never boring."

The pair found their way to the artists' hangout of Montmartre and were struck by the revolutionary fashion explosion. On seeing the hip *garçons* decked out in capes and pantaloons they felt hopelessly outdated in their teddy-boy drainpipes. When they pulled on the new-style trousers, they instantly decided that although they might be appropriate for Paris, they would never do for Liverpool.

However, another emerging fashion statement was a different matter. Meeting up with photographer Jurgen Vollmer, who was in Paris at the same time, they immediately noticed he was sporting a shaggy new hairstyle, which Paul once termed, "a kind of long-haired Hitler thing". They took to it instantly and Vollmer agreed to give them the same look. The Beatles' trademark haircut was adopted right then and there on the streets of Paris.

Things were moving ahead for them, but the most auspicious development was the entrance into their lives of Liverpool businessman Brian Epstein. His interest in them was piqued when a young man named Raymond Jones walked into his parents' record store NEMS (North End Music Stores) and requested a German import called "My Bonnie" by the Beatles. Brian promised he would try to track it down, and eventually he did. He ordered a cautious twenty-five copies, and sold out almost immediately. He repeated the process several times, then decided to check out for himself what the fuss was about.

Somewhat against his better judgement, on Thursday, 9 November 1961, the dapper twenty-seven-year-old bachelor descended the eighteen stone steps of the Cavern Club to witness at first hand this up-and-coming beat group he had heard so much about. Alistair Taylor, his personal assistant, remembered the occasion: "As for their act, I don't think they'd go down very well at the Royal Variety Performance. It seems like they've got a permanent long-running set of private jokes, which they share as they play. They crack one-liners to each other and from time to time let the front row of the audience in on it. When the girls screamed requests, the Beatles shouted back, adding their own suggestions and comments. Brian and I gave a discouraged look at each other and settled down to pay attention to the music. This isn't much, I thought. For a start, it's too damned loud, and from what I heard as we crossed the dance-floor the Beatles are a bunch of five-chord merchants.

"We sat through five numbers, four of them beat-song standards: 'Money', 'Till There Was You', 'A Taste of Honey', and 'Twist and Shout'. I might admit, however, I never heard standards played with the sort of raw excitement the Beatles put into them. Then Paul came to the microphone and announced that they were going to play a song he had written with John Lennon, 'Hello Little Girl'. Brian and I exchanged a glance. 'So they write their own songs.' "

"The Beatles were on stage raving it up," remembered Epstein. "I sensed that something was happening, something terribly exciting, although I didn't know what. There was this amazingly direct communication with the audience and this absolutely marvellous humour. There was something about it that was totally of today. I knew immediately they could be one of the biggest theatrical attractions in the world."

Brian returned to the "vile and smelly" club several more times, and then, at a 3 December meeting at NEMS, suggested to the boys that he become their manager. For some years, Epstein had felt suffocated, merely retracing his father's footsteps in running the family business. As it happened, the Beatles were quietly despairing of ever breaking out of Liverpool's local beat scene. Impressed by Brian's prominent standing in the musical community, they quickly accepted. For Brian, life looked up immediately: "They represented the direct, uninhibited relationships I had never found and felt deprived of. My own sense of inferiority and frustration soon evaporated because I knew I could help them, and they wanted and trusted me to."

TWO

Don't Allow The Day
Liverpool and London
1962–3

> "The Beatles have gained immeasurably in prestige as a result of the inquiries of their manager. That they will secure a recording contract with a major British label in the near future is certain. Their outlook is now mature and professional. They are no longer only a local attraction . . . If it is possible for a rock'n'roll group to become a status symbol, then the Beatles have made it so. They are still a phenomenon, but now their appeal is legend!"
>
> *Cavern compère Bob Wooler*

The new year rang in with the Beatles poised on an exciting new frontier. Brian Epstein had landed them their first big-time audition with Decca Records. On 1 January 1962 the band trekked down to the studios in West Hampstead, North London, to meet amiable A&R man Mike Smith. The hour-long morning session, recorded on two-track mono, featured fifteen tracks selected by Brian as most representative of their sound. Much bootlegged today, the audition highlighted three original Lennon–McCartney compositions: "Like Dreamers Do", "Love Of The Loved" and "Hello Little Girl". John thought the latter was perhaps his best from that period, inspired by the Cole Porter standard, "It's De-lovely". The classic was a favourite with his mother. "It's all very Freudian," he quipped. "She used to sing that one. So I made 'Hello Little Girl' out of it. This was one of the first songs I ever finished. I was then about eighteen and gave it to the Fourmost." The remaining twelve songs were well-worn covers of additional standards including "Money (That's What I Want)", "Take Good Care Of My Baby", "The Sheik Of Araby" and a future fan favourite, the romantic ballad "Till There Was You" from the stage show *The Music Man*.

After the session, Epstein asked how the audition had gone. Smith smiled and extended his hand. "We'll let you know, chaps," he said quietly. "Thanks very much for coming down."

As almost every Beatles fan knows, nothing came of it, and Decca recording manager Dick Rowe famously remarked to Brian that groups with guitars were "on the way out".

Despite that disappointing setback, on 7 March the Beatles made their first radio appearance on the BBC variety show *Teenager's Turn – Here We Go*, then headed back to Germany in April.

Along with Elvis Presley, Little Richard and Buddy Holly, fifties rocker Gene Vincent was also a pivotal influence on the Beatles. His Virginia roots in southern blues, black gospel and backwoods rockabilly struck a powerful chord with them, and his 1956 megahit, "Be Bop A Lula" was the first record Paul ever bought. The young Beatles incorporated several classic Vincent tunes in their early repertoire. John, who often imitated his idol's menacing on-stage swagger, later covered "Be Bop A Lula" on his disappointing 1975 *Rock'n'Roll* album.

John, Paul and George saw Vincent play every time he was in Liverpool. His close friend Bill Sheriff "Tex" Davis, who had discovered him, remembered them sitting in the front row for his performance: "They just kept looking and looking. This was before they were called the Beatles. They were learning to play like the Blue Caps. That's very important to history."

Two years later, in April 1962, Vincent played Hamburg's notorious Star Club and was "very impressed" with the emerging Liverpool legends. "We met and talked," he later recalled. "They were really good. God, I could have picked them up so cheaply, which was foolish of me. But I'm a singer, not a bloody businessman."

It was at the Star Club while the Beatles were sharing the bill with headliner Vincent, that the band saw a different side of their hero. Late one afternoon, they spotted him alone at a table, an imposing ex-marine decked out in black leather, a king-sized bottle of Johnnie

Walker in front of him. Years later, Paul noted, "He used to like his Scotch; he was a very hard drinker." The Beatles summoned the courage to approach his table. "You've already bought a drink, then," they greeted him.

"Oh, you want some, guys?" offered Vincent, happy to accommodate.

"Yeah, sure, all right," they replied, and pulled up chairs.

They shot the breeze for awhile, and Vincent invited them to his hotel on the Grosse Freiheit. For the up-and-coming, but still second-string Beatles, the prospect of hanging out with the star was thrilling. "Unlike us, he had a hotel," remembered McCartney. "The stars had hotels, but we only had this crappy little place in the back of a cellar where we froze to death! We were going down the corridor and Gene said, 'Just a minute.' He ran to the door and knocks the littlest knock you could ever knock. He knocks again and there's no answer and then whispers, 'She's in there with *him*!' So we go, 'Oh dear! Situation ruined.' We asked, 'Who do you mean, Gene?' He says, 'Henry's in there, with Margie.'"

"What do you mean, Gene?" the boys asked.

"Henry's in there with Margie and she's not answering."

"You might have to knock a bit louder, Gene," they suggested.

Vincent banged on the door and finally a woman opened it, hair in curlers. There was no sign of anyone else in the room. "It was just her on her own, getting ready for the evening," Paul recalled. "So Gene says, 'Where's Henry?' We're all thinking, Oh dear! We were wishing we weren't there. But he's such a big star, we've got to stay. We can't go, this is getting interesting."

Vincent stormed into the room heading for the bed where a pair of rumpled khaki trousers lay. "And who the fuck are these, then?" he demanded.

"They're yours, Gene," the woman barked.

"Oh, yeah?" He reached over to a bedside table and pulled out a huge silver-plated revolver.

Even by Hamburg's standards, where the club waiters carried gas guns, this was well beyond the Beatles' suburban Liverpool experience. "We didn't know if it was loaded or not," said Paul. "I mean, this guy was a former marine! Then he wanted to knock us out by showing us all the pressure points."

An enraged Vincent, pumped up on Johnnie Walker, was waving the weapon, with Margie goading him, "Go on, that's it. Give it to 'em!"

"Oh, no, *no*," shrieked McCartney, dodging Vincent's erratic aim. "John's every bit as good as me!"

"Oh, no, you'd be much better, Paul!" retorted the terrified Lennon.

They backed out of the doorway. "We gotta split, Gene. Nice seeing you, man!" They fled down the corridor and back to their dingy rooms, which suddenly seemed an inviting haven.

"In my opinion our peak for playing live was in Hamburg," George Harrison recalled in 1969. "You see, at the time we weren't so famous, and the people who came to see us were drawn in simply by our music and whatever atmosphere we managed to create. We got very tight as a band there. We were at four different clubs together in Germany. Originally we played the Indra, and when that shut down we went over to the Kaiserkeller and then, later, the Top Ten. That was a fantastic place, probably the best one on the Reeperbahn. There was a natural echo on the microphones, it was a gas. The Star Club was very rough. We developed quite a big repertoire of our own songs but still played mainly old rock'n'roll tunes. Back in England, all the bands were into wearing matching ties and handkerchiefs, and doing little dance routines like the Shadows. We were definitely not into that so we just kept on doing whatever we felt like, and ultimately it worked out."

Those early Hamburg stints honed the Beatles' edgy rock sound but were soon abandoned when Brian Epstein took over, a move Pete Best strongly criticized: "We came back playing the music the way we wanted. When Brian took us over the image started to change. At the time every group in Liverpool was copying our performance, mannerisms and the material we were playing. All of a sudden Eppie comes along and says, 'Okay, you've got to tidy the act up. I'm going to put you in suits and you're going to play the same repertoire every night.'"

Gerry and the Pacemakers, well known for their chart-topping

Mersey beat singles, shared several bills with the Beatles since their early Quarry Men days. "I was with the Gerry Marsden Skiffle Group," Gerry remembered in a 1986 interview. "We played a show together, I think I was fourteen or fifteen. One time at the Liverpool town hall* we formed a big band, it was the Beatles and ourselves. John was a good friend of mine. We spent many years together. John was not as aggressive as people say. He wasn't a Teddy Boy. John was always the last guy in a fight and that's the truth. If a fight occurred John wouldn't be the first in line. If you and John gelled then that was it. Period. Lennon wasn't that aggressive or even really sarcastic."

He explained that the emerging Mersey sound, which stood apart from other contemporary music coming out of Europe and Britain, had been spawned by American rock, specifically rhythm and blues. "Fats Domino, Chuck Berry, Ray Charles, the greatest rock in the world and the greatest jazz musicians in the world," he revealed. "We never did songs by Cliff Richard, Billy Fury or Adam Faith. We always stayed with rock.

"In Hamburg we played seven hours a night with a fifteen-minute break every hour. So we played lots of music, Ray Charles, Arthur Alexander, all the great American stars. When we were actually writing songs, the influence was chiefly American writers. The kids we played for in Liverpool loved the new songs. There was never any sort of 'Ugh, that's crap,' writing your own gear.

"John and Paul were so powerful in their composing. That's the closest I've ever come to genius, seeing them as kids writing their music. They changed the entire concept of music. Basically they were just four guys with no background, not from star school, not from the States, not too good-looking, and they proved you don't have to be all that. Their lyrics were nice, the music pleasant. Very simple songs."

On 11 April, when John, Paul and Ringo arrived in Hamburg, they were shocked to learn from Astrid of the tragic death of their one-time colleague, Stuart Sutcliffe. After a trip back to Liverpool, where he met Brian Epstein for the first and only time, Stuart returned

* Records suggest that this actually took place at the Litherland town hall, 19 October 1961.

to Germany where his health steadily worsened. "For days at a time he would not come down from his attic studio to eat or sleep," Astrid said. "The headaches became violent, they seemed like fits." Nothing could be diagnosed as Stu continued to suffer severe headaches and seizures. "My head is compressed and filled with such unbelievable pain," he wrote. "Hour after hour . . . from screaming at the frustration, pain and helplessness. I must try and pull myself together . . . I must try hard." On 10 April 1962, after a particularly violent seizure, Stuart Sutcliffe died with Astrid by his side at 4.45 p.m. He was just twenty-one. The post-mortem revealed the cause of death as "cerebral paralysis due to bleeding into the right ventricle of the brain". According to Pete Best, when John heard, he burst into hysterical laughter, then "wept like a child. I had never seen him break down in public before . . . He was absolutely shattered." Members of Lennon's family believe that his friend's death haunted him for the rest of his life.

For years it has been widely speculated whether the Lathom town hall fight in January 1961 or a Hamburg scuffle contributed to Stuart's death. Stuart told his sister Pauline that John had turned on him in May 1961. Lennon was angry that Sutcliffe seemed to be putting more effort into his relationship with Astrid than he was into the Beatles. Paul and George, too, had been complaining to John about his friend's poor bass-playing. Pauline described the attack in *The Beatles' Shadow*: "[Stuart] said John had been brooding as they walked along but they were such good friends that they did not need to be constantly making conversation. Then, like a volcano, John blew up. Stuart did not know anything until he was splayed across the pavement. He said he could smell the streets: the debris of them; that was the only sense he had as John kicked him again and again . . . Stuart said John kicked him in the head and I'm convinced that kick was what eventually led to Stuart's death." However, according to one American neurological nurse who has studied the case, it was virtually impossible for the incident to have any bearing on Sutcliffe's death. In fact, the likely cause was congenital, possibly an aneurysm. "No head trauma causes cerebral bleeding and death that long after injury," she concluded. "Therefore, John could not have been responsible for Stu's death."

Shortly afterwards the band suffered yet another upheaval. In August 1962 Pete Best was abruptly sacked. Many point to his mother's constant meddling as a key factor. Certainly, she had done many positive things for the group, particularly in convincing Cavern owner Ray McFall to book them in his then trad jazz establishment, but her role as the band's unofficial manager, to the point of overseeing their contract negotiations with Brian Epstein at her home, was seen as crossing the line, especially by the ever-adversarial John. In the end, however, it was probably Best's inferior drumming that brought about his downfall. According to Howard DeWitt, author of *The Beatles: Untold Tales*, "The protests when Pete was fired have been greatly romanticized by the press. There was very little in Best's drumming to recommend him, and many professional drummers who witnessed this little drama snickered as young girls raised a hue and cry over the loss of Pete. One Liverpool musician suggested, 'Pete's departure was regretted for chiefly non-musical reasons.' "

In a recently discovered letter from Brian Epstein to a friend, the idea that McCartney alone wanted Best out of the group was refuted. "[Pete was too] conventional," he wrote. "Didn't fit well as a drummer or a man. Beat too slow, or so George thought. I liked him though he could be moody. Friendly with John, but Paul and George didn't like him . . ."

Maybe it was true Eppie had once made a move on the handsome Best in a Liverpool car park, and he'd politely refused the advance. Pete commented, "As far as I'm concerned there was no great build-up even though the conspiracy was obviously going on. It would have been nice if I'd been in a position to defend myself or simply ask why. While Brian was dismissing me there was a call from Paul asking whether the deed had been done! It would have been nice to have them there and actually ask why." One thing he says can never be taken away from him: he racked up more hours playing drums onstage for the biggest band in history than even Ringo Starr.

When Ringo joined the group on 18 August the Beatles' outer shell was complete, while John and Paul had already written "Love Me Do" and "Please Please Me".

Shortly before Best was given his marching orders, in the sweltering summer of 1962, Brian landed the Beatles a modest recording contract with Parlophone Records, a small subsidiary of the gigantic EMI, via producer George Martin. Their first formal session took place on Wednesday, 6 June, at EMI Studios in London.

Contrary to popular myth, this historic session was *not* simply another audition, but a recording date at which the Beatles cut demonstration lacquers of "Besame Mucho", "Ask Me Why", "Love Me Do" and "PS I Love You", which were never commercially released.

"Love Me Do" and "PS I Love You" went on to become the Beatles' first single. Although generally considered to be a Lennon composition, John (who later referred to "Love Me Do" as "pretty funky") conceded, "Paul wrote the main structure of this when he was sixteen or even earlier. I think I had something to do with the middle."

"I slagged off school to write that one with John when we first started," said McCartney. "You get to the bit where you think, If we're going to write great philosophy it isn't worth it. 'Love Me Do' was our greatest philosophical song. That's what we want to get back to, simplicity. You can't have anything simpler yet more meaningful than 'Love, love me do'."

The Hamburg-period ballad "PS I Love You" was written in the form of a letter and has McCartney stamped all over it. It is sentimental and decidedly middle-of-the-road. Perhaps someone should have asked the laid-back George Harrison if he had anything lying around he might like to record. Lennon later commented that it made him cringe from the moment they struck the first note. Some music critics draw comparisons with his own "Ask Me Why", with its similar slow Latin swing, but towards the end of his life, John told interviewers, "It was shit. Paul was trying to write 'Soldier Boy' like the Shirelles. He wrote it in Germany, or when we were going to and from Hamburg."

On the afternoon of Tuesday, 4 September, John, Paul, George and now Ringo ducked into the bureaucratic maze of EMI Studios for an ambitious session. They balked at recording "How Do You Do It", a number by fledgling songwriter Mitch Murray, but George Martin decided it was perfect and proclaimed it would place the band on the map. "When I played them the tune they were not very impressed," remembered Martin. "They said they wanted to record their own material and I read them the Riot Act. 'When you can write material as good as this I'll record it,' I told them. 'But right now we're going to record this.' And record it we did, with John doing the solo part. It was a very good record indeed, and it is still in the archives of EMI. I heard it recently and it sounds quite good even today. But it was never issued. The boys came back to me and said, 'We've nothing against that song, George, and you're probably right. But we want to record our own material.'"

The real gem of the day was the haunting "Love Me Do", on which Paul and John shared lead vocals. Engineer Norman Smith recalled the genesis of the now-legendary track: "After the first take we listened to the tape. It was horrible. Their equipment wasn't good enough. We hooked Paul's guitar up to our own bass amplifier and had to tie John's amplifier together because it was rattling so loud. They were very much in awe of the studio. They didn't realize the disparity between what they could play on the studio floor and how it would come out sounding in the control room. They refused to wear headphones, I remember. In fact, they hardly ever wore them."

Lennon had to pull together the song's distinctive harmonica solo literally on the spot. The style was heavily borrowed from Delbert McClinton's intro on the Bruce Channel hit, "Hey! Baby". A few months earlier he had appeared on the same bill with the Beatles, and John had asked him for a fifteen-minute harmonica lesson. He used what he had learned to give "Love Me Do" its resulting bluesy edge.

Lennon's ad-libbed instrumental left McCartney to sing the lead vocal. "I was very nervous," said Paul. "John was supposed to sing lead, but they changed their minds and asked me at the last minute, because they wanted John to play harmonica. Until then, we hadn't rehearsed with a harmonica; George Martin started arranging it on the spot. It was very nerve-racking." After the session, Martin confessed he wasn't impressed by the trite lyrics of "Love Me Do": "That was the best of the stuff they had, and I thought it pretty poor."

Nevertheless, it was released on Friday, 5 October 1962, and peaked at number seventeen two days after Christmas. The record's modest success represented a milestone to the group. Paul remembered, "In Hamburg we clicked, at the Cavern we clicked, but if you want to know when we knew we'd arrived, it was getting in the charts with 'Love Me Do'. That was the one, it gave us somewhere to go." However, by the autumn, the Beatles, while up and away, were not yet established. The powers-that-be in London considered them a ha'penny outfit of untrained hopefuls.

Another eccentric character they encountered in the early days was the outrageous pompadour-coiffured rocker from Macon, Georgia, "Little Richard" Penniman. Although all four cited him as one of pop's founding fathers, Paul idolized the piano-pounding, falsetto-singing sensation who infused gospel, country and blues with just a touch of vaudeville. It was McCartney who incorporated Penniman's songs into the group's set list in Quarry Men days and celebrated his final day at the Liverpool Institute by whipping out his guitar, jumping on to his desk and belting out his hero's staples, "Long Tall Sally" and "Tutti Frutti". "I tried to emulate Richard and sort of had a knack," he admitted. "I had all his records and loved him so much. I wanted to sing like that."

When the Beatles were playing in Hamburg in November 1962, the openly homosexual "Queen of Rock" struck up a mentoring friendship with the young British group. "I met the Beatles and introduced them to Billy Preston who was only fourteen years old and my organist," said Richard. "The Beatles became my buddies. They used to love to hear me talk. They said everything I sang rhymed. I knew the Beatles would be famous because they sounded like four Everly Brothers. If I had known how big they were going to become I would have hung on to their coats and gone with them."

Little Richard took full – and quite reasonable – credit for teaching Paul how to use his highest vocal register, heard in such classic hits as "I Saw Her Standing There", "I'm Down" and "Oh! Darling". McCartney said that doing Richard's voice was "an out-of-body experience. You have to leave your current sensibilities and go about a foot over your head to sing it." The boys hung out for hours with Richard, "asking him questions like he was God". The rock pioneer happily held court, sitting naked to the waist with an old grey army blanket draped around him. "Remember the time you threw all your rings off Sidney Island Bridge?" they asked. They were referring to a 1957 incident wherein Richard claimed he'd had a vision from God telling him to quit showbiz and join the ministry. He had flung his treasured rings off the bridge and had to be forcibly restrained from jumping off to retrieve them. "Oh, child," giggled Richard, eyes flashing, "let me tell you about that! I was in an evangelical mood and one day . . ."

The four young men watched while he prepared a steam treatment: he poured boiling water into a basin then added a decongestant, and inhaled, a towel over his head, to clear his voice. "Then he would go to the mirror," says Paul, "and go, 'Oh, Richard! You're so beautiful! I just can't help it, *I am just so beautiful*!' We learned all this jive talk off him."

Paul also told a story of when the Beatles and Little Richard were walking back to their hotel and Richard took Ringo's hand. "Those are beautiful rings, child, where did you get those rings?" he gushed flirtatiously. "Those are *sooo* beautiful. You know, I've got a ring just like that in my hotel room. Why, I'll give you a ring like that."

"Not realizing what the gig was," Paul went on, "we were all saying, 'He's going to give Ringo a ring, we'll all come!' Not realizing that he perhaps might really rather want to get him up there on his own!"

The Beatles returned to the studio on Monday, 26 November 1962 and reaped substantial benefits. The centrepiece of the session featured a remake of "Please Please Me". The first recording of the tune, however, featured a slow tempo that George Martin didn't like.

Lennon later recalled the inspiration behind it: "It was my attempt at writing a Roy Orbison song . . . I wrote it in the bedroom in my house at Menlove Avenue, which was my auntie's place. I heard Orbison doing 'Only The Lonely' or something . . . I was always intrigued by the words of 'Please, lend your little ears to my pleas', a Bing Crosby song. I was always intrigued by the double use of the word 'please'. So it was a combination of Bing Crosby and Roy Orbison."

"George Martin's contribution was a big one," McCartney confirmed. "The first time he ever really showed me he could see beyond what we were offering him was 'Please Please Me'. He said, 'Well, we'll put the tempo up.' George lifted the tempo and we all thought that was much better and it was ultimately a big hit."

Ever the perfectionist, Martin was so impressed that he allowed a mistake to remain in the final stereo version: Paul and John sang different lyrics on one line of the last verse. In his book, *All You Need Is Ears*, he wrote, "It went beautifully. I told them what beginning and what ending to put on it and they went into number-two studio to record. The whole session was a joy. At the end of it I pressed the intercom button in the control room and said, 'Gentlemen, you've just made your first number-one record.'"

True to his prophecy, "Please Please Me", officially released on 11 January 1963, shot to number one in both the *New Musical Express* and the *Melody Maker* charts. After nearly seven years of backbreaking, largely unrewarded non-stop work, the Beatles were an "overnight success".

Twenty-six-year-old Malcolm Evans was working as a telecommunications engineer for the Liverpool Post Office when he first encountered the Beatles. One day he was out window-shopping and stopped in his tracks at 10 Mathew Street. "I heard this wonderful music coming from under my feet in the fruit cellar of this old warehouse." He later said: "It was the Cavern, domed ceilings, very low. I paid a shilling, went in and immediately became a firm fan. I was going down so often that one day George came up and said, 'Hey, you're big and ugly enough, why don't you become a bouncer, get paid, get into the band room and meet the band?'"

For the next several months Evans worked part-time at the Cavern door, where he witnessed Ringo Starr's first appearance with the Beatles. He disputed the commonly held opinion that widespread riots erupted on the streets from Beatle fans outraged over the ousting of popular drummer Best. "It was just a few rowdies causing trouble," he claimed, although he added, "Poor George got a bloody nose from one of Pete's fans."

As luck would have it, in early 1963 the Beatles tour manager Neil Aspinall fell sick. "He had a terrible cold," noted Evans, "and asked me if I'd drive them down to London in the middle of a heavy snowfall. It was 23 January. They had to do some radio shows and it was in the middle of winter. It was freezing, snowing heavy, and we'd just left London when the windscreen shattered. I had to go two hundred miles, in the middle of the night, without a bloody windscreen . . . Every time things got rough, the Beatles would say, 'It's two hundred miles to go, Mal.' Two hundred miles is the distance between London and Liverpool." When they made it safely home John couldn't wait to tell Neil – or "Nell", as he sometimes called him – the story. "You should have seen Mal! He put a paper bag over his head and tore out a slit to see through. He looked like a fucking bank robber!" Years later McCartney remembered how the Beatles all lay on top of each other in a huge pile to keep warm. "A Beatle sandwich," he called it.

That same day they were due to go out of London on another gig and fretted over how they were going to get there. Evans turned up on schedule, with the windscreen replaced. By August he was officially on their payroll as the number-two road manager. He quickly proved himself indispensable as handyman, chauffeur, *ad hoc* butler and Man Friday. He set up and tested the equipment, checked security and could repair just about anything. "It was always," noted Ringo, "'Mal, have you got an Elastoplast? A screwdriver? A bottle of this?' He always had everything and if he didn't have it, he'd get it very quickly. Mal was our bodyguard and he was great because he would never hurt anyone. He was just big enough to say, 'Excuse me, let the boys through.' He was pretty strong. He could lift the bass amp on his own, which was a miracle. He should have been in the circus."

"All my life I wanted to be an entertainer," Evans said. "Being their roadie is the next best thing . . . Everywhere we go there's always five of us, even though sometimes I'm just standing in for Neil . . . They include me in the family. I never feel I work *for* the Beatles, I always feel I work *with* the Beatles."

Mal happily took on the most menial tasks. Describing life on tour in England he recalled, "I was up at 4.00 a.m. washing stage shirts and polishing boots because I wanted the group to look their best. I was so proud of them!"

With his congenial, outgoing nature and willingness to do any job – "To serve is to rule," he liked to say – and his loyalty to his employers, Evans quickly gained their confidence. One evening when the boys were relaxing backstage, watching a television programme, Evans was told that a gentleman was waiting on stage with a brand new state-of-the-art amplifier system they had ordered. He told the Beatles, but they were so engrossed in the show that nothing could divert their attention. "Here the fellow is waiting and the Beatles aren't budging. So I picked them up one by one and carried them on stage. They got a look at these great amps and started fooling with them and totally forgot about the programme. John actually gave me a hug. I felt 'in' at last!"

In his eleven-year tenure, Mal Evans grabbed the Beatles' coat-tails and hung on for the ride of his life.

On 18 April 1963 during the Beatles rehearsals at the Royal Albert Hall in London for the BBC Radio special *Swinging Sounds of '63* the boys met someone who, especially to Paul, became an important part of their extended London period, the seventeen-year-old actress Jane Asher. Paul remembered: "We knew her as the attractive, well-spoken chick we'd seen on *Juke Box Jury*. We all thought she was blonde because we'd only ever seen her in black and white and we went mad for blondes. Then she came backstage afterwards and we all immediately tried to pull her. We went to the journalist, Chris Hutchins's apartment on the King's Road. It was all very civilized."

Hutchins remembered the increasingly embarrassing evening: "The old Regency furniture in the cramped living room was hastily pushed aside to make space for the unexpected guests, and they squatted on the dark green carpet. As the only woman, Jane was in the centre. She was pale-faced and suitably thin for the period which spawned Twiggy. When she spoke, her voice reflected her Wimpole Street background, singling her out as upper-middle-class, yet her kindly smile made the rest of us feel comfortable. I raised my glass of

Mateus Rosé, then the sophisticated drink for young Chelsea trendies: 'To the Beatles!' "

"Yeah, the fans love us so much they want to tear us to fucking pieces," Lennon remarked.

"Oh, John," said Jane, "you're such a cynic. Admit it, you adore all the attention."

"Sure I'm a cynic. What we play is rock'n'roll under a new name. Rock music is war, hostility and conquest. We sing about love, but we mean sex, and the fans fucking know it."

"But they all think you're decent, clean-living chaps," Chris chimed in.

"It's just an image, and it's wrong. Look at the Stones. Rough as guts. We did that first and now they've pinched it!"

"You can't blame them," Ringo retorted quietly.

"The fans have to dream that one day they might marry a Beatle," said Jane.

"Yeah," snapped John, "but only those who haven't reached the age of puberty. I give some girl an autograph and she wants my tie or some hair. Then she wants to have sex. Then she tells me she's only fifteen. Jailbait! Is there any more booze?"

Chris poured the last of the wine into his glass: "That's the last of it. I wasn't really expecting company."

Things went from bad to worse: "Okay, so there's no booze," Lennon said. "Let's talk about sex. Jane, how do girls play with themselves?"

"I'm not going to talk about that!" she replied, almost in tears.

"You're the only girl here and I want to know. How do you jerk off?" John demanded.

"There's only one jerk here!" ventured Hutchins, in an effort to jab Lennon out of his bad behaviour.

"Oh, fab! No booze, no birds and insults from the host . . . what kind of rave is this? Bleedin' marvellous. I'm going to search for some crumpet. Call me a fucking taxi!"

Jane was now in tears and was being comforted by a deeply resentful George Harrison. "You know, John, you can be very cruel sometimes," she said.

Standing at the front door, Lennon exclaimed, "It's the beast in me!"

Almost immediately after he had stumbled out, Jane left the party accompanied by George. However, it was Paul who would soon begin to court her: "I ended up with Jane," he said, "because I'd maybe made the strongest play, or maybe she fancied me, I don't know . . . All very innocent stuff, so from then on I made strenuous efforts to become her boyfriend."

Lennon, by this time, had agreed to a "secret marriage" to Cynthia who was pregnant with their first and only child. "I was a bit shocked when she told me," remembered John, "but I said, 'Yes, we'll have to get married.' I didn't fight it." They were wed on 23 August 1962, with Brian Epstein as best man. Lennon's family, including Aunt Mimi, refused to attend, and Ringo was so new to the group he was not even told about it. As a wedding present, Brian granted them the use of his flat at 36 Falkner Street. John noted it was "the first apartment I'd ever had that wasn't shared by fourteen other students, girls and guys at the art school. Brian Epstein gave us his secret little apartment he had in Liverpool to keep his sexual liaisons separate from his home life." Julia Baird recalled that the Beatles took almost all of his time, both personally and professionally. Even after his and Cynthia's son, Julian, was born on 8 April 1963, it was a constant tussle between home and family. Late as usual, John would come bounding up the walls of the Cottage with baby Julian slung under his arm letting out the most ear-splitting scream imaginable. "Here, Ju, take him," he said, puffing from his sprint to the door. "We've got another bloody show tonight and I'm already an hour late getting to the station. Bye-bye, son, be a good boy. See you all soon, good luck!" With that he leaped into the van and off they'd race into the late-afternoon drizzle.

When they weren't babysitting, Julia and Jacqui Baird sometimes accompanied their brother to gigs. Once the girls rode with him to London for a concert at the Finsbury Park Astoria. John, said Julia, seemed nervous: "Just because I've been doing this rubbish since I was fifteen is no reason not to be edgy," he confided to his sisters. "You've got no idea what these shows are really like, Ju, twenty minutes of blithering idiots. None of us really likes it, but still, somehow, the show must go on."

Inside the dressing room the sisters were surprised to find the other Beatles enjoying a quiet drink with Mick Jagger.

"I thought you were rivals with the Stones," Julia whispered to John.

"Only as far as the media is concerned. In real life most of the groups are all mates."

Moments later the band was called on stage while Lennon's two sisters were shown to a specially cordoned-off section in the front row. Very carefully the stagehands lowered them down from the stage, much to the surprise of the screaming girls in the audience who, for a moment, thought they were part of the performance. Once the show began, a near riot erupted. The hysterical crowd was out of control and pushed its way forward, crushing Julia and Jacqui against the stage.

"Get the girls!" shouted John, between numbers. "*Now!*"

Security men leaped from the stage and hauled them to safety.

It was the kind of hysteria that the Beatles had first become familiar with in 1963, as they toured the country; their singing almost drowned out by the screams of the audience. It was after they topped the bill at Val Parnell's *Sunday Night at the London Palladium* on 13 October that the press memorably dubbed this phenomenon "Beatlemania". Nor was this adulation confined only to Britain: a trip to Sweden later that month saw the Fab Four surrounded by more screaming girls, some of whom managed to get inside their suite at the swank Hotel Continental.

November saw the Beatles stealing the show at the Royal Command Performance in front of the Queen Mother and Princess Margaret when Lennon memorably remarked to the specially invited audience, "For our last number I'd like to ask your help. Would the people in the cheaper seats clap your hands? And the rest of you, if you'd just rattle your jewellery." The press lapped it up, even the stuffy broadsheets were won over. When their second album *With the Beatles* was released on 22 November, with an astonishing 250,000 advance orders and sales hitting 1 million by Christmas, it was clear that Britain was now officially Beatle mad.

THREE

Please Escape Me From This Zoo

America and the World

1964–5

> "When we got to America everyone was walking around in fuckin' Bermuda shorts with Boston crewcuts and stuff on their teeth. The chicks looked like fuckin' 1940 horses! There was no conception of dress or any of that jazz. We just thought, What an ugly race. It looked disgusting."
>
> *John Lennon*

The Beatles' trip to Paris in January 1964 produced another onslaught of Beatlemania outside Britain according to Mal Evans, who recorded his impressions of the free-for-all backstage at the Olympia Theatre that broke out among photographers, each vying for exclusive shots. Punches were thrown, and George Harrison was trapped with his beloved Country Gentleman guitar tucked behind his back. The gendarmes charged in, while outside fans were rammed against the crush barriers. There were riots in the streets, traffic jams and crowds mobbing the George V Hotel where the Beatles were staying.* One red-shirted man leaped on stage and started dancing with John Lennon. Evans put out one massive paw, snatched him up and discarded him in the wings.

After the opening at the Olympia, they received a telegram from London: "Beatles top American hit parade." "I Want To Hold Your Hand" was a number-one smash. The boys went wild, Evans observed,

* Photographer Dezo Hoffmann, who was also with the Beatles at this time, recalls that in fact the Parisiennes were largely indifferent to the English popstars.

like schoolchildren, racing up and down the corridors, hooting in celebration, and Paul jubilantly leaped on his back. "It was the biggest thing in their young lives," he said. "We're going through it all together. It was very exciting."

By early 1964 the Beatles were cutting an unparalleled musical and cultural swath through every international city they stormed. Now as February rolled around they set their sights on the ultimate prize: America.

Capitol Records, who had nearly rejected them when first offered the group by EMI, launched a fifty-thousand-dollar promotional campaign to drum up interest in the USA. They plastered five million "The Beatles Are Coming!" stickers in telephone kiosks, buses and even public lavatories, and issued a comprehensive Beatles press kit containing wigs – J. Paul Getty was seen sporting one – a Beatles badge and auto-pen-signed photos. The blitz paid off: disc jockeys began to play the Beatles' music and interest swelled.

Still, the boys remained wary. On the flight over Paul worried: "America's got everything. Why should we be over there making money? They've got their own groups, what are we going to give them they don't already have?"

On 7 February, the Pan Am jet touched down at John F. Kennedy airport and taxied to the international arrivals terminal where an army of teenagers, headed by around three thousand on the observation roof, awaited them. Frenzied demands of "We want the Beatles!" greeted them. Paul cried, "Jesus, this is fucking great!"

A cadre of journalists had been assigned to cover the event. Like his fellow reporters, Al Aronowitz, on assignment for the *Saturday Evening Post*, was sceptical: what could four young men from Liverpool have to offer to the USA, the cradle of rock'n'roll, which had spawned Elvis Presley and, more recently, Bob Dylan?

Aronowitz recalled his first glimpse of the British invaders. "When they emerged from the airliner to a fanfare of screeches that drowned out even the whining of the jets, they were four young men in dark Edwardian four button suits. Their names were Ringo, Paul, John and George, but they were otherwise indistinguishable beneath the manes of their windblown, moplike hair."

On the way to the Plaza Hotel, through the quarter of a million fans who lined the Manhattan streets, the Beatles witnessed the same hysteria that had met them at the airport. The police fortified the building, allowing no one to enter without proper ID or a valid room key. One upper-crust matron, horrified by the unruly exhibition, demanded to be escorted to her suite. Several famous names also checked in, hoping for a glimpse of the British sensations, while resourceful fans, who had scaled the fire escapes, were found roaming the twelfth floor where the Beatles' entourage were staying. Police even found a trio of semi-nude girls waiting in the bathtubs in the Beatles' suites. Eventually the hotel manager was forced to increase security by calling in the Burns detective agency. He even pleaded with the Waldorf to take the Beatles in exchange for Nikita Khrushchev, scheduled to arrive later that month. The Plaza, an old-money bastion, regarded the shameless assault as a blight on its impeccable standards of propriety and decorum.

But Beatlemania was the word in Manhattan and an endless queue of journalists wanted to talk to pop's irresistible young guns. Requests poured in for licences to produce Beatles merchandise, from ashtrays to sanitary towels. The hotel switchboard was so jammed that its clientele couldn't get room service.

In anticipation of the watershed *Ed Sullivan* appearance in two days, Brian Epstein was embroiled in streamlining the Beatles' promotional arrangements with CBS executives. News mogul Walter Cronkite's daughter was the only network offspring granted access to the studio for the group's rehearsal. Talk-show king Jack Parr ended a long-time feud with Sullivan when his daughter Randy pleaded with him to get her a ticket to the "really big show".

Meanwhile, the Beatles' personal press officer, Brian Somerville, retreated to his room in tears. He'd had it out with Epstein over the unforeseen media circus at the airport and threatened to resign. He left that July, whereupon his replacement, the capable Derek Taylor, received the following cable at his NEMS Enterprises office in London:

UNDERSTAND THROUGH WEST COAST SOURCE YOU PLAN TO LEAVE BEATLES. CAN UNDERSTAND TRAVELING MOST TIRING AND YOUR

DESIRE TO SETTLE DOWN. WHILE WE HAVE NO IMMEDIATE OPENINGS ON KLIF DEEJAY STAFF, WE OFFER YOU THE MUSIC CRITIC'S POSITION ON NUMBER ONE STATION IN DALLAS. SUGGEST YOU REMAIN WITH GROUP UNTIL BEATLES APPEAR IN SEPTEMBER. IT WILL SAVE YOU MOVING EXPENSES. PLEASE ADVISE. CHARLES F. PAYNE, MANAGER KLIF DALLAS, TEXAS.

Amazingly, the cable was addressed to "John Lennon, the Beatles, London"! Taylor said: "The one who quit, of course, was Brian Somerville. You know, the 'genius' behind the Beatles. I think his official reason, according to the press announcement, was that he had done all he could for the Beatles and they didn't need him any more. He said they were ready to fly on their own, ready to fly like birds."

For their part, the Beatles took it all in their stride, watching television, sipping Scotch and Coke, making phone calls home to everyone they knew, enjoying the attention. Gotham's frenetic disc jockey Murray 'the K' Kaufman brought in the Ronettes to meet them. The girls giggled and reminded the group that they'd met back in England. George Harrison was curled up in a corner alone with his transistor radio, and joined in only to remark on the dreadful room-service fare. That night he came down with a sore throat and the hotel doctor was summoned.

The Beatles played their first US concert at Washington DC's Coliseum on 11 February before 8000 deafening fans. The next day they boarded a train back to New York for a performance at the normally high-brow Carnegie Hall. The mushrooming phenomenon did not escape the attention of Ed Sullivan, who reeled them in for an encore performance on his Sunday-night variety show on the sixteenth. Live from Miami's Deauville Hotel, the 3500 seats were overbooked, which caused a near riot among ticket-holders refused entry, but it drew in a staggering 70 million television viewers. Beatlemania was sweeping the nation in a way that the lads could not fathom.

Next, the Beatles relaxed in Florida for a week. From their home base on a luxury houseboat in Miami Bay, they tried water-skiing, deep-sea fishing and even attended a drive-in movie. Britain's prime minister, Sir Alec Douglas-Home, proudly declared the Beatles "our secret weapon".

On the twenty-first, they flew back to London, and four days later they were back in the EMI studios to lay down tracks for their next album, the soundtrack for their first film, *A Hard Day's Night.* A week later they went before the cameras, under Richard Lester's direction, to begin filming the now classic pseudo-documentary that captivated critics and fans alike, showcasing their individual charm and acting talent.

Something else too was brewing on the set. Following her success in Britain's Smiths Crisps advertisements Patricia (Patti) Boyd was cast in *A Hard Day's Night* by the director. George spotted her on the first day's filming and was overwhelmed by her big blue eyes, long blonde hair and kittenish personality. Standing around behind the scenes in her Mary Quant micro-mini and pale dolly-bird makeup, she looked the epitome of swinging London at its best. At the end of that first day, Patti and a couple of her friends summoned up the courage to walk up to all of the Beatles, except John, and ask for an autograph. To an innocent like Boyd, Lennon seemed too caustic to risk encountering him in a bad mood.

During the next few days, George's attention was not on his work, and Patti often felt his eyes on her. On the second day he invited her into the Beatles' private trailer for a cup of tea. She and her two younger sisters, Jennie and Paula, were from a steady middle-class home in the south of England, raised in a strict though loving environment and loyal to their men. Patti politely declined, telling George she was "semi-engaged" to another boy. On the third day he tried again, this time asking her out for "a proper date". Once again she put him off: she had an old-fashioned view of romance, she said, and couldn't hurt her boyfriend with a casual night on the town. Later that afternoon George approached her one last time. "She accepted," he remembered, years later. "We went out to dinner together and then drove around London talking about everything we could think of. I don't know if you could actually call it love at first sight, but by the end of the first week I had already met her mum. Three weeks later we were looking at houses together, so I guess you could definitely call us a couple."

During the first heady days of their romance, they were desperate for a few stolen moments away from the madness. George decided an Easter getaway at an Irish castle would be the perfect tonic, and they decided to invite John and Cynthia along on their adventure.

It began with the boys' going incognito, wearing false moustaches, scarves and hats. However, their disguise didn't fool other travellers as they scurried through Manchester airport with their baggage and boarded a six-seater plane for the bumpy flight across the Irish Sea.

Once at their luxury suite in the remote Dromoland Castle Hotel in western Ireland, where President Kennedy had stayed, George, Patti, John and Cynthia were at last able to relax. Cynthia liked Patti's spirit and enthusiasm, comparing her with a butterfly. All four revelled in their freedom.

It was short-lived. Early the next morning they were jolted out of a deep sleep by an endless barrage of phone calls and commotion. They peered out of the window in horror at a regiment of *paparazzi* and journalists, fighting for an exclusive. Inside, the hotel teemed with reporters and cameramen stalking the corridors and cramming the lobby.

"One trip to America and everyone thinks they bloody well own us!" cried Lennon. "How are we fuckin' gonna get out of here?"

The hotel staff came up with a plan to shuttle their guests back to the airport on the sly, their main concern to shield Patti and George. The boys would be chauffeured away while the girls would put on chambermaid uniforms to push a wicker laundry cart full of dirty linen to the hotel's staff entrance. Once there, they would empty the hamper and climb in, closing the lid.

The plan, however, went awry. A security man was supposed to escort the hamper to the waiting laundry van in which Patti and Cynthia would be set free, but it was tossed in and the van sped away without him. The women were trapped.

The driver tore round hairpin curves, and the basket flew about the van, its occupants rolling and bumping inside it as if they were in a pinball machine. Cynthia recalled, "Exhausted and hoarse, we eventually gave in with arms, legs and feet scrunched up in the most unlikely positions. We completed the journey feeling like a couple of redundant acrobats from Billy Smart's Circus."

When they reached the airport, dishevelled and dirty, John joked, "Good God, you look like a couple of right scrubbers!" But the escape had been a rousing success and the girls were triumphant that they had outwitted their pursuers.

Not long afterwards on 2 May 1964, the two couples again set out on holiday, this time yachting in Tahiti. They had envisaged sunny days and tropical breezes, but they were met with monsoon rain and bitter winds. On the island they were taken to a quayside bar, rife with cockroaches, where they waited to join their yacht. They were appalled to discover that it was no more than a decrepit fishing-boat. In disbelief they followed the cook below deck to the cramped bunks, which were far from the luxury cabins they'd paid for.

By morning the driving rain had escalated into a full-fledged tropical storm. The crew, who spoke no English, were unimpressed by their celebrity passengers, tossing them raincoats and wellingtons. As they cast off, monstrous waves whipped the boat skyward and slammed it back against the sea. Everyone hung on to anything that was bolted down, as towering swells threatened to toss them overboard.

"John, I'm frightened!" cried Cynthia, through the din as her hat flew into the water. "I'll never see Julian again! Tell them to turn back!" Both girls, stomachs churning, fought their way below deck and collapsed.

When the storm passed, everyone calmed down and found the crew gracious and helpful; they even dined happily on the steady diet of potatoes. Out on the ocean no one could touch them. "When I finally found my sea legs it turned out to be a truly marvellous holiday," Cynthia acknowledged. "We felt as free as the wind, not a soul to bother us or even to care who we were."

*

A most unfortunate incident – as far as Lennon and his family were concerned – was the sudden and unexpected reappearance in John's life of Alfred Lennon in March 1964, during the filming of *A Hard Day's Night*. McCartney takes up the thread: "It was certainly a great pity when he showed up again after those many years. We got to know about it from an article in Sunday's *People*, which said something like, 'BEATLES DAD WASHES DISHES AT THE BEAR HOTEL IN ESHER.' (In fact, it was the Greyhound Hotel in Hampton Court.) I was with John at the time, and he just kind of went, 'Ooooohhh . . .' Luckily, we both had a good robust nature, so we could say, 'Oh, bloody hell, isn't it typical?' We managed to laugh it off like that. Eventually, of course, John did agree to see him."

Lennon's father had not tried to contact him since 1945. Apparently he had had no idea about John's career until 1964 when a workmate pointed out an article on the Beatles to him and said, "If that's not your son, Lennon, then I don't know what!" Almost immediately, stories about Alfred were appearing in the newspapers, but he denied that he had sought the publicity. In his words, "It just happened."

"I never saw him until I made a lot of money and he came back," said John. "I opened the *Daily Express* and there he was, working in a small hotel, very near where I was living in the stockbroker belt outside London. He had been writing me for some time trying to get in contact. I didn't really want to see him, though. I was too upset about what he'd done to me and me mum, and that he would turn up after I was rich and famous and not bother before. Originally, I wasn't going to see him at all, but he sort of blackmailed me in the press by saying he was a poor old man washing dishes while I was living in luxury. I fell for it and saw him, and I suppose we had some kind of relationship."

Contrary to most reports, however, John's old friend Pete Shotton saw him almost immediately after his first meeting with his father and said that, at first, Lennon was encouraged by it: "He's good news, Pete! A real funny guy, a loony just like me!" The initial glow wore off, however, when Cynthia invited him to spend the night at

Kenwood and three days of highly emotional scenes followed between John and his father. Later it was alleged that Alfred had tried to make a pass at his daughter-in-law.

That year, Mr Lennon teamed up with record producer Tony Cartwright, and cooked up a scheme to promote Alfred as a pop singer. Incredible as it sounds, they even landed a record deal with the Piccadilly label. Amid a flurry of London publicity, a lengthy press release was included with the promotional copies of Alfred's one and only single entitled, "That's My Life (My Love and My Home)":

> Fifty-three-year-old Freddie Lennon, father of John, has made his first record. Mr Lennon has been an entertainer in an amateur capacity most of his life. When he left the sea twelve years ago, Freddie took a job as a waiter, and later worked in holiday camps at various northern resorts. He came to live in London seven years ago. Over the years, Freddie was always interested in songwriting, but never took it seriously. Six months ago, he met Tony Cartwright, who is now his manager. Together they wrote "That's My Life", the story of Freddie's life. The song was accepted by a music publisher, and recorded.

Naturally, as a curiosity, the record received quite a lot of airplay, and Beatle Lennon came in for a lot of ribbing in the media about it. He was livid. Strangely, he wasn't angry with his father but, rather, manager Cartwright. As far as John was concerned, encouraging Alfred to make that record had been unforgivably manipulative: his father had no experience in show business and was, therefore, ripe for the taking. To top it, Piccadilly also issued publicity photos of Alfred attempting to play the guitar with his all-but-toothless mouth wide open in song. The sensitive Lennon was deeply embarrassed.

Uncle Charlie explains: "Apparently, as soon as Alfred's record started moving up the charts, Brian Epstein stepped in and somehow took control of his contract from the record company and, before you knew it, the disc all but disappeared. Anyway, Cartwright and Freddie had gone off to see John about it at Kenwood, but he just slammed the door in their faces.

"Later that night, Freddie rang me in Birmingham and told me all about it. 'I don't think he would have turned me away if I didn't happen to be with Tony,' he said, obviously very hurt. 'Perhaps it was a mistake to ever have got involved with any of this in the first place.' Frankly, I was miffed at John for treating his dad like that so I wrote him a stinking letter for acting like such a child. His response? A totally unexpected phone call from him inviting me up to Kenwood for a visit! 'It's your birthday this weekend, isn't it, Uncle Charlie?' he said. 'Why not take some time off and come see your "childish" nephew?'

"After a lot of hassle with my employer – I was scheduled to work that weekend – I finally ended up going down, but John was out doing some film work with the Beatles. I spent the afternoon chatting with Cynthia and, later that evening, John came home, as happy as a lark, going on and on about how, no matter what anybody said, he really thought deep down his dad was great. I didn't dare mention the letter for fear he might punch me in the face or something!

"Despite the controversy, though, Freddie was genuinely very proud of John. 'He's a typical Lennon all right,' Freddie often told me." According to Charlie, Freddie would reminisce about their father, a well-known entertainer who once toured America as part of the Kentucky Minstrels. " 'The talents in this family! Why, look at our dad. Mum always used to say that if only they could have afforded a piano, somebody in the family would have definitely become a pianist!' "

In June the runaway train that was Beatlemania steamed through yet another continent. In a whirlwind tour down-under, unbridled fanaticism almost turned to tragedy. Al Aronowitz wrote, "In Australia the Beatles left an estimated one thousand casualties including a man who had an epileptic fit, a girl who burst a blood vessel in her throat from shrieking too loudly and a dozen more who were kicked by horses' hoofs while trying to crawl beneath the mounted police to get to the Beatles' car. Still another girl suffered carbon-monoxide poisoning when the mob knocked her down next to the exhaust pipe of an automobile hemmed in by the crowd. The girl realized the exhaust blowing in her face might asphyxiate her but she couldn't get up as a bunch of other girls climbed on top of her to get a better view of the Beatles. She almost died."

It was against this unfortunate backdrop that the Beatles headed back to Liverpool for an official homecoming. Since they last played the Cavern things had changed among Liverpool's youth: a young man's future was no longer assumed to be a lifetime of toil on the docks, as his father's and grandfather's had been. The Beatles had blazed a trail to international adventure and prosperity, followed by acts like Gerry and the Pacemakers, Cilla Black, and Billy J. Kramer with the Dakotas. There were now some 350 beat bands within an eight-mile radius, all hoping to capitalize on the Mersey mania.

For many natives, however, the Beatles were not the great liberators the young took them for. To these stalwart citizens the boys, once the pride of Liverpool, had sold out, left town to chase the almighty dollar and forgotten their roots. They were no longer fellow Scousers but cosmopolitan, snooty Londoners. The Liverpool police even recorded several death threats against the group and their families.

On the plane to Liverpool on 10 July, the Beatles, aware of the controversy, were on the defensive. The way Paul saw it, the only significant change in them was that they were richer: "We think we've got something because we'd be idiots if we didn't. The danger is in the narrow-minded, soft people who will say it's gone to our heads. We've always had exactly the same kind of faith in ourselves. It's not conceit, it's just confidence."

As the plane landed in Liverpool, the Beatles grew excited. A couple of fans who had won a competition to accompany the group had them reminiscing about their Cavern days. Ringo raised his shirt to expose the scars from some fourteen stomach operations. Paul chatted about the racehorse he'd just bought for his father's sixty-second birthday: it had come second in its début race.

As the jet descended Paul pointed out landmarks, old and new.

"Look at that!" cried George. "A new estate!"

Any doubts that they had been missed evaporated when the plane taxied to the terminal where a crowd of some 1500 (the allowed limit) Liverpudlians were waiting for them on the airport roof. "It's bigger than when Matt Monroe landed!" Lennon exclaimed.

The band piled into their Austin Princess and followed the eight-motorcycle police escort into the city. A staggering 150,000 people lined the ten-mile route, cheering, tossing jellybabies and flowers, eventually spilling into the road to mob the vehicle, claw the windows and throw themselves on to the bonnet. Police propelled the fans off the road and onto the kerb.

At the town hall, some twenty thousand admirers were pressed against barricades fashioned from wooden pilings cemented into the cobblestones. Fans hung out of windows, from tree branches and off rooftops. No one could recall anything like it – even the Queen's visit didn't compare. In the crush of madness some four hundred were injured.

Liverpool's mayor, Louis Laplan, decked out in white tie and tails, led the boys into the town hall and up the grand staircase as the Liverpool police band played "Can't Buy Me Love". Ringo danced up the steps as they were led into the impressive second-floor ballroom with its extravagant chandeliers. Seven hundred invited guests and four hundred gate-crashers descended on the refreshments; but the moment the Beatles entered, escorted by a lone policeman, they were rushed by masses of those present, who rammed them into the table, doubling them over. Mal came to the rescue and dragged them out. His new Rolex was stolen in the mêlée.

The Beatles were paraded on the balcony to a heroes' homecoming unknown in Liverpool's history. Paul and Ringo boogied and whistled as one of their records played. As the mayor introduced them, John buried his face in the man's regalia, then gave a Hitler salute to the crowds. The mayor began his speech: "I have here a letter from the orthopaedic hospital, which says that when the children heard Beatles' songs they took a new lease on life and many were inspired to get up and walk for the first time."

The Beatles' final stop was the Odeon Theatre for the northern première of *A Hard Day's Night.* Once more their car tunnelled through a mass of hysterical girls hurling themselves at it. A few latched on to the boot and were dragged along the street, finally ripping it open. At the theatre, the band opened a telegram of congratulations from Prince Philip. All this for four young men who, only a year or so before, had had to share sandwiches in Liverpool clubs.

Finally, back at the airport for the trip to London, the Beatles were corralled in an executive suite to await their flight. Thousands of the faithful stood in drenching rain for a glimpse of their new idols. They wound down with their usual Scotch and Coke, but John refused to touch the sandwiches that had been provided: "I used to wrap them," he explained. "I worked at the airport and I used to spit in them, wipe them in the dirt and even come in them."

While they waited, the mayor produced photographs to be signed for his constituents. Paul and John joked, "Yes, Your Holiness, we'd better sign these!"

Lennon got in a political jab: "Yeah, Louie, I saw people in the crowd today without any teeth. When are you going to get them teeth, hey?" As they boarded the plane he took one final look at the assembly on the roof. "They were getting us worried," he joked. "They'll never say they don't like us here any more!"

Later that same month John and Cynthia had tired of the constant intrusions by fans at their temporary home, a walk up at 13 Emperor's Gate in Knightsbridge, London, and began house-hunting. They soon settled on Kenwood, a Tudor-style house in Weybridge, Surrey, with twenty-seven rooms. They bought it for twenty thousand pounds on the advice of their accountant, Walter Strach, who lived just down the road. Although their new home had several reception rooms, the family gravitated to the kitchen. Almost immediately John commissioned designer Ken Partridge to renovate and redecorate the property at a cost of about forty thousand pounds. Partridge had done up Brian Epstein's Knightsbridge flat and John was very impressed with the result.

"One thing I remember was a lovely handcrafted rocking-horse John and Cyn surprised Julian with a couple of months earlier," recalled Julia Baird. "The only problem was he was still far too small to sit on it without falling off. So either we would have to hold him or, better yet, ride it ourselves!"

An impressive feature of the estate was the spectacular tiled swimming-pool just behind the kitchen at the rear of the house. Lennon designed it with an elaborate "psychedelic eye" on the bottom. Upstairs, among the half-dozen bedrooms, was John and Cynthia's, with a four-poster bed, and an *en suite* Italian marble bathroom.

"At the time of our first visit," said Julia, "John was busy with his many Beatle-related duties and finally learning how to drive. Not being able to really drive himself, however, wasn't any great impediment to him buying several fine cars. Among his collection was a matte black Ferrari, the Rolls and a lovely all-white Mini with electric windows. Although he hadn't got round to taking his test, that didn't stop him insisting on taking us all for a ride. 'Might be a little risky actually driving on the road just yet,' John muttered, as Jacqui and I piled into the diminutive two-door. 'Perhaps we would be better off simply going for a little spin on the golf course?'

"'Oh, John, you can't!' squealed my sister, laughing. 'You'll be nicked.'

"'Are you kidding?' said John, indignantly. 'I'm a Beatle! No one would dare say a word!'

"Although he was obviously only kidding, it struck me that perhaps John was finally beginning to understand the unique position he was in. Off we sped, tearing into the turf with a vengeance. Up and over the hilly fairways and careering through the bunkers we all felt happy, wild and free. Fortunately, it was still early in the day and no one was golfing. Otherwise we might have had the opportunity to test John's theory of Beatle infallibility."

That August the Beatles returned to the USA and took the country by storm; it just couldn't get enough of them. Mal Evans liked to point out that although violence was rarely associated with Beatles' tours, there was the ever-present danger that thousands of hysterical teenagers presented. "At San Francisco's Cow Palace [on 19 August 1964]," he said, "we were late in arriving and normally I look after security but we didn't have the time. It was the only time I'd been drinking on the job. We'd had three days off in LA, partying. It was absolute chaos."

The boys had to be smuggled from the venue back to their hotel. "The crowds surged forward," Ringo remembered. "Had we got in the limousine we were supposed to be in we could have been killed, but fortunately we were safe in an ambulance with seven sailors. The girls smashed the roof of our empty limo."

It was downright scary when they arrived in Houston. "You can't tell the police anywhere they need security," Evans complained. "They all think, Our kids aren't like that. The children in our town are fine. We can handle them. When we landed at the airport only two motorbike policemen were waiting to control the entire crowd. They soon disappeared under the throngs never to be seen again.

"At the airport the plane had barely come to a stop on the runway when crowds of Beatlemaniacs, some 5000 strong, stormed police barricades and the aircraft. The propellers had barely stopped turning when the fans were all over the plane." Some, Evans said, even forced their way into the cockpit and locked themselves in for several hours. Things became so impossibly out of hand that a fork-lift truck was called in to raise the boys above the clamouring admirers and chauffeur them a safe distance from the pandemonium.

Security, Evans pointed out, was essential, not only for the band's safety but for the fans': "In Dallas there just wasn't an appropriate security detail at the Beatles' hotel. One young girl, overcome by hysteria, hurled herself right through the plate-glass door of the hotel. It was very dangerous."

The unquestionable highlight of the tour, however, came offstage in New York on the evening of 28 August 1964: the day the Beatles met Bob Dylan. For the Fab Four, Dylan was a league above them, the established American folk-poet laureate, and a daunting, imposing, inscrutable figure. A few months earlier, while hanging out at London's trendy Ad Lib club, John said dismissively to journalist Pete Hamill, "To hell with Dylan! We play rock'n'roll. Give me Chuck Berry. Give me Little Richard. Don't give me that fancy American folky intellectual crap!" To Dylan, the Beatles were pure "bubblegum" and their teenybopper followers a disgrace to any respectable musician. Why should he waste his time on these pimply pop idols?

In fact, Lennon wrote "I'll Cry Instead" after hearing Dylan's début album, and Dylan took up electric guitar in the wake of "I Want To Hold Your Hand". "Lennon and McCartney were doing things nobody was doing," the Minnesota-born composer was forced to admit. "Their chords were outrageous and their harmonies made it valid. I knew they were pointing the direction music had to go. I was not about to put up with other musicians, but in my head the Beatles were *it*."

Al Aronowitz, a long-time Dylan friend and now a firm Beatles' supporter, appointed himself intermediary for the summit he would later call his crowning achievement. "I was brokering the most fruitful union in the history of pop music. In many ways I saw Dylan and Lennon as mirror images, personifications of hip on the opposite sides of the Atlantic, each epitomizing the culture of his country and each emerging as a spokesman of its culture. To me Bob and John were brothers born of the same creative clay, both towering bastions of individuality. They certainly were both so different from everybody else as to make people take notice. To me, Lennon was Dylan's English reflection through the looking-glass and across the sea in the land of left-hand drive. As soon as I got to know John I started telling him he ought to meet Bob. Lennon kept saying he wanted to wait until he was Dylan's ego equal. 'I wanna meet him, but on me own terms.' "

After many attempts, Aronowitz pressed Dylan into a reluctant meeting. On that evening, following a performance by the Beatles at Forest Hills, he and Dylan drove up to the ritzy Hotel Delmonico on Park Avenue in Dylan's humble blue Ford station-wagon chauffeured by roadie Victor Maymudes. The trio ploughed their way through the crowd straining behind police barricades and into the lobby. At the lifts they encountered several burly policemen who forbade them access.

Finally Mal Evans came to the rescue, and escorted them to the Beatles' suite where hordes of photographers and reporters were camped outside, along with Peter, Paul and Mary, and the Kingston Trio, all hoping for a few moments with the occupants. Press officer Derek Taylor entertained them while they waited.

Inside, they found the Beatles finishing their room-service dinner

– Delmonico steaks, the speciality of the house. After somewhat awkward introductions, the gathering retired to the sitting room where Dylan requested his usual "cheap wine". "I'm afraid all we have is champagne," Brian Epstein apologized, and sent Evans out for Chianti while Dylan began on the Scotch. Eventually the Beatles offered their guests some pick-me-up purple hearts. This was the moment Aronowitz had been waiting for: he gestured to Maymudes who had a stash of marijuana in his pocket and said, "Hey, let's have a smoke."

To his surprise, the Beatles told him they'd never tried it. Like many, Aronowitz had assumed the line in "I Want To Hold Your Hand" was "I get high" rather than "I can't hide". "They considered pot smokers to be the same as junkies," Aronowitz revealed. "Like the DEA they put grass in the same category as heroin." Now, realizing he had introduced the great Beatles to the drug Aronowitz gave the honour of rolling their first joint to Dylan. "Bob wasn't much of a roller," he later conceded, "and a lot of the grass fell into the big bowl of fruit on the room-service table."

Another concern was the posse of New York's men in blue prowling the corridors outside. In order to prevent the pungent odour from seeping into the hallway the party placed towels under the doors and retreated to the far end of the room near the windows and closed the blinds. With the first joint now ready, Dylan handed it to John, who immediately passed it to Ringo, saying, "You try it," then muttering something about Ringo being the "royal taster". According to the reporter's instructions, Starr inhaled deeply and found it to his liking. However, he was unaware of marijuana-smoking protocol, and failed to pass the joint round, handling it like a cigarette – much to the disapproval of Dylan and Aronowitz, who knew how difficult it was to find such potent cannabis.

Before long everyone was in a very merry state, including Epstein and Taylor – Aronowitz said that the latter ended up the biggest dope-smoker of them all. Ringo was giggling, working his way up to hysterical laughter. The suddenly laid-back Brian kept repeating, "I'm so high I'm on the ceiling!" He stood before the mirror, pointed to himself and muttered, "Jew," which had the others rolling on the floor. Paul, not one to let such an auspicious occasion pass by, instructed Evans to fetch a notepad and jot down any nuggets of wisdom he might come up with. The next day he checked the paper and read, "There are seven levels." He reckoned that must have been a sublime reference to the world's great religions.

"After they met," remembered Aronowitz, "the Beatles' lyrics got grittier and Bob invented folk-rock." The change, according to music historian John Marck, came with the *Beatles For Sale* album, a work little recognized for Dylan's influence, despite Lennon's distinctly Dylanesque "I'm A Loser". "In their early works," says Marck, "Lennon, McCartney and Harrison tried to emulate, to some degree, Dylan's writing. They had been drawn to Dylan because the words in his songs were as important as the music. It was not until Dylan introduced them to marijuana that their artistic freedom surfaced."

McCartney even admitted his brassy "Got To Get You Into My Life", from the marijuana-enhanced *Revolver* album, was not about a woman but, rather, a blatant ode to the drug: "We were kind of proud to have been introduced to pot by Dylan, that was rather a coup. It was like being introduced to meditation and given your mantra by Maharishi. There was a certain status to it."

In the wake of that monumental evening at the Delmonico, the Beatles shared many such moments with "Dylan Thomas", as John liked to call him. The occasions were characteristically awkward. As John pointed out, "We'd spend time together but I always used to be too paranoid or aggressive and vice versa. He'd come to my house, can you believe it? This bourgeois life I was leading, and I used to go to his hotel." As Aronowitz noted, "For two of the greatest communicators of their time, Dylan and Lennon certainly seemed to give the appearance of being tongue-tied every now and then."

Still, there were moments of hilarity too. One time the Beatles, Dylan and Aronowitz spent the night trawling aimlessly around Greenwich Village, finally stopping for breakfast at four a.m. at the Brasserie. John pulled out a yellow toy aeroplane he'd found in Aronowitz's car, which belonged to the journalist's young son. He ran it across the table and over everyone's faces. Inevitably, during such encounters someone would pull out a joint. "Let's have a laugh!" Lennon would bellow.

Meanwhile, back in Liverpool, a sudden development was about to rattle Paul and change for ever the dynamic of the McCartney clan. Since his wife's death Jim McCartney had done his best to provide a stable home for his two boys. With Paul and Mike now grown-up and Jim having retired and moved into Rembrandt, the elegant five-bedroom home on Baskerville Road that Paul had bought for him, the McCartney patriarch found himself lonely and at a loose end.

In the autumn of 1964, Paul's cousin Elizabeth Robbins, better known as Auntie Bette, ran into her old friend Angela Williams whom she hadn't seen since their childhood holidays at Butlins. She discovered that the energetic thirty-four-year-old Angela, a secretary and the mother of a young daughter, Ruth, had been widowed two years previously. Angela explained: "She was thinking, a young widow, active, capable. Uncle Jim, living in complete isolation in Rembrandt, afraid to hire a housekeeper because if he even sent out laundry in those days they used to cut up the sheets in little bits in case Paul slept on them. Jim was a prisoner in his nice new house."

Bette suggested that she and her husband go out for an evening with Angela and Jim, and everyone agreed. As soon as Jim opened the door to her, Angela had an overwhelming premonition: "I thought, I'm going to marry this man." After a pleasant evening, Jim asked his "date" if she wouldn't mind staying on for a little while after the Robbins had departed. The two talked until dawn and began a courtship. Their dates largely consisted of family gatherings centred around Jim's sisters, the kindly but timid Auntie Millie and the gossipy, domineering Auntie Jin, known as the "McMatriarch". Both women had helped Jim bring up his boys in the absence of their mother. Breaking into this tight-knit clan was a daunting proposition, especially for a woman twenty-eight years Jim's junior.

In late November, Angela brought four-year-old Ruth to meet Jim, who was instantly smitten by her. He took her into the garden, and later gave her one of the stuffed animals that fans lavished on

Paul. Later that night he sat Angela down. "I want to ask you something," he said. "I think we both know where this is leading. How do you want to work this? Do you want to live with me, be employed as my housekeeper, or do you want to marry me?"

"I would only go for marriage," affirmed Angie. "After all, I have a daughter to consider."

Almost immediately the phone rang. "Angie, come and speak to Paul."

She heard the voice of the world's premier pop idol: "Me dad's just told me the news. You sound nice. Are you staying the night? I'll jump in the car and be there in three or four hours."

Around one in the morning Paul sprang into the kitchen to meet his future stepmother. "Is Ruth sleeping?" he asked. "Well, you've gotta get her up!"

With that, the sleepy child was carried downstairs and Paul gathered her on to his lap. She took one look at him and said, "You're on my cousin's wallpaper!" Then she lifted up her pyjama top and pointed to a recent incision from a kidney operation. "I've got a scar! See my scar?"

McCartney grinned. "Ringo's got lots of scars too."

Paul made a memorable first impression on Ruth. The next day he swept her into his Aston Martin for a trip to meet some of the family: "I remember the smell of the leather made me sick," she said. "Paul was wearing navy blue pinstripe trousers, blue loafers without socks, a white T-shirt and jacket. He had a record-player in the car and you could put three or four records on at a time. When you went round a corner, or over a bump, it used to jump and I giggled. The records would sometimes melt in the sun. I remember Paul playing a warped Elvis single and it sounding all garbled. 'One day they'll make something better than this,' he told me, and sure enough a few years later when eight-track came out he reminded me, 'See, I told you!' "

McCartney was an alert and careful driver. "My father was killed in a car crash," Ruth said, "and I was nervous of anything with wheels on it. But with Paul I felt very secure. We went round to meet the Robbins. He thought it would be good for me to meet my new cousins. Kate Robbins is a talented singer and we became really close.

Paul was very conscious of visiting family when he came to Liverpool about every three weeks. He's always been a real family boy."

Jim and Angela tied the knot on 24 November 1964 in a wedding that none of the McCartneys attended. "I don't want this to be a bloody circus!" said Jim, who wanted to avoid media intrusion at all costs. On their way to Carog church in Wales, Jim asked an unlikely gravedigger named Griff to be a witness, and Ms Williams became Mrs James McCartney as the organist played "Yesterday". For all the planned secrecy word soon leaked out and photographers snapped the newlyweds all the way from Wales to Rembrandt's back garden. When Ruth discovered she had a new daddy and a grand place to live, "It was like all my Christmases had come at once."

Later, in February 1965, Jim had an opportunity to take his bride on a belated honeymoon. The Beatles were making their second film, *Help!*, in the Bahamas, an ideal getaway spot. Arrangements were made and the couple jetted to Nassau for five weeks in the Caribbean. As it turned out, the Beatles arrived at the same time. "We walked into the [press] conference," explained Angela, "thinking Paul would be [smiling]. But he looked at his father and said, 'What are you doing here?' in front of a roomful of people. John was obviously embarrassed and quickly said, 'Hey, congratulations, you guys got married! Isn't that wonderful? Let's all get together.' It was John who diffused a very hostile situation."

Balmy nights were spent at the hotel bar swapping stories with *Help!*'s co-star Victor Spinetti and other cast members. John would hiss loudly every time Leo McKern, who played the villain, came in. To celebrate Ruth's fifth birthday the hotel's chef produced a cake in her honour. Familiar with "She Loves You", he had decorated the cake with four Beatle heads and "*Ja Ja Ja* [yeah yeah yeah]!"

The all-important metamorphosis of the Beatles from carefree millionaire young men to aspiring musical mystics began to unfold in the spring of 1965 during filming of *Help!*. Richard Lester had decided to employ local Indian musicians for some key sequences in the soundtrack, and enlisted one of Indian music's foremost composers, Pandit Shiv Dayal Batish. He was also a renowned vocalist, arranger and conductor, who had helped to popularize the emerging Indian film industry. Lester needed him to play a classical Indian stringed instrument, the *vichitra veena*.

Soon after Batish and three other Indian musicians arrived at London's Twickenham Studios the cultural differences between them and the Beatles became apparent. Batish remembered: "We'd barely finished tuning our instruments when [George Harrison] came over to us and said, 'You can't work all the time, mate! This is teatime, that's the rule!' I was taken aback by his remark. This was most unlike India where once you entered the studio you were supposed to keep working until lunchtime. Anyway, we went to the canteen and had our tea with some snacks."

Back in the studio, the Beatles inspected the instruments, fascinated by a wooden peacock's head on the *vichitra veena*. "With typical British wit," Batish noted, "John Lennon praised its workmanship. In another instant he stood near the peacock's head and pretended to lure the bird with some grain in his hand at which all of us had a great laugh."

Help! co-star Roy Kinnear revealed, "George seemed immensely interested in it all, and before we knew it, he had someone run out and buy him a cheap sitar from one of those Indian shops near the British Museum. There they all were in a little clump plucking away. None of it made much sense to me, of course, but it kept Harrison happy."

During the day-long session, Batish played several cross-cultural Beatle riffs on the *veena* and said afterwards, "Working with the Beatles not only earned us fame and popularity in the West, but also brought us great respect within the Indian community."

Back in Liverpool, Jim adopted Ruth ("I should be a proper dad to her," he decided) and the family settled into their new life. Angela, who'd left her job, put her secretarial skills to work by tackling the mail that flooded into Rembrandt from Paul's fans at the rate of two huge sackfuls a day. The requests were bizarre, to say the least: "Please have Paul chew this piece of gum and send it back," or "Have Paul smoke this cigarette and return the butt." Someone even sent a chewing-gum wrapper asking Paul to burn it and mail back the ashes.

A pair of Japanese girls corresponded for over fifteen years and mailed several expensive gifts to Ruth, including handmade slippers and exquisite Asian dolls. In turn, Angela responded to fans with Beatle tokens and letters, although she was warned not to. One incident made the reason for that precaution all too clear. "We began receiving letters from a Denise Hanes from Texas," Angela said. "As she continued to write, I noticed the postmarks were getting increasingly closer to England, at one point from Africa. One day we got a call from the Merseyside dock police saying, 'Mrs McCartney, we've got a girl here who stowed away on a ship and she said if we contacted you you would receive her.' "

"Is her name Denise Hanes by any chance?"

"Yes. Are you expecting her?"

They put Denise on the phone at which point Paul, who happened to be at Rembrandt, grabbed the receiver. "Your parents must be horrified," he told her. "You really shouldn't do this. No, I'm just leaving."

A year later Denise showed up on their doorstep, suitcase in hand, having travelled some six thousand miles. The kindly Angela invited her in for tea and she stayed until Jim motioned for his wife to get rid of her. She continued to hang around McCartney's Cavendish Avenue home, and over the years wangled her way into the family inner circle. She even befriended Linda and snapped photos of daughters Stella and Mary.

There were frightening moments too. On one quiet evening, Angela, Ruth and Jim had sat down to dinner and Paul dropped in to join them. All of a sudden they heard a violent crash outside. The family rushed to the window to see hysterical fans stampeding towards the house. Having caught a glimpse of Paul they had broken through the gates and were soon pounding on the windows. Angela rang the police: "We need your help! They've crashed the fences and are threatening to break through the windows!" Quickly she ushered Ruth upstairs where they turned off the lights and waited in the dark. "It's scary to think what would have happened had they got in," said Ruth. "They would tear you to shreds!"

As time went on, Angela and Ruth got to know the other Beatles. They visited Ringo first at his home in Weybridge on Boxing Day 1964. Ruth recalls, "I remember thinking it was the biggest house I'd ever seen. Maureen [Ringo's future wife] was so nice to me. I was running around outside climbing trees." Harrison, shy and introspective, patiently taught young Ruth Indian *ragas* on the piano while John taught her to ride a bicycle. The latter came to Rembrandt more frequently than the others and Angela remembers how everyone treated him with kid gloves because of his "difficult" reputation. Angela felt sure that this was nonsense. On one occasion he stayed overnight in Mike's room. The next morning, she had squeezed some orange juice and was about to take it up to John, when Brian phoned, wanting to tell him that another single had shot to number one. "Don't disturb him, love," warned Jim emphatically. "Just tap on his door and leave the juice outside."

Angela ignored this and rapped boldly on the door. "John, are you up? Are you decent, son, can I come in?" She opened the door as he leaned out of bed and fished for his glasses, grinning sheepishly.

"He was perfectly fine," Angie remembered. "This fear of John, this, 'Oh, watch out for John, he's in a bad mood', I couldn't fathom. Why walk on eggshells? I just didn't see the relevance. If you treat people like they're in a bad mood they will be! Yes, he was a tough kid, but I saw the warmth in him and I never had any problems. When he was at the house, John would ask if he could have a cup of tea. I'd tease him, 'Say please.' He was perfectly fine with me."

Later Cynthia confided to Angela that she was the only person John was a little in awe of. "You tell it like it is," she told her. "You never take any shit from him."

On another occasion when they were staying at Rembrandt, Lennon and McCartney decided to go antiques hunting. They each borrowed an old overcoat and a trilby from Jim, tucked their hair under their collars and bravely boarded a bus for the fourteen-mile trip to Chester. They were gone for several hours. On their return Paul told his father and stepmother, "There'll be a van coming soon.

We bought all sorts of stuff. We even stopped at a pub for a beer and a meat pie."

They shelled out a king's ransom for a miscellaneous assortment of enormous Bibles, brass crucifixes, gilded picture frames and cartons of dusty old books that Angela stashed all over the house. "Eventually," she says, "I had to hire a truck and send it all down to London."

The near two-decade-long friendship between the Beatles and comedic genius Peter Sellers was forged chiefly by their similar taste in offbeat humour. In an odd twist, Sellers became the catalyst for the marriage between producer George Martin and the Beatles. In January 1962, Brian Epstein was seeking a record contract for the band and, as Martin remembers, "Brian had been turned down by everybody and was desperate. So he tried to joke on the fact he'd been told about me because I made comedy records. When the Beatles heard about it they kind of groaned, but then pricked their ears a bit when they learned I'd made records with Peter Sellers. They were great fans of his."

What sealed the deal for the Beatles was learning that Martin had produced the comedian's popular 1960 *Songs For Swinging Sellers*. Interestingly, back in Cavern days, Sellers was offered the opportunity to invest in the band. Ironically, he had concluded it was just too much of a gamble.

For a time during the sixties, the artists' whirlwind careers intertwined. The Beatles integrated Sellers's *Goon Show* humour into their début film, *A Hard Day's Night*. Sellers returned the favour by guest-starring on the group's Granada Television special *The Music of Lennon & McCartney*, which aired in December 1965. Dressed as Richard III he gave a hilarious rendition of "A Hard Day's Night". Tony Bramwell, then PR man for the group, observed, "Sellers did this mock Shakespearian version of 'A Hard Day's Night' and he was stoned out of his mind the whole time." It was released as a Parlophone single and got to number fourteen in the British charts.

"I didn't know him too well," Paul admitted, "but I met Peter later. A very nice bloke, pretty hung up and like a lot of comedians he wanted to be a musician. He was a drummer and on this show he did a very funny impression of Larry Olivier doing 'A Hard Day's Night'."

Sellers was offered Leo McKern's role in *Help!* but turned it down. Nonetheless, he was such a fan of the group that he had his own Beatle suit made and became a frequent guest during their recording sessions, laying down several Beatles songs himself, including "She Loves You" in 1965, which was released posthumously in 1981. On 28 April 1965 he presented a Grammy to them for Best Performance by a Vocal Group:

Sellers: Welcome to the great Twickenham Studios where the boys, the Beatle, are making their new film, *Help!*. I am actually with the Beatle now to present them with their Grandma awards which they have won from America. I have had the singular honour, if you don't mind my saying so, of having been asked to present them. May I say . . .
Paul: Yes you may!
Sellers: Great pleasure. There are some more in here. Perhaps you'd like to just take one.
John: Thanks, Mr Ustinov!

Of all the Beatles, Sellers initially gravitated towards George Harrison. Later they shared a business manager in Dennis O'Brien and were keen to launch a property-development venture, but things dragged on too long for the impatient Sellers and he eventually dropped out.

One of the Beatles' most heralded appearances was at Shea Stadium, New York, on 15 August 1965 and a record-breaking number of fans turned out for their dazzling entrance by helicopter. Not wanted at the Plaza, they were bunking down at the Warwick on 54th Avenue. Once again Al Aronowitz was around with Bob Dylan in tow, along with young disc jockey Scott Ross, the assistant music director for local radio station WINS, who had tracked the Beatles from the beginning. Aronowitz wrote:

> When we entered their suite, John, Paul, George and Ringo were relaxing imperiously on the edges of a couple of beds, rapping their heads off with one another. John rises to say hello. One by one they all do. There's absolute cordiality, warm greetings. Handshakes. Smiles. Grins. Laughs. Conviviality. But no bear-hugs. There is a sort of relaxed stiffness, an inability to cross boundaries of the demureness which prevailed the first time I took Bob up to meet the Beatles.
>
> Although they always are delighted to see one another, how can Dylan and the Beatles not be aware of how psychically heavily armed they come? They have a relaxed, loosened-up way of preening, strutting and swaggering. They try to be good-natured in their boastfulness as they tell about their latest exploits. They certainly know how to turn everything into a laugh. The Beatles are always F-U-N.
>
> The trio had just settled into the group's suite when Mal popped in to announce that Sammy Davis Jr was down in the lobby asking to come up.
>
> "Tell him we're sleeping," barked Paul, brushing off the star like an irritating fly.

As had become a habit, some heavy-duty joints were rolled and the quintet dived into their favourite game of Hipper Than Thou, a snappy, quickfire often cutting verbal exchange designed to outwit each other. Aronowitz called it "a psychic tug of war between two sides separated by a mud pit of paranoia. Whether meaning to or not each side subtly tries to pull the other side into the pit." But that day, observed Big Al, it was four against one and the Beatles were uncannily almost like one person, nearly able to read each other's minds. "I detect Bob probing the Beatles' defences but he can't make a dent," Aronowitz reflected. "The solidarity of the Beatles is impregnable."

Suddenly Al noticed that Scott Ross was about to throw up and rushed him to the bathroom. The door was locked and Scott vomited over it. Neil Aspinall flew in, howling, "This is Paul's room! You'd better clean it up."

At that point the door opened and to Ross's horror, out came McCartney, zipping up his trousers. He shot the young man a look of cold annoyance and walked out. Ross made his own prompt exit, and Dylan got in the last word: "Hey, man, if any of those kids ask for your autograph on the way out, don't forget to tell 'em you're with the Rolling Stones."

On 27 August 1965 John, Paul, George and Ringo spent the evening in Bel Air with another music legend: Elvis Presley. The occasion became known as the "rock'n'roll summit". It was no secret, Elvis was a great inspiration to them. "Elvis was the epitome of it all when we started," said Paul. "Before he went into the army we idolized him. He could do no wrong. When he went into the army he became a bit subservient. We'd liked the rebel thing in him. Seeing him in uniform, getting his hair cut was a disaster for us, like the flag flying at half mast."

Lennon found his lightning rod in the snarling Presley ode to love gone bad, "Heartbreak Hotel". "It was an experience of having my hair stand on end," he stated. "We'd never heard American voices singing like that."

About a year earlier while the Beatles were on tour in America a writer from the *New Musical Express* arranged for McCartney to speak with his Memphis idol via telephone. But it was Mal who got the biggest thrill: he was a long-time Presley admirer – and president of his fan club in Liverpool. One day, as Evans remembered,

> Paul said, "Hey, Mal, come into the bedroom, I've got a surprise for you." I wandered in behind him and suddenly he's talking to Elvis! "Oh, you've got a bass guitar," Paul was saying and Elvis replied, "I've got blisters on my fingers from playing this thing!" Paul saying, "Oh, don't worry, that'll soon go away."
>
> "By the way, Elvis," Paul says, "there's a great fan of yours here. You can call him Mal."
>
> He put me on the phone and I was "Uh . . . uh . . . ummm . . . hel-lo, Elvis." I was tongue-tied. He was so polite. He was fantastic. He told me if I ever needed anything just come and see him.

Brian Epstein had been trying to arrange a meeting between Elvis and the Beatles for two years, with the delay blamed on scheduling conflicts. More likely it was Presley's manager Colonel Tom Parker making the Beatles wait for an audience with the King. "We didn't really feel brushed off," revealed Paul. "We felt we *deserved* to be brushed off."

Finally, the timing was deemed right in the summer of 1965 as the Beatles were in Los Angeles on a break during their American tour and Presley was also there, filming the movie *Paradise, Hawaiian Style*. The band left their temporary home on Benedict Canyon Road in two cars: Colonel Parker, Brian, John and Paul in one; George, Ringo and Mal in the second. "It was all very exciting," John recalled. "We were all nervous as hell. He was a legend in his lifetime and it's not easy meeting a legend in his lifetime."

According to George, thanks to a few "cups of tea" – a Harrison euphemism for smoking dope – in the limo, the band forgot where they were going. George quoted comedian Lord Buckley: "We go into a native village and take a couple of peyote buds; we might not find out *where* we is but we'll sure find out *who* we is." Formerly owned by forties' screen goddess Rita Hayworth, Elvis's house was built into the hillside and hidden from the road behind a massive seven-foot wall. "Big house, big Elvis," quipped Lennon, as they walked down the palm tree-lined drive and went into the King's house at around ten p.m. They found themselves in a darkened circular living room, with a jukebox continuously cranking out Charlie Rich's "Mohair Sam", Presley's favourite record at the time, and the television switched on without sound, as later became Lennon's habit. Elvis's ever-present entourage, the "Corporation", as he called it, seemed to pour out of the woodwork. Neil Aspinall, also on hand, said that when Brian entered the room, "Colonel Parker ordered 'a chair for Mr Epstein' and about fifteen people all came running with chairs. I remember when Brian told the Colonel he managed bands other than the Beatles, the Colonel was shocked. He said he didn't understand how Brian could handle more than the Beatles because it took him all his time to handle Elvis."

The sleek, handsome Presley, wearing a red shirt, grey slacks and a tight-fitting black jerkin, was perched on a couch strumming a bass guitar, which Ringo found "very strange". There was an awkward silence, then Elvis joked, "Look, guys, if you're just going to sit there and stare at me all night I'm going to bed."

McCartney was the first to break the ice, pouncing upon the opportunity to demonstrate a few guitar licks. "That was the thing for me, that he was into the bass. So there I was, 'Well, let me show you a thing or two, El.' "

The four-hour visit was a mixed bag of highs and lows. The Beatles were suitably impressed with the giant billiard table that swivelled silently and turned into a crap table. Brian and Ringo occupied themselves with the roulette wheel in the games room, challenging Colonel Parker to some spirited competition.

Harrison, meanwhile, spent the evening trying to "suss out from his gang if anybody had any reefers. But they were 'uppers and whisky people'. They weren't really into reefer-smoking in the south."

The conversation wasn't exactly high octane. The somewhat bewildered Elvis didn't even know the names of his celebrated guests, referring to each as "Beatle". As Ringo observed, "He was pretty shy and we were a little shy but between the five of us we kept it rolling. I was certainly more thrilled to meet him than he was to meet me."

Lennon had spotted Presley's spanking new Rolls-Royce Phantom in the drive and told the King he had one too. Then they found common ground in travel stories, swapping tales of the dangers of the skies. George, who hated flying, related incidents of an aeroplane window blowing open in mid-flight and when an engine had caught fire.

Elvis told a similar tale: "I thought my number was up. We had to remove sharp objects from our pockets and rest our heads on pillows between our knees. When we landed, the pilot was wringing wet with sweat even though it was snowin'."

Later Presley introduced his teenage girlfriend and future wife, Priscilla Beaulieu. She wore a bizarre purple gingham frock with a huge gingham bow, the "image of Barbie", as Paul put it later, her brunette locks carved into a towering beehive. The boys caught only a glimpse of her delicate beauty before she was escorted from the room, Elvis perhaps fearing that someone might make a move on her. "She didn't need to be put away so quickly," McCartney quipped.

Finally, Presley called, "Somebody bring in the guitars," and several instruments were swiftly produced. With Presley on bass, John took up rhythm guitar while Paul and George picked up guitars too and plugged into a large bass amp. Ringo, feeling a bit left out, was consoled by the King: "Too bad we left the drums in Memphis." The world's most famous pickup band then launched into Cilla Black's hit "You're My World". Lennon reportedly grinned and yelled, "This sure beats talking!" McCartney seemed to recall Elvis's tape machine being switched on, although no one else has mentioned it.

Journalist Chris Hutchins, who was along for the ride, took full note of the historic house band. "Elvis's voice rose, richer, deeper and more powerful than the others', his leg pumping up and down in time to the beat. You could feel the magic and he did it so naturally. Paul, on the piano, joined Elvis in some vocal duets (including 'I Feel Fine'), George worked in some of his neat little riffs and John, even if he were just going through the motions, didn't let his side down."

For Mal Evans, who took in the historic proceedings "with my mouth open all night", the evening was a bit of an embarrassment. In preparing for the event he'd taken his suit for cleaning. When he got it back the cleaners had sewn up the trouser pockets. In the middle of the jam Elvis picked up a guitar and asked if anyone had a pick. Paul said, "Yeah, Mal's got one. He always carries picks." When Evans reached into his pockets, he excused himself to rush off to the kitchen. There he gathered some plastic spoons and broke them up to make picks for the King. "I'd have loved to give Elvis a pick, had him play, then got it back and had it framed," he later said.

Perhaps the real highlight of the occasion was Elvis's TV remote control, the first they'd seen. "He was just switching the channels," recounted Paul, "and we were going, 'How is he doing that? It's magic!'"

Around two a.m. the evening finished. Elvis presented his guests with a complete set of his records and the Beatles invited him to their place the next day. But there was no follow-up. No doubt Colonel Parker didn't want the public to think that the King of rock'n'roll was on equal footing or, even worse, in the shadow of the Beatles.

Peter Brown, co-manager of NEMS, remembered, "The following night a few members of the Memphis Mafia showed up, but not Elvis. Paul played the gracious host and showed them round the rented house. He opened one of the bedroom doors to reveal Joan Baez stretched out on the bed, talking to George. Elvis's guys later reported, incorrectly, she was there to see George, when in fact it was John's room. Baez had developed a wild crush on John and was reportedly following him wherever he went."

After the event McCartney gushed, "He looked great, he was Elvis, he just looked exactly like him! We were just touching him, shaking his hand and that. He was really nice and he hadn't gone into the Las Vegas phase when I don't think I would have liked to have met him quite as much."

Characteristically John downplayed it: "It was a nice meeting. He played a few songs and we were all playing guitars. It was great. We never talked about anything, we just played music. There's only one thing wrong with Elvis, he's a bit square, that's all."

While George hailed the event "the highlight of the tour", Ringo said, "He was just like one of us. None of the old Hollywood show-off thing."

Presley gave Mal a jacket he'd worn in one of his films, and years later he hadn't forgotten him. Journalist Ray Connolly, interviewing Elvis in Vegas, asked what he remembered most about the Beatles. Presley answered, "The one who stands out to me is their road manager Malcolm Evans."

Although on his turf Elvis might have had the upper hand, even then the tide was swiftly turning. Presley's maverick image had long since faded and it was the Beatles and Bob Dylan who were blowing the winds of change through pop culture. As Lennon so aptly observed, "Elvis died when he went into the army. I think they cut 'his bullocks' off."

The Beatles eventually soured somewhat on the King when they learned that he had tried to "shop us", as McCartney put it, in America, telling President Richard Nixon they were "un-American and promoting drugs". "That's very sad to me," noted Starr, "that he felt so threatened he thought (like a lot of people) we were bad for

American youth. This is Mr Hips, the Man, and he felt *we* were a danger. I think the real danger was mainly to him and his fading career."

In 1970 Welsh pop crooner Tom Jones, who befriended Presley, passed on the news of the Beatles' impending break-up. Elvis, clearly in a state of denial, if not delusion, came up with this bizarre scenario: "You know what I'd like to do? I'd like it if the two of us and the Beatles would do a show together. But we'd have them only as our backing group."

Ringo ran into Elvis again, in LA in Presley's declining years, at a pickup football game with the Memphis Mafia. He accosted him and demanded to know why he wasn't in the studio putting out new music. "I can't remember what he said," Ringo reported. "He probably just walked away and started playing football again."

In the aftermath of the King's death in 1977, Paul reflected on the irony: "The great joke is that we were openly taking drugs and look what happened to him. He was caught on the toilet fucking full of them!"

In mid-October 1965, the Beatles laid down tracks for the much-acclaimed *Rubber Soul.* By early November they had finished most of the work and on the eighth they entered EMI's studio two for a vocal session for George's "Think For Yourself". They were in a particularly jovial mood:

George Martin: Ready here, then, lads!
(*The tape is rewound.*)
John: You'll just have to bear with me or have me shot! Uh, we'll just have to have a go of it, y'see.
George Martin: I know exactly what you mean.
John: Mm. It could be there, and it couldn't.
George Martin: Could be where?
John: There – or it couldn't. All right, Paul, come along, now. Come on. '. . . we close our . . . about the good things that we can have . . . we close our eyes . . .' I'm sure that wasn't the real one, but that'll do. If that works, I'm in for it!

George: That is the one.

Paul: Two say will, two say won't. It's nothing like it! Let's see what they think about this one. Ding! On with the jukebox! To say, Sir Harry, things that you do. And this . . .

(*Playback of the backing track*)

George Martin: Oh, you're a right particular one, aren't you, John?

John: I get something in me head, you know, and all the walls of Rome couldn't stop me!

Paul: Is that right, Pickled Onion?

John: Pooh, and I stink, too. I'm waiting for somebody to say something about it.

Paul: It's that, uh, deodorant you use.

John: 'Tisn't. Cynthia licked it clean before we left! Here's to a prosperous pickle!

Paul: Do you wanna fight?

John: No . . .

Paul: Let's settle it other ways.

John: You play snooker?

Paul: Yeah . . .

John: I don't. Play tennis? Somebody up dere likes me!

Paul: Who is it?

John: It's Jesus, our Lord and Saviour! Who gave his only begotten bread for us to live and die on! And that's why we're all here, and I'll tell you, brethren . . . there's more of them than there are of us. And that's why there's so few of us left!

Paul: Why such fury?

John: Condemn thou the torts of man!

George: Yeah, what is this wrath that beholds you?

Paul: Why such fervour?

John: He called, and they bloody will come!

Paul: Oh, aye! Yes! But if you look in your Bible . . .

George Martin: Are you ready?

Paul: Troy! It looks like Supercar's getting out of control, Troy! "Aqua Marina . . . How come you fuck up everything you do? Marina . . ."

John: I will be pleased to see the Earthmen disintegrated! I'm sorry,

> sometimes I feel less than useless at these sessions! I really do. Cynthia understands. I often talk to her about it when we get home. I say, "Sometimes, y'know, Cynthia, I just can't get the note." She understands a lot of things like that because she went to Bali for her holidays.

Released on 3 December in Britain, *Rubber Soul* was certainly the Beatles' most sophisticated album to date. On the same day, in Glasgow, they started what was to become their final tour of the United Kingdom. On stage at the Glasgow Odeon, their songs were, as usual, drowned out by the screams from the audience.

FOUR

Right Is Only Half of What's Wrong

London

1966

> "On our last tour people kept bringing blind, crippled and deformed children into our dressing room and some boy's mother would say, 'Go on, kiss him, maybe you'll bring back his sight.' We're not cruel. We've seen enough tragedy in Merseyside, but when a mother shrieks 'Just touch him and maybe he will walk again' we want to run, cry, empty our pockets. We're going to remain normal if it kills us!"
>
> *John Lennon*

During the high-flying, head-spinning mid-sixties the Beatles' women – Cynthia, Maureen, Patti and Jane Asher – shared a unique experience that for ever linked their destiny. There was a stark contrast between the reticent, low-key Cynthia and Maureen, and the more assertive, high-profile Patti and Jane. Cynthia and Maureen, Liverpudlians born and bred, were resolute homebodies, committed wives and mothers. Both married their respective Beatles and were ill-prepared for the overpowering tidal wave of media attention lavished on their husbands. Patti and Jane, however, were virtually weaned in the public eye. Patti, the charismatic, seductive model, had graced the covers of top fashion magazines from adolescence, while Jane, the educated, refined redhead, had been a successful actress all her life.

For this comely quartet those early, thrilling days were played out in exotic holiday destinations, sumptuous homes and extravagant cars. As Cynthia once reflected, "The excitement of the Beatles was wonderful; the experience we shared is something a lot of people were very envious of, but I think the best times were before, in the simplicity of life."

The women shared the romance of being the muses behind many of the band's classic love songs. "I get a thrill knowing it was written for me," Patti once said of George's exquisite "Something". However, Harrison later revealed that the song had originally been about Krishna (God). He had felt that singing "Something in the way He moves . . ." would be misunderstood and people would think he was a "pooftah". McCartney's numerous sentimental ballads, especially the wistful "And I Love Her" were for Jane. In a 1995 interview with *Q* magazine Cynthia confirmed, "I'm sure I was part of John's writing. In those days none of them would say, 'I'm writing this for so and so,' because it would be too embarrassing. But John actually wrote poetry to me quite a lot. The only song I thought might be something to do with me was 'Girl', but of course John isn't here to say any more. Still, whatever they were writing was about their lives anyway."

With the group's ever-escalating musical and cultural global domination came a cruel alienation from the women at home. The boys' extended absences while touring, recording and shooting films were lonely times for their families, particularly Maureen and Cynthia. "The nearer John travelled to the centre of the whirlpool," said the first Mrs Lennon, "the farther away I pulled. We became more and more distant in our understanding of each other." For Cynthia it was particularly agonizing: she had married John pre-Beatlemania, and then been forced to keep her marriage quiet until well into 1963 because Brian Epstein had ruled, "A Beatle must not be seen to be married." At one point, the ruse was so convincing that as she was getting into a waiting limousine with John after a concert she was shoved back by security, who thought she was a fan.

Even McCartney's passionate romance with Jane Asher, begun in 1963, was subject to Brian's dictum that a Beatle must remain conceptually unattached. For a February 1964 interview with the British teen magazine *Fabulous*, she had been coerced into downplaying her affair with: "We aren't engaged and certainly aren't secretly married. We're just dating. I really like Paul. He is very nice."

All four young women experienced an unprecedented intrusion into their privacy, with fans often holding them prisoner in their own homes. At one point in early 1964, Cynthia recalled, "The hysteria would deafen us, hands would pull at our clothes. Poor baby Julian would disappear from view as they crowded in on his pram. All one could see was a mass of knickers all colours of the rainbow."

Furthermore the Beatle women were almost universally disliked simply for being a Beatle's consort. Patti remembered the scene outside their Esher bungalow shortly before her marriage to George in January 1966: "Hordes of wretched little girls used to hang around waiting for me to go out to the shop. I was regularly kicked, bitten and even punched solely because I was George's girlfriend. 'You'd better leave off our George or else!' they would shout, as I drove away. George attempted to talk to them about it, but every time he came round they just fell about swooning and giggling. The next morning they'd be out in full force, screaming insults and sometimes actually threatening to murder me!"

John once discussed the often-duplicitous fan mail he and Cynthia received. "You can see through the letters. 'Hello, Mrs Lennon, may I call you Cyn? Could you please send me ninety-five autographed photographs of the boys?' "

Ringo said, "You can tell the genuine fans. They write in saying if you are going out with [Maureen], good luck, I hope you're happy. Then you get these letters from half-wits, who write saying, 'You're a traitor!' "

Maureen Cox, who was working as a hairdresser by the age of sixteen, was a regular at the Cavern Club and had even once dated Johnny Guitar from Starr's former group, Rory Storm and the Hurricanes. On a dare she fought her way into the Cavern dressing room and gave Paul McCartney a kiss, then waited for Ringo, her favourite in the group, to appear in order to do the same. Three weeks later, Starr rang her up for a date and they began seeing each other regularly. Starr found himself in the same position as John before him when Maureen became pregnant, and proposed marriage to the eighteen-year-old girl. "I was thinking about it," recalled Ringo, "and I just sort of said 'Will you marry me?' and she said, 'Yes, have another drink.' We did and that was it.' "

They married on 11 February 1965 at Caxton Hall in Westminster, with Brian Epstein again acting as best man and John and George in attendance. Maureen, by this point, had already become all too aware of the tendencies of the Beatles' female audience to treat Beatle wives and girlfriends cruelly. "The other girls were not friendly at all," she said. "They wanted to stab me in the back."

Another common thread that slowly unravelled the four unions was infidelity, often played out in the public eye. Shortly before his marriage to Maureen in February 1965 it was known to practically everyone but her that Ringo was seeing popular London model Vicki Hodge. In his defence he said, "You go with girls or you're called a queen . . . I've been called a queen! If we don't go with a girl for a couple of weeks they start saying you're a queen. You can't win. That's a real drag." Starr later confessed to a string of affairs conducted throughout his ten-year marriage to the long-suffering Maureen.

But it was the ever-charming Paul who left behind the longest trail of broken hearts. As Cynthia explained, "With the adulation of their fans came a varied choice of submissive dolly-birds, groupies willing to do anything for their new-found idols. A temptation Paul found hard to resist." In fact, she even suggested that the elegant Jane Asher was a mere trophy for him, calling her his "great prize". She was an established actress of stage and screen, intelligent and beautiful, all of which gave Paul's ego an enormous boost. It was as if he was saying, "Anything you can do I can do better."

John's frequent indiscretions were purposefully overlooked by the make-no-waves Cynthia. "I know who 'Norwegian Wood' was about," she once acknowledged, "but I'm not telling." However, it has been suggested that it was written with London journalist Maureen Cleave in mind.

While Maureen and Cynthia were content as stay-at-home mothers, raising a brood of Beatle rug-rats, Patti and Jane chafed against the northern code that women should remain subservient to their men and not pursue a career outside the home. Although early on Patti continued modelling, she all but relinquished her career when she married George – but, as she said in 1968, "I don't want to be just the little wife hanging round the house. I want to do something worthwhile." To fill the endless days of sitting at home waiting for her husband to appear, she took up a number of hobbies, including the piano and the violin, and thought she'd landed the perfect way to keep busy and help the community when she received an unsolicited plea to collect used spectacles for the needy in Africa. She scoured London's junk shops and amassed a large collection, then spent hours carefully smashing out the lenses with a hammer at her kitchen table. Needless to say, the *Daily Mirror* got hold of the story. When the publicity-shy George saw it he was furious at the intrusion into his precious inner sanctum.

Jane waged her long battle for professional independence throughout her intense five-year relationship with Paul, but it was the key to their split in mid-1968. When McCartney admitted he had tried to "break Jane down", she responded, "I've refused. I've been brought up to be always doing something. I enjoy acting. I didn't want to give that up."

Sadly, the main thing the women had in common was that their relationships were all but doomed from the start in the white-hot throb of Beatlemania.

Of the four women, Jane has been perhaps most circumspect, saying only, "I was never the dolly-bird type. I didn't particularly like going to discos and sitting up until four a.m. in a haze of cigarette smoke."

For the gentle, ever-forgiving Cynthia, ignorance shielded her from what was going on in John's life. "I'm very glad I was naïve. Naïvety can be a real bonus sometimes. If I'd known what was going on, life would have been so much harder for me. I was naïve enough and it saved me a lot of heartache."

"There are memories you'd like to bottle up and take out and look at every so often," said Patti. "I enjoy today and I will enjoy tomorrow. I haven't got stuck in a sixties groove."

*

Although by early 1966 the Beatles were unquestionably the fashionable, hip lords of London, they often found time to go home, Paul in particular. "It's been said that the Beatles never returned to Liverpool after making it, but the reverse is true," said Angela McCartney. "Especially in those early years, they wanted to hang on to their roots, trying not to be cast adrift in the impersonal madness of their fame."

Whenever McCartney came home to Merseyside, a revolving door of celebrity musicians and VIPs filed through Rembrandt – "Beatle Central" – everyone from Eric Clapton to Dusty Springfield. At the kitchen table Angela's mother Edie would read tea leaves for the diminutive pop vocalist Lulu and supermodel Twiggy. Of the Rolling Stones' Mick Jagger, Paul's stepsister Ruth recalled, "Mick was a crazy rock'n'roller, well into birds and booze. He and Paul were quite friendly, which I found odd as they were in the two biggest rival groups. He used to hang out with Paul. They both knew what a pain it was to be followed, watched and unfairly busted for drugs."

Jim's new family also paid frequent visits to the Beatles' homes. At John's Kenwood in Weybridge, a suit of armour dominated the cavernous hallway. Ringo's home, not far away, included a roomy tree-house and several handsome Airedales. He was instrumental too in putting a dishwasher on Angela's wish list. The ever-practical Jim, however, judged this new-fangled appliance impractical nonsense, until Starr took him out to the kitchen to see the spanking new dishwasher and said casually, "You have to see this, Uncle Jim, it's the best buy we ever made. You gotta get Ange one of these!" He demonstrated how it worked and shortly thereafter Angela had one.

As time went by, Mal Evans grew ever closer to the Beatles. "I have three sisters," he said, "but the Beatles are the four brothers I never had."

The "Elephant", as the boys dubbed him, became the good-natured butt of many jokes, especially from the acid-tongued Lennon. Once he teased Evans about his "black banker's socks". "Mal, we've been talking and we think you're the straightest fucking guy in the world for wearing those goddamn black socks."

"They kept rousing me," Evans related, "saying, 'It's not groovy to wear black socks, man!' They'd all started wearing orange, green and even fluorescent socks. We all got very psychedelic." It soon became a running gag. Paul had only to say "socks" as he strutted into Abbey Road, and Evans would rush out into the London afternoon to buy a huge bagful. Each of the four would enthusiastically select several brightly coloured pairs.

Evans clearly craved the Beatles' limelight, which sometimes spilled over in his direction. "It's exciting, all the autographs and photographs. It really goes to my head. I've got a bigger head than all four of them!" His warm approachability and self-effacing nature had made him a popular figure in his own right ever since the early club days when the compère often introduced him before the Beatles performed.

Describing one six-week tour of America, Evans said, "I'm getting about three hours' sleep a night if I'm lucky. I can accept invitations to parties they can't. The Beatles are virtual prisoners, locked in their hotel, all they ever see are policemen and security guards."

One of his unofficial duties was to select the band's groupies for the night, and keep any leftovers for himself. "You get chicks who'll say, 'I'll go to bed with you if you get me in to meet Paul and John,'" he recalled. "But I don't want to know about that. I want to be loved for myself . . ."

Al Aronowitz confirmed that Evans's reputation as a ladies' man took a back seat to no one. "He was a very romantic character who had more women chasing him than the Beatles. All over the world they chased him!" The Beatles themselves were significantly more discreet about their casual encounters.

Another unwritten element of Evans's job was maintaining the band's stash of illicit pharmaceuticals. He wasn't above helping himself to it occasionally, LSD being a particular favourite. On one occasion, after the Beatles' performance at the Memorial Coliseum in Portland on 22 August 1965 he tagged along to a party at the Beatles' house in Benedict Canyon, Hollywood. "Many of the guests were on acid," observed John Phillips, of the Mamas and Papas. "Peter Fonda kept coming up to George, John and Ringo saying he knew what it was like to be dead. Mal and Neil were all tripping too."

"I remember telling Fonda to fuck off, that we didn't want to know," remembered Lennon years later.

"John and George already had a hefty dose," recalled Fonda, now sixty-three, "but they called and asked if I wanted to come over, and I thought, Yeah, cool, why not? It's the Beatles, after all.

"At a certain point, Harrison got really afraid he was going to die, which unfortunately can be one of the side effects of the drug. So I was trying to console him," said Fonda. "I was saying, 'Don't worry, George, it's okay. I know what it's like to be dead.' Then Lennon looks over, all pissed off, and says, 'You know what it's like to be dead? Who put all that fucking shit in your head? You're making me feel like I've never been born.' As he said it, John's eyes went wide and he knew he had a great lyric, which he would later use in 'She Said She Said'. He never liked me – in fact, John hated my ass. He couldn't stand to have anyone intelligent or intellectual around him."

Lennon, however, remembered the occasion differently. "We were on tour, in one of those houses, like Doris Day's house* or wherever it was we used to stay. And the three of us took it. Ringo, George and I. I think, maybe Neil. And a couple of the Byrds . . . But there were so many reporters, there was like Don Short. We were in the garden, it was only the second one. We still didn't know anything about doing it in a nice place and cool it and all that, we just took it. All of a sudden we saw the reporter and we're thinking, 'How do we act normal?' Because we imagined we were acting extraordinary, which we weren't. We thought 'Surely somebody can see.' We were terrified waiting for him to go, and he wondered why he wouldn't come over, and Neil, who had never had it either, had taken it, and he still had to play road manager. We said, 'Go and get rid of Don Short,' and he

* It is now thought that the address in question was the house where Sharon Tate was murdered, then occupied by Doris Day's son, record producer Terry Melcher.

didn't know what to do, he just sort of sat with it. And Peter Fonda came, that was another thing, and he kept saying [*whispering*], 'I know what it's like to be dead.' We said, 'What?' And he kept saying it, and we were saying, 'For chrissake, shut up, we don't care. We don't want to know.' But he kept going on about it. That's how I wrote 'She Said She Said.' [*half singing*] 'I know what it's like to be dead . . .' It was just an acid-y song, it was. 'And when I was a little boy, he said.' . . . Oh, a lot of early childhood was coming out anyway."

Soon Big Mal was becoming even more valuable to his employers in the more heady, if unlikely, role of lyricist. During the writing of *Revolver*, he noted, "Neil and I were staying at a London hotel and we'd been up rather late. We finally got to bed about seven a.m., really wiped out. At nine there's a bang at the door and jolly ol' Paul comes in, smiling from ear to ear. 'Morning, lads, thought we'd come and have breakfast with you! I've been songwriting and I'm stuck for a line.' So he sits down and plays it for us. The line I came up with was 'watching your eyes/hoping I'm always there'. They used it. I'm very proud of that." The song was "Here, There and Everywhere" released on *Revolver*.

Recorded between 6 April and 22 June 1966, *Revolver* was an important musical turning point for the Beatles and deemed by many critics the most important pop album ever. Harrison was becoming a formidable writer, leading off the album with the vociferous "Taxman", and supplying the musically experimental "Love You To" and "I Want To Tell You", gaining him the most spots on a single Beatles LP ever (his standard LP contribution was two). Group efforts abounded, from the lyrics of "Eleanor Rigby" to the good-natured humour on "Yellow Submarine". Paul's compositions such as "Here, There And Everywhere" exhibited his penchant for balladry, and John's experimental nature manifested itself in new songs including "I'm Only Sleeping" and "Tomorrow Never Knows".

But the sessions did not always go smoothly. During the recording of "She Said She Said" internal arguments saw Paul quitting the session and cede bass and backing vocal duties to George. When egos collided and nerves frayed, Evans often came to the rescue:

> You do things on the spur of the moment. Things get very tense sometimes, even between friends . . . You've got four people going in very different musical directions. I was always making tea, sandwiches or scrambled eggs for them in the middle of the night. Anything to look after them and keep them working . . .
>
> I once walked into the control room one night and the air was electric. You could cut it with a fucking knife. Everyone was snarling, so I casually strolled in and dropped a tray of cups. Then they all had a common enemy! That really broke the ice, they were all laughing and hooting saying, "Look at the big dummy dropping cups all over the floor!" They were soon back doing the music again.

He was privileged to witness the germination of many a classic Beatles tune. "I'd go round to George's to visit and hang out, or take something over. He would say, 'Mal, I've got this new song.' He'd get the guitar out and I would hear it with only vocals and acoustic guitar. Then you go through all the various stages to where you've got a forty-piece orchestra on it. It would be fascinating to have an album of just one song throughout the various stages as it builds up in layers. It's like a recipe. You add things as you go."

Evans meticulously recorded the day-to-day details that went into laying down the Beatles' classic albums. In late 1966 he noted how far they'd advanced since the musically innocent days of "Please Please Me" where they had kept banker's hours and depended on George Martin and recording engineer Norman Smith for everything – mike settings, what to do with their vocals, guitars, and even the all-important mixing.

With six stellar albums under their belts they were now sophisticated and inventive professionals who took charge in the studio. Lennon and McCartney typically arrived for an all-night session between seven and ten in the evening with only a bare-bones melody in mind. Together, through excruciating trial and error, they constructed the arrangements in layers and recorded bits and pieces as they went along. Eventually this formed the backing track, to which further instrumental effects could be added. A wealth of instruments was at their disposal, which Evans laid out for them, up to fourteen guitars, a two-manual Vox organ, a variety of pianos and keyboards, George's tambura and sitar and, finally, Ringo's kit. A far cry from the early pint-sized set that often drew snickers on stage, his sophisticated Ludwig gear was custom-made of calfskin and plastic, miked in several areas to give it a richer, deeper sound and allow separate recordings of toms, bass and snare.

Musical perfectionists John and Paul typically discarded many strong song ideas, even after several days' work. According to Mal Evans, during the recording of "Strawberry Fields Forever" they spent days on the backing track. "John's faster version wasn't working," said Evans, "because the initial slower version had a wistful, dreamy atmosphere. So in the end they merged the two tracks by speeding up one tape and slowing down the other until a common tempo and key worked . . . The Beatles could easily spend an entire week laying down just one track."

By mid-1966, the group were regularly hiring session musicians to produce their increasingly complex arrangements. This was time-consuming as each part had to be scored and none of the boys could read music. That was where producer George Martin came in, as Evans explained: "John and Paul typically play the tune on piano or guitar. Martin translates each individual note into musical symbols which the session musicians played . . . Sometimes they are able to directly instruct the musicians what they want instead of going through Martin."

On 30 June 1966, the Beatles flew to Haneda airport, Tokyo, for a series of five concerts to be performed at the Nippon Budokan Hall. Newly released MI5 documents reveal that even staid British diplomats were seized by Beatlemania when the band took Tokyo by storm. Embassy staff breathed a collective sigh of relief as the group shrugged off dozens of death threats and performed under the watchful eye of some 35,000 police.

Chargé d'affaires Dudley Cheke's memo to his masters in London came to light on 12 March 1997 when the confidential papers were made public. Interestingly, they were released a day after Paul McCartney was knighted in the New Year honours. Cheke revealed how fans were enraged at being kept "ridiculously out of range" during the 1966 tour, while the Beatles were virtual prisoners in their hotel suite and never saw Tokyo. However, eager to boost the Swinging Sixties image of London, Cheke hailed the visit a resounding success: "The Beatles typhoon swept the youth of Japan off their feet," he declared, in a lengthy telegram to the Foreign Office. "They were a five-day wonder, and a Beatles mood gripped the city. The popularity of the four young 'pop' singers from Liverpool, at its height, was said to be the envy of even Cabinet ministers." Still, an army of police were mobilized when "fanatical opponents of the group and all they were supposed to stand for had threatened to have them assassinated. The Beatles, I am happy to say, were at no time in any physical danger in Japan," Cheke wrote.

He also noted that the major task faced by police was "comforting the sobbing teenage girls who found the physical presence of John, George, Paul and Ringo more than they could take". Cheke won praise for his lively dispatch, with one official scribbling on it: "This is instructive as well as entertaining. Much of Whitehall need reminding that the Japanese are human."

As usual the Beatles sang for just thirty minutes at each of their five concerts at the Nippon Budokan Hall, a venue that sparked controversy among traditionalists as the Hall was seen as a shrine to Japan's war dead. "The Hall has occasionally been used for less lofty purposes but never for anything so alien to the Japanese martial spirit as an electric guitar concert," says Cheke. "Various highly placed Japanese and foreign personalities had seen in us the only hope of obtaining tickets for themselves or their offspring."

When the dust finally settled, the Beatles' frenetic Japanese tour was seen as one of the most musically sophisticated concerts they had ever given, predicated on the songs they chose to play, including "Nowhere Man", "Paperback Writer", and "If I Needed Someone". All were far more complex pieces than the "yeah, yeah, yeah" boyish love songs they offered up at earlier venues. A pristine video of concerts filmed on 30 June and 1 July illustrates the great unrealized potential the Beatles possessed for performing accurately and convincingly even their most musically challenging compositions.

Nearly a decade before Muhammad Ali and Joe Frazier seized the world spotlight in the Philippines by going toe to toe in boxing's now legendary heavyweight bout, in the first week of July 1966 the Beatles experienced their own "Thrilla In Manila". It was perhaps the most harrowing chapter of their musical life and would hasten their exit from the public stage for ever.

When they arrived on Sunday, 3 July, in the bustling port city, the scene was not unlike others on their worldwide tours, the airport packed with thousands of screaming adolescent Beatlemaniacs. But as the band and their entourage stepped off the plane into the suffocating Filipino heat a glance told a different story. The airstrip was fortified with regiments of gun-toting military police in olive green khakis, "tough little gorillas", Harrison called them, whose morose demeanour seemed more appropriate for transporting dangerous convicts than a pop group. The Beatles had arrived in a country caught in the stranglehold of the infamous Ferdinand Marcos dictatorship and martial law. Years later, George remembered: "Manila was a very negative vibe from the moment we got off the plane."

Almost before they knew it, a member of the Filipino welcome party accosted them and ordered, "Leave your bags here and get into the car now!" Without explanation they were swiftly driven away. "Everyone had guns and it was really like a hot/Catholic/guns/Spanish Inquisition," Ringo later recalled.

The bewildered group peered out of the back window to see on the runway their briefcases – which contained their supply of marijuana. Luckily, Neil Aspinall snatched them up and flipped them into the boot of a limousine, then told the driver, "Follow that car!"

A short drive took the Beatles to a pier in Manila harbour where they were hustled from the car on to a speedboat, which shot off to the middle of the harbour and a yacht. The four were herded on board and locked into a cabin. George peered out of the porthole to see several armed guards roaming the decks. "It was really humid and we were all sweating and frightened. For the first time in our Beatle existence, we were cut off from Neil, Mal and Brian . . . There was not one of them around and we had a whole row of cops with guns lining the deck around this cabin we were in."

Thirty minutes later Epstein came to the rescue with Filipino concert promoter Ramón Ramos in tow. After a prolonged, violent shouting match the boys were finally released and taken to their hotel. Although the official word from the government had it that the Beatles were taken to the Manila yacht club to "avoid hysterical fans", to this day no one can explain their abduction. Marcos's power play, however, was a precursor of the nightmare to come.

That morning the *Manila Times* ran an article which said, in part, "President Marcos, the first lady and the three young Beatles fans in the family have been invited as guests of honour at the concerts. The Beatles plan to personally follow up the invitation during a courtesy call on Mrs Imelda Marcos at Malacanang Palace tomorrow at eleven o'clock."

The following morning, the four woke to a persistent banging at their door. It was the promoters, dressed in white lace shirts, accompanied by armed guards. "Why are you not at the palace?" they shrieked. "You must all go to the president's palace *now*! You must be at the royal engagement! Hurry up, get going! You must not keep Madame Marcos waiting!"

The Beatles ignored these orders, especially McCartney, who escaped house arrest earlier to find a decent meal and shoot some candid shots of the shantytown, just moments away, that the government didn't want anyone to see. "What are you talking about?" He sighed. "No, no. It's our day off, man. We're not going to any fucking palace!" He slammed the door summarily.

When they turned on the television, there was a queue of Filipinos in their Sunday best, lining the garish marble hallway of the palace. A reporter was saying, "The first lady is waiting for the British pop sensation who are slated to arrive momentarily . . ."

Still the Beatles made little of the event: they had not been informed about any reception and believed Brian would sort it out.

Later that day they performed two concerts, at four o'clock and eight thirty, in Manila's mammoth Jose Rizal Memorial Football

Stadium to the largest crowds in their history, a total of 80,000 feverish fans. The group was not prepared, however, for the huge throngs and suspected the promoter, Ramos, of deliberately overbooking and pocketing the cash.

The following morning they woke early to prepare for their flight to New Delhi, and their first trip to India. The morning newspapers flashed the headlines: "Beatles Snub First Family!" "Imelda Stood Up!" "First Family Wait In Vain For Mopheads!" Local television ran footage of Mrs Marcos wailing, "They've let me down!" with the camera panning across a presidential dining hall showing unused dinnerware being removed and the disappointed faces of the children. The Beatles found themselves in the middle of a full-blown, potentially perilous international incident.

The Marcos family had issued an "invitation" to the Beatles for a lunch reception at the palace, of a kind that not even the highest dignitaries dared turn down. Imelda had rounded up more than two hundred VIP guests from the Filippino aristocracy, politics and business. Brian reportedly told Neil, "I cancelled the thing," but apparently word had failed to reach Imelda. As a matter of policy the Beatles hadn't attended receptions for more than two years since an outrageous 1964 incident in Washington at the British Embassy when an excited middle-aged guest had clipped off a lock of Ringo's hair as a souvenir. "I'm sure we were the only people who'd ever dared snub Marcos," McCartney said later. He considered their action a symbol to the impoverished, voiceless victims of the corrupt regime.

The dictatorship was deeply offended and the British pop band had to pay. At the hotel all room service was immediately cut off, the hotel staff turned openly hostile and death threats were phoned into the British Embassy. "John and I were sharing a room and we woke up and phoned down for bacon and eggs. Time went by so we called down again: 'Excuse me, can we have our breakfast?'" Starr recalled.

"I didn't eat for three days," remembered Aspinall. "They would bring up food that was terrible. Even if it was cornflakes, you'd pour the milk and it would come out in lumps."

A harried Epstein tried to smooth ruffled feathers by issuing a public apology on TV but his speech was scrambled by the government.

When the band tried to make a quick getaway they found no taxis outside. The Filipinos deliberately pulled the plug on their vital security detail. When they eventually commandeered a car, they encountered roadblocks at every turn as soldiers tersely redirected them away from the airport. All along the harrowing journey, in stop-and-go morning traffic, they encountered violent mobs making menacing gestures, shouting obscenities and even throwing bricks at them. It became significantly uglier.

At Manila airport, the chaotic scene was designed to make the four young men sweat. The escalators had been turned off, leaving Aspinall and Evans to haul the heavy equipment up several long flights of stairs. At the check-in counter officials tried to put the gear on another flight; Evans had to leap over the counter to sort it out.

The group was then approached by a commissioner from the Filipino taxation authority, Mismael Vera, who insisted they could not leave the country until they had paid the appropriate tax on their concert receipts, which the promoter was still holding. Brian, quite rightly, said that the promoter was responsible for the levy, but after a heated argument reluctantly paid the man a large sum. "It was anything to get the hell out of there with our lives," Evans remarked later.

From there the party made their way to the departure lounge, where hordes of frenzied citizens behind an observation balcony pounded on the glass and shouted, "Beatles *alis dayan*!" Beatles go home! The soldiers began to manhandle the band, butting them with their rifles, shoving them against the walls, barking, "Get over there!" Passengers awaiting other flights hissed and spat on them. Suddenly punches were thrown, launching a full-scale riot. In the violent mêlée, Ringo was dropped to the floor by a vicious blow and had to crawl to Customs as he was clubbed repeatedly. A local roadie was slammed down a flight of stairs and broke an arm. Brian Epstein, who bravely took the brunt of the brutality, was struck in the face and back, and sprained an ankle. When someone yelled at John, "You treat like ordinary passenger!" he cried back, "Ordinary passenger doesn't get fuckin' kicked, does he?"

"Beatlemania was going on around us," Harrison later said, "with all the kids screaming and trying to grab hold of us, but with the adults and thugs punching us, throwing bricks and kicking us as we passed. They tried to kill us. They set the whole of Manila on us!"

Eventually they spotted a group of nuns and two Buddhist monks, whom they cowered behind for protection. Starr surmised, "We thought, It's a Catholic country, so they won't beat up nuns."

"We knew not to fight back," said Aspinall. "If we had it could have been very, very bad."

When they reached Customs, the soldiers continued to batter them while the crowd roared approval. Evans jumped into the fray to put himself between six inspectors and his four charges, only to be mercilessly pounded to the floor. Beatles' chauffeur Alf Bicknell got the worst of it, however, with a broken rib and a serious spinal injury. Only Paul slipped through unharmed.

At last the band made it on to the plane or "sanctuary", as McCartney termed it. Just when they thought they were finally out of harm's way a call rang out over the PA system: "Will Mr Evans and Mr Barrow please exit the aircraft."

The cabin fell eerily silent, all eyes on Evans and NEMS press officer Tony Barrow. Mal said: "I thought this was it. Tony and I were going to be left behind. I thought I was going to die. I'd never see my friends or family again. I remember walking down the aisle, feeling sick to my stomach and absolutely petrified. Choking back tears, I looked down at George and said, 'Tell Lil [his wife] I love her.' " When the two men reached the terminal they were told that no one in the entourage would be allowed to leave Manila due to a so-called bureaucratic error: there was no official record of the group's arrival in the Philippines some two days previously. Since they hadn't officially arrived they were now unable to leave, cited illegal immigrants.

"I had fantasies we were going to be put in jail because it was a dictatorship," Starr recalled. "You lose your rights in a dictatorship, no matter who you are. So we weren't going to get off the plane."

About an hour later, the pair were allowed to reboard. As the plane taxied down the runway and took off, the jeers of the crowds still echoing in their ears, there was speculation that it was fired upon from the tree-lined runway. President Marcos issued the following official statement: "There was no intention on the part of the Beatles to slight the first lady of the Republic of the Philippines."

A beleaguered Brian Epstein slumped in his seat, vomiting into a paper bag. It turned out that the promoter had pressured him into handing over a whopping fifty per cent of the performance fee: in fact a ransom for the Beatles' freedom. This didn't sit well with booking agent Vic Lewis, who instantly jumped on him, grabbed him by the throat and demanded, "Where's the goddamn paper-bag money?"* His reaction was understandable: he'd been hauled out of bed in the middle of the night and spirited off to the palace where he was mercilessly grilled until dawn by army officers.

On arrival in India, the fragile Brian, who had broken out in ugly welts, was rushed by ambulance to the nearest hospital where he was diagnosed with mononucleosis, from which he would suffer on and off for the rest of his life. This was the beginning of the end for him: he was overcome with guilt about what the Beatles branded "Brian's cock-up", his confidence shattered, and questioning his future role with them.

Once safely at home in Britain, George Harrison's public comments belied the Beatles' future "All You Need Is Love" mantra. He told a reporter grimly, "If I had an atomic bomb I'd go over there and drop it on them!"

As for First Lady Imelda, she got her own back by telling the press, "Oh, I never liked them anyway. Their music is horrible!"

The Beatles informed Brian that their upcoming American tour would be their last: their near-death experience in the Philippines had sent them permanently into the sanctity and privacy of the recording studio.

Still, the ugly incident was not as easily forgotten in Manila. If there was one thing Ferdinand Marcos loved even more than money

* Promoters were so anxious to book the Beatles that Brian sometimes received over £1,000 in cash on the night of the show.

or power it was his demanding wife, and he would not allow her to lose face because of these four British upstarts. It was later revealed, during the revolutionary takeover of Manila by its people in 1986, that he had secretly ordered a hit on all four Beatles in India: it was intended to look like just another of the many fatal car crashes which occurred daily on the subcontinent's dangerous roads.

According to secret documents found among the dictator's private records after his fall from power, his intelligence operatives had called upon the services of a foreign national named Juan Daga Fernandez, living in Delhi, to orchestrate the plot. The plan was simple. The Beatles would be shadowed constantly in India, and as soon as they took to the roads on a sightseeing tour, which they did, a huge cargo-filled articulated lorry would ram them head on, demolishing their rented black American Cadillac. The driver was to be paid twenty-five thousand rupees and would avoid injury by leaping out of the truck at the last moment. The scenario was right out of James Bond – according to both Filipino and recently uncovered MI5 documents. MI5, however, didn't find out about the plot until two weeks after the Beatles were back in London. It turned out that Marcos had eventually realized it might be too much of a coincidence for the Beatles to die violently only days after leaving Manila. Further, he was attempting to build a better relationship with Britain and felt his ambitions might be jeopardized if the plan went ahead. Thus, with only hours to spare, his overseas security team called off the conspiracy as quickly and quietly as it had been conceived. Ironically, when the Beatles were out and about in their Indian Cadillac they broke down and were stranded for hours by the side of the road just outside Delhi, which would have forestalled the plot in any case. To date there is no evidence that Mrs Marcos had any knowledge of her husband's aborted conspiracy on her behalf.

About four weeks after their traumatic experience in the Philippines the Beatles faced further controversy when they flew to America to start their tour. It started innocently with an article published in the *London Evening Standard* on 4 March 1966 which saw Lennon waxing philosophical about the current state of religion. "Christianity will go," he said. "It will vanish and shrink. I needn't argue about that; I'm right and I will be proved right. We're more popular than Jesus now; I don't know which will go first – rock'n'roll or Christianity." His remarks passed unnoticed in Britain but were later printed in US teen magazine *Datebook* on 29 July 1966, and within days radio station DJs, outraged at the comments, were banning the Beatles from their playlists and conducting public bonfires of the Beatles' records. In Memphis on 19 August, a firecracker was thrown at the Beatles on stage. "It went, 'Bang'," Lennon recalled, "and each one of us looked around and Ringo shouted, 'Who was shot?' in all the excitement, you know." For the first time the Beatles were playing regularly less-than-capacity in the United States and they decided to call it quits by the time they reached Candlestick Park on 29 August. Boarding the plane that evening in San Francisco, George Harrison commented, "Well, that's it. I'm finished. I'm not a Beatle anymore!"

In September 1966 while Lennon was on location in Spain shooting *How I Won the War*, for Richard Lester, he and Cynthia rented a sprawling villa in Almeria that had once been a convent. Ringo and Maureen joined them for what they hoped would be a serene holiday far away from the madding crowd of Beatlemaniacs. No sooner had everyone settled in than a series of strange incidents ensued. The electricity went on and off for no good reason and objects disappeared from one room only to turn up in another. One evening at a candlelit dinner in the villa's cavernous main hall, the party was suddenly spellbound by a clear, rapturous singing whose origin they were unable to pinpoint. They joined in with the angelic choir, which continued uninterrupted for some thirty minutes. It was as if someone had taken control of their voices.

One evening Maureen had the uneasy feeling that an unseen presence was in her and Ringo's bedroom. The lights were steadily flickering on and off as she fell asleep. The next morning she woke to find the laces on her nightgown mysteriously tied in knots when she had gone to sleep with them in bows. Starr insisted he was not the culprit. It appeared that she had been set upon during the night by a mischievous poltergeist.

During that holiday, the Lennons and Starrs, now with George Harrison in tow, received an invitation to a health spa run by a kooky couple who believed they were in contact with extra-terrestrials whose spaceships, they alleged, had landed on their property. Of course, Lennon was keen to check it out. Upon their arrival, the hosts exuberantly ushered their famous guests to a makeshift radio receiver designed to communicate with intergalactic aliens. "Can you hear them?" cried the pair. "They're trying to contact us!" All the guests could make out was static.

That night everyone was asked to participate in a seance. As the party assembled round the table, the so-called clairvoyant immediately informed Cynthia that she, too, was gifted with the power to communicate with the spirit world. As they all held hands in the darkness, it was all she could do to stop herself laughing as John tickled her fingers. As if in a scene from a bad movie, the "medium" began moaning and swaying from side to side, then a voice thundered, "Red Indian spirit!"

Following a litany of cryptic messages and predictions, the medium's voice rumbled, "Is there a Cynthia here? You must listen to her! Cynthia will lead the way!"

Afterwards, as the party went home, the Beatles proclaimed the episode a scam. As Cynthia continued to grin, John turned to her and joked, "Who ever listens to you anyway? He must be fucking mad!"

Not long afterwards, Lennon wrote his melancholy "Cry Baby Cry", which was released on the *White Album* and referred to the event in the final verse: "For a seance in the dark / With voices out of nowhere".

Meanwhile, McCartney decided to take a ten-day motor holiday along the Mediterranean, planning to hook up with John on location. He enlisted the ever-agreeable Mal Evans for company, and the pair headed out from Bordeaux in Paul's green Aston Martin DB6. On the French border McCartney purchased an antique oil lamp and Mal bought a double-barrelled shotgun that didn't make it through Spanish Customs.

They travelled down through Madrid and Cordoba to the beautiful coastal city of Málaga, but the trip ended abruptly after a call to

John, who had finished his film work earlier than scheduled and was already on his way back to London. On the spot, Paul came up with a far more exotic itinerary: "Are you up for a safari in Kenya?" he asked Mal, who, agreed enthusiastically.

The car was shipped to London, and the pair hopped on a plane back to Madrid and booked a flight to Nairobi. There, they found their African driver Moses in his brand new Plymouth, waiting to chauffeur them. First up was Tsavo National Park. McCartney, obsessed with his new 16mm movie camera, shot roll upon roll of hippos, zebra, monkeys and other wildlife. Mal's 8mm home movie of the safari is now a hot commodity on the Beatles collector circuit. Later the two bunked down in the park's luxury lodge where Paul played poker and had a few drinks with some rowdy British soldiers. Evans, meanwhile, made friends with a stunning cocktail waitress named Tess, whom he entertained in his suite until the small hours.

The pair continued on, despite McCartney's mild heat stroke, to Amboseli Park at the base of Mount Kilimanjaro. On the way to their chalet-style hut, Moses had to drive down a single-lane track with embankments on either side. Suddenly the car screeched to a halt. A massive obstacle blocked their path. "It's a whacking bull elephant!" cried Evans. It was a precarious situation: they were unable to reverse with the traffic behind them. So Moses slammed his foot on the accelerator and sped round the animal before it knew what was happening. "Both Paul and I were shit scared!" Evans admitted.

On his return to Nairobi, Mal notes that the biggest thrill of the adventure was their stay at the Treetops Hotel. It was constructed around a series of massive trees, the trunks pushing up through the middle of the rooms. It was so remote that only a Land Rover and an experienced game hunter could safely transport them there.

On their final night in the Kenyan capital, McCartney decided to camp at the local YMCA. Evans ran off to buy some souvenirs and returned to find him sitting on the lawn playing his guitar, encircled by a dozen schoolchildren.

*

Over the course of the mid-sixties Angela and Ruth McCartney had witnessed many of the highs and lows in Paul's romance with Jane Asher. The family had first met Jane in 1964 at a Christmas dinner party at her parents' home in London's Wimpole Street. Angela described the actress as elegant and artistic, an ideal match for Paul. "Jane could be a bit moody," she said, "but she had a lot to contend with. She was courting a Beatle, and coming up north to visit his millions of relations who came from a completely different background. We were as working class as it was possible to be while Jane came from a very well-educated, cultured, artistic family. She changed Paul's outlook and made him see a much broader spectrum of life." In her turn Jane taught Ruth to knit and bought her some new clothes: a kilt, a green mohair sweater and a camel coat.

Paul and Jane both delved into their genealogical histories, having their respective family charts drawn up. It turned out, while Asher's distinguished ancestors dated back to King James I, McCartney, on the other hand, descended from a long line of Irish potato farmers. "He quickly rolled up his chart and tossed it under the bed!" Ruth chuckled.

McCartney had bought his first house that year – a Georgian building in Cavendish Avenue, St John's Wood that he and Jane decorated themselves. Encouraged by Jane he also bought a farm in Scotland. On Christmas Eve 1966, when the family gathered at Cavendish Avenue, Paul and Jane announced their engagement. McCartney showed off the diamond ring he'd purchased for her and announced, "I've got a song to play you." He sat down at the piano to play the only just recorded "When I'm Sixty-four". Although he had written it when he was nineteen, he had saved it to honour his father's sixty-fourth birthday.

FIVE

The Love Inside Us All

Inner Space

1967

> "I've never really known what it's been like to be a Beatle. The Beatles is still something abstract as far as I'm concerned. Other people see us as Beatles, and I've tried to see us as Beatles, but I can't!"
>
> *George Harrison*

On 5 January 1967 at seven p.m. the Beatles gathered at EMI Studios on Abbey Road to work on "Penny Lane", which was released as a single in February. Paul laid down vocal overdubs for the song, then set to work to create an underground tape as part of a commission for "The Carnival of Light Rave" to be held at the Roundhouse on the evenings of 28 January and 4 February. Psychedelic posters for the event offered "Music Composed by Paul McCartney and Delta Music Plus". The identity of the secondary composer is still unclear. Earlier that year, underground designers Binder, Edwards and Vaughan were promoting a light show at London's Roundhouse. The trio, whom Paul had recently commissioned to detail a piano – which he uses on stage to this day – approached him to compose a musical piece for the event. The force behind the Carnival was Barry Miles, author of *Many Years From Now*, a biography of Paul, and co-founder of London's hip *International Times*. Miles asked him to write a fifteen–twenty-minute piece. McCartney enthusiasically agreed.

There are conflicting opinions as to whether the Beatles started work on what the press later called "A tape of random electronic noises" before Paul did the vocals on "Penny Lane", or after. Beatles expert Mark Lewisohn has said that it was started afterwards, but Paul recalled, "I told them, 'Look, we've got half an hour before the session starts. Would you mind terribly if I did this thing?' I said, 'Would you be into that and we'll only take twenty minutes to do it in real time?' They agreed."

The recording included four tracks: track one, drums with organ and rhythm backing; track two, distorted guitar and sound effects; track three, John and Paul screaming, "Demented old women", then Lennon yells, "Barcelona!" and McCartney, "Are you all right?", with random whistles and gargling noises added later; track four, sound effects, tambourine and tape echo.

As the boys were finishing, George Martin came in: "This is bloody ridiculous," he scoffed, to engineer Geoff Emerick. "We've got to get our teeth into something a little more constructive."

The composition was mixed down to mono, given to the promoters and played at the Carnival of Light Rave's two-day festival. It has never been heard since, not even on bootleg.

In April 2002 McCartney told *Rocking Vicar* magazine, "The tape still exists. It's very avant garde, as George would say, 'avant garde a clue'. George didn't like it, as he did not like avant-garde music." It was considered for inclusion in the *Beatles Anthology* compilation but Harrison gave it the thumbs down. "Maybe its time hadn't yet come," said McCartney.

Interestingly, two years later, in 1969, George released his own album of Moog-inspired squeaks and squawks, with the help of surrealist/New Age composers Beaver and Krause, entitled *Electronic Sound*. One man's avant garde, it seems, later becomes another's ganja-inspired gobbledegook.

Following the phenomenal success of the Beatles' two movies, *A Hard Day's Night* and *Help!*, there was great pressure for the group to star in a third. Several ideas were scuttled, including an adaptation of J. R. R. Tolkien's *Lord of the Rings* as well as *The Three Musketeers*. Then, in January 1967, producer Walter Shenson contacted playwright Joe Orton with a view to engaging him to produce a script.

Orton was a hot property in the London theatre, and Brian Epstein, too, felt he might be perfect for the job. Paul was also a firm fan – having invested a thousand pounds in Orton's play, *Loot*. Orton's diary entry for 12 January 1967 tells us that Shenson had said he had a "dull" script and wondered if Orton might take a look at it. He agreed, and on 15 January wrote in his diary: "I like the idea. Basically it is that there aren't really four young men. Just four aspects of one man. Sounds dreary, but as I thought about it I realized what wonderful opportunities it would give."

Orton based *Up Against It* on a novel he had written in 1953 with Kenneth Halliwell, his lover, *The Silver Bucket*, and on his own 1961 novel, *The Vision of Gombold Proval*, published posthumously as *Head to Toe*. He delivered a first draft on 25 February, convinced that it would be rejected: "The boys in my script have been caught in flagrante, become involved in dubious political activity, dressed as women, committed murder, put into prison and committed adultery." He was right. "The reason we didn't do *Up Against It*", said McCartney, "wasn't because it was too far out or anything. We didn't do it because it was gay. We weren't gay and that was all there was to it . . . Brian was gay and so he and the gay crowd could appreciate it. It wasn't that we were anti-gay, just that the Beatles weren't gay."

Revolver, which had been released in August 1966, paved the way for pop's most celebrated soundtrack, which underscored the 1967 Summer of Love. Recorded between December 1966 and April 1967, *Sgt. Pepper's Lonely Hearts Club Band* brims with artistic and technical innovation, and emerged almost magically from its rapidly maturing composers. Mal Evans said, "The Beatles' lifestyles changed at the time. It was a growing-up process. They experienced many different things which were included in their music."

McCartney has said that the idea was born on the flight home from Kenya, following his safari with Evans, on 19 November 1966. The two had certainly tossed around several ideas. "Me and Mal often bantered words about," said Paul, "which led to the rumour that he thought of the name Sgt. Pepper, but I think it would be much more likely it was me saying, 'Think of some names.' We were having our meal and they had those little packets marked S and P. Mal said, 'What's that mean? Oh, salt and pepper.' We joked about that. So I said, 'Sgt. Pepper,' just to vary it. 'Sgt. Pepper, salt and pepper,' an aural pun, not mishearing him, just playing with the words. Then, 'Lonely Hearts Club', that's a good one. There's a lot of those about, the equivalent of a dating agency now. I just strung those together in the way you might string together Dr Hook and the Medicine Show. The culture of the sixties was going back to the previous century really. I just fantasized, well, 'Sgt. Pepper's Lonely Hearts Club Band'. That'd be crazy because why would a Lonely Hearts Club have a band? If it had been Sgt. Pepper's British Legion Band, that's more understandable. The idea was to be a little more funky, that's what everybody was doing. That was the fashion. The idea was to use any words that would flow. I wanted a string of those things because I thought that would be a natty idea instead of a catchy title. People would have to say, 'What?' We'd used quite a few pun titles, *Rubber Soul*, *Revolver*, so this was to get away from all that."

Not everyone, however, agrees with McCartney that the concept of the Beatles taking on the persona of a fictional pop group was his. Pete Shotton has credited Mal Evans with conjuring up the idea, inventing its name, and even co-writing some of the best songs. Ringo Starr agreed in a *Big Beat* interview in 1984: "Paul wrote a song with Mal called 'Sgt. Pepper'. Mal thought of the title. Big Mal, super roadie!"

"The first song I ever wrote that was also published was 'Sgt. Pepper'," Evans remembered. "I was staying with Paul as his housekeeper. His previous housekeepers left after Paul discovered they had written an article for an Australian magazine. At the top of his house he had a small music room and we sat at the piano and wrote 'Sgt. Pepper'. It was originally 'Dr. Pepper' until we found out that was a trade name in America. So we wrote the tune. When the album came out, I remember very clearly, we were driving somewhere late at night. There was Paul, Neil, myself and the driver, and Paul turned round to me and said, 'Look, Mal, do you mind if we don't put your name on the songs? You'll get your royalties and that, because Lennon and

McCartney are the biggest things in our lives. We are really a hot item and we don't want to make it Lennon–McCartney–Evans. So, would you mind?' I didn't mind, because I was so in love with the group it didn't matter to me. I knew myself what happened."

As with "Here, There And Everywhere", Evans remained uncredited, although he reportedly received an unspecified royalty for his efforts. He seemed, at least on the surface, to take it in his stride, but his decision probably cost him millions of dollars over his short lifetime. As author Ross Benson has pointed out, "Mal really had little choice in the matter. Evans was only a hired hand. McCartney was a prince of the New Age. If the prince chose to claim it as his own, no lowly courtier was going to contradict him."

Interestingly, it was Mal's co-authored, uncredited "Fixing A Hole" that garnered rare praise from music critic William Mann, who wrote in the London *Times*, "There is hope for all these new pop genres, and 'Sgt Pepper' provides it in abundance. 'Fixing A Hole' is cool, anti-romantic and harmonically a little like the earlier 'Michelle' and 'Yesterday'."

McCartney later recalled the laborious process of recording the landmark album: "We did quite a few takes of each song, but it's just because we've changed. In the old days of *Please Please Me*, we went in and did it in a day because we knew all the numbers. Nowadays, we just take a song in and all we've got is the chords on guitar, the lyrics and the tune. So we've got to work out how to arrange it. We do a lot of takes on each one. We had a lot of people on some of the tracks, and sometimes we used them, asking them to clap and that."

As the project was being put together Evans said that with each track leading straight into the next, it was "like listening to Radio London without jingles, commercials and the deejay. Even the run-out groove [between the final track and the record's centre] is used. The Beatles came up with the idea to place a high-frequency note right at the end, which only dogs can hear. Its pitch is eighteen kilocycles, far beyond the limit of the human ear. Most people can't detect sounds above seventeen kilocycles." Lots of LSD-inspired thinking on that one, then. "But why not something for chipmunks or otters to enjoy as well?" chimed in Bonzo Dog Headmaster, Vivian

Stanshall at the time. "There's a whole new potential zoological audience just out there waiting for the Beatles."

Left out in the cold from the first true Beatles effort to be initiated and led by McCartney, Lennon felt that *Sgt. Pepper* signified both a creative peak for the group and, with touring out of the picture, the beginning of the end. "I was in a big depression during 'Pepper' and I know Paul wasn't. He was full of confidence. I, however, was going through murder." Being forced into the studio without what he considered any substantial material of his own, Lennon was obliged to knock off several songs for the new project within a short period at home in Kenwood. "Being For The Benefit Of Mr. Kite!" came easy, reading like prose from an old circus poster Lennon purchased in Sevenoaks, Kent. While "Good Morning, Good Morning" drew its inspiration from a cornflakes commercial and the television show, *Meet The Wife*. "Lucy In The Sky With Diamonds" gained its fanciful title from the now-famous drawing by Julian and the most significant of John's new compositions, the tabloid-inspired "A Day In The Life", was bolstered by McCartney's middle section based on their early Liverpool life. A Lennon–McCartney collaboration would not occur in this fashion until the roles were reversed for Paul's, "I've Got A Feeling", to which John added his short repetitious piece, "Everybody Had A Hard Year". McCartney was definitely reaching a new creative plateau with efforts such as the *Sgt. Pepper* title track, the charming Ringo vehicle "With A Little Help From My Friends", and "Fixing A Hole", a song McCartney admitted at the time was "really about fans who hang around outside your door day and night". With "Getting Better" Lennon was drawing from his own experience: "It is a diary form of writing. All that 'I used to be cruel to my woman, I beat her and kept her apart from the things that she loved' was me. I used to be cruel to my woman, and physically . . . any woman. I couldn't express myself and I hit." McCartney revived the age-old "When I'm Sixty-four" at the beginning of the LP and "Lovely Rita" was "Paul writing a pop song," commented John. "He makes 'em up like a novelist." Harrison's only contribution to the LP was the majestic and meaningful "Within You Without You", which Lennon later hailed as "one of George's best songs". The Beatles also recorded George's

"Only A Northern Song" during the sessions, but the piece was left off the LP and was released later on the 1969 *Yellow Submarine* soundtrack.

Harrison's heart at the time was still very much in India, as he was to relate decades later, "Now that we only play in the studio we have less of a clue what we're going to do. Now when we go we have to start from scratch, just thrashing it out and doing it the hard way. If Paul has written a song, he comes into the studio with it in his head. It's very hard for him to give it to us, and for us to get it. When we suggest something, it might not be what he wants because he hasn't got it in his head like that. So it takes quite a long time. Nobody knows what the tunes sound like until we've recorded them and listen to them afterwards." Through all of this, Ringo was feeling rather left out: "With *Sgt. Pepper* I felt more like a session man because we were interested in making an album with strings, brass and complex parts. Everyone says the record is a classic, but it's not my favourite album."

Evans had creative input into the equally trail-blazing album sleeve with its many graphic firsts, including printed song lyrics on the back, a multi-coloured inner sleeve and cardboard cutouts of the Pepper band. He remembered:

> Paul, Neil and I sat down to have our first discussion about the sleeve. Our first thought was that the band should be outfitted in some kind of Salvation Army uniforms. But when Berman's theatrical agency came out with materials for the costumes, the Beatles decided to shelve that idea for more brightly coloured uniforms. The stripes, tassels and lanyards were on loan from an army barracks. We hired all the brass instruments, which I spent hours polishing up for the shoot.
>
> We brought things from home, statuettes and ornaments, to be placed on the lawn. In the right-hand corner I've got a little fat soldier on guard duty that's a flower vase. John has a couple of stone heads. Paul brought a lot of instruments and we ended up using two. It is a very personal cover.
>
> It was like building a cardboard house . . . The resulting wall-

George and Paul as tidy suburban schoolboys at the Liverpool Institute, April 1956. Few know they were actually quite good mates long before the Beatles.

Lennon as a young nipper in Woolton, 1946.

Alfred Lennon, John's apparently irresponsible absentee father, c. 1966.

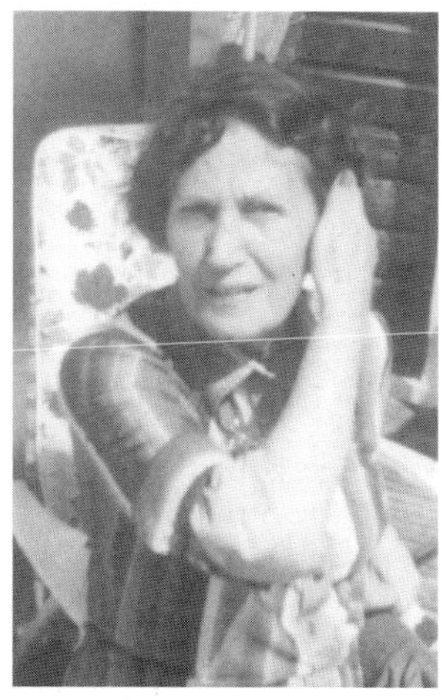

Aunt Mimi Smith at the modest home John purchased for her at 126 Panorama Road, Poole Harbour, Dorset, summer 1969.

The Beatles in Liverpool at the Grapes pub on Mathew Street, their favourite watering hole. Today this spot is maintained by the current owners as a kind of shrine to the Fab Four.

An early shot of the group, unseen these many years. Liverpool, 1963.

In yet another palatial hotel suite holding court to visitors, the folk trio Peter, Paul and Mary, New York, 1964.

John and Cyn together in London, 1965.

Lennon on holiday with the long-suffering Cynthia during the first golden glimmer of global Beatlemania.

Ringo and eighteen-year-old Maureen Cox strolling in the gardens of Beatles' lawyer David Jacobs's home at Hove, Sussex, after their brief civil-wedding ceremony.

Patti Boyd as a young model, just prior to meeting George. Every teen boy's British fantasy girl.

A rare shot of George and Patti on their wedding day, 21 January 1966.

left: The Beatles fly out to Munich for a quick, three-city tour near the end of their performing days, 23 June 1966.

opposite below: PR man Paul meets with Brian Epstein (second left) and a couple of unnamed executives, during the never-ending commercial grind that was the Beatles.

below: Working at Abbey Road Studios in 1967. A heady time for the boys as their individual dalliances with various psychedelics was in full swing.

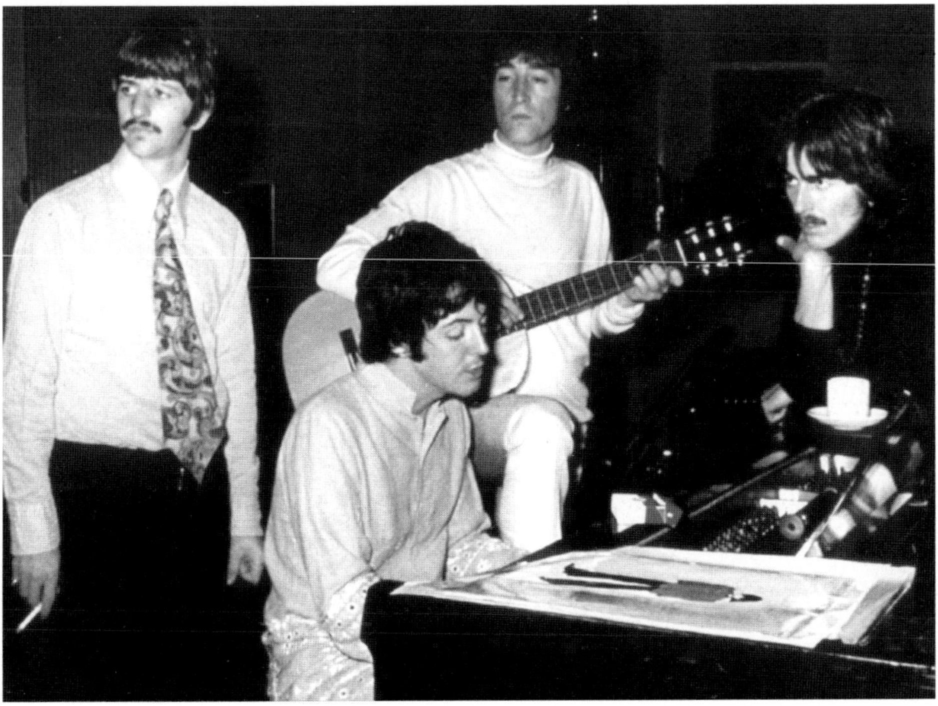

above: At the urbane press launch for *Sgt. Pepper's Lonely Hearts Club Band*, held at Epstein's Belgravia townhouse, May 1967.

left: The brilliant Dutch design team The Fool.

below: Making battle plans for the fun-filled fiasco that was the *Magical Mystery Tour* film.

John and four-year-old Julian, en route to Greece for a two-week holiday with the other Beatles.

Paul, Jane Asher and Julian at Heathrow, 31 August 1966. As a grown man Julian commented that in many ways the compassionate McCartney was more fatherly to him than Lennon.

Seeing the Lennons standing next to the Harrisons, c. 1967, it's easy to see which was the more fashion-conscious couple.

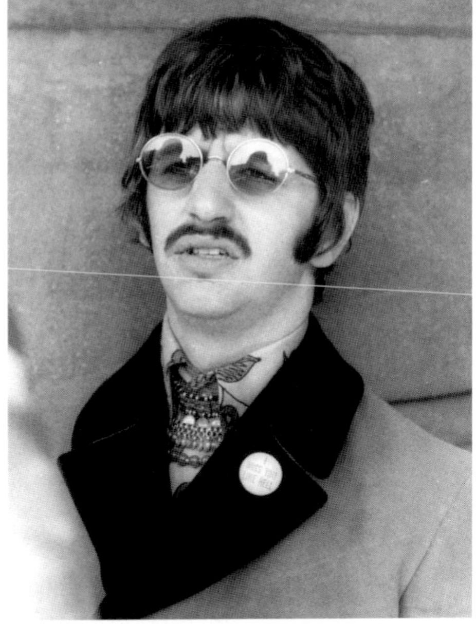

Ringo poses outside a London hospital, after his second son Jason was born, 19 August 1967.

A private audience with the Maharishi Mahesh Yogi backstage at the Hilton Hotel, London, 24 August 1967.

The Beatles arrive at Bangor with the Master.

Moments after receiving the news of Brian Epstein's death, the Beatles meet the press at Bangor Normal College in Wales, 27 August 1967.

sized collage was set up behind the Beatles in their Victorian style uniforms wearing their MBE medals.

Of the sixty-four celebrated figures gracing the cover one icon was noticeably absent. As Evans said, "Paul pointed out the one person who wasn't on the cover was Elvis. He almost punched me because we got the people together we liked. It was a family affair and we were such big Elvis fans." An Elvis cutout was made by artist Peter Blake but for some reason it was not included. Hitler and Mahatma Gandhi were also withdrawn.

Sgt. Pepper was rush-released on 26 May 1967 in the UK, although the date usually commemorated is 1 June. In the US it came out on 2 June. Public and critics deemed it a profound revolution in recorded music. The *New York Times* called the album "a new and golden Renaissance of song". Kenneth Tynan remarked that it represented "a decisive moment in the history of Western civilization". Abbie Hoffman said, "Upon hearing *Sgt. Pepper*, smoking reefers, and planning the revolution in my friend's loft, we were overwhelmed by their vision." An unanticipated amount of praise was directed, too, at Beatles producer George Martin. "The time we got really offended," Paul said. "One of the reviews said, 'This is George Martin's finest album.' We got shook. I mean, we don't mind him helping us, it's a great help, but it's not *his* album, folks. There was a little bitterness over that. A bit of help, but Christ, if he's going to get all the credit . . . for the whole album . . ."

John Lennon came under the influence of many gurus during his ten years with the Beatles, but none caused him such acute future embarrassment as John "Magic" Alexis Mardas, who first made himself known to the Beatles during the Summer of Love. Mardas had befriended John Dunbar of the Indica Gallery, London, who had been married to the singer Marianne Faithfull, and moved into his modest flat in Bentinck Street. It was there that Magic Alex met Lennon. He'd entered Britain from Greece at twenty-one on a student visa, and ultimately worked as a television repairman. He had grander visions, however, for what he might accomplish, given the opportunity, and regularly promoted these notions to Dunbar. "He was quite cunning in the way he pitched his thing," remembered Dunbar. "He knew how to wind people up and to what extent. He was a fucking TV repairman: Yanni Mardas, none of this Magic Alex shit!"

Nonetheless, Dunbar was impressed enough by him to arrange for him to work on the lighting effects for the Rolling Stones' three-week European tour of 1967. The Stones were singularly unimpressed with the results. However, Magic Alex soon found a new patron in John Lennon, who was captivated by the fantastical inventions the young man waved in front of him. "Magic Alex was a Greek bloke who was a friend of John's," said Paul. "He had a lot of knowledge about electronics. Other people disputed his ideas and said that they couldn't be done but Alex said they could."

"Magic Alex impressed John," Harrison recalled, "and because John was impressed Alexis came into our lives. He was a charming fellow for a while." Magic Alex moved quickly to isolate John from any other major influence, including his closest friends. He was introduced to the rest of the Beatles in typical Lennon fashion: "This is my new guru: Magic Alex," he announced one evening, at Paul's Cavendish Avenue home.

McCartney was astonished, but remained open-minded. "Because John introduced him as a guru, there was perhaps a little pressure on him to try and behave as a guru," Paul conceded. "But I didn't treat him that way. I thought he was just some guy with rather interesting ideas."

"He had this one idea we all should have our heads drilled," Ringo remembered. "It's called trepanning. Magic said that if we had it done our third eye would be able to see and we'd get cosmic instantly."

His "interesting ideas" ran the gamut from designs already in production by other research scientists, to an X-ray camera that could see through walls, an artificial sun, loudspeakers made of wallpaper, and a house that hovered in the air supported only by an invisible beam. Paul's pointed response was: "Well, if you could actually do that, we'd like one please." One of the few to be completed was the aptly named "nothing box", a simple plastic cube with twelve lights, which flashed at random until the battery died. Harrison was typically critical of the new guru's "creations" and later embarrassed by their gullibility: "What Magic Alex did was pick up the latest inventions, show them to us and we'd think he'd invented them. We were naïve to the teeth." Towards the end of his life he said, "There wasn't anything he ever did, except he made a toilet with a radio in it, or something."

By the end of 1967 the resourceful Alexis was living in a house John had bought for him. It was he who encouraged the Beatles to buy a Greek island during their holiday there in July 1967. It was a way for him to involve himself in the Beatles' finances, and improve the reputation of the country's military regime, of which his father was said to be a leading member. The Beatles saw the island as somewhere they could escape the pressures of life in Britain, but as Magic Alex tipped off the media as to their whereabouts in Greece, their peace was limited.

"Once on a trip to a remote hill village, we came round a corner only to find hundreds of photographers clicking away at us," Alistair Taylor recalled. Alexis selected the island of Leslo, surrounded by four smaller ones, for the Beatles and the plan had to be realized immediately for fear of John losing interest in it. The island's price tag was ninety thousand pounds, and Alistair Taylor was given the task of purchasing it from the Greek government. It took time for the transaction to get clearance from British officials, but by then the Beatles (and John in particular) had moved on. All was not lost, however, as an unexpected change in property values and exchange rates meant the Beatles ultimately made a neat profit of £11,400 on the deal.

Back on the homefront, tensions were building in the McCartney family over Paul's increasing use of marijuana. The straight-laced, old-school Jim McCartney frowned on it, but tolerated it at first because of the stress of his son's celebrity. He would send him out to the garden or to his bedroom to smoke, worrying that if the housekeeper got wind of it she might broadcast it. Ruth observed that when Paul was high on weed, "He becomes oracle-like. He knows everything and everyone else is an idiot. If you dare to argue with him there's a fight." To this day Ruth associates the smell of marijuana with bad moods.

Throughout 1967 McCartney also occasionally took stronger substances. On one occasion when Angela and Jim were at Paul's home in Cavendish Avenue, Jim and Paul went to see a noted television critic. Afterwards Jim told his wife about the experience: "This guy was coming down from an acid trip, and Paul was explaining how it expands your consciousness and helps artists to open new vistas of thinking and comprehension. I don't like the sound of it. It's flying in the face of God. I think the boys have done it. Paul more or less told me tonight they have."

At one point when Paul was getting stoned almost daily his family grew concerned over his pale, unhealthy appearance and withdrawn, irritable demeanour. On 24 July 1967 the Beatles and others took out a full-page advertisement in *The Times* advocating the legalization of marijuana. His father was devastated. "That really broke Jim up," said Angela. "He wouldn't go out, and didn't want me to go to the shops in case anyone asked about it. He was so humiliated that his son, whom he admired and worshipped, who was up on this pedestal, should be tempted by such things which tempted ordinary mortals. He'd hoped Paul would be Mr Squeaky Clean."

Eventually Jim exploded: "Don't bring that stuff into this house!"

"Whose fuckin' house is this anyway?" snapped Paul.

"Well, it's in my bloody name."

"I paid for it and don't you ever bloody forget it!"

The vibrant but fleeting summer of 1967 marked the zenith for the Beatles' Liverpool Mafia. As press officer Derek Taylor once said of the group's inner circle, "I sometimes think the people closest to them are the people the Beatles resent most. We were so adjacent to the truth, to the money, so near the fame and success and all the glamglitzscreamcheer, we got to look like courtiers covered in gold dust. Did they ever think, Goddamn them! Who do they think they are? Who needs them? We are the Beatles, we are the four!"

Even as the four were veering off on separate paths, their tightly woven band of helpmates – Peter Brown, Neil Aspinall, Alistair Taylor, Derek Taylor, Mal Evans and Brian Epstein – remained steadfastly at their posts. Although they all had fancy titles their duties were infinitely broader, merging together into one job description: Beatles' confidant. All were essentially on twenty-four-hour call, with a special hotline to their bosses, ready to bail them out of trouble or lend a sympathetic ear. As the suave, witty Derek Taylor said, "We were the link, the pipeline, the barrier, the obstacle course to be cleared to reach the big prize. We were there because we wanted to selflessly serve the Beatles."

Neil Aspinall, who had attended the Liverpool Institute with Paul and George, was universally acknowledged to be the Beatles' hardest worker. As Al Aronowitz observed, "The Beatles themselves will tell you if anyone deserved to be called the Fifth Beatle, it was Neil. If John was the commanding officer of the Beatles Neil was his top sergeant. John Lennon exercised his leverage over the Beatles by using Neil as his fulcrum."

Both Peter Brown, the smooth, capable, quasi-manager and Alistair Taylor, the no-nonsense office executive, were swept aboard the Beatles' luxury cruiser by Brian Epstein: they had been his assistants before he had taken on the Beatles. Taylor likened their duty to a forcefield that insulated and cushioned the group from the daily warzone of Beatlemania. The Beatles' late-sixties pill-popping and acid-dropping helped them to cope with the pressures of their fame, and they invited their well-paid minders to join in. Alistair remembers, "Lennon spent three weeks trying to persuade me to go on a trip but I never did. But John and Derek would spend hours trying to convince me. 'We'll be with you, it'll be great!'"

Brian faithfully championed his clients both in the press and behind closed doors. When it became clear that the media had targeted John and Paul over George and Ringo as the stars, he would have none of it. When journalists tried to book interviews with either of the band's songwriters, he partnered John with George or Paul with Ringo. When George Martin suggested that "Yesterday" should be marketed as a Paul McCartney solo single, Brian remained staunchly loyal: "That would be wrong. That would break up the Beatles. It's got to be the Beatles!"

According to Clive Epstein, who credits his elder brother with "founding the Beatles era", one of Brian's brilliant parting shots was to bring in showbiz impresario Robert Stigwood on 13 January 1967 in a shocking merger with NEMS. Stigwood, who represented acts like the Bee Gees, the Moody Blues, Cream and Jimi Hendrix, became joint managing director of NEMS. "Unfortunately he was never to see what tremendous foresight he had," says Clive. "For Brian to link up with Stigwood was quite remarkable. What Stigwood achieved is incredible. Brian was looking for something in 1967. What he would have found had he lived I don't know, but I believe it would not have been in entertainment."

In September 1966 George Harrison had travelled to India. He was already aware of the concept of mantra meditation, but became increasingly interested when he came across an album of chants by A. C. Bhaktivedanta Swami Prabhupada, founder of the blossoming Hare Krishna movement.

In Greece in mid-July 1967, he and John threw themselves into chanting while yachting in the Aegean with Paul and Ringo, their wives and entourage. "Before meeting Prabhupada, I'd bought an album he did in New York," George said. "John and I listened to it. I remember we sang 'Hare Krishna' for days, with ukeleles, sailing through the Greek islands. Like, six hours we sang, because we couldn't stop once we got going. As soon as we stopped, it was like the lights went out! It went on to the point our jaws were aching, singing the mantra over and over. We felt exalted, it was a very happy time for us."

Even Alistair Taylor, normally rather conservative and hesitant, joined John and George in their marathon chanting sessions. Later he said, "For me, the greatest moment of the trip came one moonlit evening. John, George, Mal and I, were sitting out on the deck just above the bow of the yacht, watching a glorious Greek moon. John, Mal and I had been chanting 'Hare Krishna' while George gently picked out the notes on his ukelele, but at last we stopped, at peace with the world, sitting with legs crossed. We must have been there for nearly two hours, with the rush and push of Beatlemania utterly forgotten in this new-found peace and tranquillity. At last I broke the silence. 'Just look at that moon.' 'Well spotted, Alistair!' said John. Now they won't let it go. Whenever I point out anything to them, someone says, 'Well spotted, Alistair!'"

Of all the Beatles, George and Patti Harrison were the most absorbed in cultivating their spiritual life: they were restless and unfulfilled by the glitz surrounding them. They had already endeavoured to teach themselves meditation from books but weren't making much headway. It was Patti who first encountered the transcendental meditation movement, which made a huge impact on their lives. She remembered, "I'd been trying to teach myself, but only really half doing it. One day a girlfriend told me about transcendental meditation. I went along with her to a lecture given at the Caxton Hall. Maharishi wasn't there. It was just someone talking about his work. I joined the movement, but I found the lecture very dull and rather obvious. But I got all their literature so I knew all about their summer conference at Bangor. I said yes, long before George and the others heard about it. I'd booked up weeks before."

Patti found out from a friend that the Maharishi was giving "one last farewell lecture tour before taking up a lifelong vow of silence". A vow that, for some reason, he failed to keep.

There is another version of how the Beatles first hooked up with the Maharishi. While almost everyone accepts Patti's sequence of events, Cynthia Lennon recalled, "The Maharishi was in London giving lectures on transcendental meditation. Alexis [Mardas] heard about him and suggested the Beatles go along to observe first-hand the wise teacher from India. The fact that Alexis had any influence at all over the Beatles was a feather in his cap. I must admit the best thing he ever did was point the boys in the direction of the Maharishi and away from drugs.* Although I don't believe he had any idea the Maharishi would become such a strong influence on the boys, leaving his particular brand of silly magic out in the cold, as it were."

After the Beatles got together with the teacher, Alexis realized he'd made a colossal miscalculation and publicly challenged the Maharishi in front of the Beatles insisting that he had met him in Greece, travelling under "another name" doing "something completely different". Maharishi told him he had never visited Greece and that the young man must be mistaken. Alexis, however, stuck to his guns, and goaded the old man to admit the "truth". At that point both John and George told him to be quiet, and later admonished him for speaking to a holy man in that manner. "I know what I am saying is true," Alexis shot back. "He is just a common hustler out to get as much money off you as he can." It was the first nail in the coffin of his relationship with the Beatles.

Meanwhile, Harrison alerted the other Beatles that the Maharishi was coming to London and that they could hear him speak at the London Hilton on 24 August. They went – minus Ringo who was visiting his wife and newborn son Jason in a London hospital – and were impressed. Afterwards, the Maharishi met them and invited them to go to Bangor with him, by train, the next day. They agreed. "That was one of the privileges of the Beatles, we could get in anywhere," says George. "We got backstage, met Maharishi, and I said to him, 'Got any mantras? Give us a mantra, please.' And he said, 'Well, we're going to Bangor tomorrow. You should come and be initiated.'"

McCartney remembered, "He basically said, with his simple system of meditation, twenty minutes in the morning, twenty minutes in the evening, no big crazy thing, you can improve the quality of your life and find some sort of meaning in so doing."

Also accompanying them on the "Mystical Special", as the *Daily Mirror* called it, were Mick Jagger, Marianne Faithfull, and Patti's younger sister Jennie Boyd. Everyone was excited about the prospect

* Shortly after John Lennon became a disciple of the Maharishi he buried a huge stash of LSD in Kenwood's back garden. Following his rift with the guru he reportedly dug it back up again.

of spending time with a spiritual master, but Bangor station was mobbed by hundreds of screaming fans. The next day, after the Beatles had all been formally initiated they received distressing news from London. Brian Epstein was dead.

There really hadn't been much room in their lives for him: they were all involved in their work in the studio and were unsure of his role. After they stopped touring, he remained their manager in name only. Also, although he had an active social life, he had become lonely and unhappy: he had never been able to establish a stable one-to-one relationship and had had to find affection when and where he could. He often confided to friends that he had felt cursed since boyhood.

Brian Epstein died alone in his bed on 27 August 1967 from an overdose of bromide mixed with barbiturates and antidepressants. An official inquest by the Westminster coroner's court found on 8 September that his death was "accidental, due to repeated, incautious, self-administered doses of sleeping tablets". Lennon later recalled: "We were just outside a lecture hall with Maharishi. Somebody came up to us – the press were there 'cause we'd gone down with this strange Indian. And they said, 'Brian's dead.' I was stunned. We all were. And the Maharishi – we went in to him, 'He's dead,' and all that. And he was sort of saying, 'Oh, forget it, be happy.' Fucking *idiot*. That's what Maharishi said. So we did. We went along with the Maharishi trip . . . I've had a lot of people die on me. And the other feeling is, 'What the fuck? What can I do?' I knew we were in trouble then. I didn't really have any misconceptions about our ability to do anything other than play music. I was scared. I thought, 'We've fuckin' had it.'"

"A great many tears were shed by our very unhappy group that morning," recalled Cynthia. "God and Christ must have been tired of hearing their names called, although they couldn't answer our repeated question, 'Why, Brian, why?' We all felt our world had turned upside down. We just couldn't come to terms with the fact we had lost our dear friend so tragically. It was all too much to comprehend, without trying to invoke an answer from the only God we knew."

A little later, a messenger arrived from the Maharishi's quarters inviting the Beatles' entourage to meet with him. They silently entered his flower-filled white room. Cynthia remembered that he was seated in the centre of the room in the half-lotus position with the sun pouring through the windows, filling the space with the most "glorious, iridescent colours". He held forth on the cosmic meaninglessness of the death of the body and the indestructibility of the soul. His reasoning comforted them, and he made the point that all the tears in the world could never bring Brian back but, rather, might hinder his onward spiritual journey to his spiritual destination. If they were joyful, the master said, Brian's spirit would be filled with joy and light. He even made them laugh. "Our love for Brian," remembered Cynthia, "was cemented by laughter, not tears." Then she added, "Although Eppie listened to the boys' initial enthusiastic rantings about the Maharishi, for the first time he did not show any real personal interest in his group's activities. He nodded, smiled and listened, but did not want to become too involved. When I look back, Brian must have felt great sadness at seeing his boys take off without him for the first time in six years. He must have seen, as I did, the beginning of the end."

As the Beatles emerged from having learned of Brian's death, they were pounced upon by the waiting media. Surrounded by microphones and cameras George, John and Ringo were forced to hold an impromptu press conference.

John Lennon: We've only just heard and it's hard to think of things to say. He was a warm fellow and it's terrible.
Question: What are your plans now?
John: We haven't made any. I mean, we've only just heard.
Ringo Starr: It's as much news to us as it is to everybody else.
Question: John, where would you be today without Mr Epstein?
John: I don't know.
Question: You heard the news this afternoon, I believe, and Paul's already gone down?
John: Yes.
Question: You've no idea what your plans are for tomorrow?
John: No, no. We'll just go and find out, you know.
George Harrison: We just have to play everything by ear.
Question: I understand Mr Epstein was to be initiated here tomorrow.

John: Yes.

Question: Had you told him very much about the Spiritual Regeneration Movement?

George: As much as we'd learned about spirituality and various things of that nature, we tried to pass on to him. He was equally as interested as we are, as everybody should be. He wanted to know about life as much as we do. I spoke to him Wednesday evening, the evening before we first saw Maharishi's lecture, and he was in great spirits.

Question: When did he tell you he'd like to be initiated?

George: When we arrived here on Friday we got a telephone call later that day to say that Brian would follow us up and be here Monday.

Question: Do you intend returning to Bangor before the end of the conference?

George: We probably won't have time now, because Maharishi will only be here until Thursday and we'll have so much to do in London. We'll have to meet him again some other time.

Question: I understand this afternoon Maharishi conferred with you all. Could I ask what advice he offered you?

John: He told us not to get overwhelmed by grief. And whatever thoughts we have of Brian to keep them happy, because any thoughts we have of him will travel to him wherever he is.

Question: Have you a tribute you would like to pay to Mr Epstein?

John: We don't know what to say. We loved him and he was one of us.

George: You can't pay tribute in words.

"We left Bangor in the early hours the following morning," says Cynthia. "John and I sat in the back of the car stunned, yet calm. We both felt very strange, as though we were in a cocoon. There were no tears, no fears, just silent acceptance."

When Brian died, the Beatles lost a close friend, and knew that their collective fortunes would change drastically. Lennon once commented on his relationship with Brian: "I liked Brian and had a very close relationship with him for years, like I have with Allen [Klein] because I'm not gonna have some stranger running things. I like to work with friends. I was the closest with Brian, as close as you can get to somebody who lives a 'fag' life, and you don't really know what they're doing on the side. But in the group, I was closest to him and I did like him.

"He had hellish tempers, fits, lock-outs and he'd vanish for days. He'd come to a crisis every now and then and the whole business would fucking stop because he'd be on sleeping pills for days on end and wouldn't wake up. Or he'd be missing, beaten up by some docker down the Old Kent Road. But we weren't really too aware of it. It was later on we started finding out about those things."

Pete Shotton remembers that, towards the end, the pull of the Beatles' increasingly independent lives eroded Epstein's day-to-day role in their career. Also, his escalating drug use exacerbated his sense of isolation. Formerly confined to fine wines, uppers, downers and a little marijuana, Brian had been experimenting with LSD and even, occasionally, cocaine. Evidence of his fragility was later relayed by Pete Shotton. He recalled a visit he made to Kenwood in 1967 when Lennon told him how dire things had become. " 'Eppie seems to be in a terrible state,' John told me. 'The guy's head's a total mess, we're all really worried about him. But we don't know what the fuck we can do about it. It's time for us to go off in our own direction, and that's that. Listen to this, Pete,' he added, threading a tape through one of his Brunnell machines. Whereupon there issued from the speakers one of the most harrowing performances I've ever heard. The recording was barely recognizable as a human voice, alternately groaning, grunting, shrieking and occasionally mumbling words. It made no sense whatsoever. The man was obviously suffering great emotional stress, and very likely under the influence of some extremely potent drugs.

" 'What the fuck's that, John?' I asked incredulously.

" 'Don't you recognize the voice? That's Brian! He made this tape. I don't know why he sent it, but he's trying to tell me something, fuck knows what! He just can't seem to communicate with us in his usual way any more.' "

Peter Brown remembered the grim sequence of events leading to Epstein's death. "Sunday at noon, when Brian's car was still in the same place in front of the house, Antonio and his wife Maria [his household staff] tried to rouse him on the intercom. When he didn't answer they called me at Kingsley Hill [Brian's country house], but Geoffrey Ellis [one of the Beatles' lawyers] and I had gone to lunch at a local pub. Antonio then called Joanne Newfield [Brian's secretary], who called Alistair Taylor and asked him to meet her. By the time they arrived at Chapel Street I was back at Kingsley Hill, and they summoned me to the phone. I told them not to call Brian's doctor, Norman Cowan, who lived quite far away, but to get my personal GP, Dr John Gallway. Fifteen minutes later, Joanne, Alistair and Brian Barratt, the chauffeur, were waiting outside the still-locked doors to Brian's bedroom. Dr Gallway called me and asked me what to do. I said to break down the doors. The curtains were drawn and the room was dark. In the light from the hallway they could all see him, lying on his right side, his legs curled up in the foetal position."

Although for many years the Beatles' party line was that Eppie died of an accidental overdose of carbitol which was supported by the coroner's verdict, the truth was that he had been crying suicide for months, which all of the Beatles knew. When police found a suicide note, the group's spokesmen insisted it was from a previous attempt, but the officer in charge of the investigation tersely pointed out, "Suicide notes have no expiry date." In 1984 this author interviewed Alistair Taylor, who maintained then that Brian had not killed himself, and still does. "Brian was a very complex man and there's far more to it than his just being gay. He wasn't happy. Twice I had phone calls from him saying goodbye, he was committing suicide. I've often said in many ways I would have been happier if he had. I was there, minutes behind the doctor, and I want someone to tell me where it says he committed suicide! The verdict by the coroner was accidental death and the survey confirmed it. Remember, there were only two people in that room, the doctor and myself. I've never said it was suicide. I've heard stories there was a note found but I certainly didn't find it."

But the note exists: it was found later in the bureau to the left of

Brian's four-poster bed, and was shown to me by Clive Epstein in the Adelphi Hotel in Liverpool, in 1984. It was written in black ink on his monogrammed stationery. It read simply, "My life has become intolerable. I am no longer of any productive use to the people I love, and I am sick of myself, and my eternal loneliness. I am very sorry for any hurt I may have caused. Please do not be hurt by this. I am tired, so tired. The responsibility for this act is entirely my own. I dearly love you all. Ever Brian."

As the media got wind of the full story, the Beatles' already difficult lives were made more so by the constant intrusions of an army of Fleet Street interlopers intent on filing their own exclusive stories. Privately John and George, and others close to Epstein, were certain Brian had committed suicide. "The coroner ruled Brian died from an accidental overdose of sleeping tablets," says Pete Shotton. "John, however, remained privately convinced that, for all intents and purposes, he committed suicide. Which is not to imply the actual fatal overdose had necessarily been deliberate. Nonetheless, Brian's acute distress over his imminent break with the Beatles, along with his recklessly self-destructive behaviour, suggested he didn't much care whether he lived or died."

Brian was buried in Liverpool's Jewish cemetery in a private funeral on 29 August 1967. The Beatles did not attend because of the disturbance that might have been caused by their presence. However, they were at a memorial service held at the New London Synagogue on 17 October. This occasioned some controversy: John and George, in particular, thought it hypocritical not to go in their usual psychedelic garb but eventually respected a personal request from Brian's mother, Queenie. They all turned up in nearly identical dark business suits and yarmulkas.

Now that Brian was gone, Peter Brown assumed the daily management of the group. The smooth, self-confident, highly efficient Brown guided the Beatles' roller-coaster business affairs for the remainder of their time together.

No one, however, could ever replace Brian Epstein.

*

On 5 September, a week after the death of their manager, the Beatles entered the studio to press on with their planned television special, *Magical Mystery Tour*. In Studio One at 7.00 p.m. they began laying down an angry instrumental backing for Lennon's "I Am The Walrus", which was accomplished in 16-takes. Harrison was quick to downplay the seemingly heavy lyrics: "People don't understand. In John's song, "I Am The Walrus" he says: 'I am he as you are he as you are me.' People look for all sorts of hidden meanings. It's serious, but it's also not serious. It's true, but also a joke." The track was added to the banned song list by the BBC for its supposedly indecent lyrics, something McCartney became accustomed to during his early solo career. He commented in 1967, "Everyone keeps preaching that the best way is to be 'open' when writing for teenagers. Then when we do we get criticized. Surely the word 'knickers' can't offend anyone. Shakespeare wrote a lot of words far naughtier than 'knickers!'"

Even though they were hard at work the Beatles continued their meditational practices as directed by the Maharishi Mahesh Yogi. They put aside all drug use and cleared their minds for the challenges of life without their beloved 'Eppie'.

On 29 September and 4 October 1967 John and George appeared on *The Frost Programme* to talk about the transformative effects of the Maharishi's mantras. The original tapes were destroyed, but a portion of the conversation has been preserved by collectors:

Question: One of you, I think it was Paul, commented the feeling meditation gives is the permanent version of what drugs can give temporarily. Is that true?

George: Not really, because drugs are still on the relative level . . . The thing is, you could take drugs, which might heighten your perception a little, and then maybe try and go into that subtle level with the drug. But just to take the drug and hope it's going to bring the subtle on to this gross level is a mistake. It's never worked.

Question: You've experimented with drugs, is that why you put them aside?

John: We dropped them long before the Maharishi. We'd had enough acid, it did all it could do for us. What it does mainly is help in finding out about yourself and that kind of scene. It's more psychological than anything else.

Question: Whereas meditation is not psychological?

John: With acid, it's all about yourself, but this is a bit gentler.

Question: Do you think with acid what you discovered is really yourself or just a fantasy?

John: No, it's yourself, but obviously you do have hallucinations. You could find out about other people, but they're only mirrors of yourself anyway. You find out about yourself instead of taking a hundred years, or maybe you never find out.

George: People can look at themselves objectively instead of thinking that you are the big cheese. You can see yourself from a different point of view. Consequently, it shows you a bit more truth than you've seen. You see certain things that have been there all the time, and yet you've lived with such a narrow concept of yourself you could never see them. The thing is, your true self isn't on this level, it's on a much subtler level. The way to approach it is through meditation or some form of yoga. Yoga incorporates many different techniques, but the whole point is that each soul is potentially divine, and yoga is a technique of manifesting that.

John: It's something you've always had. If you haven't been brushing your teeth all your life suddenly somebody says, "Hey, it would be a good idea if you clean them." So you try it, and it's quite good. You just add it to your routine. You add to your religion, you don't have to change your religion.

George: And you're surprised your teeth are suddenly so shiny!

John: If you asked Maharishi to give us a few rules for living they'd be the same as Christianity. Christianity is the answer as well as this. It's the same thing.

George: Christianity, how I was taught, told me to believe in Jesus and God, but they didn't actually show me any way of experiencing God or Jesus! So the point of believing in something, without actually seeing it, is no good. You've got to actually experience the thing. If there's a God, you must see Him!

John: The kingdom of heaven is within you, you know, that's all it means, to have a peep inside. There's nobody to see, some old fellow, it's just like electricity, you don't see it. Yeah, but I'm still really a Christian. Had I been told about meditation at fifteen by now I would be pretty groovy!

Question: What differences would you say there were between Jesus and the Maharishi?

John: Maharishi doesn't do miracles for a kick-off. I don't know how divine or super-human he is, that's all.

George: Some people, like Christ, Buddha and Krishna, are divine the moment they're born. They've achieved the highest state, and they choose to come back to try and save a few more people. Whereas others manage to be born just ordinary, and attain their divinity in that incarnation.

John: Maharishi was probably born quite ordinary but he's working at it.

George: By having money we found money wasn't the answer. We had lots of material things people spend their whole life trying to get. We managed to get them at quite an early age. It was good, really, because we learned that wasn't it. We still lacked something, and that something is the thing religion is trying to give people.

Question: Would you be as happy now if all the money were taken away?

George: I'd probably be happier actually, because if you have income you have income tax! If you have a big house, you have all the other headaches that go with it. So, naturally, for every material thing you gain, there's always loss, whether it's mental or in some other way. You get a headache for everything you own, so if you don't own anything, you've got a clear mind.

John: You'll get them all saying, "Give it away!"

But what about McCartney's state of mind while all this was going on? An article by Norrie Drummond published in *Hit Parader* in January 1968 sheds some light:

McCartney's huge Old English sheepdog, Martha, bounded forward, leaped up, put both front paws on my shoulders and started chewing my tie. His three cats, Jesus, Joseph and Mary, were crawling over each other underneath the television set.

Paul, dressed in a green, floral-patterned shirt and green slacks, sat cross-legged in a large green velvet armchair. Mike McGear, Paul's brother, was just leaving with several colourful kaftans over his arm. A large *Sgt. Pepper's Lonely Hearts Club Band* poster is pinned to one wall. His book collection includes many works on yoga and meditation.

At the moment, all four Beatles are on holiday, although they have been secretly recording. "When I used to tell you we didn't know what our plans were, it was simply that we hadn't been told what we were going to be doing. Now we simply just don't know." Mrs Mills reappeared, bearing cups of tea and a large cream sponge. "The only thing lined up for us is the TV show," said Paul, thoughtfully stirring his tea. "But we're still trying to work out the format. We've also been recording the past few nights, and our next album will probably come from the TV show.

"We can now sit back and pick and choose what we want to do. We're not going to turn out records or films just for the sake of it. We don't want to talk unless we've got something to say. When you don't have to make a living, a job has a different meaning. Most people have to earn a wage to live. If you don't, you take a job to relieve the boredom, but you do something which gives you pleasure.

"If three of us wanted to make a film, for instance, and the fourth didn't think it was a good idea, we'd forget about it, because the fourth person would have a very good reason for not wanting to do it."

In the past year Paul has become much more introspective. He is constantly striving to discover more about other people. What is depression? Why do people become bored? What is his ultimate goal? These are the questions to which Paul has tried to find the answers in books on meditation and in lectures by those who know more about it than he does. Maharishi Mahesh Yogi is playing a big part in developing the Beatle minds.

"I'm more tolerant now than I was, and I feel more at ease myself, but I'm less certain about many things," said Paul. "In some ways I envy George, because he now has a great faith. He seems to have found what he's been searching for. When we went to India we were amazed. So many people living in terrible poverty, but everyone was so happy. They were always laughing and smiling, even though most of them were starving. For people in the Western world to understand why these people can be so happy is a very difficult thing."

With John, George and Ringo, Paul will be flying to India shortly to study transcendental meditation with Maharishi. To a certain extent, Paul's music is his greatest emotional outlet. "Ravi Shankar discovered himself through his music, and I suppose in many ways we are, too."

McCartney is certainly more at ease now and much more tolerant and understanding. But he's still searching for something. Whether or not he'll ever find it, I just don't know. But he is determined to, somehow.

Meanwhile, out in Weybridge, Lennon continued to tout the Maharishi whenever he found a microphone in front of his face. In this case journalist Ray Connolly recorded what he said:

We want to learn meditation properly so we can propagate it and sell the idea to everyone. This is how we plan to use our power now, they've always called us leaders of youth and we believe this is a good way to lead. We want to set up an academy in London and use all the power we've got to get it moving for all the people who are worried about youth, drugs, and that scene. All these people with the short back and sides can come along and dig it too.

It's no gospel, Bible-thumping, sing-along thing and it needn't be religion if people don't want to connect it with religion. It's all in the mind.

It strengthens understanding and makes people relaxed. The whole world wants to relax and people who get to know a bit about meditation will see it's not just a fad, but a way to calm tensions.

> You learn about thoughts, the meaning of thoughts, how to trace your thoughts, and it's much better than acid.
>
> If Brian had been in on the lectures on meditation he would have understood. This is the biggest thing in my life now and it's come at the time when I need it most! It's nothing to do with mysticism. It's about understanding.

One of the Beatles' most adventurous moves as a group was the foundation of Apple Corps, formed to market their own products and to extend opportunities to other artists in need of a patron. Earlier that year their accountant, Harry Pinsker, had warned them that they had £3 million which they would lose in tax if they didn't find a long-term investment. Alistair Taylor said, "Apple was Paul's idea. McCartney was very much the man with the ideas. We set up Apple Corps and wanted to get projects in from unknown people . . . In the beginning when there was an executive board at Apple, the boys and Brian didn't want to know. It was Clive Epstein, myself, Geoffrey Ellis, a solicitor and an accountant. The idea was that we would quietly announce to the tax authorities we would be opening a string of shops. When the boys heard this they decided this could be boring, they didn't really want their name above a string of shops. The original idea was greeting cards. Imagine Beatles greeting-card shops! They didn't like that at all. Gradually they started drifting in on meetings and Apple Corps evolved from there. Later it turned into this silly philosophy admittedly. Even then it was not designed to save the world, it was really to get rid of the hassle of big business. I mean, why couldn't business be fun and pleasurable?"

Obviously, the Beatles' great interest was music, and Apple Records became the hub of the young company. As the idea developed, it included several interesting ventures – the Apple boutique, Apple Tailoring, Civil and Theatrical, Apple Electronics, Apple Films, Apple Publicity, Apple Studios, Zapple Records, and Apple Publishing. Mal Evans recalled how he was drawn into his employers' latest enterprise in February 1968: "When Apple was first starting, we all had a meeting, and Paul said to me, 'What are you doing, Mal?' and

I said, 'Well, not much at the moment, as I'm not working.' 'So,' he said, 'Right, you're going to be president of Apple.' I thought, Great, but what does a managing director do? He's got to be groovy and go out and find talent for the label. So, I found this group called the Iveys, which turned into Badfinger."

Alistair Taylor was struck by the almost reckless nature of the project, and the Beatles' desire for it to be up and running once they finally made up their mind to go ahead. "One Sunday we were sitting in Hilley House, Brian's private office, in 1968, having an Apple meeting. It was just the boys, myself, Neil and suddenly they picked up the phone, and said, 'Hey, let's get hold of Derek.' They rang Derek Taylor, it was when he was with the Beach Boys, and they said, 'Pack your bags and come on over!' Well, I said, 'What's he going to do?' 'Oh, we don't know. We'll find something.' Later, when Derek arrived, he said, 'Okay, let's set some kind of business up.' There was talk about doing one of these dispatch-rider delivery things . . .

"Now, who's going to run publishing? So Derek said, 'Hey, there's this marvellous guy in the States.' 'Well, get him on the bloody phone. Bring him here!' They were just pulling people in and saying, 'Oh, shit, what are we going to do with them?' 'Oh, it doesn't matter. We'll think of something.' Is it any wonder money was flying out?"

Initially Lennon had wanted the new venture to go in a very different direction, as boutique manager Pete Shotton remembered: "John was very keen on having a car-rental service, Apple Limousines, to brighten the drab city streets with a fleet of psychedelic Rolls-Royces modelled after his own. It was a lovely idea, but it never amounted to anything."

"They gave *carte blanche* to anyone!" says Alistair. "People were buying genuine antique desks for their offices. Ron Kass (CEO of Apple Records) had this incredible all-white office, which cost the earth. It was unbelievable! Peter Asher (A&R director) had real old-master paintings on the wall of his office.

"We had this crazy idea of having *cordon bleu* chefs in residence . . . I think it was probably my idea because here we were entertaining people, spending a lot of money in restaurants, and I said, 'Look, this is much more sensible. Here, we've got this beautiful office on Savile

Row, let's have our own cooks.' They were two girls out of the Cordon Bleu School but it was never used for that. We still took people out to lunch and the only people who ever dined at Apple were Peter Brown and Neil Aspinall, who were having eight-course lunches with Rothschild wine. There was this huge metal cabinet full of vintage wine and champagne. You'd go in and there they were, just them, no visitors. Oh, yeah, great stuff!"

The first official Apple venture was the Beatles' ultra-hip clothing boutique in central London. The Beatles insisted they wanted to retail only items that really interested them. Paul thought of selling only white things. "It didn't end up like that," said John. "It ended up with Apple and all this junk and The Fool and those stupid clothes."

In the middle of September 1967 a suitable site was found in Baker Street for the first Apple shop, and the official opening would take place on 9 November, with Pete Shotton taking time off from his Hayling Island supermarket post office complex to co-ordinate and manage the operation. He also had to contend with the Beatles' conflicting views on how the business should be run. "One morning," remembered Shotton, "Paul came into the shop and told us where to install a partition. Almost as soon as we had done his bidding, John showed up, took a good look round, and said, 'What the fuck's going on in here? What's all this stuff up for?' 'Paul told us he wanted partitions up,' I explained. 'Get that fucking lot out,' John ordered. 'I don't want these fucking stupid partitions in here!' The offending partitions were duly removed."

A group of young Dutch designers called the Fool were commissioned to produce a line of clothes for the shops. They were paid £40,000 which horrified accountant Harry Pinsker, who saw this as unnecessary expenditure. The group had previously worked on a rejected centrefold painting for *Sgt. Pepper* and completed various projects for the Beatles, but their first connection with the Beatles had come through the Savile Theatre, which Brian Epstein owned. The Fool consisted of Josje Leeger, Marijke Koger and Simon Posthuma, who had met in Amsterdam and briefly ran a boutique called the Trend. When they moved to London in 1966, they met Barry Finch and Simon Hayes, who ran a public-relations firm with ties to Robert

Stigwood and Brian Epstein. Finch soon became a full-fledged member of the Fool, while Hayes acted as business manager. Simon Posthuma explained the group's name: "It represents truth, spiritual meaning and the circle which expresses the universal circumference in which gravitate all things." After Marijke met Paul McCartney in 1967, she began to conduct private tarot readings for the Beatles, and Paul always seemed to draw the Fool card. This upset him, but Marijke emphasized that the card represented an innocent, childlike quality, and Paul was inspired with a new song. "I began to like the word 'fool'," he said, "because I began to see through the surface meaning. I wrote 'Fool On The Hill' out of that experience of the tarot." In an exclusive first ever interview, conducted in February 2003, Marijka shed considerable light on the Fool's convoluted relationship with the Beatles and company. "I never debased my interest in the metaphysical by laying the cards willy nilly. I only remembered one time I had Paul draw a single card: Death. It has been very significant in his life. The death of loved ones and the renaissance of his career."

The Fool was given tremendous freedom at the boutique, and Simon described his vision for the shop to the *Sunday Times*: "It will have an image of nature, like a paradise with plants and animals painted on the walls. The floor will be imitation grass and the staircase like an Arab tent. In the windows will be seven figures representing the seven races of the world, black, white, yellow, red, etc. There will be exotic lighting and we will make it more like a market than a boutique." The original plan was to sell a wide range of clothing, furniture, jewellery, paintings, posters, and even the fixtures that were part of the shop. The press release termed it, "a beautiful place where beautiful people can buy beautiful things". The Fool soon took off with Pete Shotton on a buying trip to Marrakesh. Marijke remembers, "Simon and I spent a lot of time in Morocco, had connections and knew the country well. Apple needed items other than clothes and so all agreed we needed to go and buy stuff, which we did; jewellery, instruments, etc.'

Numerous garments were created for the opening – an orange crushed-velvet hooded jacket, colourful minidresses with attachable long skirts, Edwardian coats made from upholstery fabric, and other items more suitable for fancy-dress parties than everyday wear. Marijke commented: "Boys and girls can't go to offices dressed quite like we are. But we have made velvet suits for boys and dresses for girls they could begin to wear everywhere." Simon, too, expounded on their overtly hippie philosophy in the same article: "In the future people will have more leisure and they will therefore develop their inner eye. They will want to get to know the supreme power: love!" He insisted that each label be made of pure silk. When Shotton found out about this he protested to Lennon, pointing out that the cost of producing each label would exceed the price of the actual clothing! John, however, told Shotton to allow the Fool's extravagances: "Remember, Pete, we're not business freaks, we're artists." "The Beatles commissioned us to do a fashion line and a series of fourteen art productions," Marijke explained. "They wanted our talent very much. We certainly didn't hold a gun to their heads!

"The Fool have been accused of stealing many garments from Apple. We only used some for public relations purposes as we were inundated by the press and constantly photographed in these outfits to advertise the boutique. We were merely trying to get the job done right, making sure the design sketches were executed as indicated, the patterns were right, the fabrics correct etc. The manufacturers may have overcharged but that was not our department. We preferred to have nice woven labels rather than cheap looking printed ones. It is absurd to say the label cost more than the outfits!"

To make the premises stand out among the drab, unadorned buildings of busy Baker Street, the Fool planned to cover the outside walls with a swirling psychedelic mural. The City of Westminster council refused permission for this but the Fool employed art students to paint their trippy images in rainbow colours. "We had about six art students working as gophers and we did all the painting ourselves over the weekend," Marijke recalled. "We did not push this mural. I clearly remember a meeting with all four Beatles in Brian's office and John on his knees begging to do the mural! Not that anyone else objected either. I don't know how much we were paid, I never had anything to do with money. As a matter of fact I didn't even carry any change!"

The grand opening party was held on 5 December, nearly a month behind schedule, with the shop officially open to the public on the seventh. Magic Alex had been commissioned to supply an artificial sun for the event to light up the sky at precisely 8.16 p.m., but it was a predictable no-show. Paul was at his farm in Scotland and Ringo was filming *Candy* in Rome, so they both missed the opening gala, which was so overcrowded with guests that a BBC commentator fainted.

Early on the shop appeared to be doing well as stock had to be constantly replenished. Much, though, was shoplifted and the venture lost nearly £200,000 in seven months. Also, within three weeks of its unveiling the outside mural had to be whitewashed due to complaints from other local traders and a stinging letter from their landlord, the Duke of Westminster. "With all the trouble in the world, it wasn't worth fighting for," said John, ruefully. Paul suggested projecting the mural on to the now all white building from across the street, but this was soon forgotten.

Incredibly, the Beatles opened another shop, Apple Tailoring, Civil and Theatrical, to be run by John Crittle, a twenty-five-year-old designer who had previously made clothes for them, the Stones and other rock luminaries. The opening was held on 22 May 1968 at 161 New King's Road, and was attended by John, Yoko Ono, George and Patti. "We won't really get teenyboppers here," Crittle said, "because the prices will be too high for them. We're pushing velvet jackets and the Regency look, although the Beatles put forward plenty of suggestions. They have pretty far ahead ideas, actually. We're catering mainly for pop groups, personalities and turned-on swingers." Harrison commented to the *New Musical Express*: "We bought a few things from him, and the next thing I knew, we owned the place!"

SIX

Across The Universe

The Beatles' Rishikesh Diary

1968

"Who was that woman who looks like Jean Simmons who kept going to Maharishi for private interviews? She must have been about forty-five. I was always trying to get an audience with the Maharishi and he kept refusing. . . . The rest of us had to wait like good American people, in line to see the master walkin' on the petals."

John Lennon

"When Ringo comes, the storm clears the passage . . . in the clear, Ringo comes!"

Maharishi

Reporter: Do you really feel this man is on the level?
John Lennon: I don't know what level he's on.

Born in Jabalpur, India, in 1918, the son of a schoolteacher, Mahesh Prasad Varma graduated from Allahabad University with a physics degree in 1942. He soon abandoned his worldly aspirations, however, and, according to his official biography, spent the next thirteen years living the life of a Hindu ascetic uncovering the delicate mysteries of meditational yoga. During that time he took initiation from his spiritual master, His Holiness Brahmaleen Jagadguru Shankaracharya Brahmananda Saraswati Maharaja or, to his followers, simply Guru

Dev. Following the master's death, Varma apparently bestowed upon himself the name Revered Maharishi Bala Bramachari Mahesh Yogi Maharaja, an unheard-of title for a mere ashram clerk. Beyond that, he publicly assumed the position of successor to his guru. Officials of the orthodox Hindu society from which he sprang believe that he was unsuited for the post as he had been born into the *kshatriya* caste – warrior/governmental class – and argue that he was also ineligible according to the last will and testament of Brahmananda Saraswati. In 1985 Robert Kropinski, a former follower of the Maharishi, met in India with Guru Dev's successor, Sri Shankaracharya Swaroopanand Saraswati, to try to shed some light on the Maharishi's lightning rise to international prominence. "If he is a follower of the Sanatana Dharma [Hinduism], he should not do what he is doing," the aged master began. "This would be against the orders of his guru! Moreover, calling himself Maharishi [a great saint] is totally inappropriate. No assembly has conferred upon him a title of Maharishi. In the ashram he was doing the work of typing, writing and translation. Then he became a *sadhu* . . . He went abroad, first to Singapore. The expatriate Indians there, thinking he was a disciple of Shankaracharya, received him and bought him a ticket for the United States. After going to America, he brought the Beatles back here. It was rumoured he did inappropriate things with them and that's why they went away. He later opened many camps and claimed he could teach people to read minds and levitate. No one, however, succeeded in learning the things he promised. He himself does not know or practise yoga. He does not know anything about such things! He used to place a picture of Guru Dev behind him, and during initiation he would have people worship it then he would give out mantras. I have met many persons who in reality had their mantras from Mahesh, but they consider themselves to be disciples of Guru Dev. But, no matter whom they consider their teacher, the fact is a person who gives a mantra is to be considered the real guru. If Mahesh thinks he is backed by Shankaracharya, then it is proper on his part to tell people to take initiation from Shankaracharya . . . I believe Mahesh has caused a severe blow to genuine Indian culture."

Professional jealousy from a less commercially successful guru, or legitimate criticism from the spiritual organization the Maharishi once represented? Cynthia Lennon comes down on the side of the old master. A decade after the Beatles met the Maharishi wrote, "I believed then and I believe now that the Maharishi is a very wise and beautiful being. The press of the world took great delight in trying to belittle him but their judgement was not founded on the experience of his teachings. No matter what anyone says about the Maharishi, he has always worked for the betterment of mankind. And if one man can even partially succeed in a single lifetime, then as far as I'm concerned he is worthy of praise not degradation or insult."

Whatever the case, in 1959 he travelled West and established the International Meditation Society. Then known as the "Beacon Light of the Himalayas", he landed in Hollywood, where he set up his Spiritual Regeneration Movement on a sunny summer afternoon in Sequoia National Park. To his twenty or thirty followers the Maharishi spoke of a time when there would be Spiritual Regeneration centres in every major city in the world and millions would embrace the technique of meditation.

Once Maharishi was involved with the Beatles he became a household name the world over. He appeared on *The Johnny Carson Show*, exchanging roses with Merv Griffin, his smiling face on the covers of the *Saturday Evening Post*, *Esquire*, *Newsweek*, *Life*, *Look*; he toured with the Beach Boys, and even played Madison Square Garden.

When veteran journalist Lewis Lapham asked one of the guru's senior American aides about the financial side of the Maharishi's international movement the man answered coyly, "The Maharishi has a head for just about anything he needs a head for." When he was told he was sending too much money out of India he simply set up companies in America and Switzerland to circumvent the problem. He homed in on US college campuses as recruiting grounds and did equally well there. In the beginning it cost only thirty-five dollars to receive a mantra from the Maharishi but rumour has it that he requested the Beatles to deposit some 10–25 per cent of their annual gross income into a Swiss account in his name. Lennon, for one, was not having *that*. Bill Harry, a friend of the Beatles, has written, "He seemed to act as if he didn't understand business affairs, but always had an accountant present at his meetings. When travelling he always stayed at the best hotels."

The Beatles' aide-de-camp Peter Brown recalls his dealings with the guru. "I had my doubts about the efficacy of the Beatles going off with Maharishi in the middle of the formation of Apple, particularly because of incidents which led me to believe Maharishi was using the Beatles' name for personal gain. One day I received a call from the lawyers for ABC Television in America. They said the Maharishi was negotiating a TV special, which would include an appearance by the Beatles. They were calling to confirm the Beatles' co-operation. I told them the Beatles had no intention of appearing on the Maharishi's show. Only a week later the lawyers were back on the phone: the Maharishi was still insisting he could deliver them.

"I called the Maharishi in Malmö, Sweden and explained the problem, but his answers were obscure and indefinite. I then decided to fly to Malmö to insist he should not represent the Beatles as being part of his projects. The Maharishi greeted me warmly but only giggled and nodded as I laid down the law. Later the lawyers, who said the Maharishi was still insisting the Beatles would appear, were soliciting sponsors with this understanding. I went to Malmö once again, this time with Paul and George. We met the Maharishi and tried to explain he must not use their names to exploit his business, and that they definitely would not appear on his TV special, but the Maharishi only nodded and giggled. 'He's not a modern man,' George said forgivingly on the plane home. 'He just doesn't understand these things.'"

In Bangor, back in August 1967, the Maharishi extended an open invitation to the boys and their entourage to travel to his International Academy of Transcendental Meditation in Rishikesh, India, to take part in his advanced teachers' training programme. Thus on 14 February 1968, Mal Evans picked up the Beatles' luggage from their homes and boarded Qantas flight 754 from Heathrow to New Delhi. John, Cynthia, George, Patti and her sister Jennie flew in the next day. Evans recalled, "Travelling from London with John and George were two reporters, Robin Turner of the *Daily Express* and Don Short of the *Daily Mirror*. Don and Robin told me George and John convinced them on the plane, just by chatting, of the value of meditation. At 8.15 a.m. on Friday morning George, John, Patti, Cyn and Jennie arrived. There to meet them and say hello was Mia Farrow. I'd already introduced myself back at the hotel and found out her brother, Johnny, was due to fly in about the same time as the two Beatles. Getting away from the airport wasn't too difficult because the press were quite polite and didn't detain anyone too long."

However, the Beatles entourage did not reach Rishikesh without incident, as Lapham remembered: "Harrison and Lennon arrived over the weekend. The Indian press pursued them to the ashram, and there were several unpleasant incidents, a photographer was assaulted, and the editorials the next day reflected a general bitterness and disillusion."

Apple bigwigs Neil Aspinall and Denis O'Dell had come with John and George, as well as Magic Alex. Paul, Jane Asher, Ringo, Maureen and a few members of the British press corps arrived at the Maharishi's comfortable mountain retreat late on 19 February. Across the path a banner strung between bamboo poles bore the single word "Welcome". Just beyond, where the path turned steeply upward, a stern guard stood before a wooden gate in a barbed-wire fence. The buildings at the higher elevations stood among shesham and teak trees, but those below the gate were erected on open stony ground. Evans later revealed that the Beatles were all relieved to discover the many amenities available to them in what was literally the Indian jungle. "Having heard a mixture of strange stories about the place, I think we all half expected to find ourselves living in tents with cardboard boxes for seats and tables. We had a very pleasant surprise when we saw the high standard of the accommodation."

"Rishikesh is an incredible place," Harrison said. "Ninety-nine per cent of the population are renunciates."

Starr began to feel unwell on his first day as Evans recalled: "When he got the chance Ringo told me he needed a doctor. It wasn't anything serious but his injections were giving him trouble. His arm was swollen and painful and he thought it best to see if any treatment was required. Our driver lost his way and led us to a dead-end in the middle of a field. The press came to our rescue, as a whole stream of cars had been following us. In the end we accepted the directions of some helpful reporters and found a hospital. A doctor assured Ringo all would be well without treatment."

Everyone relaxed as the initial excitement of the trip subsided and tensions dissipated under the spell of meditation. Surprisingly, most days it was the normally sluggish John who was first up, and after half an hour's meditation he would go for a leisurely stroll around the compound with Evans or George. "We lived in one of six little cottages," Evans recalled. "They had been luxuriously done out. Each of our rooms was neatly furnished, with twin beds, new rugs, dressing-tables, shelves and cupboards, a bathroom with toilet and shower facilities. The water supply broke down from time to time, both hot or cold. Surprise, surprise! Not a single creepy-crawly thingy in sight! So much for all the soft rumours we'd heard before we set off!"

"The Maharishi was a wonderful teacher," said Cynthia. "His lectures were humorous, enlightening, and provided truly halcyon days. John and George were in their element. They threw themselves totally into the Maharishi's teachings, were happy, relaxed and, above all, found a peace of mind denied them so long."

Harrison recalled that quite a lot of what the guru said went directly into their music: "There was a lot of things that was actually stuff the Maharishi had said, like that song, 'Come on, come on,' you know, 'Come on, it's such a joy,' whatever that song, 'Everybody's Got Something To Hide Except Me And My Monkey'. Well, apart from the bit about the monkey, that was what Maharishi used to always say."

McCartney, too, became absorbed in the master's philosophy, but Starr didn't like the food or the insects, and complained that the stifling midday heat stopped him meditating properly. "Ringo, an only marginally interested convert, found some of the curry dishes a bit hot," said Evans, "too many spices. So when I went into Delhi I collected a good supply of eggs so that we would have plenty of alternatives, fried eggs, boiled eggs, poached eggs."

"To eat communally overlooking the Ganges was a far cry from bacon and eggs in Surrey," Cynthia recalled. "A wooden trellis canopy over the dining area, entwined with creepers, sheltered us from the elements during these first weeks of cold and rain. Although our diet in India contained no meat, none of us suffered . . . The simple life suited us all. We thrived and began to evolve more as individuals without all the stress and pressure."

Lapham remembered his initial impression of the entourage and the lousy food. "The Beatles first appeared towards the end of lunch and the beginning of tea. Dressed in romantic combinations of mod and Indian costumes, they came as a group, accompanied by their wives, also in vivid trailing silks. They moved slowly, their heavy gold chains and pendants swinging against their chests, and the girls, all of whom had long blonde hair, evoked images of maidens rescued from castles. Collectively they looked like characters from a strange and wonderful movie as yet unseen. They sat in a row on one side of the table, and Paul McCartney said he'd had a dream to Anneliese Braun, an elfin woman to whom everyone applied on such matters. He explained that in his dream he'd been trapped in a leaking submarine of indeterminate colour. When all appeared lost, however, the sub surfaced in a crowded London street. Anneliese clapped her hands like a child seeing their first snowfall. 'How very nice', she said, wondering if McCartney understood. He smiled and said he didn't think he quite got it. 'Why,' she said, 'it's the perfect meditation dream!' The voyage in the submarine she interpreted as the descent towards pure consciousness through the vehicle of the mantra; the leaks represented anxiety, and the emergence in the street indicated a return to normal life, which was the purpose of all good meditation. The other people present applauded, and in the ensuing silence at the far end of the table, I heard somebody say, 'I'm sure it's Wednesday, but they're trying to convince me it's Saturday.' "

"The Maharishi never appeared at meals to eat with his students," said Evans. "He stayed in his bungalow. We were three weeks behind the rest of the meditators so he used to give us extra lessons in the afternoons. We'd all sit in the open air, sometimes on chairs on the grass or on the flat sunroof. When it was cooler we'd join him in his bungalow, sitting round on cushions. I could never cross my legs comfortably so there was this big thing about providing me with my own special chair for these sessions!"

Maharishi man Mike Dolan recalled perhaps the strangest and certainly most controversial of the Beatles' extended group. "His name was Magic Alex, who we were led to believe had the genius of both Marconi and Edison combined, he told us so himself. George once confided that Alexis was designing a solar-powered electric guitar, which would be groovy for afternoon concerts. He was summoned to India by John and George to build an electronic device he promised to be not much bigger than a trash-can lid. It was to be made out of humdrum electronic parts available at the local equivalent to Radio Shack and he modestly claimed that when assembled the device would not only supply power for the gigantic radio station, that was to beam out to the far corners of the world the Maharishi's message of meditation, peace and love but would have enough of a surplus to light up the entire region. Amazingly, all that had to be done was for the device to be assembled and then placed at a strategic point in the Ganges."

"You're sitting up there at lunch," remembers TV actor Tom Simcox, "and you think you're talking to a real person . . . then suddenly you're talking to the white rabbit."

Another of the lauded pop-star élite to join the Beatles on their pilgrimage to inner peace was the Scottish singer-songwriter, Donovan. He remembered a happy time full of promise, and the youthful hope that what was taking place on that lonely mountain was somehow of near universal importance. "One night we were in the Maharishi's room," he said. "The Maharishi was sitting on the floor cross-legged, there were the four Beatles, Mia Farrow, Mike Love of the Beach Boys, and myself, but there was a sort of embarrassed silence. I think we didn't know quite what we were expected to say or do, because this sort of thing was obviously all very new to us. To break the mood, John went up to the Maharishi, patted him on the head and said, 'There's a good little guru.' It worked! We all laughed. That gesture was very typical of Lennon, because he always said and did exactly what he felt."

As one lazy cosmic day passed languidly into the next the jangly sounds of acoustic guitars began to echo across the camp as the Beatles and Donovan got down to some serious composing. On 15 March, Mike Love's birthday, a tape-recorder captured a charming McCartney composition about both meditation and the Beatles' Rishikesh experience. Possibly entitled "Spiritual Regeneration Movement Foundation" it bears a strong rhythmic resemblance to "Back In The USSR", in addition to using the alphabet in its lyrics and thanking their beloved "Guru Dev". The performance was followed by a rendition of "Happy Birthday", and a reprise of "Spiritual Regeneration", part of which went, "I'd like to thank you Guru Dev, 'cause your children couldn't thank you enough. ABCDEFGHI Jai Guru Dev." Later American DJ Wolfman Jack got hold of a copy and it's appeared on Beatles bootlegs ever since.

Life inside the compound was structured in terms of the daily routine but very laid back. Evans recalled: "A total of about forty people were employed at the Academy, including a joiner, a full-scale printing works, cooks and cleaning staff. The room service was marvellous. On my first day I unpacked dozens of shirts and clothing and put them on shelves in my room. An hour later the lot had disappeared. The same evening they were back, all freshly washed and pressed." Ringo thought it was rather like "a sort of recluse holiday camp".

At one point the Maharishi presented the Lennons with a complete Indian wardrobe for their son Julian. A collection, remembered Cynthia, fit for a young Indian prince. Nothing was too good or too much trouble for the master's celebrity converts.

Nothing, that is, except drugs and alcohol. Still, old habits die hard, especially among the rich and famous, and Magic Alex sneaked in a supply of Rishikesh marijuana and some lethal local alcohol. A few days later the Beatles read in the local paper that dozens of locals had died from drinking it. John and George did not have any and strongly disapproved of those who did. According to Cynthia Lennon's memoirs it was only Patti, herself, Alex and two Americans who strayed.

A sparky young nurse from the USA was at Rishikesh at the same time, more to hang out with the Beatles than for the wisdom of Maharishi. Mike Dolan recalled: "My next-door neighbour in the ashram was a feisty New Yorker in her late twenties whom I will call RB. She was perkily attractive, very funny and at times combative. She would interrupt Maharishi with pointedly uncosmic questions during his lectures. She was, as a lot of people on that course, a recent meditator, one of the sudden influx of Beatles fans. It seemed to hit her all of a sudden this technique was more a part of a greater Hindu tradition than she expected. She was having trouble as the lectures delved more and more into Vedic philosophy. I believe she felt deceived by the movement . . . She was friendly but soon became very negative towards meditation in general. She wanted so badly to just go home but her plane ticket was dated for the end of the three-month course so she was forced to stay at the ashram for weeks. RB soon found a friend, however, in Alex. She stopped attending the lectures weeks before and she stayed in her room with Alex as he made plans for his revolutionary power pack. I could hear them through the thin wall huffing and puffing as they practised their *asanas* late at night. It behoved both RB and Alex to get out of Rishikesh but he couldn't leave without losing face. Magic was under some pressure from his friends/bosses to actually produce something. If he were to stay in Rishikesh he would be exposed as a fraud. The familiar smell of very happy herbs would sometimes waft out of the open door, and their behaviour was becoming notorious especially with the older establishment meditators like Walter Koch, Nancy Cooke and newly arrived president of SRM [the Spiritual Regeneration Movement], Charles Lutes."

For everyone else, though, life in Rishikesh went on as usual. "We met for ninety-minute lectures at 3.30 p.m. and 8.30 p.m. each day," Evans recalled. "People would recount their meditation experiences and Maharishi would explain the causes of the sensations and thoughts we'd had. The idea was to build up to longer meditation periods, gradually tapering off again towards the end of the course so that everyone would come out of Rishikesh more or less feeling down to earth again. To make sure we could meditate in peace we had little printed cards saying, 'Meditating, please do not disturb.' We stuck these on the doors of our bedrooms."

Lewis Lapham later recalled his initial impressions of Britain's pop-star élite and the contest to see who could meditate the longest. "The Beatles appeared to be 'straight kids', but they kept pretty much to themselves. Mia Farrow left after a week to go on a tiger hunt, but maybe she would be back. The menu consisted of rice and vegetables, all of it boiled for twenty minutes, and a lot of people were getting pretty sick of it. The majority of those present were either British or American, but the Swedes were the best at prolonged meditation, and one of them held the current record of twenty-one hours." As John Lennon commented in 1980, "That was the competition in Maharishi's camp: who was going to get cosmic first. What I didn't know was that I was already cosmic!"

One of those who perhaps went a little too far with her cosmic homework was Prudence Farrow, Mia's sister, who was spending hour after hour, day after day alone in her cottage apparently in deep meditation. This was all well and good for the more seasoned practitioner, but not a rank beginner. Her concerned friends decided that something had to be done. "All the people around were very worried about the girl," said Lennon. "So we sang to her."

The spiritually polar opposite to Farrow was the always affable Jane Asher. Canadian ashram inmate Paul Saltzman remembered: "Jane was the warmest, most emotionally open of any of the 'famous folks' who spent parts of each day sitting outside at the table overlooking the Ganges and the town of Rishikesh, far below."

Now that the whole world knew where the Beatles were, fan mail poured in and some lucky correspondents actually received a reply. I found a copy of this letter from John to a fan in a diary while researching this book.

> *Dear Beth,*
>
> *Thank you for your letter and kind thoughts. When you read that we are in India, "searching" for peace etc., it is not that we need faith in God and Jesus, we have full faith in them; it is only as if you went to stay with Billy Graham for a short time, it just so happens that our Guru (teacher) is Indian, and what is more natural for us to come to India, his home? He also holds courses in Europe and America, and we will probably go to some of them as well, to learn, and to be near him.*

A newspaper cutting from the now long defunct *Dehra Dun Dispatch* was with the letter:

A MEDITATION CELEBRATION!

Meditating with the Maharishi had its lighter side for the Beatles

RISHIKESH – You'd be forgiven for thinking every day's a birthday for the Beatles, but no Beatle has ever had quite such a birthday party as George Harrison's twenty-fifth, which he celebrated during his meditational sessions in India.

Apparently George hadn't given much thought to his birthday, probably thinking it would be spent in meditation. But the Maharishi, a quiet expert in showmanship, had some surprises up his sleeve! He had the assembly hall decked with everything colourful that could be found: flags, curtains, yards of silk, so that it looked more like a theatre than a scene for a party.

The timing of the affair was beautiful. When everyone was seated, the Maharishi entered with his priests, and sat cross-legged on a deerskin rug beneath a portrait of his Guru. A real Rishikesh rave-up followed, with the chanting of hymns and the waving of a burning oil lamp! Fashion note for would-be meditators: the shoeless Beatles and their girls were resplendent in *raja* coats, saris and silk trousers, all looking very tanned and dressed up for the occasion. A sort of "say-it-with-flowers" ceremony followed. Firstly, the Maharishi garlanded George, then George returned the gesture. Then the whole audience garlanded both George and Patti with floral sprays of yellow marigolds, yellow apparently being an auspicious colour for the event. George carried on from there by garlanding the necks of his fellow Beatles and their wives.

When it came to Mal Evans, chaos developed! The garland around Mal's neck caught on one of George's leaving them twisting and wriggling around the stage to free themselves, the whole place roared with laughter!

Mike Love, leader of the Beach Boys, who was in the audience, was then asked up on stage to speak about meditation.

Finally the Maharishi gave George his birthday present. It was a plastic globe of the world. A simple present, but actually full of meaning.

The globe had been fitted so the map of the world was upside down. "This is what the world is like today, upside down," the Maharishi announced solemnly. "It is rotating in tension and agony. The world waits for its release and to be put right. Transcendental Meditation can do so. George, this globe I am giving you symbolizes the world today. I hope you will help us all in the task of putting it right."

Accepting the globe from the Maharishi, George immediately turned it over so that the map was the right side up. "I've done it!" he shouted, and was applauded with laughter for his quick wit.

Finally everyone moved outside for a fireworks display, and as the Maharishi left, the Beatles bowed and folded their hands, murmuring, "*Namaste.*"

Cynthia Lennon remembered the lasting effect meditation had on Harrison: "Previous to George's experiences with LSD and the subsequent flower-power explosion, he had been the most tactless, blunt and often pig-headed of the Beatles. George was the youngest and least mature, but he was the one Beatle who altered most in character and temperament over the years . . . The rough edges were smoothed down and self-discipline became the cornerstone of his character. This was never more evident to me than in India."

While George and Patti prospered, though, John and Cynthia were growing apart. "John and I shared a room but found it increasingly difficult to co-ordinate our timing as far as meditation was concerned. For two people to meditate for days on end in the confines of a single room was difficult. The ideal situation was to have our own separate rooms . . . Sometimes we met at mealtimes; sometimes not at all. The closeness we felt at the time of Brian's death was slowly disappearing. We were separate entities and contact was infrequent."

A long-lost diary, written in Hindi and Nepalese by one of the *sannyasi* (renunciates), His Holiness Ravindra Damodara Swami (a younger godbrother of the Maharishi), was given to me at Rishikesh. The humble document throws considerable light on events:

Wednesday, 2.00 p.m.

This afternoon Maharishi held press conference below gate. In the morning boys set up *asana* and antelope skin. For the reporters they spread mats. Walking slowly, followed by two monks, he came from the hill carrying marigolds. The taller monk held an umbrella over his head, shading him from sun. The pressmen asked him about the difference between his teachings and Vedic renunciation. Plucking petals from a flower, Maharishi said that *vedanta* and yoga had been misinterpreted for many years. The tall monk held the umbrella, raising and lowering it as the photographers stood up to take pictures. The smaller monk squatted at Maharishi's feet, holding out the microphone of his tape-recorder. A man who'd come from South India asked if he could read a poem. Maharishi nodded and the man read in Tamil. When he finished he kissed Maharishi's feet, saying, in English, he hoped to sit at the Maharishi's feet in heaven. Maharishi asked if anyone had seen article about him in *Life* magazine. Nobody had seen it. "Too bad," he said, "huge picture." Although there were many questions from reporters I thought to write down only a bit of what was said:

Reporter: What success have you had here in India?

Maharishi: The Indian people are poor and lazy, and meditation will give them the energy and drive to work harder and better themselves.

Reporter: But surely poverty is not a simple matter of laziness?

Maharishi: With meditation they will overcome their poverty.

Reporter: What do you think about American young people?

Maharishi: They should stay in school and obey their parents and they must obey the leaders of your country who are more informed and qualified than they. I disagree with nuclear disarmament but feel America was right to be in Vietnam.

Friday, 11 p.m.

I don't like the Greek [Mardas]. He doesn't care for meditation or Guru Dev. He cares only Beatles and girls. He drank wine and gave to others, he has a girl in his room. Behind his back I saw him make funny faces at Maharishi, no one laughed. He also eats chicken which is against the rules in Rishikesh. How he got it I do not know. During lectures he does not come, or he just pretends to listen. He does not meditate. He is a bad influence on all westerners. Maharishi also doesn't like him, but he cannot do anything because he is the Beatles' good friend. He tried to touch one Indian lady who ran away. Only I saw. He is bad.

Saturday, 9 a.m.

Nice meeting with all at camp and Guru Dev. Maharishi makes everyone laugh. He likes Ringo very much. He says Ringo is always in meditation, but the others, too much brain in the way. Ringo goes by feeling, and heart. Wife is also nice, she is a very good artist. Boss Beatle John is funny, but sometimes mean to his wife who is a nice lady. George is my favourite, he is most kind to all. I do not know his wife, but she smiles and is polite. Donovan is also good, but smokes cigarettes. I tell him no, he says he can't stop. Meditation will help him. Sometimes Paul talks mean with George; he is clever, but over smart. He wants to be boss of Beatles. He also a funny man and writes good songs. The girl Jane seems afraid of India, she is quiet. Maharishi tries to encourage her, but she has no real interest I think. Today we will walk by the river, all the westerners and Guru Maharaj. I must go to Rishikesh for sweaters for Farrow sisters. They complain of cold mornings. Bananas, mangos, aggabatti and tea also not to forget.

Sunday 2.30 p.m.
I visit Maharishi's house for kitchen work. He tells me of all the Beatles George is most advanced and this is his last life. He also says John has many more to go and must not give in to his weakness for women or it will ruin him. I have to work quietly while he takes a nap. Something I have never seen him do.

John, Paul, George and Ringo went to Rishikesh hoping to further their studies in meditation and relieve the demands of fame. In the long run, however, the journey was far more valuable to John and Paul in terms of their songwriting and forthcoming album. Even with meditation on their minds, the Beatles were never without their music. John and Paul came with their Martin D-28 acoustic guitars, and George instructed Mal Evans to go to Rikki Rams in Connaught Place in Delhi and buy him the finest instrument in stock.

Popmaster Donovan became an important, if unacknowledged, musical presence for the Beatles, giving valuable feedback on the constant flow of fleeting ideas, and co-authoring some central elements in their new music. His first major contribution was to teach Lennon a distinctive guitar-picking style. Once John had mastered it he passed it on to George. It proved a valuable tool for John, who wrote "Dear Prudence" and "Julia" utilizing it.

"Dear Prudence" was written for Prudence Farrow. When she "went over the top" with her meditating as Lennon later put it, he and George were elected to coax her outside, and John wrote the song. Prudence remembered George telling her that John had written a song about her, "but I didn't hear it until it came out on the album. I was very flattered. It was a beautiful thing to have done."

Her sister Mia remembered that "In response to several frightening emotional eruptions that occurred during the long hours of meditation, Maharishi appointed sets of 'team buddies' to look out for one another. Prudence's buddies were George and John, and they took their responsibility seriously. Every morning and most afternoons they met in Prudy's room, where they discussed their respective lives, the meaning of existence and who Maharishi really was.

"Before they left the ashram, Lennon and McCartney wrote the song 'Dear Prudence' for my sister: 'Dear Prudence, won't you come out to play, Dear Prudence, greet the brand-new day . . .' "

"I guess I thought it was really nice, but I didn't know they were going to put it on an album or anything," said Prudy. "I didn't really think about it; it wasn't anything in my mind. Then much later, after India, I heard people saying there was a song. I was really grateful that it was something so nice.

"I just wanted to meditate as much as possible," Prudence told me. "It was a special time, and such a holy place. One night when I was meditating, George and John came into my room with their guitars, singing, 'Ob-la-di, ob-la-da, life goes on.' Another time John, Paul, and George came in singing 'Sgt. Pepper's Lonely Hearts Club Band', the whole song! They were trying to be cheerful, and it was so sweet of them. I was grateful, but I wished they'd go away. At first I don't think they realized what the training course in meditation was all about. They were just having fun. They didn't quite understand until later . . ."

In John's mind, "Julia" was a song about two people: his late, free-spirited mother Julia, and Yoko Ono. Lennon had first met Ono at an exhibition of hers at the Indica gallery in November 1966. By spring 1968 he had begun to exchange passionate letters with the Japanese-American artist. He was interested in producing an album by Yoko: "I was in India meditating about the album, thinking what would be the best LP cover, when it suddenly hit me. I thought, Aha! Naked! So I wrote Yoko with a drawing." This idea went on to become the cover for their first collaboration, the infamous *Two Virgins*. John snapped the photo himself in Ringo's basement apartment in London. In "Julia", Yoko was the "ocean child" (the meaning of her name in Japanese). The reference to "seashell eyes" is lifted from Kahlil Gibran's poem "Sand and Foam". The song is the only number in the entire Beatles catalogue performed entirely solo by Lennon.

Paul first showed John the chorus to "Ob-la-di, Ob-la-da" in Rishikesh, and the two played the chorus over and over while McCartney wrote the lyrics for the convoluted storyline. The title phrase was *yoruba* for "life goes on", and was first tossed at Paul by Nigerian conga player Jimmy Scott in London. Although Scott later played congas on an early version of the song, his relationship with McCartney was not always cordial. He believed he deserved a small cut of the song's royalties, having "written" the catchphrase. Paul was angered by the British press for taking Scott's side, and complained to the other Beatles in 1969 about a particular article: "It just says, 'Currently, Lennon/McCartney are doing quite well out of a riff they "borrowed" from Jimmy Scott, "Ob-la-di, Ob-la-da", which is topping the charts.' Cunts! I mean . . . you haven't got a riff when you say 'hello', that's the riff I got off Jimmy Scott! Those two words, you know, fuckin' hell, you'd really think we'd taken his life! It's not as though he wrote the song." Subsequently McCartney bailed Scott out of jail, via Apple man Alistair Taylor (the musician had been arrested for failing to pay alimony), and eventually the pair were reconciled.

Richard Cooke's visit to his mother Nancy in Rishikesh inspired in Lennon "The Continuing Story Of Bungalow Bill". Mother and son went off on a tiger hunt, and afterwards Cooke explained to John and Paul why the animal had been killed: "It was either the tiger or us! The tiger was standing right in front of us." This became the lyric

"If looks could kill it would have been us instead of him." To John the song was "a sort of teenage social-comment and a bit of a joke". Today, it is a sneaky anthem for the animal-rights movement, but it was written at a time when such matters were thought either eccentric or foolishly sentimental.

Meanwhile, Donovan had his eye on Jennie Boyd, Patti Harrison's younger sister, and wrote "Jennifer Juniper" for her. But she wasn't interested in him and spent a lot of time with John. He was suffering from insomnia, and turned to songwriting to get him through the hot nights. His compositions, such as "I'm So Tired", reflected his often dark, surly moods. Jennie remembered: "When I was at my lowest, he made a drawing of a turbaned Sikh genie holding a big snake and intoning, 'By the power within, and the power without, I cast your tonsil lighthouse out!' Sometimes, late at night, I can still hear John singing those sad songs he wrote during those long evenings."

Lennon was aware of the irony in trying to ascend to God through meditation while producing suicidal songs: "It was that period when I was really going through a 'What's it all about? Songwriting is nothing! It's pointless and I'm not talented, and I'm a shit, and I couldn't do anything but be a Beatle and what am I going to do about it?' " The self-doubt that had arisen in the *Sgt. Pepper* period remained. The Maharishi told him repeatedly that the ego could be a positive force if kept in perspective, but he believed that "I'd really destroyed it and I was paranoid and weak. I couldn't do anything." "Yer Blues" reflected this. Here Lennon's loneliness and despair were real, not masked by third-person imagery. A parody of the emerging English blues scene in London, "Yer Blues" was about the end of his marriage. He also came up with a statement against the Vietnam War, a song called "Revolution": "I still had this 'God will save us' feeling about it, that it's going to be all right. That's why I did it, I wanted to say my piece about revolution." He originally envisaged it as a faster number, but when he took it into the studio, it was slowed down, and unusable as a single. The initial recording, though, formed the basis of two songs on the Beatles' *White Album*, "Revolution 1" and "Revolution 9". The original faster version was later used as the B-side to the smash "Hey Jude".

Lennon was frustrated by not having a piano on which to compose, even though his skill on the instrument was limited. However, several of his newest songs were piano-based, including "Hey Bulldog", "Across The Universe", and, "Cry Baby Cry", which had been in his head for months. It had come from a TV advert: "Cry, baby cry, make your mother buy." In India, he reworked the idea on acoustic guitar and added several new lyrics, based in part on the nursery rhyme "Sing a Song of Sixpence". He used a similar source for "What's The New Mary Jane", a wild Lennon/Magic Alex collaboration, which drew from the A. A. Milne poem "What Is the Matter with Mary Jane?". Later the song, an unmelodious number featuring Yoko's wailing vocals, caused tensions between John and Paul, and the latter did not participate in the recording. It was dropped from the *White Album*, and Lennon attempted to recycle it as a Plastic Ono Band single, but it remained unreleased until *The Beatles Anthology 3* in 1996.

Inspired by Chuck Berry's "Back In The USA", McCartney composed the clever story of a Cold War spy returning home from America in "Back In The USSR". One morning at the breakfast table, he sang it to Mike Love, who suggested mentioning girls from various parts of Russia, such as the Ukraine, Georgia and Moscow in the lyrics. His presence at the ashram perhaps sparked in Paul the idea of using Beach Boys-style harmonies in the recording.

McCartney's "Martha My Dear" was made up of two pieces: "Martha My Dear" and "Silly Girl". "It is about my dog," he said in 1968. "I don't ever try to make a serious social comment. So you can read anything you like into it, but really it's just a song. It's me singing to my dog."

Sitting on the roof of one of the chalets, Paul introduced the chords of "Rocky Sassoon" to John and Donovan. All three, equipped with their acoustic guitars, composed the lyrics and McCartney wrote them down. He changed "Sassoon" to "Raccoon" for a more cowboy-sounding name, and likened the song to a one-act play. "I don't know anything about the Appalachian mountains, cowboys and Indians or anything . . . I just made it all up."

At this point, Paul had only the melody of "I Will". In McCartney's words, it was "a sort of smoochy ballad" that was entitled "Ballad" until suitable lyrics were found. He tried writing some with Donovan, using Maharishi-inspired imagery, but in the end adopted his own straightforward love lyrics, which he finished on his return to England. "I don't think I helped with the lyrics," said Donovan. "He is very productive and will always take over the writing in a jam. I may have helped with the shape of the chords and encouraged the imagery from tunes I wrote in India. The descending movements of my songs may have encouraged Paul to write differently." "Wild Honey Pie", meanwhile, came from a spur-of-the-moment singalong at the ashram. Two other acoustically driven numbers, "Junk" and "Teddy Boy", ended up on his first solo album, *McCartney*.

Lennon also wrote the plaintive "Look At Me", which he kept for his own *Plastic Ono Band* album. He also produced two "throwaways", which found their way into the medley on side two of *Abbey Road*: "Mean Mr. Mustard", a song inspired by a newspaper article "about this mean guy who hid five-pound notes, not up his nose but somewhere else", and "Polythene Pam", about a girl who dressed in polythene, although "she didn't wear jackboots and kilts, I just sort of elaborated. Perverted sex in a polythene bag! I was just looking for something kinky to write about."

Monkeys mating in the open inspired Paul's "Why Don't We Do It In The Road?". "That's how simple the act of procreation is . . . we have horrendous problems with it, and yet animals don't." Lennon's "Everybody's Got Something To Hide Except Me And My Monkey" was "just a nice line which I made into a song". It was a reference to his new relationship with Ono, with filler lines from the Maharishi's daily lectures. Some of these same words would form the basis for McCartney's "Cosmically Conscious", which was not released until it closed off his 1993 album *Off The Ground*.

According to Mal Evans, he turned up in one of Paul's dreams in Rishikesh, saying, "Let it be." McCartney was struck by this, and wrote a song around the phrase in late 1968 at home in Cavendish Avenue. Driving around London one afternoon he asked Evans if he minded that "Brother Malcolm" be changed to "Mother Mary". Mal had no objection. Paul occasionally slipped in "Brother Malcolm" during the extended "Get Back" rehearsals of 1969. In his own recollections after Evans's death, McCartney said the source of his inspiration was a dream about his mother, Mary.

Many evenings in Rishikesh were spent in a large hall where the Maharishi would sit on a platform to lecture, and occasionally mini-concerts took place. At one, Paul, George and Donovan composed a spontaneous tribute to him:

> When the sun is tucked away in bed
> You worry about the life you've led.
> There is only one thing to do
> Let the Maharishi lead you.

The song ended with a quiet incantation of "Maharishi". The Maharishi's lively lectures were another source of inspiration for the new Beatles music. A talk on nature motivated John to write "Child Of Nature", a song much like "Across The Universe" with its wistful, poetic lyrics. When he became disillusioned with the Rishikesh experience, he changed the setting from Rishikesh to Marrakesh. The song was abandoned and never seriously rehearsed, but it resurfaced with new words on John's 1971 *Imagine* album as "Jealous Guy". Paul was inspired by the same talk to write "Mother Nature's Son" at his father's home, Rembrandt, combining the Maharishi's wisdom with childhood memories of bicycle rides in the English countryside. "The only thing about this one, however, it says 'Born a poor young country boy' and I was born in a private ward in Woolton Hospital actually, so it's a dirty lie."

The last thing George Harrison wanted to do in Rishikesh was write, and he admonished Paul for even thinking of the next album (tentatively titled "Umbrella", at this point and then later "A Doll's House"). He wrote a verse for Donovan's "Hurdy Gurdy Man", which was eventually left off the final recording: "When truth gets buried deep beneath a thousand years of sleep, time demands a turn around and once again the truth is found." He also wrote "Sour Milk Sea" – later recorded by Apple artist Jackie Lomax – in about ten minutes: "Even though I was in India, I always imagined the song as rock'n'roll. That was the intention." He began the sleepy "Long, Long, Long" but finished it in England, using chords from Bob Dylan's "Sad-eyed Lady Of The Lowlands". Literary influence was the key to George's work in this period, and most of his *White Album* contribution came from his reading in England. His major composition in India was "Dehra Dun", co-written with Donovan, about a sleepy mountain town some twenty-five miles north-west of Rishikesh. He attempted to record it during sessions for *All Things Must Pass*, but it remains officially unreleased.

Maureen and Ringo were the first in the Beatles' party to leave, on 1 March. If anyone thought that he was leaving so early because he was now anti-meditation, Ringo dispelled the idea when he reached Britain. "The Academy is a great place and I enjoyed it a lot. I still meditate every day for half an hour in the morning and half an hour every evening and I think I'm a better person for it. I'm far more relaxed than I have ever been. If you're working very hard and things are a bit chaotic, you get all tensed up and screwed up inside. You feel as if you have to break something or hit someone. But if you spend a short while in meditation, it completely relaxes you, and it's easier to see your way through problems. If everyone in the world started meditating, the world would be a much happier place."

Despite all the high times, good vibes and great material, Paul and Jane left the ashram next, arriving home on 26 March. McCartney remembered: "I gave myself a set period, and then if it was going to be something we really had to go back to India for, I was thinking of going back. But at the end of the month, I was quite happy, and I thought, This will do me, this is fine. If I want to get into it heavy, I can do it anywhere. That's one of the nice things about it. It's, like, you don't have to go to church to do it, do it in your own room." Canadian Paul Saltzman felt that Jane Asher might have encouraged Paul's decision to leave early. "Cynthia Lennon seemed the most pleased by the Maharishi's plans for the future of his world-wide meditation organization. Jane was the least interested . . . She was less interested in the Maharishi and meditation and more interested in travelling with Paul to see the Taj Mahal."

Mia Farrow's exodus came next and has passed into Beatles legend. She left, so the story goes, as a result of the Maharishi making a move on her. Paul Saltzman remembered that many people felt something was wrong even before the mysterious incident. "Mal and I were walking up the dirt road towards the kitchen," he said. "At one point, Mia's name came up and Mal said she still felt very awkward with all the attention the Maharishi was paying to her, far in excess of any other individual there."

"Nearly every afternoon Maharishi sent for me to come to his bungalow for a private talk," said Mia. "From the start he had been especially solicitous and attentive to me, and I had responded with wary resentment. 'Not only does he send for me every single day, and not the others', I complained to my sister, 'but also, he is giving me mangos. To the best of my knowledge, he has not given a single mango to anybody else . . .' Prudence said the problem was me."

Many details of the Beatles' visit to Rishikesh and the events that led to them leaving so suddenly are still uncertain. The Farrow/Maharishi story is the most popular, but it doesn't really ring quite true. Mia Farrow was just twenty-one when she married Frank Sinatra and was an insecure, emotional young girl from a troubled Hollywood background. Like the Beatles, she was thrust into the spotlight at an early age and was still inexperienced, despite her position as a Hollywood *ingénue*. It was after her unhappy, two-year union with Sinatra that she and her sister went to the Maharishi. For years when she was asked whether the rumour that he had made a pass at her was true she did not answer. When she published her autobiography, *What Falls Away*, in 1997 she confirmed, half-heartedly, that *something* happened:

> "Now we will meditate in my 'cave'," said Maharishi, and I followed him down steep wooden steps into a dark, humid little cellar room that smelled of sandalwood. It was my first time in his cave: there was a small shrine with flowers and a picture of Guru Dev, Maharishi's dead teacher, and a carpet on which we settled ourselves in the lotus position to meditate. After twenty or so minutes we were getting to our feet, still facing each other, but as I'm usually a little disoriented after meditation, I was blinking at his beard when

> suddenly I became aware of two surprisingly male, hairy arms going around me. I panicked, and shot up the stairs, apologizing all the way. I flew out into the open air, and ran as fast as I could to Prudy's room, where she was meditating of course. I blurted out something about Maharishi's cave, and arms, and beard, and she said, "It's an honour to be touched by a holy man after meditation, a tradition." Furthermore, at my level of consciousness, if Jesus Christ Himself had embraced me, I would have misinterpreted it.

When Farrow left the ashram, some say that it was with a rich male Indian travelling companion to go tiger hunting (which seems unlikely), or on a solitary hitchhiking trip to the hippie haunts of Kathmandu and Goa. It has even been suggested that she would return to feature in a film the Beatles were planning to promote their new faith.

So what was the genesis of the final split between the Beatles and the Maharishi? Mike Dolan insists that when SRM founder Charles Lutes learned from ashram insider Nancy Cooke that the Maharishi was making plans for a film with Apple, Lutes boarded the first Delhi-bound plane he could find to put the brakes on the scheme as he already had an agreement with the guru to make a film about him, with musician Paul Horn. The company he formed, Bliss Productions, was in danger of losing the star of their movie, the Maharishi Mahesh Yogi. The Beatles were under contract to make another movie with United Artists and thus couldn't have appeared in Bliss Productions' epic. Also Lutes was apparently annoyed that the guru was spending so much time with the group.

Some say that it was the nurse from New York who became close to the Maharishi, not Farrow. Mike Dolan has said, "I am very aware that especially back in 1968 there was a knee-jerk reaction to disbelieve this young woman and stab her with her own sexuality. For [the nurse's] part she had a fixed ticket home and just wanted to get the hell out of there."

RB eventually rather mysteriously got her earlier flight, but at what price? Did she back up Magic Alex's stories about the guru screwing and thus ensure the final betrayal of the Beatles' faith? To date there have been three accounts of the event, by Mike Dolan, Cynthia Lennon and Nancy Cooke, all of whom saw Magic Alex as the bad guy. Both he and Lutes wanted to get the gullible, yet immensely powerful Beatles out of the Maharishi's orbit so that Alexis could regain his influence over them and Lutes could win back the attention of his guru and get his movie made. Ironically, they both failed.

"John and George, the only Beatles left in Rishikesh, were more than a little pissed when the advance crew from Bliss Productions suddenly arrived at Shankaracharya Nagar," said Dolan. "Charlie [Lutes] could be a buffoon at times but he had chutzpah. How could he expect the world's biggest act ever to roll over and be bit players in a movie whose profits would enrich not only the movement they loved but whoever owned the production company? John and George stayed in their rooms for much of those last few days, craftily avoiding the cameras."

Dolan continues, "On the morning of 12 April I was woken by Rhaghwendra [senior Maharishi liaison to all western disciples]. It was still dark in the very early dawn, I was to go down to the dining area and find the cooks to make tea for some guests who were leaving. It was a little startling to see Cynthia, Patti, Jennie and RB [the New York nurse] standing around in the cool morning air. Sitting in the open dining area in deep conversation were John, George, Alexis and Rhaghwendra. Cowboy Tom, RB's ex-boyfriend, sat to the side. It wouldn't have been unusual except that the simple Indian clothes were nowhere to be seen. All were dressed in stylish pop-star attire.

"I noticed Cynthia had been crying. Nobody looked happy. Patti and Jennie smiled meekly. Rhaghwendra, a lovely man, wore the grey ashen mask of the defeated. I noticed Maharishi sitting alone on a rock just outside his garden. The rain from the night before threw up a light mist giving the scene a theatrical effect. Rhaghwendra told me something had happened, there had been meetings all through the night, that John and George were upset and Alexis was insisting they all leave . . . Rhaghwendra was given the job of transporting them all to New Delhi, they were very upset when they got into several taxis. The girls, sobbing, were still trying to persuade them to reconsider, they were fighting back tears as they drove away. They started filming the Maharishi movie that morning."

"There was a big hullaballoo about him trying to rape Mia Farrow or trying to get off with Mia Farrow and a few other women, things like that," Lennon later said. "And we went down to him and we'd stayed up all night discussing, was it true or not true. And when George started thinking it might be true, I thought, 'Well it must be true, 'cause if George is doubting it, there must be something in it.' So we went to see Maharishi, the whole gang of us, the next day – charged down to his hut, his very rich-looking bungalow in the mountains. And I was the spokesman – as usual, when the dirty work came. I actually had to be leader, whatever the scene was, when it came to the nitty gritty I had to do the speaking. And I said, 'We're leaving!'

"'Why?' Hee-hee, and all that shit. And I said, 'Well, if you're so cosmic, you'll know why.' He was always intimating, and there were all his right-hand men intimating that he did miracles. He said, 'I don't know why, you must tell me.' I just kept saying 'You know why' – and he gave me a look like, 'I'll kill you, you bastard.' He gave me such a look, and I knew then when he looked at me, because I'd called his bluff. And I was a bit rough to him."

To this day many of those who were there do not believe that the Maharishi ever made a move on any of his female followers, including Mia Farrow. That list included George Harrison, fellow meditator Mike Dolan, Nancy Cooke, Paul Horn, Jennie Boyd, Paul McCartney and Cynthia Lennon, who later denounced the man she believed was the culprit.

> The finger of suspicion was well and truly pointed at the man who had given us all so much. Alexis and a fellow female meditator [the nurse] began to sow the seeds of doubt in very open minds. Meditation practised for long periods renders the meditator truly sensitive . . . Alexis's statements about how the Maharishi had been indiscreet with a certain lady . . . gathered momentum. All, may I say, without a single shred of evidence or justification. It was obvious to me Alexis wanted out and more than anything he wanted the Beatles out as well . . . A night was spent trying

> desperately to sort everything out in their minds, what to believe, Alexis and this girl's accusation, or faith in the Maharishi . . . The following morning, Alexis set the ball in motion by ordering cars to take us to the airport . . . While we were seated around the dining tables waiting for the taxis and conversing in whispers, nerve ends showing, the Maharishi emerged from his quarters and seated himself not a hundred yards from our agitated group of dissidents. One of his ardent followers asked us to please talk things over properly with the Maharishi . . . The Maharishi was sitting alone in a small shelter made of wood with a dried grass roof . . . They stood up, filed past him and not a word was said . . .
>
> The journey away from my personal Shangri-la was miserable. Although John wasn't as glum as I, he was worried. He wanted to get home, and quick. Although he had gone through the motions of rejecting the Maharishi, he was very nervous about the situation.

At the time the Lennons were convinced that as he had been well and truly defeated, the Maharishi might try to derail their getaway from the ashram by either magical or material means. Cynthia, the more sensible of the two, wasn't as worried as John until their almost derelict Ambassador taxi ground to a halt in the middle of nowhere.

> It was our luck to break down somewhere in the Indian countryside . . . The driver didn't speak English and we didn't understand a word he said but it did dawn on us when he took off down the road that perhaps he was going to get help. We found ourselves parked on a grass verge in the pitch dark without food, drink or any means of light, not a sign of life anywhere. The other taxis had gone ahead, unaware of our predicament . . . John's only solution was to stand on the edge of the road with his thumb up in the air frantically waving it backwards and forwards at the sound of any car approaching. We were about to give up all hope when a saloon car drew up and two very educated Indian men inquired after our health . . . After a great deal of humming and haa-ing we opted for the lift . . . The driver of the saloon was a very fast driver. John and I clung to the front seats like grim death . . . We were about to ask them to let us out when one of them made it known that they were aware that John was a Beatle and that they would do all they

> could to help us get back to Delhi . . . At the nearest village they bought us drinks, and arranged after a great deal of persuasion for another taxi to take us on the remainder of our long journey . . .

The final Beatles song composed in India represented for John the entire Rishikesh experience: "Maharishi, what have you done?" On the long drive to Delhi, he thought of calling it "Maharishi" until George observed, "You can't say that, it's ridiculous." He suggested the title "Sexy Sadie", which John later viewed as a cop-out. The Rishikesh experience was over, and the Beatles had left "with a bad taste", as Lennon put it. They came back, though, with a treasure trove of new material, but John emphasized that "It could have been written in the desert, or Ben Nevis." Still, the time spent in Rishikesh represented the last spurt of creativity in Lennon during his time with the Beatles: over the next two years he regularly tapped into his 1968 pool of songs.

In a moment of irreverence he spoke of the negative effects of his Rishikesh experience*: "Let me tell you something about the Maharishi camp in Rishikesh. There were one or two attractive women there, but they mainly looked like, you know, schoolteachers or something. And the whole damn camp was on for the ones in bathing suits, and they're supposed to be meditating. And there's this cowboy there called Tom [Simcox] who plays cowboys on TV and, my, did the Beatle wives go for him in a big way! I wondered what it was – it was his tight leather belt, his jeans and his dumb eyes.

"Me, I took it for real, I wrote six hundred songs about how I feel. I felt like dying, and crying, and committing suicide, but I felt creative and said, 'What the hell's this got to do with what that silly little man's talking about?' But he did charm me in a way because he was funny. Sort of cuddly, like a little daddy with a beard, telling stories of heaven as if he knew. You could never pin him down . . . His right-hand man told about the planes he saved. How Maharishi came through the storm, on a plane. The pilot was getting worried

* Lennon's words come from a tape recorded some time between April 1969 and 1972.

they couldn't land. When Maharishi looked up with one foul look, according to the man who works for him, everything was okay and they landed." Lennon, as the tape makes clear, was not convinced!

Whatever the Maharishi was or is to the world, the Beatles' time in India prompted a flood of wonderful enduring work. At home undeveloped musical ideas sprouted and the *White Album* was the result. The experience was still in John's mind a decade later, when he wrote two songs for an unperformed play, "The Ballad of John and Yoko". The first, "The Happy Rishikesh Song", is a satirical piece that makes light of the meditation and mantras that promised all the answers. Of special interest is its coda, which, in sharp contrast to the title, is reminiscent of the lyrics in "Yer Blues": "I feel so suicidal, something is wrong."

In the second tribute, "India", John remarks that he left his "heart in England" with Yoko. It touches upon the search for answers in India, but recognizes that the truth will not come from Rishikesh but is already in his mind.

"Whatever anybody said there seemed especially wise, and nobody could make any serious mistakes," Lewis Lapham recalled. "Even Farrow's abrupt departure from the ashram could be explained, as could her wandering in the south of India. They wanted me to stay, partly because they thought I'd begun to attain God-consciousness and partly because, later that afternoon on the shore of the river, Donovan promised to sing. At the time both reasons seemed entirely plausible. I can remember thinking how pleasant it would be to follow the others into the garden, where the Maharishi sometimes would speak to us in a voice that was both high and musical, like the piping of a flute."

Today, alive and well in a sprawling former monastery in Vlodrop, the Netherlands, Maharishi, now well into his eighties, continues to oversee his ever-expanding worldwide conglomerate of real estate holdings, schools and clinics worth a reported $3.5 billion. "What strikes you is his energy and vitality," says Martin Smeets, a former mayor of Vlodrop and an occasional visitor to the ninety-acre compound from which the guru seldom strays. "You get the impression he's still at the forefront of all these global activities."

Those activities include roughly a thousand transcendental-meditation centres in more than a hundred countries, a chain of five-star hotels, an international health-food distribution network and a library of instructional books and videotapes. Maharishi and the late magician Doug Henning, spent years trying to launch a $1.5 billion theme park in Ontario, Canada, called Veda Land. It was intended to feature a levitating restaurant and a journey through a giant flower. "They have so many businesses and properties, the movement is basically a corporate religion," says Dutch journalist Caroline Verhees, who on meeting Maharishi was impressed by him. "Even from a distance, you could feel the charisma of this man sitting cross-legged and chanting."

"He introduced meditation to the West and made it mainstream," said Deepak Chopra, who was Maharishi's top assistant for nine years. "Yet he never took anything too seriously. We called him the Giggling Guru."

During his last days, George Harrison visited the Maharishi for solace and advice, and vehemently insisted in *The Beatles Anthology* that the guru had never been anything but a sincere spiritual guide, a genuine inspiration and a lifelong celibate. Recently, even Paul McCartney and his new wife Heather have made secret visits to another of the Maharishi's homes high in the Swiss Alps. Ringo, too, professes only fond memories of the Beatles' time at the feet of their first guru. That the Maharishi brought them a measure of much-needed inner peace and planted in them a lifelong ideal of spiritual enlightenment independent of the material body is sure. Always laughing and happy as he taught the 5000-year-old art of Vedic meditation, the Maharishi did more good than harm in his mission to transcendentalize the world. As Cynthia Lennon said, the fact that he tried so hard for so long makes both his life and mission an unquestionable success.

SEVEN

Mother Superior Jumped The Gun

Ascot, Henley, St John's Wood and Surrey

1968

"I know John thinks we hate Yoko and that we're all a bunch of two-faced fuckers running around behind his back snivelling and bad-mouthing her, sticking pins in our homemade Yoko Ono voodoo dolls, but you know and I know what's happening, and that's not happening at all. No one in this building hates her. Hate! That's a very strong accusation and an extreme assumption. I can't say as I blame him for thinking that sometimes, but the reason he feels that way is because we don't *love* her!"

Derek Taylor

1968 was a turbulent and eventful year for all of the Beatles, both personally and professionally. Together the Beatles launched Apple Corps Ltd, *Sgt. Pepper* won four Grammy awards, the National Theatre produced a play based on John's book, *In His Own Write*, Apple took over offices at 3 Savile Row near Piccadilly, the Apple boutique closed, the Beatles' authorized biography was published and the *White Album* was released.

But this was only what the eye could see. Internally the Beatles were slowly coming apart. Was it simply, as John once suggested, that wedding bells were tolling the end of their remarkable time together? Or perhaps that George and Ringo were tired of being bargain-basement Beatles, their work continually shifted to the back-burner in favour of Lennon and McCartney's compositions. Maybe it was the continuing effects of their drug-taking. Some suggest that the constant demands of fans, fame, media and big business eroded the fragile foundations of the magic that made up the group. Perhaps it was a subtle combination of all of the above that pushed the four to find success on their own terms and in their own time.

Cracks in the Lennon's marriage had been visible for some time, and were very clear to one newcomer to the family. The previous year Alfred Lennon had presented his celebrated son with the disturbing news that he planned to marry a nineteen-year-old Beatles fan, Pauline Jones. "I was really terribly shocked when he first rang to tell me the news," remembered Charlie Lennon. "I said, 'What? Isn't one fallen marriage enough for you? Do you have to go out and do the same thing again, and with a younger girl at that?' "

Freddie, however, was adamant. He would marry the former Exeter University student and, hopefully, if John and Cynthia were willing, perhaps they might employ her as their personal assistant. John wanted to please his father as far as he could, so that was what happened.

Life at home with the Lennons in their Weybridge mock-Tudor home was fiercely guarded from public scrutiny. At least, it was until late October that year when Pauline Jones was installed at the Surrey mansion to do secretarial work and help with Julian.

She noted that John was definitely the king of his castle. As he shuffled about the house in his socks, he was condescending to Cynthia and everyone else. His day started around noon, when he wolfed down a breakfast of mushrooms on toast that Dot, the housekeeper, placed before him. Then he would isolate himself for the entire day to work at the piano. During the evenings, friends would gather in the drawing room to listen to music and pass joints. Lennon played benevolent dictator, manipulating the course of conversation but holding his guests in rapt attention.

On one rare evening he and Pauline sat down to watch a television documentary on heroin addiction. As the junkies told their stories Lennon remarked, "It must be fucking terrible to end up like that." An ironic statement, considering that he was soon to be entrenched in his own battle with the deadly drug.

Pauline was struck by the overwhelming sense of foreboding and loneliness in the house. A narrow staircase that led to the upper floors was creepy, especially when one of John's cats, who congregated in the attic, jumped out and scampered down. The cats were allowed to run wild throughout the house, and the black Wilton carpet on the ground floor was ruined by their urine.

Pauline's room was in the attic, next to one where Lennon's recording equipment was stored and which served as his painting studio. The Beatles' gold discs were tossed carelessly about in it.

The tension between John and Cynthia added to the heavy atmosphere. Essentially, as Pauline witnessed, they went their separate ways. If one came home late he or she would sleep in the guest room. Their rare conversations invariably took place in the study over a drink. John would park himself in a velvet armchair, restless and edgy. "You're getting pretty fat, aren't you?" he would snipe at his wife. Cynthia was coldly silent.

For all her obvious devotion to hearth and home, however, Cynthia was rarely at Weybridge. She frequently went clubbing with Patti Harrison, or the singer Lulu and her boyfriend Maurice Gibb of the Bee Gees. The next morning Cynthia would spill the details of her evening to Dot. John's father, however, deemed it inappropriate for his daughter-in-law to be out unescorted in the middle of the night, and once reprimanded her. John found out about this, which led to a row between himself and his father. "If you can't learn to keep your bloody mouth shut," he raged, "the feud between us will be on again and we'll see what Fleet Street makes of it!"

During her two months at Kenwood Pauline looked after five-year-old Julian. He was a bright little boy who loved to burst into her room and pounce on her. Like his father, Julian was bossy among his playmates, which was fuelled, in part, by the constant fawning of guests. Cynthia, perhaps in deference to John, chose not to overtly discipline him. Pauline, however, wouldn't stand for it. Once, when Julian told her to "Shut up!", she smacked his bottom. Mrs Lennon came in in time to see her do it and shot her a frigid look but said nothing.

During the Beatles' drug-taking days, Cynthia feared for her son because of the suspect company her husband kept. Marijuana-smoking and LSD-tripping attracted unsavoury hangers-on who attempted to tap into the Beatles' coffers. The police once tipped off the family about a kidnapping plot. For weeks Cynthia zealously watched over her son, who had round-the-clock armed guards, and the police kept vigil outside his school and at Kenwood's heavy iron gates. Each night John would check and recheck the window locks and those on the glass patio doors. Ten years later, his second son Sean also faced the threat of abduction from an extortionist claiming to belong to a Puerto Rican terrorist organization.

As for his father's marriage, Lennon had this to say, "At fifty-six, my father married a secretary, who later did some work for the Beatles, and ultimately they had two children, which, I must admit, was rather hopeful for a man who lived most of his life as almost a Bowery bum."

The working arrangement between Pauline and the Lennons, however, was fraught with difficulty almost from the beginning, and after two months, John dismissed Pauline. He wanted his ageing father to be happy, though, and generously bought him a flat near Kew Gardens, London. In addition, he arranged for Freddie to furnish his new home courtesy of Apple, as well as establishing a generous weekly payment to him of thirty pounds to offset expenses. Eventually, the couple moved to Brighton where John agreed to cover their living expenses in a lovely flat near the sea. Their children, David and Robert were born in 1969 and 1973. Only David met his famous half-brother – once, in 1970.

As the Lennons' marriage eroded so John's feeling for Yoko Ono grew. By the spring of 1968, John Lennon was besotted with his new girlfriend. The two were inseparable, which was not lost on either the ravenous British media or poor Cynthia in suburban Surrey. Ono possessed just the off-beat charisma Lennon had previously believed beyond the scope of any woman. Cynthia, for all her virtue as a loving wife and caring, attentive mother, admitted that: "At times, I did give a very boring, practical impression of being just an ordinary housewife instead of a swinging extroverted pop-star's consort." John claimed that he drew from Yoko the intellectual challenges he had previously only encounted from a man, as well as the insight and intuition generally associated with women. "I've never known love like this before," he proclaimed, some months later, "and it hit me so hard, I had to immediately halt my marriage to Cyn. I don't think that was a reckless decision, because I thought very deeply about it and all the implications that would be involved. When we are free, and we hope that we will be within a year, we shall marry. Of course, there is no real need to marry, but there's nothing lost in it either. Some may say my decision was selfish. Well, I don't think it is. There is something else to consider, too. Isn't it better to avoid rearing children in the atmosphere of a strained relationship? My marriage to Cyn was not unhappy. But it was just a normal marital state where nothing happened and which we continued to sustain. You sustain it until you meet someone who suddenly sets you alight. With Yoko, I really know love for the first time. Initially, our attraction was a mental one, but it happened physically, too. Both are essential in the union, but I never dreamed I would marry again. Now the thought of it seems so easy."

Cynthia remembered, "I didn't blame John or Yoko. I understood their love. I knew there was no way I could ever fight the unity of mind and body that they had with each other . . . Their all-consuming love had no time for pain or unhappiness . . . Yoko did not take John away from me, because he had never *really* been mine."

On 11 May 1968, John and Paul flew from London to New York to join Peter Brown, Neil Aspinall, Magic Alex and the other directors of Apple for the official opening of the Beatles' holding company. In a five-day PR blitz arranged by the firm Solters and Roskin, there was a press conference at which Lennon made several disparaging comments about the Maharishi and talked about his ambitions for Apple. McCartney chimed in whenever John said something he probably shouldn't, a skill in which the media-savvy Paul excelled. "The aim of this company isn't a stack of gold teeth in the bank," Lennon ventured. "We just want to help people who want to make a film about anything. So they won't have to go down on their knees in somebody's office – probably yours!"

After appearing on *The Tonight Show* with John, Paul disappeared into Manhattan to meet up with a young blonde photographer he'd met at the Bag O'Nails Club in London on 15 May 1967. Her name was Linda Eastman. She had approached him and slipped him her phone number. Although Lennon and he were staying at the St Regis Hotel, he decided to meet her at attorney Nat Weiss's East Side apartment, afraid that if they went to the hotel they might be photographed together, the result of which Jane Asher might see in London. For the next several days the couple stayed in the flat and Paul looked after Linda's little daughter, Heather, while she went to a photo shoot at the Fillmore.

Several weeks later, on 21 June, McCartney was back in the USA accompanied by Ron Kass, to attend the annual Capitol Records convention in LA. None of the other Beatles would have ever considered attending such a publicity-seeking event, but Paul excelled in such situations. After a showing of a specially made film about Apple, he spent the afternoon shaking hands with everyone in the room. He was staying in a three-bedroom bungalow at the Beverly Hills Hotel, and that evening he entertained several young women there. Jimi Hendrix's occasional consort, the super-groupie Devon, had one bedroom and a popular young Hollywood actress another. Kass, who was sharing the bungalow with Paul, referred to the interlude as "The Paul McCartney Black and White Minstrel Show." That Sunday morning, Linda Eastman rang from the lobby. Kass asked Devon and the starlet to pack and leave. They paraded, in tears, past Paul and Linda, who were talking calmly together in the living room. The next day they went sailing with John Calley, an executive at Warner Brothers.

On the point of flying back to New York with Kass and Paul, Linda almost got everyone busted: she was carrying two kilos of grass, some acid and a bag of cocaine when, due to a security alert, everyone had to be searched. Kass, in a skilled last-minute manoeuvre, kicked the bag under a row of chairs in the VIP lounge, thinking the matter resolved.

However, after the search, Eastman made a beeline back to the lounge and retrieved her bag. During her thirty-year marriage to

McCartney Linda would perpetrate several more drug-smuggling adventures.

Paul first met New Yorker Francie Schwartz in April 1968 when she approached him at Apple with an idea she had for a film. "Paul was upset with John for bringing Yoko to the studio the night before, so he grabbed the nearest, weirdest chick he could find which was me," Francie said. "It was like saying, 'Okay, if you're going to bring a weird chick, I'm going to bring a weird chick!'" Thereafter she moved into Cavendish Avenue for a time.

She recalled a telling visit to Liverpool when McCartney took her to meet his family. Paul, according to Francie, introduced her to his family as "Clancy" because he didn't want to say "Schwartz", an obviously Jewish surname. Perhaps Paul was worried how his family would react to his having a Jewish girlfriend (though it must be said that he clearly had no such concerns when it came to his future wife Linda Eastman, also Jewish). The visit was uncomfortable for Schwartz for other reasons too.

Angela and Ruth McCartney were on a plane en route from Austria to England, chatting with the drummer of the Bee Gees, when they saw a newspaper article saying that Jane Asher had appeared on the 20 July *Simon Dee Show*, announcing that she had broken her engagement to Paul. Later, mother and daughter phoned home to ask Jim if he knew anything about it. "Actually, Paul's here now and he's got somebody with him," spoke Jim gruffly. "That girl who used to work at Apple."

When Paul's stepmother and -sister came home Francie was still at Rembrandt. "Francie hung around for a day or two with Paul and he basically ignored her," Angela remembers. "She was like a spare part. She'd just stand there or he'd go out in the car and not even speak to her. He brought her home and then she was an embarrassment to him. I felt sorry for the poor kid. He actually took her out to Auntie Jinnie's because Jim said, 'Look, you brought her here, son, you just can't ignore her.' I remember Paul said to her, 'I'm going to Auntie Jin's, do you want to come?' That was the only interaction between them. After that, we never saw Francie again."

Francie says: "That night all of these cousins and friends showed up, and Paul was very disturbed because when he got drunk – I mean, really falling-down drunk – he got really upset. He was in a bar that was paid for by him, I guess. One of the cousins had asked him for some money way back when, they purchased a pub and it was like a hang-out and these were very down-to-earth people. I didn't have a problem with them. But I was somewhere else, and someone came up to me and said, 'Hey, Clancy, you'd better take Paul out of here.' He was behind the bar, and was back up against the wall. His face was really red, and he was practically in tears. He was way out of control, too much Scotch, and I said, 'Come on, babe, let's get out of here.' Everybody was sort of frozen and we went out into the street and he literally fell on his knees, and was pounding his fists into the cobblestones saying, 'It's just too much! They don't treat me like I'm me. They treat me like I'm him. And I am not him, I'm me!' I said, 'What do you mean?' He said, 'It's the money, I've given them all this money!' I said 'How much?' And he said, 'About thirty thousand pounds.' Which then, was about a hundred thousand dollars or something. I thought, That's not a lot of money to him. Then I understood what upset him so much. They were all afraid if they were straight up with him, they were candid with him, if they said, Hey! You're acting like an asshole! he would demand the money be repaid or something . . . He's very conflicted about money, which stands to reason because he was raised poor. His father made twelve shillings a week working in a cotton mill. He still has the fear it can always be taken away. That was one aspect of his personality. I felt bad for him, it wasn't pleasant."

Another example of McCartney's inner conflict became evident in other anecdotes Francie told. "The fan mail was delivered to the house in sacks as Apple knew John and Yoko were living with us. Paul never paid any attention to that mail. I never, ever saw him open a single piece of it. But because John and Yoko were subject to a lot of bad press, hate mail and so forth, they didn't understand why people were reacting like this. It's because they were in love and it was so powerful. It was such a merger, a meeting of souls. That morning it was late. I walked into the living room, and they had taken their mail in their room. I noticed this envelope on the mantel above the fireplace. It was just a note, it had no postmark, and it was typed, 'To John and Yoko'. John took it down and opened it. I didn't understand what it was doing there . . . He opened it and showed it to me. It read, 'You and your Jap tart think you're hot shit!' John was wondering who would do something like this. He was extremely hurt . . . She [Yoko] didn't think about what it meant to her only how hurtful it was to John. Paul walked in, saw the expression on John's face and on my face and said, in his most cute Liverpudlian accent, 'Oh, I just did that for a lark!' I think it was as close as he could come to expressing his great envy of Yoko. The truth is Paul McCartney has been twice widowed. The first great love of his life was John Lennon, and the second, Linda. And they are both gone. But when it was happening it felt like betrayal. For me that was the end of the partnership."

Meanwhile, Paul and Jane's often turbulent five-year relationship was about to come to an acrimonious end. In July 1968, returning from an extended Old Vic tour of the provinces, Jane turned up unexpectedly at Cavendish Avenue. One of the Beatles' loyal groupies, nicknamed the Apple Scruffs, was waiting outside and buzzed Paul to alert him, but he was preoccupied and brushed her off. Jane entered the house and climbed the stairs to the bedroom she and Paul shared. Thinking he was asleep she gently knocked on the door. McCartney leaped up as though he had been hit with an electric cattle prod. "Who's there?"

"It's Jane, silly."

As Paul hurried to the door, Jane peered into the room and spotted Francie Schwartz standing awkwardly by the bed, dressed in the Oriental silk dressing-gown Jane had given Paul for Christmas. The circumstances were uncannily similar to Cynthia Lennon's discovery of John and Yoko in their Weybridge home: Yoko was wearing a dressing-gown that John had given his wife. As Paul groped for words, a shattered Jane raced downstairs, out of the house and McCartney's life for ever.

Meanwhile, back at Rembrandt, McCartney was showing his softer side. When Angela's sister Mae fell ill, he offered to send a private ambulance to drive Edie, their mother, to Rembrandt so the family could look after Mae. During Edie's visit Paul spent time with her in the back bedroom where she was staying. One morning Edie complained, "I can't sleep. This bloody blackbird, in the dead of night, cheep, cheep, it sings all sodding night." According to Ruth and Angela, a few nights later Paul went into Edie's room with a tape-recorder. He held the microphone outside the window and recorded the bird. "Ultimately," says Angela, "the tune 'Blackbird' was written, which incorporated that recorded bird song. It makes me very happy. Paul was very good to my mum." He even dedicated an unreleased recording of the song to Edie.

McCartney often worked late into the night and invariably woke the family to listen to his latest masterpiece. One was "She's Leaving Home". "I wept when I heard it," Angela admits. "It was such a beautiful song. I thought of it in terms of how I would feel when Ruth left home. Another time he got us up in the middle of the night to hear 'Norwegian Wood'. He was very proud of it, although it was mainly John's. It was a great song but it didn't mean anything to a lot of us. He told us it was based on a real experience of John's."

Ruth was the inspiration for Paul's "Golden Slumbers". The seven-year-old was at the piano one afternoon, practising a lullaby. "Hey, you're butchering that bloody song," Paul called. "What are you doing in there?" He sat down beside her at the piano, staring at the sheet music, which he could not read. "It might as well have been Chinese," joked Ruth. "Anyway, we ended up learning to play it together and he said, 'That's nice, what is it called?' I said, 'Golden Slumbers'."

It is well known that Paul wrote "Hey Jude" for another child, Julian Lennon, when John left Cynthia for Yoko. Angela added, "When Cyn came home from holiday and found Yoko sitting at her kitchen table wearing her bathrobe, Paul evidently felt some responsibility. John wasn't taking care of her so it was his job. He apparently bought her a single red rose and then drove out to where Cynthia was staying and asked her jokingly to marry him."

Ruth recalled when Paul first played the 1968 "Hey Jude" to his stepfamily. "We were all looking at each other like this was the emperor's new clothes. It was a good song and then it went into all this 'na-na-na-nananana' and went on for hours!"

When Paul pressed Angela for her opinion, she told him, "'All that repetition at the end doesn't really cut it. Take it out.' Of course that was the biggest-selling record they ever had! So after that he'd always say, 'Ask Ange anything you want about our songs. If she hates it, it will be a hit.'"

Another tale told by both Francie Schwartz and Alistair Taylor relates to Paul's attempt to publicize "Hey Jude" by using the old Apple boutique as the backdrop. It all started with a phone call to Taylor at his home on 7 August 1968.

"Hey, why don't we use the Apple boutique to promote 'Hey Jude'?"

"But it's empty," Taylor replied. "What are you thinking?"

"We won't do anything except paint 'Hey Jude' in huge white letters on the front window. It'll be like a big poster on one of the busiest streets in the West End. I'll get Mal and a mate so tomorrow's rush-hour will stop in front of it! '*HEY JUDE, The New Beatles Single'!*" Taylor rang round several local shops and had the necessary materials sent to the Baker Street shop.

"There was Paul, myself, Mal, another guy and Francie Schwartz. This really did seem like five minutes' work, until McCartney had another idea," Taylor remembered. "It was too simple just to paint the words on to the window. We were going to paint the entire window, then wipe out the title! My arm was aching after half an hour, so we knocked off, had a Scotch and Coke, then went back to it. Paul wanted 'Hey Jude' on the front window and the title of the flip-side ['Revolution'] on the side window."

They finished in the early hours of the morning. A little later the police came to Apple HQ to report that during the night the window of the Baker Street boutique had been smashed.

The culprit was a middle-aged Jewish death-camp survivor, who had been driving past the shop just before dawn. He'd had a drink and the words "Hey Jude" had taken him back to the thirties in Germany. The Nazis had written "Jude", or "Juden", in big white letters on houses and businesses owned by Jews as an open invitation to smash them. "Just seeing 'Hey Jude' there on the window was enough to trigger his old anger," said Taylor. "He threw a soda siphon, which had been in his car, through the window. We thought, we'll try to keep this one out of the papers."

To her credit Francie was unwilling to be anyone's doormat, no matter how celebrated they were. She soon decided her relationship with Paul was going nowhere and that she wanted out. "I got sick, or I had the flu or something. I was run-down, never sleeping more than two hours at a time. I was emotionally spent and he nursed me. He fed me this hot milk spiked with gin. I was passing out in bed, and as he was tucking me in, he said, 'Look, I'm really sorry and as soon as we finish this album I'll take you to Scotland, to the farm, and we will rest.' So I fell asleep thinking, Hey, maybe he will turn out to be a decent guy, after all, and he really is going to try and have a relationship. The next morning, I was better, my fever had broken, and I stumbled downstairs. There he was, like a mean schoolteacher, and he said, 'When are you leaving? I don't like your accent, I don't like your lips, when are you leaving?' So I thought, This is it! I can't live with these 180-degree turn-arounds. I can't live with this schizoid Gemini bullshit!' So I said 'I'll go tomorrow.' I said, 'Just get me the money for a ticket and I will go.' I went into the kitchen to call my mom, and he came up behind me, rubbed up against me and put his arms around me and said, 'Don't cry. I'm going out for a while, will you fix dinner?'"

Out went Francie and in came Linda, both intelligent, accomplished women.

Although McCartney was always keen to be involved with films and composing scores the idea had never occurred to George Harrison until his new friend, director Joe Massot, began pre-production on a film called *Wonderwall* and invited him to write, arrange and supervise the recording of the soundtrack. Massot remembered, "At a happening laid on by the Fool – Simon Posthuma, Marijke Koger, Barry Finch and Josje Leager – I asked them if they would paint the 'Wonderwall' as well as design some clothes for actress Jane Birkin. I also invited them to appear in the party scene in the film.

"At the opening of the Beatles' boutique, on 5 December 1967 were the Stones, Traffic, Clapton, The Who, girls and more girls, a real sixties event! Simon [Posthuma] introduced me to George, who was very much into Indian music, learning how to play the sitar and *sarod*, a twelve-string instrument, very difficult to master. I had various choices. The Bee Gees were interested in doing something and came down to Twickenham to see me. It seemed the movie created a real vibe as Graham Nash from the Hollies also wanted to join in. George told me he'd been working on *Magical Mystery Tour*, but that it was really Paul's project. He said he would like to do something solo. I told him he would have a free hand to do anything he liked musically. That was what interested him in the picture.

"Harrison came down to the studio the following day to see the rough cut. In my enthusiasm I began to wax lyrical about film-making, saying the studio is only the factory, assuming, in my innocence, George was a complete novice. He smiled knowingly and took it in good heart. After all, he was the veteran of two major films, countless television appearances and studio recordings. George proceeded to take notes and timings by watching the whole picture on a Moviola."

With his status as a Beatle, Harrison was given freedom to accomplish the soundtrack in any way he chose, and decided that half of the music should be western and the other half Indian. At home at Kinfauns, he made what Mal Evans called "tape-recorded outlines". When he got into the studio, however, there were significant communication problems because he could neither read nor write music and had to whistle and hum what he wanted to the session men. Evans reported: "Sometimes a short bit of music was needed. George would say, 'Now, give us a bit of happy banjo-picking.' He'd listen and then redirect the musician by adding, 'No, what I want is something more like this,' and he'd hum a few bars."

After several weeks, the western music was almost complete and just after Christmas Harrison decided to move to Bombay to finish the project. To accomplish this, EMI London got in touch with EMI

Bombay and tickets for George, Neil Aspinall and Magic Alex were booked on Air India for Sunday 7 January. The journey itself was torturous, with prolonged stops in Paris, Frankfurt and Teheran.

Shambu Das was waiting at the airport for them and soon got down to organizing the Bombay sessions. He was Ravi Shankar's right-hand man, and almost never gives interviews, but during the mid-eighties he spoke to me: "George wanted to do the *Wonderwall* soundtrack and requested some help, as he wanted to record it almost entirely in India. I was taking care of all the musical arrangements . . . I personally played sitar on *Wonderwall*, and a few of my friends played other Indian instruments too. George and I were consulting a lot in those days. Just throwing ideas back and forth. Anyway, we recorded for almost an entire week, and while he was there he started to use his hands to eat."

Naturally, the bigwigs at EMI Bombay were delighted to have the world-famous George Harrison recording with them, and kept dozens of India's top musicians in an adjacent room just in case he decided he needed something from one of them. "After we'd finished *Wonderwall* George decided it would be a pity not to make extra use of all those great Indian players," recalled Evans, "so we taped large groups of them, up to ten at a time, and made recordings which George wanted to find use for on the next Beatles' album."

In fact, none of these ideas were used by the Beatles, except in the backing for the magnificent B-side to "Lady Madonna", "The Inner Light". It was now obvious that India had penetrated deep under George's skin: it showed in the way he ate, dressed, talked, worked and thought. His passion for the culture, philosophy and, more importantly, the religion of India sparked off a worldwide interest in gurus, mantras, sitars and Indian fashion, which soon became mixed with the hippie culture, part of the fabric of today's multiculturalism.

On 15 May 1968 George, Patti, Ringo and Maureen all flew to the South of France to attend the première at the Cannes Film Festival. They stayed for four days, meeting the press and enjoying Harrison's first solo success.

*

As for the much-publicized romance between John and Yoko, signs of trouble soon began to appear. In late May 1968, an audiotape was recorded on which the insecure Lennon grilled his new lover about her sexual history. In it, Ono rambles on about her two loveless marriages, to Japanese composer Toshi Ichiyanagi and New York filmmaker Anthony Cox, whom she had used, she said, to further her career. Lennon demands to know every detail of her past erotic encounters. He even pushed her to compare the penis sizes of her lovers. Poor Toshi was apparently cursed with only a "small purplish" organ. "But I'm not one of those women," she is quick to add, "who's always sizing up pricks."

Ono went on to discuss an affair with her husband Anthony's best friend while he was staying with them. She tried to justify it by telling John she felt very vulnerable following the birth of her child, Kyoko. "I just needed some consolation and a good lay," she says. "I was just using Tony. I was becoming a fuckin' prima donna. I had no inhibitions. He was living in the same flat with us."

"How long was it before you made it with him?" John asked.

"About a week," Yoko answered.

John was also keen to explore her admitted attraction to members of the same sex. They discussed being aroused by models in television advertisements and John remarked that Yoko got the same buzz from them as he did. She suggested that if they were to bring another woman into their relationship she would worry that John might fall for her. John fired back, "Sounds like you're more worried *you* might, if you're more attracted to women."

Lennon asked Ono to tell him about her brief relationship with a room-mate at Sarah Lawrence with whom she shared a house. Yoko insisted that she had only been going through a phase of curiosity and experimentation. "I was probably just flattered a woman loved me," she explains.

John persisted: the relationship was as important as any she'd had because "you're more interested in women than in men".

When Yoko declared that she was then only a "spiritual whore", John snapped, "You're a physical whore too!" In an attempt to defend herself, Ono claimed that in fact she rejected most men. "I'm pretty particular. Not like you who's so undiscriminating."

"Well," Lennon snapped, "undiscriminate is your version of what I was, from what I told you I did!"

He then asked her about an affair she'd had with an art teacher at an Ivy League college. "I was objective," she says. "So he's pretty good, but it's just sex, isn't it? He was just on the level of a chick you would lay."

To which John replies, "Art teacher, that's a good fucking gig, isn't it? Apart from going into it for the money they know they can also make the students."

The Beatles went back into the studio on 30 May, but questions remained as to what their schedule would be, and how many tracks would make up the new album. "We're just recording until we're finished," said McCartney. "We have the studio booked for a couple of weeks initially and then we'll go from there. We might record all thirty songs and pick fourteen or so for an album. Or it could turn out to be two albums, or maybe even a three-pack."

Harrison was in favour of issuing multiple albums: "I suppose we've got a vague idea of the overall concept of the kind of album we want to do, but it takes time to work out. We could do a double album, I suppose, or maybe even a triple. There's enough stuff there." In fact, the first triple album to be issued was Harrison's *All Things Must Pass* in 1970.

The Beatles began by taping eighteen takes of "Revolution" in their first session. With Ono now central to Lennon's life, she too was there, which compromised the privacy of the recording studio. After an introduction to the personnel at Abbey Road, she remained by John's side for the remainder of the Beatles' recording career. At one session on 4 June, Ono taped an audio diary on a portable cassette recorder. In it she voiced her innermost thoughts, and opinions on those around her, and the state of her often paranoid, increasingly obsessive relationship with Lennon.

Not to be outdone by John, Paul invited Francie to attend the session. When she arrived at around eight p.m. she found the Beatles standing around a piano, with Yoko sitting about twenty feet from them in a corner, whispering into a microphone. The first words she uttered became the prevailing motif of her stream-of-consciousness soliloquy. "John, I miss you already again. I miss you very much," she said breathlessly, although they had not been apart for five minutes that day. In her summary of the day's events, she mentioned that John had told her the as-yet-untitled *Two Virgins* album would have to be issued under her name only, or under a pseudonym, and suggested "Doris and Peter". "Either idea is terrible," Ono believed. She preferred the idea of a limited-edition release given privately to friends, but was convinced that it had to be publicly released in the long-term "because the message is going to be so beautiful. It's going to light up the world, especially with the two of us naked, taken with a fisheye lens and all that. Just that message is beautiful." Ono was dead against using fake names on the record not only because she disliked the sound of "Doris and Peter", but also because, "John and Yoko" had real "name value. There's a dream to the name and that has to come across too." Ono could not understand why John's name should be removed from the project when its release would potentially be more harmful to her: "I just can't imagine what it's going to be like, but it's going to be hell for sure . . . like the female fans would all hate me or something.

"If I can get over this scary feeling, everything's going to be all right," she continued, and confided that her paranoia and fearfulness stemmed from her relationship with John. "It seems almost unbelievable . . . and yet . . . there's no way of turning back. Every day I think, oh, it can't be, I'm not going to miss him at all . . ." She characterized their relationship as one that could only exist "maybe once every two centuries . . . It's amazing the only time I remember my promiscuity is when I feel so insecure I have to bring that out in me, to protect myself."

Her prime concern was with Lennon's long-suffering wife. "I don't know what's going to happen tonight. Cindy's coming back maybe. Aren't sure if we go back to Weybridge or going to stay here."

Then her mind strayed to her daughter. "I'm very worried about Kyoko." She had just received word that her estranged husband had left for Paris with the child. "I hope she doesn't resent me when she gets older."

After a brief pause, her thoughts were back with Lennon: "I wish John was in me right now . . . sex, in other words . . . reaching each other and giving something, and the fact that you gave me your sperm I don't know, probably at some time of your life you had a situation where you became scared of a straight relationship, of giving to each other, and instead of giving to women, you'd rather spit on a sky or shoot it to the sky kind of thing."

Then Yoko further analysed her situation: "When I used to like somebody very much, I was too shy to tell him, and then it's easier for me to make it with someone I don't love, and imagine I'm making it with a guy I like . . . Each time I make it with you, I want you and I express my want to you. I'm making a fantastic effort because playing straight is so difficult, so embarrassing . . . I wish I could get rid of my paranoia and, like, relax . . . rather than think every day is the last." Yoko then noticed that John had stopped playing, and remarked on his appearance, then made a connection between his handwriting, his state of mind and his marriage. "All your letters are leaning backwards, which means tremendous insecurity. But today I've seen all your letters were leaning forward . . . Leaning-backwards handwriting is typical of a terribly insecure high-school girl. It's very rare to see it in a man." His insecurity and paranoia came from a single source: "I really think that had a lot to with her, your marriage . . . Seems a long relationship like that would really screw somebody up."

Lennon became curious as to what Ono was talking about at such length. He wandered over and asked. "I'm just saying how I miss you," Yoko replied.

John answered into the microphone: "Well, ladies and gentlemen, I also miss her, and it's a terrible feeling. All alone in a crowded room."

Once Lennon had got back to work with McCartney on "Revolution", she talked about Paul. He was now being very nice to her, having overcome "the initial embarrassment", and was readily chatting with her about Apple. "I feel like he's my younger brother . . . I'm sure that if he had been a woman, he would have been a great threat, because there's something definitely very strong with me, John and Paul." Ono saw the other Beatles neither as a threat nor as important: "[With] Ringo and George, I just can't communicate . . . I'm sure George and Ringo, they're very nice people. That's not the point."

The threats to their relationship, as Yoko saw them, were almost too much for her to bear: "At least if I knew I had another week with John – this situation almost reminds me that in the war I used to carry a poison pill, thinking any minute I might have to die." But the depressing thoughts were fleeting. "It's amazing, what John did on 'Revolution', with his voice, it's really beautiful. It's so sexy too, and now he has his blouse off, he only has an undershirt on. I think he looks too sexy, really. John is such a genius. I almost get jealous of his talent. I was never jealous of any artist. I almost feel like kneeling down and kissing his feet."

Lennon left the studio for a long time, and Ono worried that he was checking up on Cynthia. "He's been with her for over a decade and their other child [Julian], I don't know what to make of it . . . Either he had a terribly weak character or he is in love with her . . . I just get so jealous I almost think I'm going to go insane."

John was absorbed in his work, but was evidently at the other end of the happiness spectrum. "Take your knickers off and let's go!" he called at one point. "I'm happy to be here, it's wonderful."

Yoko finished with a fragmented but ominous message: "Probably I should be asking . . . I just don't have the courage. I know tomorrow probably we'll . . . stop pretending."

Over the next few days Lennon worked on the lyrics of "Revolution" changing the words slightly, particularly the line "when you talk about destruction, don't you know that you can count me out". Politically sensitive, he was still unsure if he wanted to be counted "in" or "out", but on "Revolution 1" he settled for both. For effect, he recorded the final vocal lying flat on his back with a boom microphone positioned directly above him.

The Beatles turned next to recording Starr's first solo composition, a bouncy country-and-western tune brought to the studio with the curious working title "This Is Some Friendly". Curious, because in 1963, when the song was first being written, Ringo had called it "Don't Pass Me By". Early takes featured Paul and Ringo laying down piano and drums, with a sleigh-bell added to the mix. Starr manually double-tracked his vocals, while McCartney added a new bass track to the recording. They took time out that afternoon, 6 June, to record an interview with the BBC's Kenny Everett. Lennon remarked, "We've just done two tracks, both unfinished. The second one is Ringo's first song we're working on this very moment. He composed it himself in a fit of lethargy. We got to a stage with one where the next bit is musicians, so we'll have to write the musicians' bit."

The remainder of the interview was typical of the verbal word play in which Lennon excelled.

Kenny Everett: What can we expect from you in the next few months?

John Lennon: There's a lot in the brown-paper bag, Kenny. We're working very hard on that at the moment, the boys and me.

Kenny: Anything tuny?

John: Oh, yeah. There's a lot of tunes we've found in the bags, actually.

Kenny: You don't come in here with the idea of doing an album, do you, it just falls out at the sessions.

John: Mmm. Well, we have a vague idea, Kenny. (*Singing*) "As I was only saying the other day, we had a vague idea, but very vague." Just a bit of laughter, ladies and gentlephones!

Kenny: Do you ever get to where you've done your bit and decide it would be good on its own, and forget the musicians?

John: Yeah. (*Singing*) "Somebody stole my gal, somebody stole my pal."

Kenny: So that's what India taught you! Did you come back with anything incredibly fantastic?

John: Yes, a beard.

Kenny: I met Donovan the other day and he looked a little better for it.

John: Yes, it was very healthy.

Kenny: I saw a photograph of you in the *Daily Mirror* standing in a sheet. You look very peaceful.

John: That's called a *benuse*, Kenny, and I got it from Morocco. Standing in a sheet, what do you mean?

Kenny: Well, it looked like a sheet.

John: Well they do. *Benuses* look very, very like sheets, you see, so the lower classes in Morocco don't feel too put out, having only the sheets to wear. Very hot, though, Ken. Black clothes. Very hot, indeed!

Kenny: Are you composing this straight out of your head?

John: This is *ad nauseam*, straight from the mouth that bit me.

Kenny: Sing goodbye to me, it's my last show next week.

George Harrison: Is it? Got the sack, did you?

Ringo Starr: (*Singing*) "Goodbye, Kenny, see you in the morning. Goodbye, Kenny, see you at the dawning. Goodbye, Kenny, it's nice to see you back. Goodbye, Kenny, we hear you got the sack!"

With "Don't Pass Me By" set aside for the day, Lennon began work on the intense sound collage that became "Revolution 9". Often cited as a John and Yoko composition, it has long been unacknowledged that, with the exception of Paul, the other Beatles also contributed to it. Decades later Harrison recalled, "Ringo and I compiled that. We went into the tape library and looked through the entire room, pulled several selections and gave the tapes to John, who cut them together. The whole thing, 'Number nine, number nine', is because I pulled box number nine, some kind of educational programme. John decided which bits to cross-fade together, but if Ringo and I hadn't gone there in the first place, he wouldn't have had anything." The next day George and Ringo left for the USA, so it was up to John to compile the sound-effects tapes while he continued to search for new effects in the Abbey Road library and his own collections.

While Lennon was in studio three, McCartney recorded "Blackbird" in thirty-two takes in studio two, and finished mixing it into mono in a single six-hour session. The singing blackbird on the recording was culled from the tape *Volume Seven: Birds of a Feather* in the Abbey Road sound-effects collection.*

When George and Ringo returned from America, Paul left, and the three remaining Beatles finished "Revolution 9", occupying all three studios at Abbey Road to accomplish the marathon task. "John was really the producer of 'Revolution 9'," tape operator Richard Lush recalled, "but George joined him that night and they both had vocal mikes and were saying strange things like 'the Watusi', 'the Twist' . . ."

Lennon's off-the-wall prose consisted of lines such as: "His legs were drawn and his hands were tied, his feet were bent and his nose was burning. His head was on fire. His glasses were insane. This was the end of his audience." Random phrases were later injected into the mix: "onion soup", "economically viable", "financial imbalance", with Harrison saying quietly, "Eldorado". To top things off, George and John whispered into the microphone six times, "There ain't no rule for the company freaks." Later John remarked, "He hit a light pole so he better go and see a surgeon. Must have been hit between the shoulder-blades. Anyway, they gave him a pair of teeth, so he joined the fuckin' navy and went to sea." It was a week before Paul listened to the results and, as Richard Lush noted, "I know it *didn't* get a fantastic reaction from McCartney when he heard it."

The reunited foursome then began a series of rehearsals to perfect the rhythm tracks, a method that became an integral part of the *Get Back* sessions. The first song done in this way was Lennon's "Everybody's Got Something To Hide Except Me And My Monkey", which was initially recorded *sans* title. Its upbeat tempo contrasted nicely with what was to be the album's finale, a wistful Lennon ballad, "Good Night". Written for five-year-old Julian and pegged as Ringo's contribution, John worked extensively on it, providing a warm electric guitar, while Starr improvised a charming introduction on each take. The unscripted bits made the timing of his vocal entry difficult, with lines like, "Come on, children! It's time to toddle off to bed. We've

* This conflicts with Angela McCartney's recollection that Paul recorded the blackbird sounds live in Liverpool.

had a lovely day at the park and now it's time for sleep." Producer George Martin made copies of the finished take fifteen to create an orchestral score in accordance with Lennon's instructions. In the end, none of the early takes, instrumentation or vocals for "Good Night" were used in the final recording.

McCartney was eager to record "Ob-la-di, Ob-la-da", which went through two remakes over the course of a week. The first version contained sax, piccolo and bongos, the latter supplied by none other than Jimmy Scott. Engineer Geoff Emerick recalled, "There was one instance just before I left when they were doing 'Ob-la-di, Ob-la-da' for the umpteenth time. Paul was rerecording the vocal yet again and George Martin made some remark about how he should be lilting on to the half-beat or whatever, and Paul, in no refined way, said something to the effect of, 'Well, you come down and sing it.' "

On 8 July, after he had attended a screening of the Beatles' most recent film, *Yellow Submarine*, McCartney commented on the current sessions: "I am pleased with its progress. We get new ideas every day, but I hope it will be made much quicker than *Pepper*. We want it out before the *Yellow Submarine* LP. We are family grocers. You want yoghurts; we give it to you. You want cornflakes, we have that too. Mums and dads can't take some of our album stuff, so we make it simple for them on our singles."

Ringo, too, revealed his own unique contribution: "I have already recorded my song for the next LP. It has two titles, so I can't say what it will be called yet."

Harrison also expressed a desire to finish the album quickly, saying, "I have written ten songs for the next LP. We have about forty in all and we don't know yet which ones we'll use."

The Beatles returned to the studio that evening to record the first remake of "Ob-la-di, Ob-la-da", with Lennon providing a new blue-beat piano introduction fuelled by his towering boredom and frustration. However, he was not the only one who wanted to move on to something else: "I remember sitting in the control room before a session, dying to hear them start a new one," said Richard Lush. This session can be pinpointed as the start of real acrimony within the Beatles and the atmosphere was tense. "The first cracks appeared in the Beatles on the *White Album*," Starr remembered. "We never really argued. That was the funny thing. We always held back a bit. Maybe if we had argued a bit more, it wouldn't have got to the stage it got to."

McCartney pressed on with another remake of "Ob-la-di, Ob-la-da", then decided the first remake was better. After overdubbing what seemed a flawless vocal the next day, he realized he had sung, "*Desmond* stays at home and does *his* pretty face" instead of Molly. "Oh, it sounds great anyway," he decided. "Let's just leave it in, and create a bit of confusion there. Everyone will wonder whether Desmond's bisexual or a transvestite."

Lennon broke the monotony by introducing a new, faster version of "Revolution". He obtained the fuzz sound on guitar through what the engineers termed an "abuse of equipment". George Martin recalled, "John wanted a very dirty sound on guitar, and he couldn't get it through his amps, so we just overloaded one of the pre-amps." The drum tracks were compressed giving them a harder sound, and John did a screaming introduction, double-tracking his vocal intermittently, leaving the mistakes in to maintain the live feel. The electric piano was added in a special overdub by Nicky Hopkins, but was later played on solo albums by John, George and Ringo.

The "musicians' bit" was finally added to "Don't Pass Me By", with Jack Fallon, a former booking agent for the group, playing a rambling violin overdub. The mono mix was to contain an extended ending, featuring additional fiddle playing. "I thought they had enough so I just busked around a bit," said Fallon. "I was very surprised they kept it in, it was pretty dreadful." Rehearsals and laying down the bedtracks for John's "Cry Baby Cry" came next. It was during this time that the atmosphere became so taut that engineer, Geoff Emerick, quit the sessions. He did not work with them again until 1969. "I lost interest in the *White Album*," said Geoff, "because they were really arguing among themselves and even swearing at each other. I went down to the studio to explain it to the group and John said, 'Look, we're not moaning and getting uptight about you, we're complaining about EMI. Look at this place, studio two, all we've seen is bricks for the past year. Why can't they fucking decorate it?'

Admittedly the studio did need smartening up, but I knew this was just an outlet for a bigger problem. They were falling apart."

With a new engineer, Ken Scott, filling Emerick's role, the Beatles set about recording several long, slow versions of "Helter Skelter"; take three lasted twenty-seven minutes eleven seconds, the longest recording the group ever committed to tape. It drew its length from extended instrumental passages and off-the-cuff jams, and featured a superb McCartney vocal backed by bass, heavy guitars and drums. John vented his *angst* about the Maharishi in "Sexy Sadie", and briefly demonstrated to Paul his original vision for the song: "You little twat, who the fuck do you think you are? Oh, you cunt!" Paul advised him that this approach did not make the piece more sympathetic to its composer. Yoko offered her opinion on the "Sexy Sadie" recordings during playbacks. "Yeah," said Paul, "you mean we can do it better?"

John cut in: "Well, maybe I can."

Moving into the large studio one to record the orchestra for "Good Night", Starr began to record his vocal around midnight, telling jokes and breaking into laughter between takes. The outtakes were preserved on a "Beatles Chat" tape they had begun to assemble some ten days earlier. Back in studio two, John recorded a new vocal for "Everybody's Got Something To Hide Except Me And My Monkey", and did several frenetic screams in the fadeout of the song. The next day he led the group through the first of two remakes for "Sexy Sadie". Forty-seven takes later he was satisfied.

Harrison had yet to bring in one of his new songs for consideration, but eventually on 25 July he submitted "While My Guitar Gently Weeps". "I worked on that song with John, Paul and Ringo," he said, "and they were not interested in it at all. I knew inside of me it was a nice song." Take one was recorded on the first day, featuring an overdubbed organ near the end, and was released three decades later on the retrospective *Anthology 3*.

McCartney was already thinking of "Hey Jude" as the next single, after he and John had put the final touches to it at his home. On the second day, a camera crew from the National Music Council of Great Britain arrived, in the process of making a documentary entitled *Music!*, and shot hours' worth of footage, yet unseen, of the Beatles at work. A frustrated Harrison was to be found in the control room: "I remember on 'Hey Jude' telling George not to play guitar," said Paul. "He wanted to echo riffs after the vocal phrases, which I didn't think was appropriate. He didn't see it like that, and it was a bit of a number for me to dare to tell George Harrison, who's one of the greats, not to play. It was like an insult. But that's how we did a lot of our stuff."

The Beatles then moved to Trident Studios in St Anne's Alley in Soho, which had more modern eight-track recording facilities, to record the final version with a thirty-six-piece orchestra. The session musicians were given an extra role, as George Martin recalled: "We also got them singing on the end, because we wanted this general big noise. I don't think they liked doing it very much. In fact, one of them asked me for a special fee afterwards, which I think he got."

While "Hey Jude" was being remixed at Abbey Road, George ran through his new composition "Not Guilty" with the rest of the Beatles, recording an incredible 101 takes over the next two days. The song featured a distinctive harpsichord solo and was subjected to numerous guitar overdubs, which brought the total number of takes to 102. After the Beatles had left for the day, Paul laid down "Mother Nature's Son" and "Wild Honey Pie" acoustically on his own. He also recorded the unreleased "Etcetera", and took the tape home after only one take.

On the next session, Harrison wanted a particular atmosphere to record his lead vocal for "Not Guilty", as engineer Ken Scott remembered: "George had this idea he wanted to do it in the control room with the speakers blasting, to get more of an onstage feel. We had to monitor through the headphones, setting the monitor speakers at a level he felt comfortable with and so it wouldn't completely blast out his vocals." Acetates were eventually cut, but "Not Guilty" progressed no further and was not slated for inclusion on the album. George re-recorded the song on his 1979 *George Harrison* album, and the superlative Beatles version, with a verse edited out, was officially released on *Anthology 3*.

After remaking "Sexy Sadie" for the second time, Lennon acted on an idea given to him by Ken Scott during vocal overdubs for "Not

Guilty": "I remember John Lennon came in at one point," said Scott, "and I turned to him and said, 'Bloody hell, the way you lot are carrying on you'll be wanting to record everything in the room next door!' That was where the four-track tape machines had once been kept; it had no proper studio walls or acoustic set-up. 'That's a great idea', John replied. 'Let's try it on the next number!'" Thus, the blues pastiche "Yer Blues" was recorded live in the small room next to studio two. The engineers, Paul noted, "were worried about separation but what we did was turn the amplifiers to the wall and put a microphone in there, so we actually got amazing separation on them." The song was virtually finished in that room, except for a second vocal overdub and a count-in edit later recorded by Ringo.

John, George, Mal and Yoko then set about recording "What's The New Mary Jane", featuring Lennon on piano and Harrison on guitar in four takes, the final one lasting over six minutes, after which Lennon commented, "Let's hear it, before we get taken away!" McCartney recorded "Rocky Raccoon" with the others and had it mixed in mono in a single session, with John bringing the harmonica out of mothballs and George Martin overdubbing a piano solo. Then Harrison took off for a four-day holiday in Greece.

John tied up loose ends on his recordings, predominantly "Revolution 9" and "Yer Blues", while Paul focused mainly on brass overdubs for "Mother Nature's Son". Relations between the Beatles were taking a turn for the worse, said Ken Scott: "Suddenly, half-way through, John and Ringo walked in. You could cut the atmosphere with a knife. An instant change. It was like that for ten minutes and then as soon as they left it felt great again. It was very bizarre."

Ron Richards, another producer at EMI, noticed on 22 August that Starr, in particular, was getting fed up with the sessions: "Ringo was always sitting in Reception waiting, just sitting there or reading a newspaper. He used to sit there for hours waiting for the others to turn up." As recordings for "Back In The USSR" began, Paul told him, not for the first or last time, how to play his drum part. The normally laid-back Ringo was infuriated and told the others he was quitting immediately. "I'm sure it pissed Ringo off," remembers McCartney, "when he couldn't quite get the drums to 'Back In The

USSR', and I sat in. It's very weird to know you can do a thing someone else is having trouble with."

Starr was also tired of sitting through endless sessions and having to deal with the ever-tense atmosphere. "I had to leave," he reflected later. "I thought the other three were together and I wasn't with them. I was separate. I was feeling down. Also, I thought I wasn't playing right. But I went round to each one, and said, 'Look, I've gotta leave. I can't make it.' But, then, each one I went to said, 'I thought it was you three, and I was on my own.'" Lennon recalls, "Ringo quit because he felt he was no longer necessary in the group and nobody knows what they're doing." Francie Schwartz was very much around at the time: "Ringo was just having a blast to get a song on this album. He was so happy, and nobody fucked with it very much. I was there for part of the drum track, because I remember that night Paul interrupted him and got in Ringo's chair and did a drum riff. The tension was so thick you could really cut it. It showed so little respect for Ringo. Paul's rationale was that he wanted to make this product as good as possible and he considered himself more sophisticated musically. But that's Paul, and the force of his personality. Eventually that led to Ringo's quitting . . . That was really tough that night. Franco Zeffirelli, Twiggy, Justin, Lulu, Davy Jones, it was like a mob of people. It got bad, but it was their own fault, because they weren't getting along with each other and so it was kind of like, 'What the heck? We might as well let other people in and see if we can get back to the fun times.' Because it was rapidly becoming hard work. Each night there were discussions. Paul almost wanted this album to have a booklet and each song a photo. I remember him saying 'Ob-la-di, Ob-la-da' was a story, so they would take a picture of a dirt road that looked like Jamaica and there would be a Desmond, a black guy in a flashy suit, who looked like a trashy lounge singer. He had a lot of ideas, but John really didn't give a shit about that kind of stuff. So there was conflict. Ringo was under Paul's direction always telling him how to play. Ringo is the nicest person on earth, but he had pride. So for Paul to tell Ringo how to play, that created a great deal of tension."

Starr flew to the Mediterranean to spend time on Peter Sellers's yacht, while the other Beatles continued recording, with Paul taking over as drummer. "Back In The USSR" was to have three drum, bass and lead-guitar parts, all adding to the massive sound of the recording. The final touch, the jet aeroplane taking off and landing, was added at the remix stage.

The three remaining Beatles decided to record the haunting "Dear Prudence", at Trident Studios, taking advantage, once more, of the eight-track machine available there. They recorded each instrument over and over again, with each successive attempt being wiped. This technique led to "Dear Prudence" having only one take. Once again Paul played the drums in Ringo's absence, and Jackie Lomax, whose album was being produced by George, joined in on backing vocals. Back at Abbey Road, the Beatles had an eight-track machine installed so that George could fashion a backwards guitar solo for "While My Guitar Gently Weeps", though these overdubs were not used.

Starr returned to the group just in time to shoot promo films for "Hey Jude" and "Revolution" on 4 September, and he was glad to be back. "Paul is the greatest bass-guitar player in the world," he said later, "but he is also very determined. He goes on and on to see if he can get his own way. While that may be a virtue, it did mean that musical disagreements inevitably arose from time to time." Returning to EMI Studios the next day, Ringo found his drum kit decorated with flowers, courtesy of Mal Evans. Once he had had the opportunity to listen to the tracks made in his absence, he deemed the drumming excellent on "Back In The USSR", but sub-standard on "Dear Prudence". The second remake of "While My Guitar Gently Weeps" was then taped, and George brought in Eric Clapton to record a guitar solo. "I was going into the session," he explained, "and I said, 'We're going to do this song. Come on and play on it.' He [Eric] said, 'Oh, no. I can't do that. Nobody ever plays on Beatles' records.' I said, 'Look, it's my song, and I want you to play on it.' So Eric came in, and the other guys were as good as gold, because he was there."

At this point George Martin took a rare holiday, and left assistant Chris Thomas in charge, although the Beatles essentially produced themselves in most of the sessions. Thomas was unprepared for the welcome he received from Paul: "Well, if you wanna produce us you can produce us. If you don't, we might just tell you to fuck off!"

McCartney's mood perfectly suited the song they recorded that night, the final remake of "Helter Skelter", which had quickly become his heaviest and most raucous number. It was drastically speeded up and, to increase the cacophony, John added a discordant sax part and Mal Evans played a maladroit trumpet. Thomas recalled, "While Paul was doing his vocal, George set fire to an ashtray and was running around the studio with it above his head, doing an Arthur Brown! All in all, a pretty undisciplined session, you might say!" Instead of going for length as they had the first time, the Beatles focused on making a tighter, more frantic performance. Each take lasted around five minutes. "We tried everything we could to dirty it up," said Paul, "and in the end you can hear Ringo say, 'I've got blisters on my fingers.' That wasn't a joke: his hands were actually bleeding at the end of the take, he'd been drumming so ferociously. We did work very hard on that track." He added that "Unfortunately it inspired people to evil deeds," referring to Charles Manson, whose bizarre interpretation of the song led him, with his group, to murder Sharon Tate and the LaBiancas in August 1969. "He's barmy," John said of Manson, in 1970. "He's like any other Beatle fan who reads mysticism into it . . . I don't know what's 'Helter Skelter' got to do with knifin' somebody, you know?"

False interpretations of the Beatles' lyrics was the source of inspiration for John's sharp "Glass Onion", the next number to be recorded on 11 September. "I was just having a laugh," he said, "because there had been so much gobbledegook written about *Sgt. Pepper* . . . This one was just my way of saying, 'You're all full of shit!' "

Paul worked with John and Ringo to complete his ballad "I Will", lapsing into brief jams or improvisations between the sixty-seven takes, including a short piece, "Can You Take Me Back", a portion of which found its way on to the album following "Cry Baby Cry".

For the session on 18 September, McCartney wanted to create a spontaneous tune: "We thought, Why not make something up? So we got a riff going and arranged it around this riff." The song was "Birthday", and after they had laid down the rhythm track everyone went to Paul's home in Cavendish Avenue to watch *The Girl Can't Help It*, a 1956 film starring Jayne Mansfield. Vocal overdubs for

"Birthday" featured not only John and Paul, but also Yoko and Patti singing backup in the chorus. Harrison's superlative "Piggies" was recorded the next day, with Chris Thomas supplying harpsichord and John the sound-effects tape of pig grunts. Before taping began, George débuted another composition, "Something", but it was not recorded for another year. John's "Happiness Is A Warm Gun In Your Hand" (the last three words were dropped from the title) was recorded over three days. "They all said it was about drugs," Lennon remarked later, "but it was more a history of rock 'n' roll."

With George Martin back from holiday, the Beatles again moved to Trident to record three more numbers, this time Paul's "Honey Pie" and "Martha My Dear", and George's "Savoy Truffle". John was significantly less involved in the recording of these three songs although, according to George, he played the guitar solo on "Honey Pie": "John played a brilliant solo on 'Honey Pie' . . . sounded like Django Reinhardt or something. It was one of them where you just close your eyes and happen to hit all the right notes. It sounded like a little jazz solo." Returning to Abbey Road, George, with Paul and Ringo, worked on "It's Been A Long Long Long Time", later to be shortened to "Long Long Long". Harrison was in great spirits throughout the recording: "There was a bottle of Blue Nun on top of the Leslie speaker during the recording," he said, "and when our Paul hit some organ note the Leslie started vibrating and the bottle rattled. You can hear it on the record, at the very end."

When Lennon returned on 8 October he was impatient to complete the rest of his numbers, and recorded "I'm So Tired" and "The Continuing Story of Bungalow Bill" in one sixteen-hour marathon session. "That night went really fast," said Chris Thomas. "Everyone who was in the vicinity of the studio joined in on 'The Continuing Story of Bungalow Bill'. Yoko sang her line and I played a mandolin-type mellotron bit in the verses and the trombone bit in the choruses."

With the current songs at the mixing stage, McCartney taped his "Why Don't We Do It In The Road?" solo, with the drum part overdubbed later by Ringo. "That's Paul," John said. "He even recorded it by himself in another room . . . We came in, and he'd made the whole record. I can't speak for George, but I was always hurt when Paul would knock something off without involving us. But that's just the way it was then." The last piece to be recorded for the *White Album* was a Lennon solo effort, the acoustic ballad "Julia". It was the only song he recorded by himself during the Beatles' career, although McCartney offered his input via the studio intercom. John double-tracked both his vocal and guitar parts, perfecting the song in a mere three takes. "That was John's song about his mum, folk finger-picking style, and a very good song," Paul later remembered.

On 14 October Ringo left for a holiday in Sardinia, and George flew to Los Angeles on the sixteenth, so John, Paul, George Martin and the engineers were left with the task of mixing the album and deciding on the final order of the tracks. Time was running out, and they spent an entire twenty-four-hour session from the sixteenth to the seventeenth trying to finish the album. "What's The New Mary Jane" was dropped, as was "Not Guilty", which left thirty tracks. Lennon and McCartney decided to cross-fade the takes, eliminating the silence between numbers, much as they had for *Sgt. Pepper*. Little sections from the "Beatles Chat" tapes were added to the mix: Paul's "Can You Take Me Back" ad-lib, and a humorous exchange between Alistair Taylor and George Martin in the control room. The album was released on 22 November in Britain and on 25 November in the USA. It had sold an estimated 6.5 million copies by the end of 1970.

"Paul was always upset about the *White Album*," says Lennon. "He never liked it because, on that one, I did my music, he did his, and George did his. He didn't like George having so many tracks. He wanted it to be more a group thing, which really meant more Paul. So, he never liked that album. I always preferred it to all the others, including *Pepper*, because I thought the music was better. The *Pepper* myth is bigger, but the music on the *White Album* is far superior. I wrote a lot of good stuff on that. I like all the stuff I did on that and the other stuff as well. I like the whole album."

In the middle of the sessions for the *White Album*, McCartney decided to go off for a weekend in the sun in Sardinia with a comely barmaid named Maggie McGivern. He'd met her while making the rounds of the exclusive private clubs that catered to the rich and famous in the London pop scene. Alistair Taylor received a phone call on Friday morning telling him to "find" Maggie and invite her along as his companion. "I've lost her address, Alistair. I'm sure you can take care of it for me. Pick her up around midnight."

When Taylor arrived at the club, he was dismayed to find it closed, but luckily met an employee who told him where Maggie lived. He drove through Chelsea and pulled up in front of a tall building. When he rang the bell a beautiful blonde woman appeared. "Are you Maggie McGivern?" asked Alistair.

"Yes."

"Do you think you might come down here for a moment? Paul McCartney has sent me round to collect you. You're off to Sardinia this weekend for a holiday together."

"Great!" she said. It wasn't the way most people get dates but, of course, Paul McCartney was a member of the greatest rock'n'roll show on the planet, and pulling girls wasn't ever a problem.

When they arrived at Luton airport at around one a.m., Paul, Maggie, McCartney's cousin and his girlfriend boarded a private jet. At the last moment Taylor was persuaded to go with them.

Just before landing in Sardinia, the plane suddenly banked steeply causing a table of wine glasses to crash to the floor. The Italians on the ground, it seemed, had forgotten to turn on the landing lights, so the pilots were unable to locate the airstrip. After several dangerous circles around the island's high mountains they touched down just after four in the morning. Waved through Customs by a sleepy guard, everyone wandered into the airport bar and Paul stopped at the souvenir shop to buy some postcards made of cork. The two couples climbed into a hire car and drove to their rented villa, leaving Taylor to deal with refuelling the plane and preparing for the return trip.

Several years later, Maggie remembered the weekend in a brief online interview. "Paul was a very interesting man. He was obviously very used to getting his own way, which is reasonable, I suppose, based upon his position. Actually we all had a really good laugh.

Though nothing really came of the relationship, I have fond memories both of Paul and a very special time in my young life."

In those days, by his own admission, McCartney was very much Jack the Lad and met, befriended and bedded so many gorgeous young women that one wonders if today he would even remember Maggie.

Around the same time the Lennons' marriage was formally ending.

On 22 August 1968, Cynthia filed for divorce on grounds of John's adultery and was granted a decree nisi on 8 November 1968. She was understandably heartbroken and dropped from sight. It was later revealed that she had gone off to Italy where she became romantically linked with Roberto Bassanini, heir to the Bassanini Hotel fortune. Eventually they married, but the union seemed doomed to fail from the start and they soon divorced. Cynthia and Julian returned to northern England.

On Friday, 18 October 1968 at around 11.30 a.m., while John and Yoko were living in Ringo's basement flat at 34 Montagu Square in London's Marylebone, they were busted for drug possession by Sgt. Norman Pilcher. The Stones had been busted earlier in 1967. Their drug-taking had widely been reported, in scandalized tones, by the *News of the World* and it was probably inevitable that the Establishment would take action. One weekend a party including Mick Jagger, Marianne Faithfull, Keith Richards, George and Patti drove down to Richards' weekend cottage in Sussex. On the Sunday George and Patti left around 6 p.m. and then the police swooped in. According to Philip Norman, Richards has always been convinced that, had George stayed, they would have been safe such was the reverence in which the Beatles were held. By 1968 it was a different story. It was clear the Beatles were no longer the lovable moptops they once appeared to be. Pilcher's motives for pursuing such a high profile case were his own, but it seems clear that the word still had to have come from somewhere higher up than the London Drug Squad in the case of both John and George. There is some speculation that these two were, in the minds of many, the most radical Beatles with Harrison's weirdo Hare Krishna connections and Lennon's public political jabbering and up front pro-drug posturing to the media. In short, the two "bad" Beatles were no longer squeaky-clean middle-class role models and therefore they must be made to pay! Says Lennon, "I guess they didn't like the way the image was looking. The Beatles thing was over. No reason to protect us for being soft and cuddly anymore, so fucking bust us!"

In a long-forgotten interview on the event Lennon has said: "It was a bit strange, because we were lying a-bed, and there was a knock, so Yoko goes to the door and says, 'Who is it?' and a woman's voice says, 'Uh, I'm the postman.' Yoko says, 'The postman is a man!' And then, 'I have a special message for you.' So we're panicking, because it's either the press or some mad fan. Yoko's intrigued, so the fucker opens the door. I'm still in bed but I can hear it going on. I just stop and peep and there's a few people at the door, all in plain clothes, so you couldn't really tell who it was. So Yoko runs back in, she's panicking, and pregnant. She's recovering on the floor, and there's this banging on the window. I thought, Oh, they've got me, not the police, but whoever it is that's trying to get me. I open the curtains and this giant super-policeman is against the window. We didn't have any clothes on, the guy is against the window, I'm trying to hold it down. 'What is it?' I don't know whether he said, 'I'm the police!' But I'm saying, 'Ring the police.' It was like the Marx Brothers, but it didn't feel like that at the time."

A previously unseen police case file reveals not only the police view on the bust but also the particulars of the case against John and Yoko:

> I said, "We are police officers and we have a warrant to search the premises for dangerous drugs. Open the window and let me in." Lennon leaned on the window preventing me from opening it and said, "I don't care who you are, you're not bloody well coming in here!"
>
> DS Pilcher told Lennon that unless he opened the front door it would be forced. Lennon still refused. DS Pilcher then left me and I heard banging coming from the front door. Lennon moved away from the window shouting, "All right, I'll open it." I opened

the window and entered the bedroom. Lennon said, "Oh, well, you're in now."

Items Seized from the Scene
Statement of Michael Ansell, MA.
Occupation of Witness: Senior Scientific Officer
On the 22nd October 1968, I took possession of the following sealed items. Description: One binocular case containing binoculars and herbal mixture. Result of Analysis: 12.43 grammes (191.8 grains) of Cannabis resin. Description: One tin containing herbal mixture. Result of Analysis: Traces of Cannabis resin. Description: One envelope containing herbal mixture. Result of Analysis: 1.77 grammes (27.3 grains) of Cannabis resin. Description: One cigarette case. Result of Analysis: Traces of Cannabis resin. Description: One box containing a phial of brown tablets. Result of Analysis: Three 'Omnopon' tablets. Containing a total of 30 milligrammes (½ grain) Morphine.

Towards the end of his life Lennon remembered the turmoil caused by the bust: "It's strange when you hear people are snorting in the White House, after the misery they put a lot of people through, and the night they busted us in England. I have a record for life because the cop who busted me and Yoko was scalp-hunting, making a name for himself. I've never denied having been involved with drugs. There was a question raised in the House of Parliament: 'Why do they need forty cops to arrest John and Yoko?' That thing was set up! The *Daily Mail* and the *Daily Express* were there. Before the cops came, he'd called the fucking press! In fact, Don Short told us 'They're coming to get you', three weeks before."

The couple were taken to Marylebone police station on 18 October at around one p.m., charged and released on bail. On 28 November at Marylebone magistrates' court they pleaded guilty to possession of cannabis resin and were fined £150 plus court costs. John was afraid that Yoko, who held an American passport, would be deported, and also pleaded guilty to a charge of obstructing the police in the hope that Yoko would be exempted from any legal liability.

The event was so upsetting for them both that Yoko miscarried her baby, ending up in Queen Charlotte's Hospital, London where John camped out next to her bed in a sleeping bag.

Lennon thought that with payment of the fine the matter would be closed, but it came back to haunt him in 1972, when the Nixon White House used it as a reason to attempt to deport him. Recently he had been politically outspoken, and the move was designed to weaken the growing left-wing youth movement intent on dethroning Nixon. In 1975, while John was fighting deportation, he revealed more about the events of 18 October 1968: "We were feeling very clean and drugless . . . I thought it was the fucking Mafia at the door. There was a banging at the bedroom window, and a big policeman was there, growling and saying, 'Let me in!' I said, 'You're not allowed in like this, are you?' I was so frightened. I said, 'Come round to the front door. Just let me get dressed.' He said, 'No, open the window, I'm going to fall off.' Yoko held the window while I got dressed, half leaning out of the bathroom so they could see we weren't hiding anything. Then they started charging the door. I had a dialogue with the policeman, saying, 'It's very bad publicity if you come through the window.' He was saying, 'Just open the window, you'll only make it worse for yourself.' I was saying, 'I want to see a warrant!' Another guy comes on the roof and they showed me this paper, and I pretended to read it, just to try and think what to do.

"Then I said, 'Call the lawyer, call the lawyer!' But Yoko rang Apple instead. I was saying, 'No, not the office, the lawyer!' Then there was a heave on the door, so I opened it, and said, 'Okay, I'm clean anyway,' thinking I was. So he says, 'Ah-ha, got you for obstruction!' I said, 'Oh, yeah?' because I felt confident I had no drugs. I said, 'Well, what happens now? Can I call the office? I've got an interview in two hours, can I tell them I can't come?' He said, 'No, you're not allowed to make any calls . . . May I use your phone?' Then our lawyer came. The police brought some dogs. They couldn't find them at first, and they kept ringing up, saying, 'Hello, Charlie, where are the dogs? We've been here half an hour!' I'd had all my stuff moved into the flat from my house, and I'd never looked at it. It had been there for years. I'd ordered cameras and clothes, but my driver brought binoculars, which I didn't need in my little flat. Inside the binoculars was some hash from last year. Somewhere else in an envelope was another piece. I'm paranoiac, anyway, we both are, especially about people coming to the door. But it was better it happened. But it's not too bad; a £150 fine. I think they should make some differentiation between hard and soft drugs. I think maybe they should have pot bars, if they're going to have alcohol. I'd sooner ban sugar. I knew what Britain's Establishment were. I'd been around it a long time. It's just the same as anywhere else, only with a stiff upper lip. They don't show any happiness or sadness."

The drugs found in Lennon's possession constituted a minor misdemeanour, especially by today's standards. But there is evidence that John, and perhaps others close to him, were using heroin. Although Lennon only admitted to "sniffing a little when we were in real pain", the Beatle's taste for heroin went well beyond experimentation. From the recollections of Paul McCartney, Hare Krishna house guest Dhanajaya Dasa, Yoko Ono, and John's aide Frederic Seaman it is now clear that between late 1968 and early 1971, and possibly longer, John Lennon was a full-blown junkie.

But why did the Lennons become involved with heroin in the first place? Yoko said it was "as a celebration of ourselves as artists". She also said: "Of course, George says it was me who put John on heroin, but that wasn't true. John wouldn't take anything he didn't want to. John was very serious, he asked if I had ever tried it. I told him that while he was in India with the Maharishi, I had a sniff in a party situation. I didn't know what it was. They just gave me something and I said, 'What was that?' It was a beautiful feeling. John was talking about heroin one day and said, 'Did you ever take it?' and I told him about Paris. I said it wasn't bad. I think because the amount was small I didn't even get sick. It was just a nice feeling. So I told him that. When you take it . . . 'properly' isn't the right word, but you get sick right away if you're not used to it. I think maybe because I said it wasn't a bad experience, that had something to do with John taking it."

Lennon tried heroin for the first time at a friend's flat. "People were giving us such a hard time," he said. "I've had so much shit thrown at me and especially at Yoko. People like Peter Brown shake my hand and don't even say hello to her. That's going on all the time. We were in so much pain we had to do something . . . We took H because of what the Beatles and their pals were doing to us. But we got out of it. They didn't set down to do it, but things came out of that period and I don't forget!"

"It was a very intense period," remembers McCartney. "John was with Yoko and escalated to heroin and all the accompanying paranoias. He was putting himself way out on a limb. As much as it excited and amused him, at the same time it secretly terrified him. 'Don't Let Me Down' was a genuine plea, 'Don't let me down, please, whatever you do. I'm out on this limb, I know I'm doing all this stuff, just don't let me down.' It was saying to Yoko, 'I'm really stepping out of line on this one. I'm really allowing my vulnerability to be seen, so you must not let me down.' I think it was a genuine cry for help. It was a very good song.

"We were very disappointed John was into heroin because we didn't really see how we could help him. We just hoped it wouldn't go too far. In actual fact, he did end up clean but this was the period he was on it. It was a tough time for John, but often that adversity and craziness can lead to great art, as I think it did in this case. When John and I used to meet, he'd say, 'Do they try and set you against me like they try and set me against you?' And I'd say, 'Yes, often. People say, "Oh, did you hear Lennon threw up before he went on stage in Toronto?"'

"They'd always tell me the juicy things, in case I wanted to go, 'Did he? The bastard! Well, serves him right, ha, ha, ha.' We'd hear it as gossip and derive some petty satisfaction from it, but on a deeper level it was like, 'Yes, but the amount of drugs he was on, he would be throwing up, never mind anything else.'

"It was a fairly big shocker for us because we all thought we were far-out boys but we understood we'd never go quite that far out. I don't think people understand what was happening but there was still a lot of affection." On another occasion McCartney recalled the ill-effects of heroin on his partner. "Unfortunately, he was drifting away from us at that point, so none of us actually knew. He never told us; we heard rumours and we were very sad. But he'd embarked on a new course, which really involved anything and everything. Because John was that kind of guy, he wanted to live life to the full as he saw it. John'd always wanted to jump off the cliff. He once said that to me, 'Have you ever thought of jumping?' I said, 'Fuck off. You jump and tell me how it is.' That's basically the difference in our personalities."

Referring to his first solo appearance with the Plastic Ono Band at the Rock & Roll Revival in Toronto, John said, "I threw up for hours until I went on. I nearly threw up during 'Cold Turkey'. I saw a review in *Rolling Stone* about the film of it – which I haven't seen yet – and they're saying, 'I was this and that.' And I was throwing up nearly in the number, I could hardly sing any of them, I was full of shit."

"I was very frightened of drugs," said Paul. "Having a nurse mother, I was always cautious . . . I did some [heroin] with Robert Fraser, and some of the boys in the Stones. I always refer to it as 'walking through a minefield'. I was lucky because had anyone hit me with a real dose, I would have been a heroin addict. Robert Fraser once said to me, 'There's no problem with heroin, even if it is addictive. You've just got to have a lot of money. The problem is when you can't pay for it.' Which, of course, is absolute bullshit.

"This was the way he put it to me and for a second I was almost taken in but then my northern savvy kicked in and I said to myself, 'Don't go for all of this. This is all very exotic and romantic but don't go for it. A lot of his friends messed around with heroin. A lot of his lords and ladies were addicts and had been for many, many years . . . I did sniff heroin with him once, but I said afterwards, 'I'm not sure about this, man. It didn't really do anything for me,' and he said, 'In that case, I won't offer you any again.' . . . I was often around when they'd all be doing it. They'd repair to the toilet and I'd say, 'I'm all right, thanks, no.' One of the most difficult things from that period was the peer pressure to do that."

Eventually Lennon saw that he had to kick heroin. This led to several unsuccessful attempts at withdrawal, including a stint at the London Clinic for four days' detoxification. Upon discharge he went on to methadone in an effort to wean himself off the drug. But his fame made it difficult for him to check into a hospital as someone on the staff would tip off the press. Yoko remembered, "We were very square people in a way. We wouldn't kick in a hospital because we wouldn't let anybody know. We just went straight cold turkey. The thing is, we never injected. We were hooked, but I don't think it was a great amount. Still, it was hard. Cold turkey is always hard."

Lennon managed to keep the matter out of the press, but not from the other Beatles. Paul, for one, was concerned and annoyed that John could be so stupid as to involve himself in such a potentially lethal pastime, when so many around them had already killed themselves by it. George too, was aghast: he had adopted a Hare Krishna lifestyle, which eschewed drugs. When John moved to America in September 1971, he had still not abandoned the drug. According to musician Jesse Ed Davis, author Albert Goldman, and several members of Lennon's staff, he enjoyed it on and off for the rest of his life.

EIGHT

Good Evening and Welcome to Slaggers

Central London

1969

"I was very disappointed in 1969 when suddenly everybody starts kicking each other and stabbing each other in the back after the whole Love Generation. Where did they go? Where are you? Suddenly it became all this hate and deceit."

George Harrison

"We started Apple like a toy, because we weren't businessmen, and we didn't know what it involved. We'd started this great empire thinking we could do it whenever we felt like it. But it ended up we couldn't, we had to go in! So what we're really doing now is paying for when we played about. We used to keep everybody on for ever just because they were mates. They never did their jobs . . . Now if they can't do the job they have to leave, which is fair. If you don't do your work then you've gotta go somewhere else. It's not a playground anymore!"

Ringo Starr

In many ways 1969 represented the Beatles at their best and their miserable worst. It was an intense time for all of the group with not only a lot of band stuff happening, but myriad solo projects as well. Personally, it was a time of change. Paul and Linda married, as did John and Yoko. George worked with several artists, both as a producer and anonymous sideman, while Ringo stepped out as a charismatic, capable film actor. *Abbey Road* was recorded and released. Lennon founded the Plastic Ono Band and played for peace in Toronto as the death knell sounded for the Beatles as a musical collective.

On 14 January 1969 Peter Sellers dropped in on the boys at Twickenham film studios while they were shooting a documentary. With the cameras rolling, the Beatles, minus Harrison, decided to have some fun with their famous guest. Abruptly Lennon brought up the subject of drugs. "Remember when I gave you that grass in Piccadilly?"

Peter Sellers: I sure do, man, it really stoned me out of my mind. It was Acapulco Gold, wasn't it?

John Lennon: Exactly!

Peter: That was really fantastic. I'm not selling any right now, though, I'm sorry.

John: No, we [the Beatles] have now given up, you know, as stated by Hunter Damier [*sic*] in the Beatles' actual life story.

Peter: Well, I'm sorry about that fellows. If I'd known I was going to see you I would have had some on me. Because I know how much you all love it.

John: Dig it.

Peter: Sure, I dig.

Paul: Sure. Gotcha, Pete! Can you dig it?

Peter: Oh, yes, dig it, dig it.

Just before the montage was cut off, Lennon wryly added, "Just don't leave any needles lying round in the loo. We've got a bad enough reputation now with me getting busted and that. I know what it's like for you showbiz people, you're under a great strain and you need a little relaxation."

Ringo: That's why he's going to bed!

John: If it's a choice between that and exercise, drugs win hand down. I say *hand* down.

Yoko: Well, shooting is exercise.

John: Shooting is exercise, oh, yeah.

Around this time Sellers was cultivating a particularly close friendship with Ringo. They bonded through their shared love of drumming, movies and partying. Starr had read Terry Southern's 1958 novel *The Magic Christian*, and thought it would make a great film. He was instrumental in getting it into production. He knew Sellers would be perfect in the lead role as Sir Guy Grand, the world's richest man, and called him. Straight away, Sellers was on board. In February 1969, they began shooting. Starr, who played the role of Sellers's adopted homeless son, Youngman Grand, quickly discovered the actor's scene-stealing abilities. During one scene he had every line while on the other side of the room all Sellers did was pick his nose. The audience was riveted to Sellers, all but ignoring Ringo. "I would never let anybody do that again in a movie," Starr affirmed. Sellers taught him another lesson: "Peter would always say, 'It's your eyes, Ringo, it's your eyes. They'll be two hundred feet up there, you know.' "

On the set Ringo and Peter played practical jokes on cast and crew. Once they collected everyone's coats and jackets and tied all the belts together. On another occasion one of Ringo's friends turned and wondered why everyone was laughing. Eventually he discovered that a variety of items, including cigarette packets and matchboxes, had been taped to his back by the pranksters.

As Starr found out, Sellers had a somewhat Jekyll and Hyde personality: he would have his guests howling with laughter at a dinner party and the next morning would turn up at the studio morose and even nasty. Ringo noted, "It would be 'Hi, Pete,' and then, Oh, God, we'd have to knock the wall down again just to say hello. Sometimes we'd be asked to leave the set because Peter Sellers was being Peter Sellers."

Producer Walter Shenson observed that Sellers, like so many comedians, suffered from a profound sense of insecurity. "Peter once said to me, 'The hardest thing for me to do is be Peter Sellers. I can hide behind an accent or some makeup or costume and be anybody you ask me to be but, God, there is no Peter Sellers!' "

Due, no doubt, to Ringo's easy-going manner the two were soon constant companions, jet-setting around the globe and hosting parties. Once they threw a party at London's trendy Les Ambassadeurs night club, with such luminaries as Sean Connery, Michael Caine, Richard Harris, Roger Moore and George Peppard among the guests. In May

1969 they sailed to New York on the *QE2* with their wives. One earlier jaunt in the Mediterranean inspired Starr's bouncy "Octopus's Garden". "I went to Sardinia," says Ringo. "Peter let me use his yacht. The captain of the boat gave us squid and chips. I said, 'What's that?' He said, 'Squid and chips.' I said, 'We don't eat squid, have you got any fish?' I was hanging out with the captain and he told me how octopuses go around the seabed picking up stones and shiny objects to build gardens. I thought this was fabulous because at the time I just wanted to be under the sea too. I wanted to get out of it for a while."

Starr even purchased his home, Brookfield in Elstead, Surrey, from the actor for £70,000 – just after Sellers had poured £50,000 into renovations. John Lennon also really liked the property and offered him double, but Sellers kept his word to Ringo, who eventually sold the fifteenth-century house, with lake, walled gardens, barns, gymnasium, sauna and private cinema, to Stephen Stills of Crosby, Stills, Nash and Young.

In January the Beatles were hard at work recording their new album "Get Back", later retitled *Let It Be*. They had agreed to allow themselves to be filmed for a documentary directed by American filmmaker, Michael Lindsay-Hogg, which later became the film *Let It Be*. Drawing largely on tapes and notes made by Apple gofer Kenny McCainn and given to this author, these excerpts give a rare insight into the inner dynamics of the Beatles at this time.

Wednesday, 8 January 1969

"I don't care if you don't want it on your show, I don't give a fuck," George caustically pronounces as he introduces his latest composition, written the previous evening, to Ringo, having just arrived at Twickenham. "I Me Mine" is complete lyrically and musically (though elements of the song would change when it was finally recorded a year later for the *Let It Be* album). Harrison's mood improves as he begins to discuss John's *1969 Diary*, a comical little book passed out to friends. "It's really too much," George laughs. "It's just his diary, filled in for the year. It starts: 'Got up, went out, came home, went to bed' . . . and then Saturday night is: 'Got up *late*, went out, came in, fucked the wife, went to bed.'"

Harrison eagerly talks about television the night before, revealing how it inspired "I Me Mine", a moving diatribe against egoism. "There was some science-fiction thing on but then suddenly it turned into all this crap about medals and things. That's what gave me the idea, because suddenly they were all coming into a ball, I think it was Austria, and they all had their medals, and some music was playing, like a 3/4 thing. I had that in me head, just the waltz thing and it fit 'I me mine'. There were no words to it." Harrison ponders aloud whether or not the line, "flowing more freely than wine", is grammatically correct. "Is there such a word as freer," George asks, "is it f-r-e-e-e-r?" Director Michael Lindsay-Hogg is quick to respond. "No," he says. "It's f-r-e-e-r." Paul cannot resist adding: "Like queer, freer. A freer queer!"

With Lennnon recently arriving, Harrison mentions a recent newspaper article. "Legalize pot!" he reads. "It's less harmful than alcohol, yet the penalty is up to £2000 and ten years in prison. Just think of it!" (John's reference to the article later in the session, "Queen says no to pot-smoking FBI members", found its way into both the *Let It Be* LP and film.)

"All Things Must Pass", another new Harrison composition, is given a full rehearsal by the Beatles, but little progress is made. "Do you fancy doing it on your own with an acoustic?" Paul asks, though doubts George's actual ability to do so. "It's a bit of a stretch vocally for you." The next piece to be given extensive treatment is "I Me Mine", though it is met with nothing but criticism from John. "Is that the end?" Lennon asks, commenting on the song's length. "We'll use it for a commercial. Sounds hard to do, I mean, for you. 'I me mine'! Run along, son, this is a rock 'n' roll band, you know!" As if John's comments weren't enough to cement his profound disinterest, Lennon drops out midway through rehearsals to waltz around the studio with Yoko.

While a new PA is being installed, a short conversation takes place between Lennon and McCartney. At the heart of the matter is John's obvious dependency on heroin and his ability to come up with substantial new material. The two speak in almost comical tones, but the issues they discuss are far from their typical "Laugh-In" style repartee.

Paul: Haven't you written anything else?
John: No.
Paul: We're going to be faced with a crisis, you know.
John: When I'm up against the wall, Paul, you'll find I'm at my best.
Paul: Yeah, but I wish you'd come up with the goods!
John: Well, look, I think I've got Sunday off.
Paul: Yeah, well, I hope you can deliver.
John: I'm hoping for a little rock'n'roller.
Paul: I was hoping for the same thing myself.

As the session winds down, Lindsay-Hogg rants away at length, discussing ideas for the proposed upcoming live show, until the Beatles finally give up and jokingly agree with everything he says. "Yes, all right, just shut up!" Lennon humorously retorts. Michael doesn't heed the advice, and says that he wants to put up posters around Twickenham advertising the live date as 20 January 1969. John, perhaps more realistically with the state of the sessions, predicts the date to be "the nineteenth of February 1982". Michael then becomes a bit too familiar, and refers to Paul as "darling", McCartney answers back with "lovey". "I was brought up in California, you must forgive me," offers the embarrassed director.

The topic of discussion now turns to the possibility of performing a concert on an ocean liner, finishing off with a performance at the (as yet undecided) final destination. Harrison is immediately direct in his opposition. "What is the point of going abroad?" he wonders. Lennon answers back: "Every time we've done an album, we've said: 'Why are we stuck in EMI? We could be doing it in LA! We could be in France!' Here we are again, building yet another bloody castle around us!" Ringo, too, is against travelling outside the country, he has been since the beginning of the project, and when asked to give one good reason to back up his argument by John, Ringo replies they should stay in England for their fans. Lennon suggests they could take the fans with them on the boat. McCartney suggests that the first thousand people in line could receive a free concert and trip. "It's impractical to lug all them people there and try and get all that equipment," Harrison reminds them. Michael, who has nicknamed Ringo "Russia" and George "France" for no particular reason, is still very much for the idea: "I think the sense of adventure, Christopher Columbus, will make it and I don't think there's a gimmick in it." Paul, apparently fed up with Michael's annoying use of wordplay, replies: "I think you're d-a-f-t." John, uncharacteristically enthusiastic about the planned live show, says, "It'll be like on the roof in India, only we'd be fully equipped" (referring to the Beatles' extended jam sessions the previous year with Donovan and Mike Love in Rishikesh). Harrison, however, stands by his view. "I think the idea of the boat is completely insane," says George. "It's expensive and insane!" Lennon thinks they can get a boat for free because of the publicity the show would generate. "They won't even give us a free Fender amp!" Harrison replies incredulously. Preparing to leave, George sings out a song aptly summing up his mood: "Cut out the bullshit, cut out the bullshit, cut out the bullshit, good night!" John then leaves final directions: "Don't forget: a boatload of mental deficients and five dwarfs for Friday!"

The new Beatles LP is still very far from becoming a reality, though Lennon explained its concept earlier in the day to George Martin: "Well, it's a very small LP, with a large hole in the middle, and a picture of your behind on the label, saying, George Martin Presents . . ."

Thursday, 9 January 1969

The Beatles conduct extensive rehearsals for "Get Back". Most of the lyrics to the songs at this stage are largely improvised although John and Paul try and organize the words.

As McCartney groped for the song's lyrics he opened a kind of Pandora's box when he referred at length to the political hot potato of Pakistani immigration into Britain as well as the sensitive issues of Puerto Rican immigration, Native Americans and the emerging gay movement. On the surface, the lyrics could be interpreted as racist, but Paul was clearly liberal in both his politics and lifestyle. He was certainly being ironic, or even condemning such archaic ideas by playing devil's advocate. At any rate, the tape of that long-ago afternoon survives. The excerpt taken from roll 97, camera A, slate 184 recorded on 9 January 1969 shows that the bouncy tune was originally entitled "No Pakistanis" (or "Commonwealth"), and Paul sings, while he is trying to come up with suitable lyrics for his new melody: "'Dowdy came from Puerto Rico and he joined the middle class. Where I come from we don't need no Puerto Ricans coming from another land. So get back, get back to where you once belonged.'

"'A man came from Puerto Rico . . . came to live in New York among the Puerto Ricans class. Get back, get back, get back to where you once belonged.'

"'Albert Domoray was a Puerto Rican . . . don't need no Puerto Ricans in the USA. Get back, get back to where you once belonged.'

"'Suddenly there is Pakistanis all over the land, taking the English jobs, riding on the buses, man. Get back, get back to where you once belonged.'

"'Siddhi Aboramy was a Pakistani but he came to leave his home. All the people said, "We don't need Pakistani, boy, you better travel home." Get back, back to where you once belonged.'

"'Louisa was the one who thought she was a woman but she was another man. All the friends around her said she got it coming but she gets it while she can. Get back, get back to where you once belonged.'"

John: "We don't want no black men!"

"Don't dig no Pakistanis taking all the people's jobs! Get back, get back to where you once belonged.

"All the folks around said partly a Mohican. Get back, get back to where you once belonged."

"Siddhi Aboramy was a Pakistani living in the Underground. All the folks around, 'Don't need no Pakistanis taking all the people's jobs.' So get back, get back to where you once belonged."

Friday, 10 January 1969

"For the first verse of 'Get Back' Paul sings about Tucson, Arizona, and California grass in the first person, quickly coming up with characters such as 'Sweet Loretta Marsh' (later to become 'Martin') and Jo, though they have a difficult time coming up with a last name for the latter. John and Paul trade several ideas in search of a western-sounding name: Carson, Williams, Dandy, while Paul finally settles for Jo Jo Jackson. The second verse retains the Pakistani immigration theme, although they now realize their new characters do not fit the storyline: "The California grass bit is daft," says Paul. "We'll straighten it out later."

McCartney is having difficulty singing over the two guitars and asks George to play only on the offbeat. Harrison grumbles that perhaps they need Eric Clapton, who will obligingly play whatever he is told. John and Paul both affirm they need only George. McCartney then argues with Harrison over a chord in the chorus, which Paul thinks is *passé* and they have used before, comparing it to "drainies" (drainpipe trousers). George disagrees, and says they are only chords, and that some suit songs better than others.

Paul envisions John and George each taking a solo during the song, and an abrupt ending featuring feedback from Lennon's guitar. He also suggests changes to Ringo's drum intro and even George, who has remained mostly quiet during the rehearsal, pitches a few ideas. McCartney reiterates his desire to keep things simple, and plays bass riffs from "Long Tall Sally" and the theme from "The Beatles Cartoons" as examples. A riff in "Get Back" reminds John of Perry Como's "Catch A Falling Star", and he sings a few lines. Lennon observes that they have never learned so many new songs at one time, McCartney suggests moving on to "Two Of Us", which John mockingly calls his "favourite". The tune is much harder at this point, featuring electric guitars with a galloping guitar riff, entirely different from the gentle acoustic arrangement it will receive once the sessions move to Apple Studios on Savile Row on 21 January. Paul remarks, "It's a bit faceless." John agrees and suggests they record a demo and give it to the band Grapefruit, new Apple recording artists. This does not occur, but another Apple group, Mortimer, will go on to record a version of "Two Of Us" which remains unreleased. Paul believes the song is not the problem but, rather, the arrangement. Lennon is at a loss for making it sound interesting on electric, and adjusts his guitar to be more suitable for strumming. McCartney proceeds to give yet more directions, and makes a mess of the middle-eight. Everyone then takes a break, having accomplished little, and it is over lunch George finally makes up his mind concerning his future with the group.

Returning to filming, Lennon plays a riff from Chuck Berry's "I'm Talking About You", and Harrison calmly stops playing to inform him he is leaving the band immediately. He sarcastically suggests they place an ad in the *New Musical Express* for a replacement. Mal says he'll talk to George Martin about finding someone, but George replies they shouldn't bother when they have Apple to handle matters like this. All Lennon can respond with is: "We aim to please!" George then packs his things and walks out to the inappropriate accompaniment of happy whistling.

The remaining Beatles don't really know how to deal with Harrison's departure and aren't really convinced he means it. John turns up the distortion on his guitar and begins a jam on The Who's appropriately titled "A Quick One While He's Away", jokingly calling for George to take the solo. Yoko soon takes centre stage wailing into a microphone and screaming John's name, while Paul coaxes feedback from his amplifier, and Ringo madly thrashes his kit. Yoko continues her painful vocal warbling for several minutes until John calls for "I've Got A Feeling", and they proceed to blithely massacre it. Lennon screams his entry to the song, and laughs at the sound of his voice, but he is obviously far from content. Continuing to vent their frustration, the trio begin a drunk-sounding "Don't Let Me Down", and John uses a high falsetto to parody Paul's silly "Maxwell's Silver Hammer".

Rehearsing anything seriously is pointless with George out of the picture, so the Beatles take to parodying several standards, including "Till There Was You", "Don't Be Cruel", and Conway Twitty's "It's Only Make Believe". Under the cacophonous noise, Lindsay-Hogg, Neil Aspinall and George Martin attempt to carry on a conversation about Harrison. "The trouble is," Michael says, "once you leave, it's very hard to come back." The Beatles join the conversation and

Michael presents the idea to Paul of not announcing the date of the planned live concert and allowing the seats to slowly fill up, starting with only one audience member. McCartney calls the idea "inane" and "imbecilic". Michael asks him to seriously consider it, but McCartney insists he is quite serious. Hogg wonders what their next move will be, and Lennon facetiously replies that it will be to "split Harrison's instruments", which causes everyone to laugh. Engineer Glyn Johns is reminded during the ensuing conversation of one of George's parting lines he had said to the Beatles that afternoon: "See you round the clubs."

John and Yoko return from speaking with an interviewer from the Canadian Broadcasting Corporation, and Paul announces them as the winners of the *Mersey Beat* award for Best Cover of the year, then nominates them for "Irritant of the Year", an honour currently being offered in *Private Eye*. They reminisce about the touring days, and John jokingly comments that Jimmy Nicol (who once stood in for Ringo) is now making a living as the 29th Beatle in New Mexico. Paul retreats back to the piano, and plays a bit of his recent composition "The Long And Winding Road", "Martha My Dear", and a classical instrumental piece. Yoko asks for a mike, and John states firmly that if George does not return by Tuesday they will ask Eric Clapton to replace him in the live show.

Cream, Lennon notes, was a group of three soloists, and Clapton would have free range to improvise freely in the Beatles and would be happy to join. "The point is, if George leaves, do we really want to carry on the Beatles? I certainly do," says John. "If he leaves, he leaves, you know." Once again Yoko begins screaming John's name into the microphone. Lennon replies to her calls first with "What?" then "Anything you say, dear," and "Stop that." Ringo humorously chimes in with his own: "I'm afraid he's not in." Yoko mercilessly continues. "He's busy!" John retorts. "Bloody mad!" Paul has not stopped playing, and continues with "Martha My Dear", which leads to some further piano improvisations. Yoko joins in with her calls to John, occasionally rising to an ear-splitting climax. Lennon quickly becomes bored and joins in on guitar. Ono bleats and shrieks, and Starr picks up his tambourine to add percussion to the mix.

When the chaos is finally over, Lennon calms things down with guitar instrumentals of "Sun King" and "Dear Prudence". Michael psychologically analyses the jam sessions which have taken place after George left, pointing out Ringo's hard playing, and Paul's retreat into his amp like he was "going into a closet". They plan to meet again on Monday, and John promises to bring "Eric, Jimi and Tommy" along with him. Michael returns and wonders aloud what to do with the project at the end of such a day, and Lennon, as usual, supplies the answer: "Stick it up yer arse!"

Monday, 13 January 1969

Starr wonders whether they actually have enough footage for a documentary and Michael replies that if they are allowed to show everything, then yes, but if they are "hiding", then all they have is a few days' footage wherein things didn't quite work out. Paul arrives and sorts through some photographs by Ethan Russell, and Linda comments on how great John looked the previous day. Michael asks who he was wearing, and Paul laughs: "Why, Yoko Ono, the celebrated Japanese actress!"

"What's wrong with him? He won't sing the words!" McCartney growls as they listen to Arthur Conley's cover of "Ob-la-di, Ob-la-da". Paul and Ringo remark on how cover versions of the song always leave out "bra" after "life goes on". McCartney says he prefers the Bedrocks' version. He mentions the first record he ever bought was "Be Bop A Lula", and how Lonnie Donegan's "Rock Island Line" didn't really move him enough to run out and buy it: "I liked it, but I thought it was a bit too British."

McCartney hopes to finish off some lyrics and rehearse the unfinished tunes, but Starr questions the point with Harrison still absent. Lennon, typically, is still at home in bed. Neil Aspinall mentions how the previous day George requested a meeting with only the four Beatles present, everyone agreed, but Harrison didn't believe John would show up without Yoko. They go on to discuss John and Yoko's relationship and Paul believes they are quite serious about what they are doing, but wishes he could write with John without Yoko present. He finds it especially difficult to start from scratch on a new song with John and Yoko, mentioning he begins on a "Yoko beam", writing about "white walls" just to get the two interested. "I give them too much credit for what I think they'd like," Paul said. Linda says Yoko did all the talking at the last Apple meeting: "She was speaking for John, and I don't think he really believed any of it." Neil comments it could never be a serious meeting with Yoko there, as it would just turn into a circus.

McCartney sees two options: either fight to get the Beatles back to just the four of them without Yoko, or realize that John will not split with her for their sake. Neil feels that whenever he speaks to John, in reality, he is speaking more to Yoko. Then, surprisingly, he defends Ono, mentioning that when John and Paul tried to write the last verse to "I Will", Yoko politely stayed out of it. "Okay, they're going overboard about it," McCartney admits, "but John always does, and Yoko probably always does, so that's their scene." Paul confesses he told John he prefers Yoko not being there when they write, and feels their songwriting partnership has gone downhill since they stopped touring. McCartney believes the current situation is silly because either side is too afraid, "or uptight" to compromise: "It's going to be such an incredibly comical thing in fifty years' time. They broke up because Yoko sat on an amp!" Paul then talks about a "sensational" idea for the Beatles' planned live show Neil finished off the night before. The television special would contain Beatles' performance footage coupled with several fast action news stories, with the final bulletin being that the group had broken up.

They again bring up the last meeting where George walked out, waiting for it to start. Michael suggests drugging Yoko's herbal tea to get a moment alone with John. Paul criticizes Hogg's use of quick cuts in The Who's performance in the Rolling Stones' show, "Rock 'n' Roll Circus", telling him he prefers long shots and studies of a subject. He suggests the Beatles' documentary should be built up like a Picasso painting, with the songs being the artwork, but Michael expresses a profound dislike of the idea, viewing it as too much like Andy Warhol. Paul disagrees, but in the end, his ideas for the film are never used.

Over lunch, Kenny overhears the Beatles' conversation in the Twickenham cafeteria. "So where's George?" Paul jokingly wonders aloud to John, who's just arrived. Yoko feels the Beatles can easily get Harrison back into the group, but Lennon disagrees, believing it to be a festering wound allowed to go even deeper the day before. "It's only this year he realized who I am or who he is, or anything like that," says John. "Half of me says, 'I'll do anything to save you, to help you,' and the other half says, 'Well, serves him fucking right! I've been through fucking shit because of him for five years, and he's only just realized what he is doing to me!' "

McCartney assumes, however, that ultimately Harrison will be coming back, but Lennon wonders what to do in case he doesn't. Paul can only say that would be a new problem. John still wants the four Beatles together, but mentions George is becoming less satisfied with the Beatles. To Lennon, the mystique is all but gone in their recording, their music no longer containing the creative surprises for them it did in the days of *Revolver*. John says he prefers the Beatles' songs individually, with each tune authored separately, still he somehow finds the final product unsatisfactory. McCartney expresses the sentiment that he often hesitates before presenting the other Beatles with new material, because he knows at least one of them will not like it, so this inhibits him.

Paul explains he prefers getting on the piano, and performing a song the way he wants to but in a way everyone might like. He hopes for a time they can all sing and play without telling each other what to do. John reminds him that Paul tells Harrison how to play because that's the way McCartney wants it, and feels sorry for the way they treated George during sessions for the *White Album*. Lennon's only regret about the past, he says, is when he allowed McCartney to take a song in a direction he didn't want it to go, and his only recourse was to leave it to George Martin. Lennon references "She Said She Said", a song which Martin took "as is", and which Paul didn't play on due to disagreements between them. Lennon wants to be able to listen to their suggestions and accept or reject them instead of having to feel guilty over making a decision. He points out that during sessions for the *White Album* he was drunk most of the time, and didn't bother to tell Paul how to play. He was mainly concerned with his singing performance over anything. John mentions how he and George would never suggest anything for Paul's songs, because their ideas would ultimately be rejected anyway, although Lennon agrees that a lot of the time it was for the good of the song. McCartney tries to think of ways to avoid their ego-issues in telling Harrison what to play.

The Beatles then return to the studio to rehearse a frantic version of "Get Back". Paul settles for the moment on the lead character's name being "Sweet Loretta Marvin". McCartney works further on the "Jo Jo" verse, and then decides to call it a day. He asks Michael to cancel their performance scheduled for 18 January. As proof he will be returning the next day, Lennon leaves his favourite guitar behind, and Paul too promises to leave his cherished Hofner bass. McCartney then dons a posh voice and bids farewell: "And so I'd like to say to the cast of this production, good night and thank you very much for having us. It's been wonderful working with you. I know it's been wonderful working with me, but it's been wonderful working with you too . . . Which way did John go?"

Tuesday, 21 January 1969

With George now back in the fold, sessions for "Get Back" resume and move to the new makeshift Apple studios in the basement of Savile Row. The Beatles, and John in particular, are taken aback by Michael Housego's article in the *Daily Sketch* entitled "The End of a Beautiful Friendship?" which dealt with George's departure on the 10th. John tells Denis O'Dell he wants to sue, and is especially upset over the inference he and George came to physical blows. "It's never got to that, except for a plate of dinner in Hamburg," says John, who laughs at the unrecorded memory. He has different feelings, however, towards Harrison's photo, which accompanies the article. "The picture's great, yeah. George Harrison, the sane one, speaks out!"

With Harrison temporarily out of the room, John parodies George's departure for Ringo. "I quit," says John. Starr asks him to repeat himself, and Lennon reiterates he is quitting. Ringo replies: "Yeah? Well, you've got to fight me first!"

Because the Beatles' current project is being extended indefinitely, Starr's filming for *The Magic Christian* has been pushed to 24 February. Lennon conducts a lengthy discussion with Lindsay-Hogg on the making of the Rolling Stones' "Rock 'n' Roll Circus", of which Lennon and Ono were participants. The project will eventually be shelved, but Michael reports many segments of the film are edited and finished. Michael suggests to John he should record an introduction for the Rolling Stones' segment of the show and, surprisingly, Lennon obliges. Only two words of this intro ("And now . . .") will be used in the final cut, which will finally see official release some twenty plus years later.

After rehearsals for "Dig A Pony" and "I've Got A Feeling", between small bursts of various oldies, Lennon gets hold of a newspaper article chronicling Harrison's recent legal troubles, and frantically reads it beneath an instrumental backing. "'Beatle George May Face French Jail,'" John says, as he reads the title. "'Nice, France. Beatle George, above, is due in court here today to answer assault charges. If he does not appear he will be given an immediate jail sentence. French law provides the defendant must appear at court in person. This case may carry a possible sentence of more than two years. Harrison is accused of assaulting a photographer last May, as he and Beatle Ringo Starr left a nightclub.'" (Harrison failed to appear in court the previous day, but instead of being jailed, was fined a thousand francs.)

In between introducing his catchy new composition "Every Night" to the group, Paul expresses the opinion that they do not need a press department and John agrees, preferring "a conceptual press department that just says, 'Press.' Or an answering service that says simply, 'No comment.'"

The Beatles' jamming inspires Paul to read the Housego article in a dissonant, dismembered voice, while John spouts twisted lines from "Roll Over Beethoven" and "Good Rockin' Tonight". McCartney begins: "'The awful tension of being locked in each other's arms snapped last night at a TV rehearsal. Beatles, Paul, John, George and Harold . . . at the very least, a few vicious phrases took place.'" McCartney leaves out or twists lines that might offend the other Beatles, and is often drowned out by Lennon's voice. "He, the mystical one who lost so much of the Beatles' magic. She, the nudie." Though reading the article in an unimpressed tone, Paul can obviously sense that some of the lines ring all too true. "'Having scaled every known peak of show business, the Beatles never came home again. They went their own private ways, found their own friends, and became less reliant on each other for guidance and camaraderie. Today, all of them find acute embarrassment at the stories of one another's oddball adventures and conduct. Harrison's escapade with his favourite mystic from India . . .'"

The next sentence, in particular, captures Paul's attention, as he is to repeat it later in the session. "'Drugs, divorce and a slipping image played desperately on their minds and it appeared to them the public was being "encouraged" to hate them. But that still doesn't amount to a complete break-up of the group.'" John and Paul now compete to be the loudest. McCartney rushes to complete the article, stressing the last line. "'Whatever talent they had . . . and who can deny it, their capacity to earn is largely tied in to their performances as a group. They stay together, out of necessity. But I can't say never, as the friendly foursome are tied irrevocably to each other until it's all over. They will never be exactly the same again.'" John is still singing his improvised rhyme: "Hold my baby as tight as I can. Tonight she's gonna be a big fat man. Oh, baby, with your rhythm and blues."

Lennon attempts to lead the group back to serious rehearsal, by introducing another Lennon–McCartney original entitled "All I Want Is You", but this reference brings Paul back to "Too Bad About Sorrows" (one of the early songs from the 1950s). This ends in cacophony, with George eager to move on to something else.

Paul: I don't want peace, man. I want violence!
John: [singing] After forty years in the desert, he couldn't find his balls.
Mal: What time are you waiting until?
Ringo: What time is it?
Mal: Seven o'clock.
Ringo: That's time enough.
John: I know I'm a vulgar bugger!

Their current list of songs, as contained on their lyric sheets, is then read aloud by Paul:

All I Want Is You [Dig A Pony]
The Long And Winding Road
Bathroom Window [She Came In Through The Bathroom Window]
Let It Be
Across The Universe
Get Back (To Where You Once Belonged)
Two Of Us (On Our Way Home)
Maxwell's Silver Hammer
I've Got A Feeling
Sunrise [All Things Must Pass]
I Me Mine

Among the eleven compositions, seven belong primarily to Paul, with John and George having only two each. The title "Sunrise" catches both Harrison and Lennon by surprise. McCartney explains that it is, in fact, Harrison's "All Things Must Pass" (which wouldn't receive a serious rehearsal in any of the Apple session dates). John is relieved by the revelation: "You threw me there, I thought I was away a day you learned a fuckin' tune!"

By the spring of 1969 it was clear the Apple experiment was failing. The first casualty had come the previous year. Things had been heading downhill as management of the Apple Boutique changed hands: former theatrical director John Lyndon took over from Pete Shotton, but was soon replaced by Caleb, a tarot reader known only by his first name. He had been assisting decision-making at Apple through divination, but had tired of making record-chart predictions for the staff and left.

On Saturday, 27 July 1968, the Beatles ended their venture into the world of fashion by closing the Apple Boutique and handing control of Apple Tailoring to John Crittle. "Our course just isn't shopkeeping," George commented, with philosophic aplomb. "It's not really a mistake, the only mistake anyone ever made was getting born. All the rest is just life." The Fool soon realized their time was up and left for America to record an album with Graham Nash entitled *The Fool*, then pretty much disappeared from view.

Yoko Ono came up with the idea of giving the remaining stock of the boutique away free to the public and this was done, although not until after the Beatles and their hangers-on had taken what interested them. McCartney released a press statement with the help of Derek Taylor, which ran: "Our main business is entertainment, and communication. Apple is mainly concerned with fun not frocks . . . We had to zoom in on what we really enjoy, and we enjoy being alive, and we enjoy being Beatles." The great giveaway began on 30 July, and customers were casually informed everything was free. "It was fantastic," said Apple assistant Jeni Crowley. "Mothers with children rushed in and took anything they could lay their hands on. An old-age pensioner came in to buy a cushion. When we told him he could have it for nothing, he couldn't believe it. He kept touching his cap as he backed out of the shop. Later, the management tried to limit people to one gift each." The big send-off lasted until the next day, but the Beatles were still stuck with paying tax on the goods. Nevertheless, John was pleased with their final decision: "That was the best thing about the whole shop, when we gave it all away." McCartney commented, "We should never have tried to beat Marks & Spencer at the boutique business."

More promising was Apple Records, which the Beatles were hoping would attract the kind of blockbuster talent that would skyrocket their fledgling label. As it happened, supermodel Twiggy saw a television talent show in which a young Welsh folk-singer performed. She passed on the girl's name to Paul, who was equally impressed and signed her up. Four international hits later, including the 1968 smash "Those Were The Days", arranged in a scant ten minutes by Paul, the Welsh songbird Mary Hopkin was one of Apple's greatest discoveries.

Paul, she said, took a major hand in producing her work. "He sang a lot of the parts. He would say, 'I want the string parts to do this and the guitar to do this.' Then he actually played guitar, just bits and pieces. He took a great interest in it."

For her part, Hopkin sang backup on "Let It Be", and collaborated with Donovan. "It was a lovely experience sitting with Paul and Donovan on guitar," she remembers. "They sat on the side playing guitar and I just read straight from a book of Donovan's lyrics."

Of all the Beatles, Hopkin remembers Harrison most fondly. One day in the studio when the band was working on "Happiness Is A Warm Gun" Mal beckoned her to come out into the reception office. There, lying on the desk, was an exquisite Ramirez classical guitar. "It was a present from George," she said. "He'd just spent an hour hunting around town for a guitar for me and didn't say a word. It was the day of the première of [the film] *Yellow Submarine*, so when I saw him later that evening I thanked him. But he's always been a sweetheart."

James Taylor, too, had his start on the new label. Peter Asher took him on and produced his first album. Asher admits that although the record was over-arranged and produced, the project was successful in exposing the new age of the singer/songwriter. "Joni Mitchell, Ian Anderson and people like that," Asher has said, "who were just starting to makes waves in America but they were still pretty much folk-singers in a sea of rock 'n' roll. My intention was to get people to pay attention to James and realize how good he was."

Another artist to jump on board the Apple cart was R&B singer/composer Jackie Lomax. Harrison co-produced Lomax's release *Is This What You Want?* with most of the tracks laid down in Zsa Zsa Gabor's home in Beverly Hills. Ringo was on drums, Paul contributed bass and Eric Clapton played guitar on five songs. His breakout single, George's "Sour Milk Sea", was released unfortunately at the same time as "Hey Jude" and Hopkin's "Those Were The Days". "So mine didn't get much notice," said Lomax. "I did a song with Mal Evans called 'New Day Dawning'. It was added to the album later on a second release. I was quite proud of that. George came back from India and put some great guitar work on it. I even did a session with Paul as producer when George was away. He picked the Drifters' 'Thumbin' A Ride' for me. But it was never released."*

* In fact, Lomax's version was released later as the B side on 'How the Web Was Woven' on 6th February 1970.

Keyboardist and long-time friend of the Beatles Billy Preston also signed with Apple for two high-powered albums. "George did most of the co-producing with me. Originally it was supposed to have been all four Beatles producing a couple songs for me but that's when all the disturbances came up. So everybody kind of split up. But me and George hung in there."

The glory days at the pioneering label didn't last long. Apple was a conceptually novel idea, which suffered from an unrealistic ethic. It aimed to give young artists the scope to explore their creativity but also attracted endless untalented dream-seekers who helped to bleed it dry. As Alistair Taylor said, "Apple was never meant to save the world, despite popular myth. It was set up purely and simply as a tax-saving project."

McCartney, known for his often bossy ways, was one of the first to realize that Apple was veering away from the Beatles' original ideal of a kind of "western Communism", as John dubbed it. One of Paul's principal concerns was the pool of young songwriters they had working at Apple on spec. In 1969, he tried to inspire them, penning the following notice, which he pinned to the bulletin-board in Apple's reception area.

> Dear Songwriting Chums,
> We at Apple feel that songwriters need deadlines to work to, and sometimes produce their best work when they are writing with a definite aim in mind.
>
> So how does this grab you, music lovers?
>
> 1 Write Mary Hopkin's next single.
> 2 Write Billy Preston's first hit.
> 3 Write a Tom Jones golden classic.
> 4 Or, finally, just write a commercial, that is, a commercial song for a week from today.
>
> So there's your deadline, if you want it. If you don't, ignore this request, and swallow the letter.

Unfortunately no such hit songs were forthcoming under this particular scheme.

Considerably less successful than Apple Records was Apple Electronics, headed by Magic Alex who was paid forty pounds a week, plus 10 per cent of profits made on any of his inventions. "I'm a rock gardener, and now I'm doing electronics," said Alexis at the time. "Maybe next year I make films or poems. I have no formal training in any of these, but this is irrelevant."

"Magic Alex invented electric paint," Ringo remembered. "You paint your living room, plug it in, and the walls light up! We saw small pieces of metal as samples, but then we realized you'd have to put steel sheets on your living room wall and paint them."

"One invention he had was amazing," said George, "a small square of metal, like stainless steel, with two wires coming out of it to a flashlight battery. If you held the metal and connected the wires one way it would very quickly become so hot you had to drop it. If you reversed the wires it got as cold as ice."

He was given a rented garage in Boston Place in which to work, but though the Beatles often visited him, there was never much to see. "I'm trying to remember why we even bothered getting involved now," McCartney admitted. Much to their dismay, Alexis's workshop fell victim to a mysterious fire before any of his inventions could be properly presented, and thus he remained in their favour for the time being. When they wanted a new studio in the basement of their Savile Row offices, naturally Alexis was commissioned to pull it together. He took to spying on the experts, and visited George Martin at Abbey Road. There, he observed the techniques and technology being used, while denouncing it as profoundly out of date. "I found it very difficult to chuck him out," said George Martin, "because the boys liked him so much. Since it was very obvious I didn't, a minor schism developed."

When the Beatles finally left Twickenham Studios to begin recording *Let It Be* at Savile Row in 1969, they discovered the truth about Alexis's "state-of-the-art" recording studio. Harrison later termed it "the biggest disaster of all time". Alexis didn't know the first thing about putting together a studio, and it showed. "If you'd had a few Revoxes you'd have done better," said John Dunbar, on seeing the many pricy purchases Alexis had made at Apple's expense. "He'd charge them thousands of pounds and buy the stuff second-hand!" He had installed sixteen small speakers to mimic a sixteen-track studio, the room was without soundproofing, and the recording console was installed beside the building's central-heating unit, rendering any recordings useless because of its constant hum. To top it off, there were no ports connecting the studio to the control room, so it was impossible for sound emanating from the microphones to reach the mixing desk. Everything was dismantled and the Beatles asked George Martin to borrow a four-track mixing console from EMI. He was so annoyed that they hadn't listened to him and had fallen for Alexis's promises that he left much of the day-to-day work to engineer Glyn Johns.

The failed studio, however, opened the Beatles' eyes to Alexis's failings, and he soon made himself scarce, although he hung on until Allen Klein closed Apple Electronics. How had he become so close to the Beatles? Perhaps his perplexing comment relating to his choice of career most accurately describes the enigma of his involvement with the Beatles' empire: "Man is just a small glass, very, very clear, with many faces, like a diamond. You just have to find the way, the small door to each face."

With Apple now losing money at the rate of some £20,000 a week, the company was in such disarray that soon there was not even enough money to pay the taxman. Businessman Allen Klein, who'd managed the Rolling Stones' finances, was brought on board on 8 May 1969 to save the company. The New York mogul wasted no time in making wholesale firings, including Peter Asher, A & R director, and Ron Kass, head of Apple Records, the one division to show a profit. Only Peter Brown and Neil Aspinall escaped the axe. It was no secret that Paul McCartney detested the brash, working-class Klein, and campaigned instead for Linda's lawyer father, the refined and elegant Lee Eastman, to run their multimillion-dollar empire. John, however, trusted Klein: "He's one of the lads, whereas Eastman and all them other people are automatons," he quipped.

"Apple started to get pretty weird," said Peter Asher. "It was crumbling and there was a lot of dissension among the Beatles. Allen Klein came in and was changing the character of Apple, John was all for him and Paul was against him. It became clear Apple was on its last legs."

"It wasn't me who wanted to do Apple," George has recalled. "Paul decided to do Apple and was aided and abetted by John . . . Of course, it was a good idea, but it wasn't subtle enough. Shouting to everybody about what you're going to do before you even know what you're doing yourself."

On the heels of Paul's breakup with Jane Asher, then Francie Schwartz, Linda Eastman was on the scene, but the ever-secretive Paul kept her tightly under wraps away from his family until well into 1969. One day when Jim called Cavendish Avenue an unfamiliar female voice answered. Then Paul was on the line. "Oh, that's Linda," Paul said, obviously not wanting to discuss her. Soon afterwards a reporter telephoned Rembrandt, informed the McCartneys that Paul had posted banns at London's Marylebone register office, and requested confirmation of the coming wedding. Shocked, Jim telephoned his son. Afterwards he told his wife, "Paul's getting married tomorrow. He meant to tell me but he said he was too busy." Brother Mike was hastily pressed into best-man duty and had to race from a Scaffold performance in Birmingham to London. Apart from Mike, the ubiquitous Mal Evans and Peter Brown no other family or friends attended the ten-minute ceremony on 12 March.

A few days later Paul telephoned his father to say that he and Linda, with his bride's seven-year-old daughter Heather, were coming to visit. Heather blew in like a tornado: "Hang up my coat! I'm the boss of the dogs," she told Ruth, in New York cabbie dialect.

Once Linda was ensconced in the family she insisted that Rembrandt must be redecorated. She hired a regiment of top designers and painters from London and put them up in a local hotel for the three months it took to complete the job. The new Mrs McCartney ripped out the elegant carpeting and curtains and installed a loud green and red plaid. The wallpaper would be replaced with the finest silk: "I want all the walls covered with the colours of Delsey Tissue." Since the company was unknown in Britain, Linda ordered a box from

America. Still, the pinks weren't quite pink enough, the blue too blue, so it had to be done over and over again. Linda was meticulous and demanding. By the time it was finished, "It looked like a padded cell," Ruth joked. Angela was pressed into service to buy a special split mattress for Paul and Linda, which allowed each side to move independently. The newlyweds installed an antique bed they'd bought from a second-hand shop, which was heavily infested with woodworm. When Angela tactfully suggested treating the bed, a shocked Linda protested, "Ange, don't fuss, they've got a right to live too!"

One room Linda didn't touch was Paul's. It was kept almost as a shrine. Surprisingly, the furnishings were quite Spartan, except for McCartney's prized Hofner bass. There was also a blinking road-construction lamp. "He ripped off one of those hazard lights from the motorway," Ruth laughed. "They dumped it in the back of the Rolls and put a coat over it as it wouldn't stop blinking. You could see the bloody thing flashing through the curtains. Dad used to have a fit."

As Angela observed in 1994, "Linda was everything to him: photographer, business partner, trusted friend, mother of his children and psychological nursemaid . . . Paul seemed to need someone to hide behind. First it was John, then Linda. This could be why he insisted on Linda becoming part of Wings against all the odds."

One of Linda's quirks was noticed at a McCartney family party. She always had a drink in her hand, but didn't touch it. "Oh, I'm tipsy," she would gush. "Oh, God, I'm so drunk!" Angela spotted her pouring a drink into a potted plant. "Presumably," she reflected, "that was to assist people to let their guard down and not be aware she was watching them."

On another occasion Linda, Paul, Jim and Angela were going out for a drive. Paul got into the driver's seat and Jim went to the passenger side to get in next to his son. "Hey, outta there!" Linda bellowed. "Get in the back!"

Shocked, Jim protested, "But I always sit in the front when Ange is driving."

"Well, you don't sit in the front with Paul! Get in the back," Linda repeated sternly. "I'm sitting with my husband."

"Look, Dad, what you don't understand is, that's all well and good in England but in America it doesn't work that way," Paul explained. "Linda's my woman and she wants to sit up front with me. You just get in the back."

McCartney often displayed his generous and charming side to his family. One day, not long after his wedding, he took Linda, Ruth and Angela in his Rolls for a sightseeing tour of Liverpool. He pointed out the site of the Casbah, the Liverpool Art Institute, the Beatles' boyhood homes and the Anglican Cathedral. There, he introduced himself to the archdeacon and they climbed the tower for a breathtaking view of the city. Finally, they stopped at 10 Mathew Street, the famed Cavern Club. At three o'clock in the afternoon the place was deserted, except for the cleaning women. "Hi, I'm Paul," he said, as the employees marvelled in awe and delight. "This is Linda, she's an American. Do you mind if I show her around?" Paul sat his wife and stepmother and -sister on some wooden chairs in front of the famous stage. "Ladies, the show's about to begin." He bowed and took the stage. "He did this charming song-and-dance routine," said Ruth. "Then he said, 'For my next trick,' and sat down at the drum kit to play a cracking drum solo. He moved on to an upright piano in the corner and sang a little song for Linda. It was like this amazing private concert. It was great!"

For George and Patti Harrison, life in serene Esher was good. They had many close friends, exciting careers and, of course, each other. Patti's sisters often came to stay for weeks at a time, and kept her company when George was recording. Later, they had a small boutique in Kensington Market, called Juniper in honour of Donovan's "Jennifer Juniper". When George was at home, he took an active interest in the garden. He and Klaus Voormann even painted a swirling psychedelic mural on an outside wall of the house, as well as one of his many cars.

Some days, when there were no pressing engagements, George would take his antique ivory pillbox and pick out a small pastel-coloured tab of LSD and quietly trip out. Wandering through nearby Claremont Park, he would sink into a dreamy haze of warm sunshine and good vibrations. Other times he and Patti would stay in and, after a hearty home-cooked meal, quietly pass the time with friends, smoking strong black Moroccan hash or drinking vintage wine. As a hippie George Harrison maintained exacting standards.

The beginning of the end of the Harrisons' Esher period came early in the evening of 12 March 1969, when Patti answered a knock at the door and found half a dozen policemen outside.

"Drugs Squad, madam," announced DS Pilcher. "We have a warrant." Immediately several constables and a couple of drug-sniffing dogs began their search of the long, low house.

"I think perhaps I should ring my husband," said Patti calmly. She darted into a nook between the sitting room and the study, then dialled the Beatles' secret number at Apple. George spoke to his wife, hung up and told Apple fixer Peter Brown what was happening. Brown rang Martin Polden, one of London's top lawyers.

Meanwhile, George telephoned Pete Shotton, who lived nearby, and asked him to go over and stay with Patti until he could get there. Prior to that the charming Mrs Harrison tried her best to entertain the police by playing them Beatles records and even serving tea.

When Harrison arrived some time later with Derek Taylor, he found at least ten police cars and a Black Maria outside the house. "Everything was in uproar," Shotton remembers. "The coppers had tipped over virtually all the furniture and were tearing through the cupboards when George suddenly burst in."

Everything came to an immediate halt. "Just what are all these men in silly felt hats doing in my fuckin' home anyway, giving all my friends bad vibes?" shouted George.

"Mr and Mrs Harrison," began Pilcher, "I am charging you with the illegal possession of cannabis resin. I'm afraid I must ask you both to come down to the station for questioning."

Harrison inquired if they had actually found any or if they had supplied their own. "And you needn't have turned the whole bloody place upside down either! All you had to do was ask me and I would have shown you where I keep everything."

They were taken to the cars, the police so close to George and Patti that they could hardly walk. "I'm not gonna run!" cried George.

"Give us a little room, will you?" Before anyone knew what was happening, a photographer jumped out of a nearby hedge and popped off a series of flashbulbs in George's face. Harrison dropped to the ground then bounced up and charged the cameraman with the London Drug Squad hot on his heels. "I'm gonna fuckin' kill you, you bastard!" he bellowed. The photographer dropped his Nikon and never stopped running. George stomped on it, wrecking it, before the police restrained him.

At the Esher police station George and Patti were charged and subsequently released on bail. The couple were then driven home and got changed for a party, given by London artist Rory McEwen at his studio in Chelsea. They arrived fashionably late and were greeted by their host, who steered them in the direction of his other celebrated guests, Princess Margaret and her husband Lord Snowdon. "Guess what?" said George sheepishly. "We've been busted. Sergeant Pilcher and his goons planted a big block of hash in my bedroom."

"How terrible," said the Princess sympathetically, herself a seasoned secret pot smoker.

"Do you think you might possibly be able to get the charges dropped?" asked George.

"I don't think so. It could become a little sticky. Sorry, George."

As if all this wasn't awkward enough for the Princess, Patti's youngest sister, Paula, strolled up and offered Her Royal Highness a joint. Shortly thereafter the Princess left.

Nineteen days later, at Esher and Walton magistrates' court, the Harrisons pleaded guilty to unlawful possession of cannabis resin. The prosecutor, Michael West, said the couple "had been of impeccable character hitherto". He also told the magistrates: "It is infrequent to find quite as much of the drug as one found in this case. There is something like 570 grains, which would result, when used, in a large number of cigarettes. It would be wrong to draw the inference, however, that there was any intention to sell it. It is quite clear on the evidence this was purely for personal consumption only and no more than a private supply."

Polden pointed out that Patti had allowed the police to search everywhere they wanted without obstruction and made no attempt to hide the box on the living-room table that contained the drug. He also said that the other powders, crystals and joss sticks in which the police had taken an interest were harmless and associated with the Harrisons' well-known interest in yoga. Of the drugs found in the Harrisons' wardrobe, Polden said: "The couple cannot explain this find. They know nothing about it to this day. The large amount of cannabis found, however, does not indicate theirs is a household of corruption or debauchery. There is certainly no question of addiction."

The magistrates fined the Harrisons each £250 plus costs. They were allowed to keep an ornamental Native American pipe that had been confiscated in the raid. As he left the court, George told the reporters outside, "We hope the police will now leave the Beatles alone."

Shortly afterwards, the couple began the laborious task of house-hunting. Amazingly, George offered to give Kinfauns to Pete Shotton, who turned it down.

Alistair Taylor told of an amusing episode in the Harrisons' quest for a new home. One day Patti asked him to play the part of her husband on an all-day country outing in search of a suitable property. Inside the limousine, she introduced him to James, their uniformed chauffeur for the afternoon.

"Where to, old boy?" the driver asked, turning to Taylor.

"Good Lord, George, it's you!" Alistair cried.

"Everyone's out to screw the Beatles, so we decided to let you be the buyer this afternoon," replied George.

The Harrisons' attempt at anonymity, however, was short-lived. At one of their final stops, an impressive Georgian mansion just outside London, the agent inquired if "Mr Harrison out in the car" might want to look round it as well. All George and Patti could do was laugh.

Shortly after that George found the house he came to love dearly, and remained his home for the rest of his life: Friar Park on Paradise Road at the upper edge of Henley-on-Thames, Oxfordshire. His friend Shyamasundara Dasa remembers it as sorely neglected just after the Harrisons moved in during 1970. "In those early months at Friar Park, we all crashed out in sleeping-bags. There were a hundred rooms, no heat, no furniture. On those early mornings when George returned from all-night sessions, we piled into the kitchen, the only warm room in the house, he and his rock'n'roll sidemen alive with some new tune hatched that night. "Hey, what do you think of this one, Shyamasundara? We call it 'My Sweet Lord' – Hare Krishna!"

John and Yoko were married in Gibraltar on 20 March 1969 in a quiet civil ceremony, attended only by Peter Brown, who acted as best man. Their honeymoon was spent first in Paris then Amsterdam where, like many newlyweds, they went straight to bed. Except John and Yoko invited the entire world to attend by holding a nearly week-long peace protest starting on 25 March.

They held a second Bed In for Peace in Room 1742 at the Queen Elizabeth Hotel in Montréal. From 26 May to 2 June 1969 they met with the media, advertising world peace. It was a surprisingly effective stunt, in a world torn apart by the war in Vietnam. Among the many celebrity guests who dropped in were Tommy Smothers, Timothy and Rosemary Leary, and *Li'l Abner* cartoonist Al Capp, an irascible old character with only one leg. From the moment John and he met, sparks flew.

Lennon was never one to back away from anything and handled Capp with aplomb.

"So far you've been confronted mainly with admirers, and I may wind up one," said Capp on arrival.

"We have had all sorts here, believe me," John replied pleasantly.

"One of the things which interested me was the message you have chosen to inspire peace," said Al.

Lennon charged in: "We're trying to sell it like soap. The only way to do it is to focus attention on peace and sell it every day."

The cartoonist then asked if it was more conducive to success for the couple to stay in bed rather than sit on chairs. John replied that as they were speaking to the media pretty much non-stop it was "functional" to be lying down.

"Being in bed is one thing, but you could go further – you could shower together!" Capp offered.

"We just did!" John countered.

From there things went rapidly downhill:

Capp: What about during World War Two. If Hitler and Churchill had gotten into bed, which Hitler would have clearly enjoyed, do you . . .

John: I think that if Churchill and Hitler had got into bed, a lot of people would have been alive today!

Capp: I see. It's a way of doing it. Now, suppose Montgomery had gone to bed with Rommel . . .

John: Beautiful!

Capp: Do you like that, John? Do you feel that this continent is the one place to preach peace or will you preach equally in Peking?

John: Sure. We're going to find out. I believe it's easier to get into Moscow than it is to get into the States, for a kick-off.

Capp: But, don't you feel that they need you now in Peking and Hanoi?

John: If we're needed at all, we're needed everywhere, but you can't be everywhere at once.

Capp: But, I do hope that you plan to make them as peaceful as you've made these blood-crazed Canadians.

John: The best thing we've done so far is talk to the people at Berkeley* and we think we had some influence in holding back the violence that was going to come out of that. And we believe that, and we talk to them solid every hour.

Capp: You haven't talked to them during this last week!

John: Ah! We talk to them everyday. We talk on the phone, on the radio station live . . .

Capp: I saw them throwing rocks at cops just a couple of days ago. You'd better talk to them a little more.

John: Well, no one got shot this time, did they?

Capp: No, nobody got shot . . .

John: And what are you doing about it?

Capp: What am I doing about it? I'm cheering the police. That's precisely what I'm doing about it.

Yoko: Why? Why?

Capp: Now, now, you people have a home in London. Are you

* A reference to student rioters at the university.

permitting people to come in and defecate on the rugs, smash the furniture? No. Then why do you want them to do it at Berkeley?

John: We don't want them to do it at Berkeley. We tell them to protest some other way. If they had stayed in bed at Berkeley, they wouldn't have got killed!

Capp: Now, simmer down, simmer down, just rest.

Yoko: Can't we have a conversation instead of, you know . . .

Capp: I'll be delighted with any conversation.

Yoko: Okay.

Capp: Good God, you're an unbelievable couple. [Laughter fills the room]

John: Nice try.

Capp: I can see why you want peace. God knows you can't have much from my own observations. But, anyway . . . From my point of view, I am sorry for you. Now, I read something that said you were actually very shy people.

Yoko: Yes, we are.

Capp: And yet . . . [showing John and Yoko's naked *Two Virgins* album cover]

John: Does that prove that you're not shy?

Capp: Certainly not. Only the shyest people in the world would take pictures like that.

John: Do shy people ever become naked or not?

Capp: If that is a picture of two shy people, I'd like to know what shyness is.

Yoko: May I ask you. Would you consider yourself shy?

Capp: Oh, I'm just normal. I think that everybody owes it to the world to prove they've got pubic hair. And you've got it, and I applaud you for it. [More laughter]

Yoko: If you want to prove it, you can prove it.

Capp: I don't feel there's any great deal of interest in it. Clearly, you must have felt that the world wanted to know what your private parts looked like and now the world knows. Now, you wrote a song, and one of the lines, and correct me if it's wrong, says, "Christ, it ain't easy" . . .

John: Rubbish! I didn't say that. The lyrics go, "Christ, you know it ain't easy, you know how hard it can be, the way things are going, they're going to crucify me," and you, baby.

Capp: But in the lyric, you said they're going to crucify you.

John: Yeah, you can take it literally.

Capp: So, how did you mean it?

John: It means everything you want it to mean.

Capp: What did you want it to mean?

John: They're going to crucify me and you and everyone else.

Capp: I'm upset that they're going to crucify me. Who's going to make the time to crucify you?

John: Everyone!

Capp: But, you said, "They're gonna crucify me."

John: Oh, if you're going to take everything literally.

Yoko: Me is you.

Capp: I don't permit you to speak for me. Who are you speaking for?

John: I took that liberty, Mr Capp.

Capp: There's too much of a liberty.

John: I'm speaking on behalf of people in general, you know.

Capp: You're speaking for yourselves.

John: I'm sorry that it upsets you.

Capp: It doesn't upset me.

John: I can choose to sing about whatever I want in whatever fashion I wish.

Capp: Yes, but you mustn't include me. Now, you're not my spokesman, are we agreed?

John: I'm everyone's spokesman.

Capp: You're not mine.

John: You're mine and I'm yours.

Capp: I don't say, "I'm speaking for John Lennon."

John: As a representative for the human race, I'm speaking for us all, whether you like it or not.

Capp: Whatever race you're the representative of, I ain't a part of it.

John: What do you write your cartoons for?

Capp: I write my cartoons for money, just as you sing your songs. Exactly the same reason, and exactly the same reason much of this is happening too, if the truth be told.

John: Do you think I couldn't earn money by some other way than sitting in bed for seven days, taking shit from people like you. I could write a song in an hour . . .

Capp: Now, now, look here. You got into bed so people like me can come and see you.

John: Right, but not for money, like what you're saying.

Capp: Er . . . it won't do any real harm, except it might give you bed sores. I'll tell you what'll do you harm . . .

John: I can earn money by easier ways than doing this.

Capp: So can I. I can make a lot more drawing people like you than confronting you, and I must say it's more appetizing drawing them, 'cause I can leave. What you've just done now is, when you said, "Taking shit from people like you," now, I was invited here. You knew I was coming . . .

John: So, we're not doing it for money. You indicated I was doing it for money. Do you have manners?

Capp: I'm your guest.

John: And I'm yours.

Capp: No, I'm not. This is your bedroom.

Capp [to Yoko]: I'm delighted to have met you, Madam Nu. You are our answer to Madame Nu. But, I'm sure the other three guys, the other three, are gentlemen.

John: What does that mean?

Capp: Think about it!

Derek Taylor: Get out!

John: I'll try and work it out now, Derek.

Capp: Oh, really, come on.

Derek Taylor: I'm not having these people spoken to like that.

John: We asked him here.

Derek Taylor: Forgive me.

Capp: Derek, it's not for me to forgive you. It's for your psychiatrist.

John: And yours, baby. You've just done a great deal for peace, Mr Capp.

Capp stormed out of the room and John sank down in the bed, scratching his beard and saying to no one in particular, "What a fucking asshole!" So much for the meeting of two great minds from the pop-culture arena of the late 1960s.

Despite his well-known public persona as a wisecracking, freaked-out peace politician, John often used his status and sexual charisma as weapons to express anger and resentment against those he identified as having hurt him. For example, as I revealed in my book *Lennon in America*, John had a meaningless fling with Linda McCartney. As the late Harry Nilsson once confided to me during a telephone conversation in May 1986, "It wasn't Linda John wanted to fuck, it was Paul!" He sought a perverse empowerment by adding friends' and colleagues' spouses to his long list of sexual conquests, including Mal Evans's wife Lil, and even Maureen Starkey in 1967, on a lonely beach in Greece, while the Beatles were together on holiday.

John's indiscretions were potentially catastrophic to the Beatles' delicate infrastructure. Although it is uncertain how many others ever knew about the liaisons, several people close to him did, including Harry Nilsson, Derek Taylor, Mal Evans and latter-day Lennon aid in New York, George Speerin.

According to Speerin, Lennon revealed details of two encounters with Linda. "John told me not to tell," Speerin ventured to this author, "but he told so many people it didn't seem to me as if confidentiality were really too much of an issue. Actually, he seemed rather proud he'd gotten one over on Paul by screwing his old lady." Asked why John would ever risk so much for a quick lay when he was still basking in the glow of his marriage to Yoko Ono, Speerin replied, "John told me many times he regretted marrying Yoko within just days of their marriage." Suddenly, he said, in John's mind the charming, coolly artistic geisha was gone and in her place stood a bossy, take-no-prisoners, aspiring pop diva. Lennon felt trapped. He'd burned his bridges with Cynthia and Julian, and also strained his partnership with the other Beatles through his relationship with Yoko. His public image had plummeted. "He told me Linda was always after him and even admitted it was him she fancied in the beginning, not McCartney. The first time apparently was at Paul's house by Abbey Road," Speerin confided. "The second was in the back of his white Rolls around the corner from EMI Studios in late 1969 during sessions for *Abbey Road*. The car apparently had a bed in the back, black windows and very good locks." Speerin chuckled. "John told me that one evening as he was watching TV Linda wordlessly slipped into the backseat and gave him head before Paul even knew she had left the studio. Yoko, John told me, was at home in bed with the flu."

How reliable a witness is Speerin? Well, it is true Lennon sometimes sat in his car between McCartney's long, laborious, musical overdubs. His chauffeur Anthony would park at a discreet distance from the studio to avoid the hordes of silly young girls who would inevitably appear whenever a real live Beatle was sighted. "John used to tell me that while he liked Linda well enough for her up-front American personality he was never really interested in her, despite her constant come-ons. He once told me he thought Linda was a nymphomaniac and that he'd heard from people around town she once allowed herself to be gangbanged while travelling on the road as a photographer with Cream in 1967." We should remember, of course, that this was the Swinging Sixties and attitudes towards sex were far more liberal than today.

One June Sunday afternoon in 1969 an avid Beatles clique of half a dozen or so Apple Scruffs went to McCartney's home and found it empty. It wouldn't do any harm to check out the garden, they agreed. One girl scaled a wall and opened the gate for the others.

Finding little of interest in the grounds, they discovered a ladder and spotted an open window. Throwing caution to the wind, the most petite of their group, Little Diane, climbed up. As she reached the window, the ladder fell away, leaving her clinging to the sill with no choice but to haul herself up and tumble into the house. She ended up in Paul McCartney's bathroom.

The others followed, and they roamed round the house, collecting mementoes – dress shirts, the trousers Paul had worn in India, even soiled underwear. In addition, they took several boxes of slides, snapshots and a prized framed photo of Paul and his father.

The following day, McCartney hauled in the suspects, telling them of the break-in. "I think it was one of the girls," he said, "because mostly photos were taken." He told them the slides were needed for the coming *Let It Be* film. "There was also a picture of great sentimental value to me," he added. "It was in a gold frame. The picture was of my dad."

The girls, however, weren't ready to plead guilty. Then Paul confessed that he couldn't fathom how they had got in. When the ladder was pointed out to him, he declared, "Girls can't climb ladders!" Finally, however, he conceded it was the only logical explanation. Eventually one of the Scruffs returned the items, although several of Linda's photos were not among them. When Linda pointed this out, McCartney said, "I don't care about those."

Before the culprit left he managed a wry grin. "By the way, I've written a song about the girls who broke in. It's called 'She Came In Through The Bathroom Window'."

The Beatles trudged back to the studio in July 1969 to wind up their final album, *Abbey Road*. Although they set aside their acrimony long enough to complete it, the tension between them was at an all-time high.

One evening John, George and Ringo were gathered at the studios for an important all-night session. Paul did not appear. Three hours later John was seen pacing outside, looking in the direction of McCartney's home. Suddenly George came out to tell him that Paul was on the phone.

Minutes later John burst out of the studios and raced down the street towards 7 Cavendish Avenue. He flew over the gate and pounded on the front door. As Paul opened it, John shoved him aside and marched into the house. "What the hell do you think you're doing," yelled Paul, "bursting in on Linda and me? I told you on the phone I was having a special dinner with Linda. I told you I wasn't coming in tonight!"

"You just decided to fuckin' blow us off!" roared John. "You knew long before today we had this session! You never had any intention of coming in. We all came in from the country to do some tracks but you didn't even think to pick up the phone and save us a wasted trip! Not to mention the money down the fucking drain for the studio. You've got a bloody nerve, man. Listen," he blazed, "I don't cancel fucking bookings for anniversaries with Yoko! Who do you fuckin' think you are to inconvenience us all this way?"

In his rage he spotted a painting he'd done for Paul hanging on the wall. He yanked it down and stuck his foot through it, then stormed out with a barrage of expletives.

A week later the four Beatles assembled in Lennon's ground-floor office at Apple for a late-afternoon business meeting. The air was filled with hostility. Finally, Linda, who was pregnant and still outraged over the episode at the house, laid into John about his boorish behaviour. In retaliation, he leaped to his feet and charged towards her, fist raised. Paul jumped between them and physically restrained John. Ringo, appalled, stood mutely to one side, and George, who was embarrassed and wanted no part in the skirmish, moved to the opposite end of the room. Paul grabbed Linda and they made a swift exit, followed by George and Ringo. It was some four hours later before Lennon, still visibly upset, was seen leaving the building.

One of the things that had been taken away from John when he became a Beatle was the pure joy of performing as a musician whenever he felt the urge with whomever he wished to play. On Friday 12 September 1969, he was in his office at Apple when he received a phone call from Canada inviting him to play solo at the Toronto Rock 'n' Roll Revival. Fortunately for the promoters, he was in just the right state of mind to agree. He summoned Mal Evans into his office to get the ball rolling. Evans remembered, "I overheard John saying he'd been asked to appear at a rock 'n' roll show in Toronto. I paused only to grab a handful of leads and a couple dozen plectrums. Then John mentioned he hadn't got anyone to play with . . . It didn't take long to get hold of Klaus Voormann and Alan White, Alan Price's ex-drummer. They both immediately agreed. John particularly wanted Eric Clapton to make up the foursome, but we couldn't get hold of him at home, or at any of the clubs. We telephoned until 5.30 a.m. the next day. Our plane was due to take off at 10 a.m., and by 9.15 a.m., most of us had arrived at the airport. Then John turned up with Yoko and told us it was off because they had not been able to reach Eric." Shortly thereafter we learned Eric had finally surfaced and would be able to make it. He'd been in bed at his house, Hurtwood Edge, in Ewhurst, Surrey, recovering from a night of non-stop partying and hadn't heard the phone. Just before he gave up his all night search, Terry Doran, George's personal assistant, sent a telegram to Eric's house. It had been opened by Clapton's gardener, who woke him to tell him about the concert."

Mal continued: "As Eric couldn't make the airport, we cancelled our flight and rebooked on the 3.15 p.m. from Heathrow. Everyone arrived for the flight. Everyone being the Lennons, Eric, Klaus, Alan White, Anthony [Fawcett], John and Yoko's assistant, and Jill and Dan Richer, who have been putting all of John and Yoko's recent activities on film. That's when it hit me: none of these people had ever played together before! John obviously thought about it too because he and Eric walked down the aisle to the back of the plane after a quick snack to have their first rehearsal. John, Yoko, Eric, Klaus and Alan had to work out the songs they were going to perform and also run through them together. A big bundle of sheet music had been delivered to London airport that morning, and they played through dozens of numbers, pointing out the ones they knew pretty well. They eventually managed to settle on eight, which would probably be okay, provided they got a bit more time to rehearse before they actually went on stage."

The Toronto Rock 'n' Roll Revival took place at Varsity Stadium and the stage was a twelve-foot dais in the middle of the football pitch, facing half of the arena where the audience sat. The 27,000 strong crowd was thrilled they were about to see John Lennon. Still, he and the rest of the band had other things to worry about. They gathered together backstage, plugged their guitars into one small amp, and started running through the numbers they were going to perform. "Actually, John wasn't feeling well," said Mal, "but he was determined to put on a good show. Allen Klein, who had also flown over, arranged for the performance to be filmed. Finally, at midnight, Kim Fowley went on stage to announce the Plastic Ono Band. He had all the lights in the stadium turned down and asked everybody to strike a match . . . Then John, Eric, Klaus and Alan went on stage, and lined up just like the old Beatles set-up.

"Yoko had been inside a bag howling away all through John's numbers. She sang two numbers, 'Don't Worry Kyoko' and 'Oh John (Let's Hope For Peace)'. At the end of 'Oh John', all the boys stood their guitars, still turned on, against the speakers on the amps and walked backstage. While the feedback started to build, John, Eric, Klaus and Alan stood back and lit cigarettes. Then, I went on and led them off stage.

By late 1969, John Lennon was heavily addicted to heroin and thus spent a lot of time at home in bed. At the time, thanks to George, several Hare Krishnas were in residence helping to renovate and run Tittenhurst, the house Lennon bought in May 1969. One tells the story of an intriguing offer made to John by the Doors' unpredictable frontman, Jim Morrison. John wasn't particularly a fan of the Doors' hypnotic music and once referred to Morrison as "dopey" in an interview. He therefore reacted with some surprise when a rambling letter from the singer was dropped onto his bed by his assistant Anthony Fawcett. "What the fuck does he want?" John wondered, as he ripped open the envelope, which bore Morrison's address and the elegant Elektra Records logo. "I've never even listened to one of his fucking records all the way through," he snarled. He began to read the contents aloud to Yoko. Just inside the room, stripping white paint from the fine oak moulding, the young Krishna kid was within earshot and was summoned by Lennon to come and hear Morrison's rambling missive.

Jim had in mind the formation of a super-group consisting of the Beatles and the Doors for some recording and even a series of concerts. Interestingly, this was an idea that had already occurred to John, but with different personnel. Some time later he articulated a similar concept to Eric Clapton: perhaps a huge ocean liner could be turned into a floating apartment complex, recording studio and arena for a series of worldwide performances with an ever-changing assortment of artists, including various Beatles, Clapton, Klaus Voormann and Billy Preston – John's preferred sidemen. Of course, such ideas were in no short supply at this time, but ultimately came to nothing. However, John's typed letter to Clapton concerning the venture survives. An excerpt reads:

> How about a kind of *Easy Rider* at sea? We'd take eight-track recording equipment with us (mine probably) and movie equipment. We'd rehearse on the way over, record if we want, play anywhere we fancied. Say we film from LA to Tahiti, we stop there if we want, maybe have the film developed there, stay a week or as long as we want, collect the film (of course). We'll probably film wherever we stop (if *we* want) and edit it on board, etc. Having just finished a movie we made around our albums *Imagine* & *Fly* – it's a beautiful *surreal* film (*very surreal, all music*, only about *two words* spoken in the whole thing!). We know we are ready to make a major movie. Anyway, it's just a thought, we'd always stay as near to land as possible and, of course, we'd take doctors, etc., in case of any kind of bother. We'd always be able to get to a place where someone could fly off if they'd had enough. The whold [*sic*] trip could take 3–4–5–6 months, depending how we all felt (all families, children whatever are welcome, etc.). Please don't think you *have to* go along with the boat trip to be in the band. I just wanted to let you know everything we've been talking about. (I thought we'd *really* be *ready* to hit the road after such a *healthy restful rehearsal*.)

Morrison, however, was suggesting that John and he get together to do some writing and even expressed an interest in working with Yoko in the production of her avant-garde material. But Lennon had little interest in Morrison as a performer, and even less in working with him. The letter was tossed to the floor where it lay for several days until it was picked up by the cleaners and thrown in the bin.

Although George Harrison, the quiet, deep-thinking Beatle, was hardly the principal Beatles heart-throb, he was lusted after by a corps of Abbey Road groupies, determined to add him to their list of superstar conquests. This made for many intense rivalries, spearheaded by a fiery Puerto Rican replica of Patti named Alfie. The sultry, aggressive beauty seduced George one night with a bottle of champagne. But it was the founder of the Apple Scruffs, Carol Bedford, a tall, leggy brunette from Texas, who caught George's eye and briefly, in 1969, his heart. For several months he engaged the Texan in long conversations – at the studio, at Apple headquarters, even in his car – about eastern philosophy. Mal Evans acted as go-between, passing notes and messages to Carol about when and where she should meet up with George.

At the annual Apple Christmas party, George pulled Carol into a cubicle off the dance-floor. "He smiled, putting his face close to mine," recalled Bedford. "His right hand stroked my left breast, and hesitated on the nipple. 'I'll always be with you,' he breathed. 'We're part of each other. I wrote a song about us the other day. It goes like this: "I, I, I love you; You, You, You love me. We're together always. We're in each other."'"

On another occasion he arrived unannounced at her Abbey Road flat. He went in and wrapped his arms around her, then Carol took his hand and they made their way to her tiny bedroom. "He looked very shy," she remembered. "I thought he just wanted to hug me as he had when he arrived. But he kissed me. Needless to say, I happily responded."

Not long afterwards, Carol received a visit from Evans who came with a proposal. George, he said, wanted to arrange for her to live in Los Angeles where he would rent an apartment for her. She pressed him for details. "He can't take you out places here," Mal pointed out. "He'd like to take you out to restaurants and places but he's married." He explained that George was waiting for the right time to seek a divorce and until then could not be seen with other women.

Carol, however, had no desire to be a kept woman. "I'm no one's mistress," she told Evans brusquely. "Not even George's."

This was great news to Mal: he swept her on to his lap and began to kiss her. She would have none of it, and ordered him out of her flat. Soon afterwards, she put her Beatles days behind her and went on to become a successful record-company executive.

One long-lasting liaison that developed while the Apple empire crumbled was between Harrison and the devotees of the Hare Krishna movement. They were determined to make contact with the Beatles, hoping they would be attracted to the philosophy and help to spread the word, and a small band came to Britain with this aim. It was a million to one chance, but it worked. The group's leader, Shyamasundara Dasa, forged a friendly relationship with George, who introduced his friends to the group. Some months later, he recorded an album of vedic chants with them.

As time went by, Harrison became increasingly involved with "Krishna consciousness", and was anxious to help the group in any way he could. One of the first European converts to the religion, Dhananjaya Dasa, remembered, "Shyamasundara was very anxious to see our temple at Bury Place turned into a proper temple. The building soon became a construction site, so he mentioned to George it was very difficult for us to live there with so much dust and noise, as they were putting up reinforced metal beams [paid for by Mick Jagger] and a lot of work had to be done there. Shyamasundara asked George if he could help us in any way and he said, 'I will speak to John because he has just acquired a big property and might be able to put you up.'

"At that time, Harrison was living in Esher, he didn't have a big house, and he knew John's house was huge. George hadn't yet moved into Friar Park, and I am sure he would have invited us to stay with him, it was just due to the circumstances. John agreed, he thought it was a really good idea. In fact, he was incredibly favourable. He offered us five acres of land, and the estate had seventy-six acres. He wasn't into farming or anything. Prabhupada [the group's founder and master] said we should utilize this land to grow fresh vegetables and fruit.

"In the beginning, John was much more interested than Yoko. In fact, one evening John and Yoko invited Prabhupada over to hear a song Lennon had just recorded. This was just after John's twenty-ninth birthday. He wrote a song called 'Cold Turkey'. The significance of that piece was about Lennon's withdrawal from heroin. While we were living there, John was constantly shooting up heroin.

"I had to clean up an office one time, and when I moved a filing cabinet I came across all of these used hypodermic needles. There were also some very unsavoury characters living there. There was someone called Alexander Troki. He was a Scotsman who moved to New York and had written a book about his visions on heroin. Also William Burroughs, who had written *The Soft Machine*, was invited. So the Lennons were into the drug culture looking for an identity or something.

"They also made another record called, 'John And Yoko Forever' [possibly later retitled 'The Ballad Of John And Yoko'] because Yoko's whole consciousness was fixed that somehow or other she wanted to live with John Lennon for eternity. When she asked Prabhupada this question, he said, 'Of course this is impossible. At the moment of death you are immediately separated.' At that instant she lost all interest.

"That night was like a private party. It was Prabhupada, his secretary, John and Yoko. Only Trivikrama Swami and myself knew about the meeting. We also knew the layout of the house, because we were stripping paint off this beautiful oak panelling. In the main living room, there were these huge french windows looking out into the garden.

"So, without Prabhupada or John knowing, in the pitch dark we snuck over to the french windows. Although the curtains were drawn, there was a slit for us to see in through. John put his equipment next to the window. He wanted Prabhupada to hear the master recording of his new song. Prabhupada also had been recording some *bhajans* he wanted John to hear.

"Prabhupada entered the room and was invited to sit on a very large, comfortable sofa. Yoko was seated in a chair next to him, and John said, 'I made this recording I would like you to hear.' Then he came over to the equipment and started to fiddle around with the knobs. The tape started to move, but he couldn't get it to work. After a minute or so, Prabhupada realized he was having difficulty, so he said, 'It seems you are having trouble. I have also done some recording, and I have my own recording machine.'

"So instead of Prabhupada having to hear this horrific song, 'Cold Turkey', he was able to play his music to John Lennon. After a few minutes' conversation, Prabhupada said he had to finish some translation work and left."

The Hare Krishnas' residency at Tittenhurst came to a screeching halt a few days later when Prabhupada was once again invited to the Lennons' inner-sanctum. This time he noticed a nude glass statue of John and Yoko based on the infamous *Two Virgins* cover. A variation on the tale has John showing him the album cover. Either way he was not impressed, and later said to his disciples, "This is not a good place for us to stay any longer. Mr Lennon has been very kind to us but now we must go and find new quarters." The next morning the devotees loaded their belongings into a waiting van, ordered a car for Prabhupada and left Tittenhurst. John was genuinely interested in the Bengali master's philosophy of devotional yoga: Shyamasundara remembers him once walking into the kitchen, sitting down at an upright piano and playing the Hare Krishna mantra in a wide range of musical styles including country and western, classical, and rock'n'roll, complete with new melodies. At John's request he carved a figure of Krishna into the base of a prized grand piano. Yoko Ono, however, had felt threatened by the influence the charismatic master had over her husband and was glad to see them leave.

On 1 December 1969 Ringo Starr gave an interview to *Line-Up* host Tony Bilbow. He talked to him in a tiny rowing-boat on the Thames. The sound of the wooden oars hitting the side of the boat can still be heard on the tape.

Although Ringo was meant to be plugging *The Magic Christian*, the conversation ranged much more widely – to the bemusement of Bilbow. "I really can't believe this is the only planet with anything going on," said Starr. "There's a law of averages. There's fifty billion planets in the solar system, but that's only in our solar system. There's millions of other solar systems! So if you take the ratio of that in our system of more planets, there's the earth where there's something living for sure, because we're all here. So, on average, there's got to be somebody else out there. George has a theory where, like, Mars – we say there's no one on it, but there is someone on it, because it's just in another time dimension we can't see! Also, it's like earth, there's another race going on here as well for which the time is just slightly different. So where all our houses are there's other things as well, but in this other time we're, like, theirs. So everything is like one thing . . . There could be like a hundred races living on just this one planet, which is fantastic! I really think it could be like that because we don't know much about time, in respect to it being different from our time . . ."

Starr then talked about the various dimensions possible within the impossible sphere of existence in which we all find ourselves. "We know there's three dimensions, and there's theories about a fourth dimension, but there could be fifty dimensions, we're just not bright enough to catch them all. In America, there's a guy who's building a time machine," Ringo continued enthusiastically. "You just get in and press a button, open the door, you're somewhere else, but purely in time. This guy's building it on instructions from another planet. You hear all these weird stories about spaceships landing, UFOs, which they keep trying to squash. I mean, how many sightings are there? All those people can't be wrong! I just wonder why the government is trying to squash that. This time machine is being built. I believe it could happen. I can't put it down. I really think it's possible."

It is exactly this kind of charming unpredictability in Ringo and the other Beatles, that made them so widely appealing. Certainly Frank Sinatra and Fabian never talked like this! Still, these were the days of consciousness expansion.

John Lennon had made up his mind some time ago that the Beatles were over, although he kept the news within the group's inner circle. Mal Evans remembered what happened on 20 September 1969: "All of them left the group at one time or another, starting with Ringo, but the real ending was when John came into the office and said, 'The marriage is over! I want a divorce,' that was the final thing. That's what really got to Paul, because I took him home and I ended up in the garden crying my eyes out.

Although the collapse of the Apple business empire would legally spark the group's split, the four individuals involved were more than ready to move on, as evidenced by the solo albums they released: George's *Wonderwall*, Ringo's *Sentimental Journey*, Paul's *McCartney* and John's freaky quartet: *Unfinished Music I & II, The Wedding Album* and *The Plastic Ono Band's Live Peace In Toronto*.

"In the old days Paul and I would knock off an LP together," Lennon has said, "but nowadays there's three of us writing equally good songs and needing that much more space. The problem is, do you spend a good three or four months making an album and maybe we get only two or three tracks on each LP? That's the main problem." Creatively, he was also feeling stifled: "What was there left to sing about? On *Abbey Road* I sing about 'Mean Mr Mustard' and 'Polythene Pam', but those are only bits of crap I wrote in India. When I get down to it I'm only interested in Yoko and peace. I don't write for the Beatles, I write for myself."

"There were just too many limitations based on our being together for so long, everybody was sort of pigeonholed," Harrison added.

Yet even with the empire collapsing around him, Paul refused to give up. One late September day in 1969, at an Apple meeting, he even suggested the Beatles recharge their creative batteries by doing a tour of the club circuit.

"I think you're daft," John said. "In fact, I wasn't going to tell you, but I'm leaving the group. I've had enough. I want a divorce, like my divorce from Cynthia."

"Our jaws dropped," Paul remembered. "He went on to explain that it was a rather good feeling to get it off his chest, a bit like when he told his wife about a divorce . . . Which was very nice for him, but we didn't get much of a good feeling."

While the four agreed to keep quiet about the pending split, an awkward situation confronted them concerning Paul's solo album *McCartney*. He wanted the release date set for April, but Allen Klein blocked this as 17 April was when *Let It Be* was scheduled for release. Tempers flared and Ringo was sent in to mediate. At Paul's Cavendish

Avenue home, he said, Paul finally went over the top. "He went completely out of control, prodding his fingers towards my face saying, 'I'll finish you all now! You'll pay!' He told me to put on my coat and get out. Whether he was right or wrong I felt that, since he was our friend and that the date was of such immense significance to him, we should let him have his way."

As expected, John was livid, accusing Paul of staging the announcement to coincide with his album release, to cash in at the expense of the other three. "The Beatles were my fucking band," he said later. "I put the band together and I took it apart!"

Shortly after the split George Martin said, "People talk about the breakup of the group as though it was a tragedy, which is nonsense. They don't say it's amazing how long they lasted together. What other group has lasted as successfully as they? And as amicably? For nearly a decade. It really is pretty remarkable. It's amazing to me, human nature being what it is, that they didn't break up earlier under the strain of superstardom. They were living in a golden prison all the time and not growing into individual lives. Now they're living individual lives and enjoying it. Good luck to them."

In the face of the public shock and outcry, John downplayed the whole Beatles phenomenon: "Whatever wind was blowing at the time moved the Beatles too. I'm not saying we weren't flags on the top of the ship, but the whole boat was moving. Maybe the Beatles were in the crow's nest shouting, 'Land ho,' or something like that, but we were all in the same boat."

Most significantly, the breakup of the Beatles marked the end of the Lennon–McCartney partnership. The blow of their professional severance notwithstanding, it was perhaps even sadder on a personal level: the friendship of the young men, who had bonded through music and the loss of their mothers, had ruptured with bitterness and acrimony.

At the time of their split, the Beatles had sold over $200 million worth of records worldwide. They'd earned Grammys, Oscars, numerous Novellos; they'd been film stars and filmmakers. They'd gone from being teenagers' heart-throbs to MBEs, and their music had been hailed as the best since Beethoven's. It was no surprise that they were eager to get on with their separate lives: what more could they accomplish together? And yet, although they had found other partners, and each would work with a succession of talented new collaborators, none would re-create the magic that was the Beatles. This, after all, had been a partnership for the age.

NINE

Heads Across the Sky

New York, Los Angeles and London

1970–9

"All I'm doing is acting out the part of Beatle George . . . you just do what you can. Even if it's being a Beatle for the rest of my life, it's still only a temporary thing. We're all just characters in the same play, aren't we? And He's writing the script up there!"

George Harrison, 1970

In January 1970, John – perhaps hoping to impress his wife with his love of children – produced an audiotape of her daughter, Kyoko, singing and storytelling. It begins with Kyoko singing about her family. She refers to John as her father, rather than Anthony Cox. At one point, Julian is described as "a friend who lives in London", and at other times as her "brother". Both John and Yoko are "stars". Kyoko also mentions the chauffeur Les Anthony, who drove their Rolls, the family cats and John's electric guitar.

Clearly, she had taken on board the Lennons' mantra of peace and love. "You've gotta believe in peace," she cries out, "and an end to war and world hunger!"

As the tape rolls, Lennon accompanies her on guitar, with a basic percussion track. Like her mother, Kyoko exudes a confidence that explodes into boisterous precociousness. Before long she is directing the session, telling John to change the tempo and what to sing. "I'm too clever," she declares.

Throughout the proceedings Lennon displays rare patience. He instructs the child on the proper use of the microphone, warns her not to touch any buttons and suggests she might sing better without chewing-gum in her mouth. They run through Kyoko's morning routine, her day at school and cartoon characters Tom and Jerry. The tape offers a fascinating glimpse into John's lovable side. He and Kyoko sing little duets, and he provides sound-effects of whistles, barking dogs, mewing cats and yawns during a spontaneous "lullaby for grown-ups". The little girl croons, "I love you, John!"

At one point Kyoko creates a story about a jewel in the sky, which leads to John's final tale about a magician and a boy fairy. Here Kyoko interrupts: "Hey, only girls can be fairies!"

The long-lost tape was presented for sale at Christie's auction house as the only copy in existence. It sold for $75,250 on 1 May 2002. Unknown to the vendor, however, I have held a copy of it for the past twenty-five years.

By the spring of 1970 the Lennons' marriage had become so fragile that they agreed to undergo primal therapy as described in *The Primal Scream*. Psychotherapist Arthur Janov's basic premise centred on releasing the repressed fears and pain of childhood by reliving those experiences and thereby exorcizing them by engaging in a "primal scream". After undergoing several sessions at home in England in April the Lennons flew to Janov's Primal Institute in Bel Air, California, for four months' intense counselling. In a tape made during the therapy, Yoko was clearly frustrated and disillusioned: to her it seemed to be doing more harm than good.

According to Ono, Janov blamed John's secret battle with impotence on her because she treated her husband "like a big baby". She suggested that the programme might have been responsible for perpetuating John's innate chauvinism and blatant inconsideration of his wife. She claimed that the therapist himself supported the male-dominated society from which she could only escape by becoming "butch". "I'd rather be a bachelor," she declared on the tape. "I refuse to be a woman in the sense of what society expects. If that's being a lesbian, then society is making me one! I have the choice of becoming an incredibly neurotic masochist who doesn't accept women or becoming a normal person who doesn't accept these masochistic traits. If I am frigid from the treatment of society, then society is responsible."

What seemed to be a factor in her distress was her resentment of John's near mythical, hero-like status. Even Janov had fallen under the spell of the "John Lennon fantasy", as she termed it. On the tape she complains that while John can compose a song that sells itself, her own projects, which required a more intensive marketing effort, are all but ignored.

While Ono acknowledges her husband as a suitable father-figure for Kyoko, she complains that he often behaves like a bachelor, viewing women as sex objects. He is constantly obsessed with sexual imagery, she says, and she is fearful of his masochistic tendencies. Apparently he enjoyed various sado-masochistic practices, wanting Yoko to spank him, whip him and even drive her spike heels into his flesh. "I would hope his violence will disappear and all the feverish talk about sexual images . . . as if he's scared about something. I'm desperate to get out of John's violence and the nastiness of it."

Yoko was concerned that primal therapy might encourage this behaviour rather than curb it, and that her husband was enjoying the shrieking, weeping and rolling on the floor that hallmarked the treatment. Later John categorized primal therapy as the ultimate fix.

On 10 April 1970, newspapers around the world reported that Paul McCartney had declared the Beatles would never work together again. Almost the entire youth population of the world was in shock. A week later, the contentious solo *McCartney* album was to be released over the strong objections of the other three Beatles. George recalled the controversy: "As a director of Apple, Ringo had to sign a letter he wrote with John ordering Paul not to release the *McCartney* album on a day which would conflict with the issue of the next Beatles LP, *Let It Be*. When the letter was finished, Ringo volunteered to deliver it as he didn't want Paul to suffer the indignity of having it handed to him by some impersonal messenger. He gave the letter to him and said, 'I agree with it.' Then he had to stand there while both Paul and Linda screamed at him. When he finally returned, he was so drained his face was white . . . The point is we're writing too much to put it all on one Beatles record anyway."

Later that same day George spoke to Paul from Apple. It was not a happy conversation. "He came on like Attila the Hun. I had to hold the receiver away from my ear. I don't want to say anything bad about Paul," he laughed, "but I can be egged on!"

On the last day of the year McCartney filed a lawsuit in the London High Court seeking dissolution of the partnership of the Beatles & Co. and the appointment of a receiver to handle the group's ongoing business affairs. In his affidavit to the court,* he listed his grievances against his former colleagues:

1970 No. 6315

IN THE HIGH COURT OF JUSTICE
CHANCERY DIVISION GROUP B

JAMES PAUL McCARTNEY Plaintiff
- v -
LENNON & OTHERS Defendants

AFFIDAVIT of JAMES PAUL McCARTNEY

SWORN the 31 day of December, 1970
FILED the 31 day of December, 1970
on behalf of the Plaintiff

Ashurst Morris Crisp & Co.
17 Throgmorton Avenue
London, E.C.2.
Solicitors to the Plaintiff

I, James Paul McCartney of 7 Cavendish Avenue, London N.W.8, the above-named plaintiff, make oath and say as follows:

By a Writ of Summons issued out of this Court on _ December† 1970 I have applied to the Court for a decree of dissolution of the partnership between me and the defendants. The partnership was formerly constituted between us for the purpose of

* This is not the complete document, but rather selected portions, so the numbering of McCartney's and Allen Klein's points is not strictly chronological.

† The copy in the author's possession has the day left blank.

performing in various branches of the entertainment industry as a group of musicians known as "The Beatles". By a Deed of Partnership made on 19th April 1967 between the defendants and myself the defendant company was admitted as a partner in the partnership business previously carried on by the individual defendants (to whom I shall refer by their first names or collectively as 'the other three') and myself. Thereafter the defendants and I carried on business as "Beatles and Co". A true copy of the Deed is now produced and shown to me marked "J.P.M. 1". The name of The Beatles Limited was later changed first to Apple Music Limited on 17th November 1967 and then on 12th January 1968 to Apple Corps Limited (hereinafter called "Apple").

1 I have been driven to make this application because (a) The Beatles have long since ceased to perform as a group, (b) the defendants have sought to impose upon me a manager who is unacceptable to me, (c) my artistic freedom is liable to be interfered with so long as the partnership continues, and (d) no partnership accounts have been prepared since the Deed of Partnership was entered into.

2 Until 1965 the group enjoyed increasing success on tour, culminating in audiences of over 50,000. But in that year we decided to stop touring and make records instead. Whilst we had been touring the relationship between us was very close, both at work and socially. The drift became more marked after the death on 27th August 1967 of Brian Epstein who had been our manager since the formation of the group in Liverpool. Brian ran the group, being trusted by all four. We always left all our business matters and tax planning to him and advisers selected by him.

3 During the making of the *White Album* Richard Starkey (whom I shall call Ringo) announced that he was leaving the group, saying that he was "not getting to the rest of us". He came back after two days. At this stage none of us wanted the Beatles to finish, but we were becoming musically less compatible and were beginning to drift apart. Each began to look to his own interests rather than those of the group.

Musical differences became more marked, particularly between myself and John. He and I had been the principal collaborators in writing the songs. By the time that *Abbey Road* was recorded we were openly critical of each other's music, and he was no longer interested in the performance of songs which he had not written himself.

4 During the recording of the music for a film called *Let It Be* (then planned as an album called *Get Back*) George had a row with the rest of us about the performance of songs, as a result of which he walked out. We next saw him a few days afterwards at a meeting in Ringo's house when he told us he was leaving the group. He later agreed to continue at least until the recording was finished.

5 During the early part of 1969 John and Yoko had launched various ventures separate from the Beatles, including *Plastic Ono* and other recordings, picture exhibitions and personal appearances. John told the rest of us at the end of January 1969 that Allen Klein was to be his new business manager, and suggested that we as a group should employ him. At about this time against the wishes of the other three I left a meeting which was attended also by Klein. I believe that the meeting went on until about 2 a.m. and resulted in some sort of arrangement being made between the other three and Klein. Thereafter the other three told me that they could go ahead without me. George and Ringo also became keen on the idea. I was not keen. I distrusted Klein in view of his bad reputation and wanted the New York law firm called Eastman and Eastman to represent me because quite apart from the fact that John Eastman is my brother-in-law I trusted him. This was the first time in the history of the Beatles that a possible irreconcilable difference had appeared between us. Hitherto we had always decided matters unanimously after appropriate discussion. I was most anxious not to stand out against the wishes of the other three except on proper grounds. I therefore thought it right to take part in discussions concerning the possible appointment of Klein, though I did not in the least want him as my manager.

6 At a meeting with Klein and the other three on 1st February 1969, Klein promised, among other things, to secure full and detailed accounts with respect to the Beatles' affairs. He promised a statement of the financial affairs of the Beatles shortly, and undertook as his very first task to show that he could do the job of putting the accounts in order. But to this day I still have not seen any accounts. These are now produced and shown to me marked "J.P.M.2", a bundle of letters or copy letters between my American attorneys and the defendants or Klein or their accountants in course of which information about the affairs of the partnership of Beatles & Co. and Apple has been demanded without avail.

7 On Friday 9th May 1969 it became clear to me that the other three had already signed the agreement on the previous day without my knowledge, and that it was going to be ratified later that day. That evening I met the other three and Klein and Peter Howard (then of Joynson-Hicks & Co.) at a recording studio. I said, "You know that you have outvoted me." I told them I wanted at least until Sunday (11th May 1969) to think it over. The other three said that if they wanted the agreement they were entitled to have it. John told me I was always stalling and that I had already had two days to think it over. Klein said he wanted the agreement at once so that he could put it before his board. He left that evening by plane. A copy of the Agreement as signed by the other three is now produced and shown to me marked "J.P.M.3". I have never signed or ratified it. I have never accepted Klein either as my manager or as manager of the Beatles.

8 In September 1969 I was still keen that the Beatles should continue as a group. I therefore proposed that we should get the group together again, and play live before small audiences. Ringo agreed with this proposal and George was noncommittal. Later at a meeting John said: "I think you're daft. Look, I might as well tell you, I'm leaving the group. I wasn't going to tell you until after the Capitol deal. When I told Allen (Klein) last night he said I was not to. I've had enough. I want a divorce, like my divorce from Cynthia

(formerly his wife). It's given me a great feeling of freedom." He then said in effect our recording activities had come full circle, because the photograph on our very first album was almost exactly similar to the photograph then planned for the album called *Get Back*. The rest of us were shocked by this announcement: I certainly had not thought along these lines at that stage. But we all agreed that it would be best that nobody should know that the group was finished.

9 The Capitol deal was signed in September 1969 shortly after the withdrawal of John. We all treated the group as finished at that stage, although I think all of us (except possibly John) expected we would come together again one day. We told Klein it seemed a "tricky" agreement to enter into, as we would not be making any more records together. But Klein said that there was no objection to entering into the agreement. I was reluctant to enter into the Capitol deal since it had been negotiated by Klein.

10 The idea that I should also leave the Beatles gradually formed in my mind during the early part of 1970, when I was making a record of my own. During this period I telephoned John and told him I was leaving the Beatles too, to which he replied, "Good! That makes two of us who have accepted it mentally." I also told him in the same conversation that I was handing over all my business arrangements to Eastman and Eastman (John Eastman's firm). My intention was hardened by the treatment which I received from Klein in relation to the release date of my own record, and the alterations to *Let It Be* hereinafter referred to.

11 In March 1970 I telephoned Apple's offices and spoke to Neil Aspinall and Jack Oliver about the release date. They asked me to postpone it for a week from 10th to 17th April 1970 so as not to clash with an impending new record by Ringo. I am informed by John Eastman and believe that on 25th March 1970 he attended a meeting at the offices of EMI and found that Klein without reference to me had stopped my album on 20th March 1970. On learning this I telephoned George who said that he was not stopping it, and this he agreed to

confirm by telegram. On 27th March 1970 George sent a telegram to this effect to the other two and me and also to Klein with a copy to Apple. I passed on the telegram to EMI. On 30th March 1970 Klein however went back on the telegram on the grounds that he had now fixed the release date for *Let It Be* in April 1970. Instead he offered me 4th June 1970 as a release date for my record. I telephoned to the offices of United Artists, and spoke to David Picker, President of United Artists, and was told that there was no release date yet fixed for *Let It Be*, since no agreement in relation to it had ever been signed.

12 At this stage I was disputing the deal which Klein had made in relation to *Let It Be*. Ringo told me if I would agree to the *Let It Be* deal, they would let my album come out. I rejected this suggestion. At this stage also Ringo visited me, bringing two letters signed by George and John with which he said he agreed. These letters confirmed my record had been stopped. In an angry conversation Ringo suggested that my record was not really ready for release, and I told him that Klein had no release date for *Let It Be* from United Artists. After telling Ringo how furious I was with the other three for impeding the release of my record, I told him to get out. He appeared shaken, and I believe that shortly afterwards Peter Howard telephoned EMI and gave Apple's consent to the record being released on 17th April 1970 as it eventually was.

13 I received the acetate copy of *Let It Be* in late March or early April 1970, accompanied by a letter from Phil Spector, whom Klein had engaged to re-mix the album, saying that if I wanted any alterations I should say so. I found in the recording of my song "The Long And Winding Road", Spector had not only "mixed" the recording, but had added strings, voices, horns and drums, and had changed the recording of my other songs considerably. This had never happened before and I regarded this as an intolerable interference with my work. I therefore telephoned Spector but was unable to contact him. I then telephoned the other three who approved the changes. On 14th April 1970 I wrote a letter to Klein. Although in my opinion

there would have been enough time to have made the required alterations, none were in fact made.

14 Between April and August 1970 there were no meetings and hardly any communication between the other three and myself. In August 1970 I wrote a letter to John suggesting that we should "let each other out of the trap". He replied with a photograph of himself and Yoko, with a balloon coming out of his mouth in which was written, "How and Why?" I replied by letter saying, "*How* by signing a paper which says we hereby dissolve our partnership. *Why* because there is no partnership." John replied on a card which said, "Get well soon. Get the other signatures and I will think about it."

15 I feel that all mutual confidence and interest has been lost, and that the group could not possibly be re-formed. I believe John takes a similar attitude, especially since he has never revoked his withdrawal of September 1969. I particularly resented the threat to my artistic freedom constituted by the attempt by the other three to stop or at least delay release of my record. I am also advised by my lawyers and accountants and believe the continuing failure of the defendants and Klein to furnish any accounts of the partnership is of the utmost gravity for my financial position and especially my tax liability. For the reasons which I have mentioned, the continuation of the partnership business has become impossible, and in default of any information about the very substantial sums of money which must have been received by the partnership by way of royalties from the sale of records I believe that its assets may be in jeopardy unless they are safeguarded by an independent person. I therefore ask the Court, pending a declaration that the partnership be dissolved, to order that partnership accounts be taken and to appoint a receiver in the interim.

As to the mountain of legal documents flying back and forth between the parties, few have survived, but Allen Klein's affidavit has. Part of it reads:

1 On 28th January 1969 at 3 Savile Row London W.1 at about 9 p.m., I met the Plaintiff, with Mr Lennon, Richard Starkey

(Ringo Starr) and George Harrison (the other Beatles) and had a general discussion about the proposed purchase of NEMS. The relevant information about the position of The Beatles (and their companies) themselves remained to be ascertained. The Plaintiff said the proposal was strongly recommended by John Eastman and he (the Plaintiff) was pressing it. I therefore suggested that there was no point in debating the matter in the abscence [*sic*] of John Eastman and it was agreed that we have another meeting on Saturday 1st February, with John Eastman present.

2 During the meeting on 28th January I said I was going to make enquiries into Mr Lennon's financial position. Mr Starkey and Mr Harrison asked me to do the same for them. (At this stage the Plaintiff had left the meeting.) I spent the remainder of that week largely in the offices of Bryce Hammer & Co., chartered accountants [who were the Beatles' personal accountants] with Mr Harry Pinsker, a partner in that firm, obtaining information about the personal position of the Beatles but, as I had not had time to make a full investigation into the affairs of their companies, I was not really in a position to assess their true financial position overall.

3 On Saturday 1st February, the meeting arranged for that date, with John Eastman present as well, took place as arranged at Apple's headquarters, 3 Savile Row, London W.1.

4 At this stage John Eastman launched an attack on my personal integrity, producing a copy of the Cameo-Parkway Proxy Statement mentioned above and clippings from newspapers. He alleged that I had a bad reputation in general and raised questions about Cameo-Parkway in particular. I pointed out that the Cameo-Parkway Proxy Statement made, in accordance with the stringent requirements of United States law and practice with respect to securities transactions, a full and complete disclosure of the "warts" of Cameo-Parkway's career and was there for all to see. I also invited him to make specific charges or criticisms which would enable me to answer them, but he did not do so. In any case I think my answers must have satisfied the Beatles. I suggested the position of John Eastman

should be that of legal adviser to the Beatles and all their companies. He rejected this on the grounds that he did more than an English lawyer normally does, the meeting broke up and another meeting was arranged for the following Monday 3rd February 1969, again at Savile Row.

5 On the morning of 3rd February 1969, I went to 3 Savile Row and saw the four Beatles, John Eastman, and a few principal staff members of Apple, who were informed that my company (then still called Cameo-Parkway) had been appointed to look into the affairs of the Beatles and all their Companies. At this meeting John Eastman agreed he would, after all, act as legal adviser to the Beatles and all their companies.

6 Apple issued two press announcements, one relating to my Company's appointment and a separate one relating to the appointment as lawyers of John Eastman's firm, Eastman & Eastman. Cameo-Parkway also issued a press announcement of its own.

While the world was devastated by the Beatles' split, insiders like Alistair Taylor were not really all that surprised. "If you weren't there, you can't begin to understand the pressure. I don't give a damn how many books you've read or people you interview, I can't convey to you what it was like. I was close to them and even I was under pressure, and I was not remotely in their league. It was unbearable and they just had to do something. Imagine, you can't walk down the street, you can't go out in a car, you can't do anything without being torn to shreds, day in, day out, night in, night out.

"They were breaking up from almost day one. More than once in the early days I had to go and find George, he'd say, 'I'm not doing this,' and he'd piss off. So it was nothing new. I think the pressures got so bad towards the end I'm astonished they stayed together as long as they did."

While all of the Beatles later rejected Klein, he ingratiated himself with Lennon by making a big fuss over Ono's talent and soon brought Harrison on side by promising to concentrate on elevating him from his perpetual second-class status within the group. It was the same with Starr, who'd spent far too much time waiting for his three partners to cast off their hang-ups and get on with it. "When Paul administered Apple the company lost a million dollars," Harrison complained at the time. "I wish Klein was our manager nine years ago. The thing about Paul is that, apart from all our personal problems, he's having a wonderful time. He's got horses and a farm in Scotland and he's much happier with his family. I can dig that." According to media sources the Beatles earned a total of $17 million in their first seven years together. After Allen Klein took over, they reportedly earned that in just seven months. The Beatles were finally on target again, but at what price?

The extended dissolution of the Beatles' partnership snaked slowly into 1971. On 19 January the case came before the court but was adjourned for thirty days. McCartney, hidden behind a beard, appeared on 26 February to testify. The others were heard only via written affidavit. By 12 March, the judge ruled in Paul's favour. At the end of April, Lennon, Harrison and Starr abandoned plans to appeal against the decision and a receiver was appointed to control the finances of their publishing firm, Maclen (Music). He would act in that capacity until 31 December 1974. Signifying the end of an era, the Official Beatles Fan Club closed its doors for ever on 31 March 1972. Exactly a year later the Beatles' management contract with Klein expired. Suffice to say, it was not renewed. To no one's surprise on 2 November, Lennon, Harrison and Starr sued Klein, his ABCKO company, claiming gross misrepresentation. Klein countersued. From there the writs flew back and forth, eventually culminating in a settlement with the final dissolution of the Beatles' partnership on 9 January 1975.

1970 was a particularly distressing year for John Lennon. The Beatles had broken up, he was heavily strung out on heroin, and living with Yoko was difficult at the best of times. An unexpected visit from Alfred Lennon, his young wife Pauline and their baby David, on Friday, 9 October 1970, John's thirtieth birthday, added fuel to the fire. In her book *Daddy Come Home* Pauline remembered, "The John we'd known a couple of years ago was now unrecognizable. He sported a fiery red beard which made our birthday gift of aftershave laughably inappropriate . . . Behind his granny glasses his pupils were heavily stoned, maybe on heroin. 'I'm cutting off your money and kicking you out of the house,' he snapped, stiffly taking a seat at the table and fixing Freddie with a penetrating gaze. 'Get off my fucking back,' he spat.

"My initial reaction was that this must be some kind of sick joke, although it was clear from the look of sheer hatred in John's eyes he was deadly serious. 'It was your choice to give me an allowance,' Freddie countered.

"'Have you any idea what I've been through because of you?' Lennon yelled. 'Day after fucking day in therapy, screaming for my daddy, sobbing for you to come home.'

"'You can't put all the blame on your dad,' I protested. 'Your mother was just as much to blame for your problems.'

"Astonishingly, the mere mention of Julia triggered a vicious attack on his mother, whom he reviled in the most obscene language I had ever heard, referring to her repeatedly as a 'fucking whore' . . . 'Look at me!' he screamed at his father. 'I'm bloody mad, insane! I'm due for an early death like Hendrix or Joplin and it's all your fucking fault!' Yoko then launched into a lecture on the seriousness of parental responsibility and the consequences to children in the event of separation from their parents. 'Do you know what it does to a child to be asked to choose between his parents?' John roared. 'It tears him apart, blows his bloody mind. You call yourself a father?' he sneered. 'You think screwing some bird gives you the right to call yourself a father? You've treated me like shit, just like all the others. You've all ripped me off, the whole fucking lot of you!'

"'You've no right to treat your father this way,' I shouted, incensed.

"'Mind your own fucking business!' he screamed. 'If you ever tell anyone what happened here, I'll have you fucking killed!' he hissed. 'You'll be cased up in a box and dumped at sea, right in the middle of the ocean, twenty, fifty, or would you prefer a hundred fathoms deep?'

"'Come on, pet," Freddie whispered, in an unfamiliar, empty

voice. John hardly seemed to notice our departure and remained sitting at the table staring fixedly in front of him . . . Only Yoko rose as we moved, in an incongruous attempt at civility. Throughout John's tirade I had been aware of her powerful presence as she sat beside him. In this respect I couldn't help but compare her with Mimi, herself a woman of powerful intensity. Although there the similarity ended, as Mimi was as narrow-minded in her attitudes as Yoko was outrageously avant garde."

That was the last time Lennon saw his father. Alfred Lennon died in the cancer ward of a Brighton hospital on 1 April 1976 at the age of sixty-three. Towards the end of his life John rang him nightly and talked to him for hours; the old man listened intently but was unable to utter a word. John was unable to visit him because he was in New York, and his request for citizenship was before the courts; to leave might have prejudiced the outcome of his case. When he died, John offered to pay the funeral expenses, perhaps out of guilt, but Pauline refused.

George Harrison's 1970 move to Friar Park was of monumental importance to him, both personally and professionally. He immediately fell in love with its secret passages, underground caverns and the cryptic quotations carved above almost every door and fireplace. It inspired much of his solo work, and was a refuge from the vile blows and buffets of Beatlemania.

The mansion had housed a convent of Salesian sisters for a number of years, and eventually became a girls' school, which closed in 1969. Model Kirsten Grepne remembered her carefree schooldays at Friar Park: "I moved to Henley when I was sixteen and went to school at Friar Park. The nuns took us on nature rambles through the caves, tadpole-hunting and roly-poly down the hill. We had a lovely time amidst all the gnomes and things. The light-switches were in the shape of friars' noses, with big grins on their faces. There were loads of gargoyles, particularly in the chapel. There were, however, certain things about the gargoyles the nuns didn't like. They did little paintings to disguise their private parts!

McCartney, Jane and Cynthia at the Maharishi's de luxe Himalayan retreat in Rishikesh.

A pensive and exhausted-looking Lennon, London 1968. All the Beatles were pretty much confirmed workaholics, and John's constant drinking and drugging didn't help.

McCartney at Abbey Road studios during sessions for the *White Album*, with then live-in girlfriend Francie Schwartz, 1968.

At a London press event, surrounded by Blue Meanies, to promote the Beatles' innovative animated adventure, *Yellow Submarine*, 1968.

A tender moment during John and Yoko's six-day Bed-In in Amsterdam, March 1969.

A break during the Montreal Bed-In. The ever-diligent Derek Taylor mans the phones.

above: Paul, Linda and Heather arrive at 7 Cavendish Avenue following their wedding on 12 March 1969. Note the rather unhappy female fans.

above left: Homebody Harrison in his walled back garden at Kinfauns, Clairmont Drive, Esher.

left: The Harrisons outside Esher and Walton Magistrates Court, 18 March 1969, after being arrested for possessing cannabis.

above: McCartney with several female fans outside his St John's Wood home, 1969. John arrives for work on *Abbey Road* amidst a throng of adolescent, camera-toting fans, St John's Wood 1969. To Lennon, fans were much more of a nuisance than a blessing.

left: George and Patti at Heathrow, after dropping off Bob Dylan and his wife Sarah for their flight to New York, September 1969.

below left: The Beatles sit at the feet of their musical guru, Bob Dylan, for a rare performance at the Isle of Wight Festival, August 1969.

right: George, Patti and Mal Evans.

Beatles producer George Martin checks the music for "Octopus's Garden" with Ringo, December 1969.

Lennon goes over the wall at McCartney's house following a rift between the two during sessions for *Abbey Road*, the final album the Beatles actually recorded together.

The McCartneys leave a London court after attending a hearing about the dissolution of the Beatles – a time Paul later described as the worst in his entire life.

top: Ringo with *Magic Christian* co-star, Peter Sellers (centre) and Richard Attenborough.

above: A rare smile from the normally sombre Beatle, 1970.

left: Leaving Apple during John Lennon's short-lived London power-to-the-people heroin phase, 1970.

McCartney at his Campbeltown farm in Scotland with his two best gals, Jane Asher (above left) in 1967 and Linda McCartney in 1971 (above right). Also pictured is sheepdog Martha, the inspiration for the song "Martha My Dear" on the *White Album.*

Ringo Starr and the Lennons in front of the Roxy in Hollywood, where they'd been to see Bob Marley and the Wailers in the early seventies. More than any other Beatle, Ringo tended to be friends with everyone else in the group.

Ringo in London in the early to mid-eighties, a difficult time personally and professionally for the drummer.

Squire Harrison inside his Friar Park recording studios during the mid-eighties, a time when the troubled singer/song-writer was seldom photographed.

"One day I was standing near the gates waiting to be picked up by my father. There was this person rustling around in the bushes dressed in wellington boots with very long hair. He was in the trees and he peeped through. I did, in fact, recognize him, as everybody in town knew one of the Beatles had bought Friar Park. He had on a brown felt hat and asked, 'Are you waiting for a bus, luv?' I said, 'No, it's okay, I'm fine.' He said, 'Would you like to come up for a cup of tea?' I said, 'No, it's quite all right.' "

Friar Park was Harrison's ultimate toy. Although to this day many of the rooms remain closed off and unheated, he set about restoring it with the intention of returning it to how it looked in the nineteenth century. "It has a thousand telephones that won't ring," said George in 1970. "It's like a horror movie, but it doesn't really have bad vibes. I've got over any of those dark corners in the back of my mind. It's had Christ in it for sixteen years, after all."

Enchanted with the pastoral beauty of Friar Park, and charmed by Henley, George found a peace there that allowed his innate spirituality to flourish. "Everybody's doing all the time, it's very difficult to stop, but that's my ambition. I thought after moving into my new house I wouldn't do a stroke. If you don't go out, you don't get into trouble."

After John and George had been convicted of drug offences, the authorities on both sides of the Atlantic harboured suspicion about them. Certainly, the Establishment in both Britain and America were no longer Beatles fans and to many the four men were now very bad news, influencing the young to become involved with left-wing politics and the drug culture. Both Lennon and Harrison were seen as ringleaders, especially in Nixon's America, and were subjected to a lot of hassle whenever they sought to enter the USA. Evidence of this can be seen in a recently declassified top-secret FBI document concerning them, written by the notorious J. Edgar Hoover himself.

Although Lennon always claimed that the Beatles only followed trends that were already establishing themselves in the sixties and early seventies, he was also keenly aware that those in power in London and Washington blamed the Beatles for a generation of youth gone wild. Hoover wrote:

Date: 23 April 1971
Subject: John Lennon, George Harrison, Patricia Harrison
These individuals are affiliated with the Beatles musical group. Lennon will be traveling under the name of Chambers and the Harrisons are using the name Masters. They will remain in Los Angeles for business discussions with Capitol Records and other enterprises. They will travel to New York for further discussions. Waivers were granted by the Immigration and Naturalization Service in view of the ineligibility of these three individuals to enter the US due to their reputations in England as narcotic users.

While Lennon and the Harrisons have shown no propensity to become involved in violent anti-war demonstrations, each recipient of this memo should remain alert for any information of such activity on their part or for information indicating they are using narcotics. Submit any pertinent information obtained for immediate dissemination.

During this period Al Aronowitz was a frequent house guest at Friar Park. He was struck by the fact that George had moved his entire extended family on to the thirty-seven-acre estate. His eldest brother Harry lived in the gatehouse with his family, and brother Peter in what was called the Middle Lodge. After George's mother died on 7 July 1970 his father, Harry senior, a retired bus driver, moved in as well. He grew his white hair down to his shoulders and tiptoed into rock 'n' roll, listening patiently as his son talked about his Hare Krishna beliefs and flirting with the many pretty young women who called in. He even, briefly, became a vegetarian at George's insistence. Aronowitz was fond of the old man, and impressed that he had crafted an energetic new life for himself after losing his wife. "Harry and I became buddies during my trips to Friar Park and he was curious to see what Las Vegas was all about. So I took him to Vegas. Patti came along too. I won a bunch of money."

It was at Friar Park that the Harrisons' marriage began to show the strain of too many wild years in the public eye. It was well known that as the seventies had worn on their love had worn off. Harrison was a contradiction in terms: an aspiring celibate orthodox Hare

Krishna who loved women in a decidedly unspiritual way, a wine and pot connoisseur who railed publicly against drugs and alcohol, the gentle, ethical vegetarian who occasionally tore into a chicken breast or sole fillet when the spirit moved him. But it was his womanizing that caused the main problems between him and Patti. As time went by, discretion lost its importance to him. As Peter Brown once put it, "George was not a very good husband."

"Although Eric Clapton was often at the Park to jam with George, I obviously was too thick to notice the budding romance between Eric and Patti," Aronowitz remembered. "George had another buddy, Terry Doran, a Liverpool auto salesman who ran with the Beatles for years. There was one night when George surprised me by stealing away to his bedroom with the woman I thought was Terry's girlfriend. She wasn't Terry's squeeze at all. Terry, it turned out, was gay."

The moral dichotomy that played itself out in the life of George Harrison was by no means unique to him but, rather, the classic dilemma for many with one foot on the spiritual path and the other in the material world. However, the level of temptation available to George was beyond the reach of almost anyone. Although it is now clear that Harrison's near-lifelong search for ultimate yogic union was what drove him, he often wavered from the strictest requirements of the path by indulging in worldly pleasures that included the best cocaine, the finest wines, fastest cars, most palatial homes and, perhaps most distracting of all, the most exotic, beautiful, willing women available to a man in his rarefied position.

Patti was dedicated to George, but way out of her depth when it came to his philosophical and spiritual interests. That is not to say, however, she wasn't interested in her husband's quest and was more than willing to adopt many of the precepts that came with the package, including ethical vegetarianism, rejection of hard drugs, daily meditation and devotions. But celibacy (in pursuit of transcendence) and the orthodox rituals of worship weren't as important to her as they were to George: she was happy with her life as it was. Harrison's sometimes preachy, often hypercritical and terse manner, with his philosophical meanderings, ultimately pushed them apart – and his philandering. Peter Brown remembered, "George seemed to want to seduce every woman he laid eyes on. He even once suggested to Neil Aspinall they swap wives . . ."

Perhaps George's most extraordinary indiscretion was his ill-advised, extended affair with Ringo's wife, Maureen, during the early seventies. Why he took up with the wife of one of his closest friends is a mystery. When asked for an explanation he replied simply, "Incest!" Peter Brown said: "Maureen and Ringo moved into Tittenhurst Park*, and one evening in September 1973 they invited George and Patti for dinner. Afterwards they all sat around the long white dining-room table, with George strumming his guitar singing love songs. Suddenly, he blurted out he was in love with Maureen. Mo turned red and shook her head, Ringo stormed off, and Patti burst into tears and locked herself in the bathroom. The couple left soon after. A few weeks later Patti returned to Friar Park from shopping in London only to find George in bed with Maureen." The couple often met secretly at the Park and in London.

When Patti left George for Eric Clapton in July 1974 it was by default: the man she loved was certainly George, but he was so conflicted and emotionally insecure that the marriage could not survive.

The seeds of the affair had been sown four years earlier. By 1970 the Harrisons' marriage was on the rocks: the years of Beatlemania had taken their toll. George confided to a friend, "Love is not enough." In 1972, when Patti defied her husband's stay-at-home decree and accepted a modelling assignment with designer Ossie Clark, Harrison left for India on a tour of the holy places of Vrndavana. It was no secret that George's close friend Eric Clapton had fallen for Patti: his song "Layla" a now historic musical declaration of his love. At first, Patti tried to use him to bring her husband to heel, but by 1974 she and Eric were deeply in love, united by their common loneliness and Patti's determination to help Eric kick his addiction to heroin.

Harrison separated from his wife that year, and took up with Rod Stewart's old flame, model Kathy Simmonds. In 1977 he talked about

* Bought from John on 18 September 1973.

his pending divorce in a lengthy interview with Crawdaddy: he admitted that he and Patti had grown apart and that he harboured no ill-will towards Clapton: "I didn't have any problem with it," he stated. "Eric had the problem. Every time I'd go and see him he'd really be hung up about it and I'd be saying, 'Fuck it, man, don't be apologizing,' and he didn't believe me. I was saying 'I don't care.' "

Unfortunately, while George eventually found stability with his second wife Olivia, Patti's subsequent marriage to Clapton, celebrated on 19 May 1979, foundered. Perhaps because they were unable to start a family, and also because of Clapton's battle with alcoholism.

Despite Harrison's frailties he was generous to a fault: he was a friend and benefactor to many causes, from the Hare Krishna movement to London's homeless. As Aronowitz recalled: "With our three young children, my wife and I were living in a cockroach-infested Manhattan tenement at the start of her five-year battle against cancer. George enabled her to live out her life in rented suburban comfort by giving me a loan of $50,000 he knew I could never possibly repay. To me, George's loan was an exhibition of saintliness unequalled by any superstar I ever knew.

"There was also one Thanksgiving when my wife insisted on inviting George and Patti to share a turkey dinner with us . . . My dying wife, who at that time had to wear a neck brace, was living on a diet of painkillers that would get her so stoned she would sometimes fall asleep at dinner with her face in her plate. Although both George and Patti were vegetarians, they graciously ate the turkey my wife so arduously prepared. Harrison was a truly great man."

During the summer of 1971 Jim and Angela McCartney, along with Ruth, drove up to Campbeltown to visit Paul and Linda at High Park Farm on the Mull of Kintyre. Following the twelve-hour drive they were unceremoniously ushered into a garage for the night. Jim and Angela had a mattress on the concrete floor, while Ruth had a makeshift bunk bed and the blanket that belonged to Jim's racehorse, Drake's Drum. Dinner with Paul and Linda was likewise an adventure in roughing it, as Angela explained: "One time we were having supper under a glass skylight and several flies buzzed around and fell into the milk jug. Jim, who was very fastidious, suggested getting some fly-killer. To which Linda replied, 'Oh, don't be so fussy Jim, they're all God's creatures.' " The McCartneys were notorious, too, for their odd eating hours and Spartan fare, often leaving family and friends to fend for themselves. Angela was forced to stock up on chocolate, hiding behind the barn to eat it. Paul and Linda's brand of lite hospitality was well documented by many visitors to the farm, including members of his own band, Wings.

Another day Paul and the heavily pregnant Linda took Angela and Ruth for a walk across the fields. Toddler Mary was wrapped inside Paul's jacket as her parents smoked a joint, passing it from one to the other. Then Linda put it to Mary's lips and jokingly cooed, "Come on, baby, come on, puff for Mummy."

Around that time, during the recording, in Manchester, of the album Paul made with his brother which was backed by his newly formed band Wings, and entitled *McGear*, the McCartneys came to stay at Rembrandt for three months. A typical day in the life of the McCartneys went something like this. Paul and Linda would get home from late-night recording sessions, during the small hours and scurry into the children's room, waking them up. "Hi, we're home," Linda would bellow. "Hugs and kisses for Mom! Mummy loves you!" Then, in the next breath, "Now go back to sleep!"

Angela was often expected to look after Heather, Mary and Stella until Linda got up at around two o'clock in the afternoon. On one occasion Linda made bacon and eggs, brought the frying pan into the living room and dropped it on to the carpet. They would leave wet towels on the bed, soiled nappies, dirty underwear and dog shit on the floor for Angela to clean up. "They were pigs," stated Ruth quite simply.

The children enjoyed playing in the master bedroom, which Angela had redecorated in white. One afternoon Angela went in to find them drawing with crayons all over the wallpaper and furniture. "Hey, girls, you mustn't do this," she admonished them. "I'll get you some colouring books and paper to draw on." At that point Linda charged in: "Oh, Ange, let them be! I'll buy you more furniture if you want. Don't inhibit them. You're always saying, 'Don't do this, don't do that.' You'll give them a complex, just let them be!"

The privacy-obsessed Linda apparently thought nothing of freely intruding on others. Angela liked to keep her diary and handbag in the kitchen drawer. One morning Linda popped into the kitchen and breezily announced, "Hey, Ange, I see you're due to start your period today."

"I beg your pardon?" Angela murmured, shocked.

"Oh, yeah, I was reading your diary last night. There's some pretty interesting stuff in there." From then on Jim's wife locked her personal possessions in her bedroom.

Angela could never really relax as Jim McCartney's wife. Despite her best efforts she could never win. She once accepted a ticket to an early Wings show, not imagining that she would have to seek approval for such an outing from her stepson. When she returned home that night she overheard Jim on the phone: "No, son, I'm not gonna get rid of her. She's a good woman and I love her. You can't tell me to do that. I'm old, I'm ill, she takes cares of me. No, son, I won't do it!" Then he told his wife, "Paul's really mad because you went to that show as he hadn't invited you." Why was Paul McCartney threatened by the woman who had given his father so much happiness and stability?

In late 1971 Paul and Linda were up at the farm in Scotland. One evening Jim telephoned them, Heather answered, and told him that her parents were out in the field, adding, "I think they've had a fight." The following day Jim rang again. This time he spoke to Linda, whose voice was taut and drained: "Paul's not here. As a matter of fact, he's been gone a couple of days. I don't know where he is." She asked him to let her know if Paul called him.

Three days later, McCartney turned up at Rembrandt, looking rough and unshaven. He muttered a quick hello and walked past his stepmother, looking very guilty. Later that day Linda rang and Paul took the call upstairs. He had a long conversation with his father, then informed the family that his wife was coming the next day with Mary and Stella.

Linda arrived with the children, the McCartneys' two large dogs and tons of luggage. "When she came to the door," Angela recalled in the mid-nineties, "she looked just awful, shocking. I put my arms round her and said, 'You poor little thing,' and we both cried. She said she was all right and let's just forget it. Obviously I wouldn't dream of asking any questions. What the hell it was all about I still don't know. But when people malign Linda, I always say, 'Look, her life can't be easy!' She was up there bewildered and alone with the kids in such a remote place. It's unbelievable."

By the mid-seventies, Ruth, now in her teens, started dating. The young men would arrive at the McCartney home, and if Paul was around they were often subjected to an intense interrogation. On one such occasion he said to a boy, "Now, son, just what are your intentions towards my sister? You lay a hand on her, mate, I tell you . . ."

"The poor guy!" Ruth said. "We went to the fairground and he threw up!"

In 1975 Ruth, now fifteen, was attending stage school and developing into a gifted dancer and choreographer. Mike McGear had co-written a song with Paul called "Dance The Do", which was about to be released as a single (it came out on 4 July) and showcased on a special for Granada Television. Ruth showed him a routine she'd worked up using Russian Cossack moves. "Hey, that looks like fun," he said. "Let me talk to the producers about using your idea." They decided to go ahead with Ruth as lead dancer, a coup that meant she would be eligible for an Equity card and her first professional fee of fifty pounds.

Ruth was thrilled and rang Jim to tell him. "That's great! Why don't you give Paul and Linda a ring and go round to see the kids?"

When she phoned and told big brother Paul her news she detected a sudden change in his demeanour, which, in her excitement, she dismissed. "We'll be home this evening, so why don't you come over now?" he offered.

Ruth entered the secret code to the gates and went into the house. Linda was upstairs, but Paul met her in the corridor between the kitchen and dining room. Ruth was unprepared for what happened next. Instead of congratulating her, an angry McCartney put her straight on the reality of the situation as he saw it. Pointing out that she was just a kid, he insisted that she'd only got the job because of him – that Granada were using her and Mike because they wanted Paul to appear on one of their shows. Ruth raced out of the house, tears streaming down her face, her humiliation increased by having to run the gauntlet of fans hanging around outside. Her stepbrother had succeeded in stripping her of her fragile self-confidence. It was only when Mike told her that she shouldn't let Paul get the better of her that she was persuaded to go ahead with the show.

McCartney's conflicted attitude towards his family wasn't restricted to his stepsister. When Angela's sister Mae died suddenly, her friends were invited to the house to support her. As it happened, that day Paul and Linda were heading up to Liverpool. One of the Beatles' iron rules was "No guests when we come to visit." When they arrived to find others gathered there Paul exploded to Angela, "Listen, this is my fuckin' house! Don't ever forget I put every fuckin' crumb of food into your mouth and your kid. If it wasn't for me you'd be out on the bloody street!" When Aunt Millie intervened, Paul lashed out, "Keep out of it, Millie! This is my fuckin' place! I paid for it and I feed all of them. So shut the fuck up!"

In the mid-seventies Jim was unable to afford the upkeep on Rembrandt, which he sold back to Paul, and settled into a bungalow on Beverly Drive, half a mile away. By now Jim suffered from crippling arthritis and his health was deteriorating.

Even when Jim's family was no longer at Rembrandt, Linda and Paul made it their first stop whenever they came into town. "The first thing they did," says Angela, "was come over to his dad's to pick up the keys and some milk. Linda would then go into my freezer and take things. 'Oh, you got these little chicken pies! I'll take some of those if you don't mind, Ange.'" The next day Linda would invariably ring up to say, "We're leaving. You can come round and clean up now." Angela had no option but to pick up the rubbish, and strip the beds. More often than not she'd find the frozen foods melted, still in the plastic bag.

As 1976 unfolded, Jim McCartney became something of a recluse, not caring to go out or invite anyone to the house. During his final weeks he told his wife, "I'm a creaking gate. Promise me you'll never let me finish up in a hospital bed. If I look up and see a sea of faces looking down I'll hate it. So promise me that when the end is near you'll let me die peacefully in my own bed."

No sooner had he said this than his sister-in-law Joan, married to his brother Joe, appeared on the doorstep, suitcase in hand. "Hi, Ange," she announced, and barged in. "Millie, Jin and I have worked it all out. We're going to take turns staying with Jim to give you a break." Although Angela knew they meant well she resented them taking over in her own home, telling her how to look after her husband and mostly ignoring Jim's wishes. She told Joan tactfully, "I appreciate your motives, but I don't want you to stay every night and give him the idea he's not got much longer and that the family is starting to gather round the bed. Let's play this the way Jim would want it. Believe me everybody's welcome but, please, only one at a time."

Nevertheless, during the final weeks of his long illness, when he was lapsing in and out of consciousness, Jim was admitted to a nearby hospital for tests. Paul and Linda were at Rembrandt, preparing to fly to New York from Manchester. Paul helped lift his father into the car and drove him to hospital. There, he gathered Jim into a wheelchair, pushed him up to his room and helped him into bed. "They were both very tender, emotional and tearful with each other," Angela recalled. "We all had to leave so they could begin the tests and Paul and Linda had to get ready for their flight. As we drove home, both of us were very quiet all the way. I remember just outside the house, Paul squeezed my hand and said, 'I'll never forget what you've done for my dad.' "

Once inside, Angela retreated to the kitchen to cook breakfast. Paul went into the dining room, sat down at the piano and "The Long And Winding Road" wafted through the house. Angela and Ruth were overcome with emotion. "Jim used to say how much he loved that song and how it reminded him of the drive up to Scotland. To this day when I hear that song it upsets me because it reminds me so much of poor Jim."

Five days before Jim's death Cynthia Lennon called in to see him, with family friend Billy Hatton of the Fourmost. Paul spent a lot of time alone with his father, then Linda and the grandchildren came in to kiss him.

On 18 March 1976 Jim McCartney died at home from complications of arthritis. After he had drawn his last breath, Mike's little daughter Abby said, "Look, Poppy's stopped!" Angela immediately rang Paul, who was at a press conference at the Royal Garden Hotel to promote his forthcoming tour with Wings. "Are you sure?" he said. "Okay, I'll call you later. I'm in the middle of this thing here," and went back to finish the conference as if nothing had happened.

Other than Mike, no one in the family came to the house. The clan was freezing Angela out, probably because they felt they had been shut out of Jim's final days. Still, Angela was determined to rise above such pettiness and offered Jim's brother Joe something belonging to his brother as a keepsake, like a scarf or umbrella. No sooner had she put down the phone than Joan arrived with Millie's huge blue suitcase to raid Jim's wardrobe. He had only been dead eight hours!

That night Mike convinced Angela and Ruth to call in on Millie. "What are you doing here?" Millie snorted. "I don't want anything to do with you. And I'm not coming to the funeral!" Other friends remonstrated: "Please, Millie, the poor woman just lost her husband." But Millie hissed, "She wouldn't let us near him when he was dying."

No family, not even Paul (who was rehearsing in Paris for the Wings Over America tour), came to Jim's funeral. However, Paul issued Angela with specific instructions: "Do some nice flowers from me and Linda and little posies from the children." To make matters worse, the notorious British press painted Angela as having married Jim only for his money. During the funeral, she spotted an old friend and was caught by a photographer in a smile of surprise. It was published in the *Liverpool Echo* bearing the caption, "Angela McCartney smiling at husband's funeral".

To offset the day's disheartening events, a beautiful bouquet arrived from George Harrison and Ringo Starr. The card read,

"Thinking of you, to Ange and Ruth, love George and Ringo." Also enclosed was a generous cheque for arthritis research. It was only later that night, when Angela switched on the radio and heard Mike McGear singing "The Casket" that she collapsed in grief.

As quickly as Angela and Ruth entered the family some twelve years before, they were as abruptly cut off. The annual allowance Paul paid to his father, due in April, did not arrive. When Angela swallowed her pride and offered to help Linda with some bookkeeping, Linda was amazed at their situation and immediately wrote them a cheque for three thousand pounds.

In a desperate attempt to make ends meet, Angela and Ruth formed a management agency with pop singer Gary Glitter as their main client. A series of disastrous business decisions followed and Angela had to sell the bungalow for considerably less than it was worth. Later they were evicted from their small flat and forced to live in an empty office building in King's Lynn near Cambridge, sleeping on the floorboards. Eventually Angela had to apply for help from Social Services. When she handed in her papers, the clerk spotted the signature and asked, "Aren't you Paul McCartney's stepmother? Why isn't he helping you?" Angela replied curtly, "Because he apparently chooses not to."

With no other option Angela and Ruth sold off prized personal mementoes, such as tickets to Beatle premières, gold discs, autographed concert programmes, all of which Angela inherited on Jim's death. Angela also sold Paul's birth certificate, which exploded into a media nightmare and infuriated McCartney.

By 1972 Maureen Starkey was deeply disillusioned with her husband's lifestyle and the constant demands and disappointments of being married to someone so famous. She had been in love when she married Ritchie and remained so for several years. Now, rightly or wrongly, she was sure Ritchie was seeing other women, so there was no reason why she shouldn't find someone else. Her affair with George Harrison was over, and she was restless, unhappy and insecure. Unsure whether to end the marriage, take the children and move on, or stay and live her own life, she drifted from day to day, drawing and taking photographs. Ringo was generous, allowing his family *carte blanche* to buy whatever they wanted, but it was not enough.

For several months, Starr had been working on an ambitious documentary about the career of his close friend, T. Rex star, Marc Bolan, filming for which started 18 March. Maureen was the project's unofficial still photographer and soon developed a sisterly relationship with the dark-haired glam rocker. For his part, Ringo was not only producing and directing the film, *Born To Boogie*, but also intimately involved with the editing. In a bid to relax he partied with the crew, which isolated Maureen even more from him. According to a family friend and co-worker, one evening, Bolan rang the house needing to discuss something with Starr. He was out, so Marc and Maureen chatted together for a couple of hours then agreed to meet at the Dorchester for drinks the following evening.

Maureen arrived at around seven and met Bolan in the bar. "Hey, Mo!" he said, and embraced her. "Let's get a drink." Two hours and several champagne cocktails later, he got up and led her out to the parking lot where he kissed her. Maureen reciprocated. Within the hour, they were at Bolan's place making love. At just after two, Maureen dressed and drove home to her three children.

The next time Maureen saw Bolan was at the London première of *Born To Boogie* on 18 December. Hugs and kisses were exchanged all round, and Bolan said nothing about their night of passion. He spent the evening talking to Ringo and Mal Evans. Maureen was relieved: she had worried that Starr might spot the attraction between her and Bolan.

In 1977, Marc Bolan died in a car accident. Both Ringo and Maureen attended his funeral service.

When John and Yoko moved to the USA in September 1971, they continued their flirtation with left-wing politics. In a 1973 letter to a magazine they aired their grievances against rumours that the Beatles might reunite. Entitled, "Newswecanalldowithout", the piece was written in John's hallmark *Through The Looking Glass* style.

Although John, Yoko and George, and George and Ringo, had played together often, it was the first time the three ex-Beatles had played together since they last played together. As usual, an awful lot of rumors, if not downright lies, were going on, including the possibility of impresario Allen De Klein or grABKCO playing bass for the other three in an as-yet-untitled album called, "I Was A Teenage Fat Cat". Producer Richard Perry, who planned to take the tapes along to sell them to Paul McCartney, told a friend: "I'll take the tapes to Paul McCartney."

The extreme humility that existed between John and Paul seems to have evaporated: "They've spoken to each other on the telephone, and in English, that's a change," said a McCartney associate. "If only everything were as simple and unaffected as McCartney's new single, 'My Love', then maybe Dean Martin and Jerry Lewis would be reunited with the Marx Bros and *Newsweek* could get a job," said an East Anglican official.

Yours Up To The Teeth,
John Lennon and Yoko Ono.

During the 1970s assembling three Beatles in a room was a formidable task, but the circumstances in March 1973 forced a meeting. John, George and Ringo met in the grand Capitol Records Tower in Hollywood to discuss the latest Beatles release. The compilation, to be titled *The Best of the Beatles*, was separated into two double albums, which bore the uninspired names, *1962–1966* and *1967–1970* and would later be known as the "Red" and "Blue" albums. They had been generated as a response to the forthcoming bootleg release *Alpha Omega*, which within weeks would be blatantly advertised for sale on American TV. The three men had to discuss the albums' postponement: all four Beatles, especially Lennon and McCartney, disliked the hastily assembled track selection and quick mixes. Unfortunately, thousands of copies of the albums had already been shipped to warehouses and were awaiting distribution. They accomplished little during their meeting, but John and Ringo later attended a screening of *Last Tango In Paris*, starring Marlon Brando. With them was Richard Perry, Ringo's record producer. George had already seen it.

Starr had already begun recording his eponymous album, at Sunset Sound Recorders Studios in Los Angeles. Soon after his arrival there Harrison dropped in to observe the proceedings. "I'm knocked out by what you've done," he said enthusiastically, after listening to several tracks, and offered to play on the album. He returned for the next session, adding backing vocals behind Ringo's lead. The next day, 13 March, John and Yoko appeared – three of the Beatles were reunited in a studio. Harrison contributed a song, "Sunshine Life For Me (Sail Away Raymond)" and John brought "I'm The Greatest", which he had intended for *Imagine*, but had dropped from the final selection, fearing that as it was based on the famous Muhammad Ali line, it might be somehow misconstrued. However, he viewed it as perfect for Ringo, and changed the lyrics slightly to suit his old friend. At this point the Beatles were on much friendlier terms. "I've talked to Ringo a lot recently," said Lennon, "because he's just moved into my house at Ascot, which is nice because I've always got a bedroom there. I haven't talked to Paul since before he did the last tour with Wings. I heard *Red Rose Speedway* and it was all right." Richard Perry recalled that the session with John, George and Ringo happened "just like that: with no planning. The three ex-Beatles recorded one of John's songs. Everyone in the room was just gleaming . . . It's such a universal gleam with the Beatles!"

A high-quality tape of the song circulating among collectors runs at just over eighteen minutes, and features numerous false starts with Lennon trying in vain to determine a definite tempo, in addition to three complete takes. Later that year, John recalled: "The three of us were there and Paul would probably have joined us if he were around, but he wasn't. I got a call from Ringo asking me to write a track so I did. It seemed the natural thing to do . . . For the track I was on piano, Billy Preston on organ, Ringo drums, George on guitar and Klaus was on bass." Also present was keyboardist Nicky Hopkins, who was quick to downplay rumours of a Beatles' reunion when news of the sessions leaked to the media: "All it was was the people turned up, which has happened many times before in England. For example, Ringo worked on George's upcoming album and Harrison helped out on my own forthcoming LP."

McCartney, meanwhile, made his contribution to Starr's project back in London: "The others did some tracks in Los Angeles and then the material was brought over for me. I worked on a track called 'Six o'Clock' . . . so in a way there's been some . . . I'm happy to play with the other three and I'm sure they are too if it's physically possible. But more important for me is Wings, because I really get turned on by new ideas."

Although this was to remain the last collaboration between all four Beatles on one new album, they were still open to the possibility of future projects. "There's always a chance," John said. "As far as I can gather from talking to them, nobody would mind doing some work together again. There's no law that says we're not going to do something, and no law that says we are. If we did something, I'm sure it wouldn't be permanent. We'd do it just for that moment. We're closer now than we have been for a long time."

By March 1974, the stage was set for what became a final, short-lived Lennon–McCartney reunion. It had taken four years for the deepest wounds to heal, as John put it, after all the in-fighting in the press and sometimes not-so-subtle attacks on each other in their solo music. Calling for a Beatles reunion at this point was wildly premature but, none the less, three-quarters of the former group somehow found themselves in Los Angeles.

John had recently become estranged from Yoko, and fled with his lover May Pang to confront his self-destructive tendencies during what he called his "lost weekend". He stayed briefly at the home of record executive Harold Seiders, where Starr reintroduced him to Harry Nilsson. In 1968, John playfully named Nilsson his "favourite American group"; Nilsson had become a friend when his Beatles medley, based on "You Can't Do That", was first brought to the attention of Derek Taylor in 1967. While John was in LA, Nilsson encouraged his alcohol-fuelled antics, which rose to a climax on 12 March when the pair were thrown out of the Troubadour Club for heckling the Smothers Brothers. While he was escorted to his car, John said to a parking attendant, "Don't you know who I am? I'm Ed fucking Sullivan!"

It was clear that the Lennon–Nilsson act needed a creative outlet, and fortunately John realized this. His current rock 'n' roll oldies project had ground to a halt when the album's eccentric producer, Phil Spector, disappeared with the session tapes. When John rented a luxury beach-house in Santa Monica with May Pang it quickly became a popular rendezvous for musicians and celebrities. Among those participating in the regular Sunday-night sessions were Nilsson, Ringo, Keith Moon and Klaus Voormann. John came up with the idea of producing a Nilsson album, focusing on covers of their favourite songs. He had written a new song, "Mucho Mungo", which he knew would suit Nilsson's vocal style. Nilsson, though, was having problems. "He'd lost his voice. I don't know whether it was psychological or what," Lennon recalled. "He was going to doctors and having injections and didn't tell me until later he was bleeding in the throat, or I would have stopped the sessions. But he had no voice. So what do you do?"

May Pang concurred with his assessment of Nilsson's health: "He lost his voice in early 1974 just before working on *Pussy Cats*. He'd get acupuncture during the day and would drink and abuse himself by night. He haemorrhaged in his throat and didn't tell anyone. I don't think his voice was ever back to the greatness he had but it was close. Harry always lived close to the edge."

Nilsson remembered, "We were getting very bored at a Joni Mitchell session one night, peeing in ashtrays and that sort of thing, when John jumped up and said, 'I'm gonna produce Harry Nilsson!' I didn't know whether he was drunk or what, so a couple of days later he says to me, 'What do you think?' I said, 'If you're serious about it, man, you bet!' We'd wake up in the morning, well, about one o'clock actually, and eat breakfast prepared by this couple we had serving us. Klaus [Voormann] went out for a swim in the ocean quite a lot. My wife, Una, used to take long walks on the beach. John and May would sleep late, I'd sleep later, and then at six the limos would show up and we'd drive over to record, finishing about two in the morning. Then we'd come home, open up the brandy, and listen to the tapes very loudly, get drunk, and tell each other how wonderful we were.

"There were a couple of tunes we started. We wrote one called, 'You Are Here'. [It was later released on John's *Mind Games*.] It's something we never really finished. We used to send tapes back and forth to each other, and postcards. He would sign them 'You Are Here'. I miss him so much! I'd like to say I was close friends with the man, but I wasn't. No one was a very close friend to John other than the Beatles.

"Someone recently told me they once saw John walking on the street wearing a button that said, 'I Love Paul'. The girl asked him, 'Why are you wearing a button that says, "I Love Paul"'? And he said, 'Because I love Paul!'"

Another on-site musical miscreant was Peter 'Dougal' Butler, full-time babysitter to Keith Moon, who did everything he could to keep The Who's drummer in line for the already difficult sessions. He recalled the controlled anarchy: "*Pussy Cats* is one of the high points of my life, because it is through this album I met Lennon . . . It soon turned out he was a nice, relaxed sort of bloke and quite one of the lads. I personally never saw him awkward or hoity-toity as many people claim he was. Far from it, he was a great laugh in the studio and a considerable hand at partying afterwards. He loved Moonie's drumming and rated Keith as one of the all-time greats. In fact, he and Keith struck up quite a friendship and spent some time together.

"Then Nilsson requested Moonie to play on *Pussy Cats*, to be produced by Lennon. The gig necessitates several flights to California, where Harry arranges a suite in the Beverly Wilshire. We take over the suite directly from Bob Dylan . . .

"Meanwhile, Nilsson, John and Ringo hired a beach-house in Santa Monica. It once belonged to the Kennedys, and is apparently where they invited Marilyn Monroe, among others, to view their etchings and indulge in private performances.

"It is not long before Nilsson, Lennon and Starr invited Moonie to stay at the house with them. A daily routine now began whereby I'd drive out to the studio every day to meet Moonie and his mates. We complete the session and then repair back to the beach-house for some epic partying . . ."

Sessions for the album began on 28 March 1974 at Burbank Studios. Two special guests attending that first evening were Paul and Linda McCartney. Wings had been in rehearsals earlier in the month, and travelled to Los Angeles where the McCartneys attended the annual Academy Awards and met up with Lennon backstage. Paul was eager to work with John again, and they played together for the first time in over four years after the initial Nilsson session, jamming with the others on the old standard "Midnight Special". As everyone prepared to leave, John invited Paul to join in the next Sunday-night jam session. It was then, on 31 March, that the final Lennon–McCartney studio collaboration was recorded. John recalled the event in a BBC interview: "I did actually play with Paul. We did a lot of stuff in LA. But there was fifty other people playing, and they were all just watching me and Paul!"

"Don't get too serious, we're not getting paid," John instructed the *ad hoc* musical troupe gathered there that night. "We ain't doing nothing but sitting here together, and anybody getting bored with me, please take over!" The recording equipment assembled at the house had been borrowed from Burbank Studios, and John spent much of the session berating the engineers: "Just turn the fucking vocal mike up . . . McCartney's doing harmony on the drums." The ensemble consisted of Paul on Ringo's kit; John, Danny Kortchmar and Jesse Ed Davis on guitars; Stevie Wonder on electric piano; a producer named Ed on bass; Bobby Keys on saxophone; Linda on Hammond organ; May Pang and Mal Evans on tambourine; and Nilsson showcasing his ruptured vocal cords.

"Do you want a snort, Steve? A toot? It's going round," John asked, before things got under way. A classic Lennon stream-of-consciousness improvisation followed: "I fell upon my ass, nobody seemed to notice, I was wearing mother's bra and she was wearing Otis, but no one seemed to care, over there, they didn't have the bus fare. Later on, a distant relative passed away, so distant I didn't even notice, but I had to go to the funeral, just to see if they'd left me any gold in their teeth or any jewellery. So I say, 'Never trust a bugger with your mother,' she'll always wear you out and saying anything on paper ain't worth a dime. But I like the suit just cut this way, ah, gee, it's been such a fun time. When I look at Jack Lennon, and I look again, I feel him coming all over me . . . it's so wonderful to be waiting for my Green Card with thee . . ."

He also tried desperately to find a tune everyone knew. "Somebody think of a fuckin' song! I've done 'Ain't That A Shame' in twenty studios on these sessions." Paul suggested "Little Bitty Pretty One", but John was not familiar with the 1957 hit recorded by Bobby Day and the Satellites. He settled on Little Richard's "Lucille", and called for anyone to join in on vocals. Paul obliged, providing harmony under John's raucous vocal, and the group gave the best performance of the evening. They next tried the Shadows' instrumental, "Midnight", but John quickly lost interest: "Come on, let's do something! Somebody give me an E or a snort . . ."

Then John asked Mal to fetch everyone some drinks, and the band attempted "Stand By Me", which instantly broke down as Lennon complained about the mix in his headphones. "Turn the organ down in the ears . . . It's gone all dead, dead in the earphones, you know . . . dead, man!" With continued microphone problems, they got through a full version of "Stand By Me", followed by short snatches of Sam Cooke's "Cupid" and "Chain Gang", and the traditional Leadbelly song "Take This Hammer".

In the early-morning hours Paul and Linda left for their nearby hotel. Ringo, meanwhile, had been out socializing with Keith Moon, and upon his return, noticed something was different. "Who's been fiddling with my bloody drums?" he asked. "Paul," the others replied. "Paul's been here." McCartney returned to the beach-house that morning and, with John still in bed, played a medley of Beatles tunes on the piano with Moon and Nilsson happily joining in. Afterwards Nilsson offered him some angel dust but he refused thoughtfully. After Lennon awoke around three o'clock, the group relaxed around the pool, and Dougal Butler snapped the last known photo* ever to be taken of John and Paul together.

The album originally to be titled *Strange Pussies*, was wisely renamed *Pussy Cats*. "The main thing was we had a lot of fun," said Lennon. "There was Moon, Harry, Ringo and me all living together

* There are thought to be many still unpublished family shots from the McCartneys' various visits to the Dakota in the late seventies.

in the house and we had some moments. But it got a little near the knuckle. When I straightened out, in the middle of that album, that's when I realized: There's something wrong here. This is crazy, man! I was suddenly the straight one in the middle of all these mad, mad people. I suddenly was not one of them. I pulled myself back and finished the album as best I could. We'd already spent the money . . . Everything was booked. We had the tapes. Me and Harry had the best out of it, because we spent a few good nights together."

Pussy Cats was the first in a string of several unsuccessful albums for Nilsson. Soon after its release on 19 August 1974, John was reunited with Yoko, the party ended, and he withdrew from making albums for the next five years.

A few months later at five a.m. on 21 December John "worked" with George Harrison for the last time. It took place during Harrison's musically ground-breaking Dark Horse tour and the two spent the evening at Harrison's hotel after the show. Two or three journalists were in attendance, invited as part of the extended entourage, and captured the last public utterances made together by the two men.

Question: How do you feel about George's new tour?

John Lennon: They attack the Stones who have just done one of the greatest albums they ever made. Mick's singing like a beauty, and people are saying it's the same old stuff. It isn't the same old stuff, it's great Stones! If you do change, you're attacked for changing, right? The audiences have been digging George's shows – because I've got good spies – but the critics don't like it, because he's changed. If he'd done everything the same, he would have been attacked for not changing it!

Question: What Beatles songs do you particularly enjoy?

George Harrison: There's lots of songs I thought were pretty good, and there's ones I thought were sensational. To quickly say which ones I really enjoyed is very hard. I liked "Strawberry Fields". I enjoyed the ones which were inventive. I enjoyed "Norwegian Wood" because I felt it was coming from the heart. I remember I was alongside John or Paul as they were writing things. Occasionally I might have said a line or a word, like my mother would say a line or a word, which they'd use. I can think of a million times I wrote a few lines or verses for "Eleanor Rigby", or something . . . John helped in as much as he gave me a tip, he was just being observant. And that is that once you get in the motion of starting a song, it's handy to try and finish it. I remember John did an interview with a certain magazine and I remember the day he disagreed with what he'd said. But the man who interviewed him denied him the right to change his mind, even though it was two and a half years later. He still went ahead and published something John said he no longer agreed with himself on. Which means the dream was over, yet certain people wouldn't allow him to have his dream over. Nudge nudge, wink wink!

John: Imagine if you accidentally bang your head, and you shout, "Ow!" and that's the end of it. Right? It doesn't go on for the next five years, right? We all do that.

George: We've been at parties full of people who have got the shiniest shoes, the biggest heels, the funniest glasses and the biggest hats. I can't get on with that scene. I just met David Bowie who they call "Boowie" in America. Who I know Ringo also thinks is great. I met him in Memphis and he was in the shower room with the band, just before we went on for the second show. I had to pull David's glasses off and say, "Let's have a look. Let's see where you are, David Bowie." These were my very words, and I hope he wasn't offended. I pulled his hat up from over his eyes and said, "Hi, man, how are you?" You know, "Nice to meet you. Do you mind if I have a look at you, to see what you are?" because I'd only ever seen those dopey pictures of him. Every picture I've ever seen of David Bowie or Elton John, they just look stupid to me.

John: I thought he looked great.

George: Well, I think he looks dopey. I want to see who the person is.

Question: What about a Beatles reunion?

John: There's problems with immigration for me, George and Paul, right? So every time George or Paul want to come here they have to ask permission, eighteen months in advance. It's impossible for

> more than one or two of us to get in at the same time. The most that were ever here were me, Paul and – who was the other one? – Ringo, and a lot of children of theirs didn't come. So, it's impossible for us even to get in a room together, so the only way we talk is either over the phone or through some paper.

As the decade unravelled Harrison steadfastly put his Beatles days behind him and got on with life, renovating Friar Park, writing and producing his own music and chanting "Hare Krishna". By late 1974 his well-known Krishna-consciousness aspirations had led to a serious collaboration with Ravi Shankar on an album of Indian classical music with just a touch of pop, rock and fusion. Entitled *Shankar Family and Friends*, here was the popular beginning of new age/world music, the creation of which, was, in large part, due to George. The LP's only single, "I Am Missing You (Krishna Where Are You)" failed to register on the charts (as did the album), but served as one of the anthems for Harrison's musically controversial 1974 Dark Horse tour as well as attracting praise from Bhaktivedanta Swami himself.

In the late 1970s Harrison received a call from his old friend, the musician Gary Wright, who invited him down to his villa in Portugal for a few days. George accepted, jumped into his Mercedes and took off through the front gates of Friar Park. As he headed for the ferry, he began to chant the sixteen-word Sanskrit mantra: "Hare Krishna, Hare Krishna, Krishna Krishna, Hare Hare, Hare Rama, Hare Rama, Rama Rama, Hare Hare". In a 1983 interview he remembered the trip: "In the life I lead, I sometimes have opportunities when I can really get going at [chanting], and the more I do it, I find the harder it is to stop, and I don't want to lose the feeling it gives me. I once chanted Hare Krishna all the way from France to Portugal, non-stop. I drove for about twenty-three hours and chanted all the way. It gets you feeling a bit invincible. I didn't even know where I was going. I'd bought a map, and I knew basically which way I was aiming, but I couldn't speak French, Spanish or Portuguese. But none of that seemed to matter. Once you get chanting, things start to happen transcendentally."

Bhaktivedanta Swami's magic mantra, it seemed, performed equally well in times of distress. "I was once on an aeroplane in an electric storm," George told Mukunda Das Gosvami. "It was hit by lightning three times, and a Boeing 707 went right over the top of us, missing our plane by inches. I thought the back of the aircraft had blown off so I started chanting 'Hare Krishna'. This thing went on for about two hours with the plane dropping hundreds of feet, all the lights were out and there were several huge explosions. Everybody was terrified! I ended up with my feet pressed against the seat yelling, 'Hare Krishna,' at the top of my lungs. For me, the difference between making it and not making it was chanting the mantra."

George Harrison's deep faith was to sustain him in the best and worst of times for the rest of his life.

By the end of 1975 the Beatles' devoted minder Mal Evans, now aged forty, was a pretty much broken figure, lost in the fading afterglow of the most famous band in history. Since the group's split he'd worked on and off for all of the Beatles, assisting on sessions and running errands, but it was mainly George Harrison who went out of his way to find work for him, even appointing him to oversee daily operations at Friar Park. He had most recently given Mal a small role in 1974's *Little Malcolm and His Struggle Against the Eunuchs*, his first film, which was based on the 1965 David Halliwell stage comedy. Evans also co-wrote a song with Bobby Purvis, which was used in the movie *Lonely Man* and performed by Splinter, a two-man group he had discovered and signed to George's Dark Horse Records. (Evans also discovered Badfinger – in a Swansea pub. They were then known as the Iveys.)

The film was a disappointing adaptation of the play and never went further than a few festival showings, and Splinter, despite George's involvement, went down as a mere footnote in pop history. Essentially, since 1970, Evans had been abandoned by his erstwhile employers and moved to Los Angeles. He was reduced to scratching around in the record industry for meagre freelance production jobs for which he was ill-qualified.

On the surface he seemed much the same, telling friends he had many big-time irons in the fire, spreading the word that he was producing the group Natural Gas, fronted by Badfinger guitarist Joey Molland, which he proclaimed as "the next big thing". At Beatles conventions, he was often the key speaker and enjoyed cult status among hardcore fans. On the dais he could relive the glory years, and it was painfully clear that he had never moved on. "It's like being a Beatle for a weekend," he gushed to fans. "The Beatles are my favourite subject. I could live on it. It's better than food or drink!

"I keep in touch with them all and we reminisce about the past. It's like, 'Let me take you down Memory Lane' every time we meet. George and Ringo were in town recently and we went over a few times, we hang out. I've just been speaking to Paul who was in town over the weekend. I shared the Beatles as a whole entity; I also shared trips with them individually. It's always 'remember this, remember that', it's nice." But in truth, contact between the four Beatles and Evans was minimal. He was no longer an integral member of their circle and it hurt.

Soon there were disturbing signs that he was heading for a breakdown. Even as he boasted on LA local radio about his "big-time" publishing company, Mal Content Music, he was forced to admit that his client list consisted of "only me". One comment was particularly revealing: "I've never had to do anything for myself in the past. Working for a Beatle was always doing something for somebody else. I can always cope with somebody else's problems. Doing it for yourself is a bit difficult."

His personal life, too, was increasingly shaky. His wife Lil was talking of divorce just before Christmas.

As America's overblown bicentennial year opened, he was finishing his memoirs for the publishing giant Grosset and Dunlop. The working title was *Living the Beatles Legend*, although he wanted to call it *Two Hundred Miles To Go*, signifying the distance from Liverpool to London. "The book at the moment is my whole life," he said. "I want all four Beatles to love it. My life's dream will be realized if they were to ring me and say, 'I love what you're doing.' I was talking to Ringo about the book and I said, 'You know I wouldn't put you down.' Starr said, 'If you don't tell the truth don't bother doing it. You, Mal, of all people, have to tell it like it was.' There's a few things I'm sure they'll get mad at me about."

Earlier that year Evans had obtained written permission from all four to use their names in the book. Lennon wrote to him, "I've been dying to read your diary for the last thousand years! Make a buck but don't buck it!" And Paul said, "Sure you can do your book, as long as you tell 'em how lovely I am." He signed off, "You great big POOFTAH!"

Interestingly, the other two Beatles took a much more formal approach. Harrison's reply read like a legal brief: "This is to confirm our conversation that you have my approval to use my name and likeness in relation to your forthcoming project . . ."

Starr, despite his advice to Evans to tell the truth, was the only one of the four to express concern about the content: "I wish you great success with it," he wrote. "I would, however, like to read the book before it is published." What might he have been worried about – and what unhappy truths might Evans have exposed?

The end of the project, however, had a devastating impact on Evans. In writing about those years, Mal could keep his treasured memories alive, but the final draft closed that chapter of his life and reality kicked in. Once the former Liverpool telecommunications worker had jet-setted around the world with the biggest musical sensation of the twentieth century. He'd acted in films, held a prestigious job at Apple Corps and lived on lavish expense accounts. Now he was existing in virtual obscurity, scraping by, too proud to ask his former employers for help. It was as if putting the final touches to the book took away his purpose in life. Like so many others cast adrift by the entertainment industry, Evans eventually turned to barbiturates, alcohol and dope to escape the pain of obscurity. Observers noted that when he was drunk, he often griped, "No one loves me for me. It's only because I worked for those bloody Beatles . . . A lot of people try to use you, but every now and again I meet somebody who likes me for myself and that makes it all worthwhile."

On the night of Sunday, 4 January 1976, a deeply despondent

Evans, at home in his motel apartment at 8122 West Fourth Street in LA, snapped. First, he phoned his writing collaborator John Hoernly, imploring him and editorial assistant Joanne Lennard to make certain the manuscript was delivered by its 12 January deadline. Hoernly rushed over to attempt to calm him but was apparently unable to do so. They went to a bedroom where Evans picked up a 30.30 rifle, which Hoernly later insisted was unloaded. They scuffled over it, but Hoernly, only half Evans's size, was unable to take it from him. Evans's live-in girlfriend, Francine Hughes, rang the police and told them, "My old man has a gun, has taken Valium, and is totally screwed up." Next, Evans allegedly ordered Hughes and her young daughter out of the apartment at gunpoint. Shortly thereafter, four police officers arrived. David D. Krampa and Robert E. Brannon cautiously went upstairs.

Mal was reportedly clutching the lever-action rifle as police surrounded his home. Telephone records indicate that he made two calls during the standoff, one to an unknown LA exchange and the other, lasting just under a minute, to John Lennon's apartment at the Dakota in New York. That call, a possible distress signal that might have proved pivotal in the outcome, was apparently not put through to John.

"Police officers!" came the shouts from the hallway. "Give yourself up!"

"No!" Evans screamed. "I'm not coming out! You'll have to blow my fucking head off!"

The officers kicked in the door and stormed the room. "Drop the gun!" they demanded. Evans, on the bed, cornered and desperate, levelled the barrel at them. They had no choice: four shots rang out. One hit the side of Evans's nose, another his lower leg. Lieutenant Charles Higbie of LA's robbery and homicide division then fired two fatal strikes to the chest, dropping him to the floor in a shower of blood and bone. The police claimed that Evans's weapon was loaded with five rounds of ammunition, one all ready to go in the firing chamber.

An unnamed Evans insider, however, told the story this way: "Hughes found him despondent and when friends couldn't persuade

Evans to release the unloaded rifle he was holding they called the police." In a drunken stupor Evans became uncontrollably violent, attempted suicide then pointed the rifle at an officer, who shot him six times in self-defence, four bullets hitting him. Some accounts even insist that Mal was brandishing a harmless air pistol.

The following day Francine Hughes sought refuge at Harry Nilsson's home. She blamed herself for the tragedy, saying Mal had been drinking heavily. "He probably doesn't even know he's dead, wherever he's at," she groaned.

In the aftermath, Francine's claim that Evans had been drinking and "flipped out" on drugs was disputed by the post-mortem, which showed alcohol levels consistent with one drink and a moderate amount of Valium. It has been suggested that Evans goaded the LA police into "suicide by cop". "If Brian Epstein was the fifth Beatle," Evans's lawyer John Mason said, "then Mal was the sixth." Evans's body was cremated in Los Angeles on 7 January; Harry Nilsson and several other close friends attended.

Later Paul McCartney blamed Francine Hughes for Evans's death because she had panicked and called the police. "Mal got shot by the LA police. It was so crazy, so crazy. Mal was a big lovable bear of a roadie. He'd go over the top occasionally but we all knew him and never had any problems. The LAPD weren't so fortunate. They were just told he was upstairs with a shotgun. They ran up, kicked the door in and shot him. His girlfriend told them, 'He's upstairs, he's a bit moody, he's got a shotgun and some downers.' Had I been there I would have been able to say, 'Mal, don't be silly.' In fact, any of his friends could have talked him out of it without any sweat because he was not a nutter. But his girlfriend, she was an LA girl, didn't really know him that well. She should not have rung the cops but that's the way it goes . . . A thump on the door. 'Where is he? Where's the assailant?' Bang, bang, bang, bang. They don't ask questions, they shoot first."

The final insult was that Evans's ashes were lost on the way home to Britain. John quipped to Peter Brown that Mal's remains probably ended up in the dead-letter office. Although it was said Lennon exploded into hysterical laughter when he first heard of Evans's demise, Harry Nilsson claimed John later broke down in tears, as he had when he heard of his mother's and Stuart Sutcliffe's deaths. His off-the-cuff verbal reaction to the news said it all: "Jesus, man. My God! America is so fuckin' quick with the gun! Mal had no real life after the Beatles. He had no art to fall back on. No real future as a producer or anything. But he was the perfect fuckin' roadie! And he was a friend. When he was shot, murdered by the cops, I felt like smashing my fist through a goddamn window or something! Mal was the last fucker to hurt anyone, even though he certainly could have, had he been so moved. He was a gentle giant. His heart was as big as the man. I'd seen him in LA towards the end but every time I asked he just said he was okay. Obviously we know now he wasn't, but whatta you gonna do? He stayed with me for awhile in a madhouse I had at the beach with Keith Moon, Harry Nilsson and Klaus Voormann. He was a very proud guy. He wouldn't take any money from us so we would all try to find odd jobs for him after the split. Still, it wasn't the same as being an important cog in a famous functioning group. He was alone, even though he had a so-called girlfriend. I'm sure it must have been hard for him to even come to me as a slight indiscretion occurred on my part with someone close to him and that really hurt him a lot. All of which made me feel doubly terrible when he died. Mal was easy. Too fucking easy. Sometimes even his best friends took advantage of that fact. Or, shall I say, especially his close friends most of all."

Harrison later reflected, "Mal was killed by his own despair and loneliness. The LAPD were only the weapon. Mal's personal pain and disillusion were the trigger. As far as I'm concerned it was suicide by cop that really killed him. It's very, very sad because we all loved him so much.

"He loved his job, he was brilliant and I often regret he was killed. To this day I keep thinking, Mal, where are you? If only he was out there now. He was such good fun but he was also very helpful. He could do anything. He was very humble but not without dignity. It was not belittling for him to do what we wanted so he was perfect for us because he was exactly what we needed."

Some two decades later, in 1997, Mal Evans's widow Lil, then sixty, approached Sotheby's auction house with Paul McCartney's handwritten lyrics to "With A Little Help From My Friends". She was working as a secretary when she discovered them among her late husband's papers. They were valued at about $100,000.

When Paul heard about it he immediately sought a High Court injunction to block the sale. As he saw it, the lyrics had never belonged to Evans who had simply kept track of them as part of his official Beatles duties. "This text was only picked up by Mal," he claimed. "It ought to be returned to its rightful owner. There is no question they ever belonged to anyone other than the Beatles."

Lil quickly drew public sympathy when she was interviewed by the BBC about her plight. "I don't know why he [Paul] would want to do that," she said. "It wouldn't be for the money as he lets other people sell, so I don't know why he would want to stop me."

McCartney's spokesman, Geoff Baker, quickly issued damage-control: he pointed out that Paul had twice offered to help out Lil but she had declined. "I don't wish to cause any trouble for Mrs Evans or her children, whom I remember fondly," said Paul, "but I do feel strongly these original manuscripts should be returned to their rightful owners."

When the press took Lil's side, he retreated from his position, dropped the legal action and said he wanted to reach an agreement with Evans's widow to make sure she was "taken care of".

It wasn't the first time that Lil had dipped into her estranged husband's effects to make some quick cash. In 1984 she auctioned a 1960 Hofner Senator acoustic guitar that John Lennon had given to him. She even provided a letter to her from George Harrison saying it was "one of the first guitars of John's going back to Liverpool". The instrument sold for some fifteen thousand pounds at Sotheby's.

Interestingly, in 1998 a notebook containing lyrics, including those to "Hey Jude", and the original cover designs for the *Sgt. Pepper* album went to auction. The notebook had been compiled by Evans and was relayed to Sotheby's by an "anonymous vendor". It fetched an impressive $167,000. Stephen Maycock, Sotheby's rock specialist, said, "The notebook is one of several items from the collection of the late Mal Evans. It is the ultimate memento of the group's career, and documents the integral role Mal played in the heart of the Beatles organization."

As for Evans's memoirs George Harrison hinted to me in 1983 that, due to legal entanglements, they would never be published. Were certain parties paid to bury the revelations Evans had suggested the Beatles might "get mad" about?

A source who asked not to be named was called to the editorial offices of the publishing house some days after Evans's death. There, several editors had found a large box containing original Beatles memorabilia, several pages from Evans's memoirs and even a dummy copy of the book complete with a provisional cover. Having realized that the book would now never be published, the firm didn't know what to do with the material and called in my source for his advice. There were letters from the Beatles to Evans, handwritten lyrics, friendly postcards, many unpublished Beatles family photographs and, of course, a small portion of the manuscript. Attempts to contact anyone from Evans's estate failed. In the meantime, an employee called an unnamed Beatles insider and informed them about the treasure trove. The insider contacted a Beatles lawyer, who used various legal manoeuvres to assert that the contents of the box were the exclusive property of unnamed parties within the Beatles camp. The box was subsequently handed over to the lawyer. As a memento, however, my source kept the dummy for the book, and has it today as a souvenir of what would have been an authorized Beatles biography.

This new information, of course, clashes with other reports that Evans's book was finished, or very nearly, at the time of his death. Perhaps, the reason that the book was never published was that it had not, in fact, been written.

After Apple all but collapsed when the Beatles split in 1970, all that was left was to guard the kingdom against incursion by those anxious to loot the Beatles' legacy. The producers of the musical *Beatlemania*, which appeared on Broadway and in every major college town in America, were the first to have a go. With the public's hunger for the Beatles at an all-time high, they held auditions around the country and hired several casts of young men to play them on stage. The two-hour-plus show was basically a live concert, featuring the Beatle lookalikes against a backdrop of high-tech multi-media phantasmagoria. Robin Williams hit the nail on the head when he remarked that people were running out to buy the soundtrack for *Beatlemania* when they already had the real thing in their record collections at home!

"We have and always have had a company called Apple (long before there were the computers) but nobody knows Apple Records or Apple Films," George Harrison complained in a mid-1980s interview. "The four of us were directors at the time, now we have designated the directorship to our personal managers or representatives because there is still so much that goes on [including] Neil Aspinall who's been with us, who Paul and I knew since school. It's like any other company who owns something, that is our property, and people come along and try to use that, by getting permission, licensing, went through years, and there is a lot of stuff like that now. There are things like *Beatlemania*, which was run everywhere. It became a free-for-all where people would think the Beatles were public domain like Mozart or something. With *Beatlemania* we were going to settle with the manager and they refused. So we went to court and they awarded us $11,000,000. We settled for a figure well beneath that."

John Lennon spent the last few years of his life in kingly comfort at home with his son Sean and Yoko in the Dakota on New York's Upper East Side. He became increasingly sentimental about his Liverpool family. In particular, he felt guilty for having neglected his ageing aunts and two young half-sisters, Julia and Jacqui. In late 1976 he reached out to them for the first time in years. Julia remembered, "Quite honestly, if it wasn't for John's great wealth, we probably would have been in touch long before. We would have had a better chance of remaining close if he had been a sheep-rancher in Australia or something. As it was, with the seemingly gargantuan aura surrounding 'John Lennon' it sometimes made it difficult to maintain any sort of relationship at all. Truthfully, as far as I was concerned anyway, his financial situation only served to keep him more out of reach of his family."

One Saturday morning John contacted Julia through their aunt Harrie. Thereafter they spoke semi-regularly for several months. "Look at the way the damned government is trying to boot me out of America," John complained to her. "And for what? A couple of lousy grams of hash! From now on, every time I have a smoke, I practically lock myself inside a fucking vault! Do you realize those bastards are actually tapping my phones? Some geezer here in New York recently gave me a special number that if you called it and it rang busy then your line was tapped. So, anyway, one day I did and it was."

"John was always a highly spontaneous spur-of-the-moment character," says Julia, "as evidenced by an unexpected phone call I received from him early one Sunday morning. 'How would you like your very own island, Ju?' he asked. 'Pardon?' I stammered, only half awake. 'What on earth are you on about, John?' 'Way back in the sixties, I bought this uninhabited island off the coast of Ireland through Apple called Dornish. Yoko and I only went there once, with Pete Shotton, and other than a wandering tribe of California hippies who stayed on for awhile no one has set foot on it since. What do you think?' 'Well . . . Hold on a minute, John,' I said. 'Allen . . . wake up a sec, do you fancy having your own island then? Listen, John wants to give us an island he owns off Ireland!' Allen was struggling to pull himself up from under the bedclothes and just beginning to comprehend what I was talking about. 'An island? Yeah, sure, I guess. It would certainly save on the bus fare to work.' 'Very funny,' I replied. 'Okay, John, we'll have your island. Thanks very much.' 'It's yours, then, and you're more than welcome. I'll get in touch with what's left of Apple in London and see that the title is transferred into your name.' "

The line went dead. John had said what he wanted to say and had rung off, apparently happy that he had finally "done" something for his sister.

"Although nothing ever came of John's offer, it makes me very happy to know he cared enough to make it in the first place. I couldn't ever really see us all tramping off to the Irish Sea to live on a remote island without any buildings, electricity or even water. But it was a nice fantasy for awhile, and every once in a while, Allen and I still chuckle about it. My mad brother, John, what a truly extraordinary fellow he always was."

It was 1980 before Ruth and Angela McCartney spoke to Paul for the last time to explain why they had had to sell off the family memorabilia. McCartney railed at his stepmother for selling a piano he had used throughout the turbulent Beatle years. "Yes, we were guilty," she acknowledged. "We sold the piano for six hundred and eighty pounds, along with a load of other furniture we couldn't use any more because we were being evicted by the mortgage company and were flat broke."

McCartney, of course, had been wealthy for many years and had not experienced the kind of money troubles facing Angela and Ruth. It seemed to Angela that he would prefer her to stay at home quietly and be a proper widow, and he was extremely discouraging about Ruth's prospects in the music business. The exchange between McCartney and the two women became heated. Said Ruth, "I actually dared to put the phone down on him that day. I was his stepsister, we'd shared a bathroom, so I didn't see him as a god. I was one of the very few people left in his life who would tell him to fuck off. I'll never forget his last words to me. He said, 'You can't put the phone down on me. I'm Paul McCartney!' I never heard from him again."

Today Ruth McCartney is happily married to a talented musician and lives in California, the successful owner of her own multi-media company of which her mother is an administrator and controller. Ruth would like nothing better than a reconciliation with her famous stepbrother. "I don't particularly like him but I still love him. He's my brother. If he ever needed me I wouldn't question it, I'd go help. I feel sorry for the poor bastard because he's trapped inside all that bullshit and he's not man enough to come out. Will the real Paul McCartney please stand up and let me love you?"

TEN

The Love There That's Sleeping

Home

1980–95

"How many Beatles does it take to change a lightbulb? The answer is four: John, Paul, George and Ringo. Whatever history thinks, that's what it was."

George Harrison

"What a great time it was, and how close we all were. We tend to forget that. We did live in a box, and saved each other's lives."

Ringo Starr

The year 1980 proved fateful for everyone in the Beatles' orbit. January marked McCartney's notorious Japanese drug bust, in which he was jailed for possession of marijuana then deported. According to Fred Seaman, Lennon's personal assistant, John followed the story with gleeful relish, asking Seaman's father to buy all the British papers so that he and Yoko could share a good laugh over Paul's predicament. "I can just picture him sitting in a bare jail cell," John said. "They've taken away his shoelaces and his belt so he won't hang himself if he becomes despondent singing: 'Yesterday, all my troubles seemed so far away.'" It was John's theory that Paul subconsciously wanted to get busted "to show the world he was still a bad boy".

The same year also brought the end of Wings, fuelled by co-commander Denny Laine's bitter defection over money disputes. The grounding of Wings ended an astounding chapter in pop history: over the group's decade-long career they had sold more records even than the Beatles.

November marked a new beginning for John, with his first release in five years, the melodic yet challenging *Double Fantasy*. He had hit forty and was finally at peace with himself, which showed in the McCartney-style themes he took on in his music of home and family, displaying a tender, even sentimental side of his nature. Of the first hit single from the LP, "(Just Like) Starting Over", he remarked, "That's what I'm doing. It took me forty years to grow up. I'm saying, 'Here I am, now how are you? How's your relationship going? Did you get through it all? Wasn't the seventies a drag? Well, here we are, let's make the eighties great.'

"I never could have written 'Starting Over' in 1975. I'm finding myself writing like I first used to. These past five years have helped me liberate myself from my intellect, and my image of myself. I could write again without consciously thinking about it, which was a joy. This is like our first album . . . It's fun to be rocking and rolling now, but if it gets not to be fun, I'll just walk away. Because I know I can walk away now."

According to Fred Seaman, even ten years after the collapse of his partnership with Paul, John was still taking up the gauntlet his former partner had flung at his feet: "After years of lying dormant John's competitive nature had been aroused. As long as Paul kept turning out mediocre 'product' John felt justified in keeping his own muse on a shelf. But if Paul were actually writing good music, John felt compelled to take up his challenge. It was a conditioned reflex, nurtured during years of friendly (and later fierce) rivalry in the Beatles. John told me Paul was the only musician who could scare him into writing great songs, and vice versa. That was the nature of their relationship, creative sibling rivalry."

Shockingly on 8 December 1980, at 10.49 p.m., John Lennon was brutally cut down outside his Dakota apartment by a faceless punk with a cheap Charter Arms revolver. Mark David Chapman, a troubled drifter from Hawaii, had lain in wait for the former Beatle the entire day, even brazenly asking Lennon to autograph a record album when he left the building earlier that evening. When John and

Yoko arrived home that night from a recording session at the Record Plant the former security guard stepped out of the shadows and fired five shots at Lennon's back, four bullets finding their mark.

Lennon was rushed in the back of a patrol car to New York's Roosevelt Hospital where doctors cracked open his chest to perform open heart massage in a desperate, last ditch attempt to save his life. But the impact of three massive, hollow-point bullets had shattered his heart beyond repair. The beloved music icon was pronounced dead at 11.15 p.m.

McCartney was overcome with grief. He gathered his family close and cried for days. "We just couldn't handle it, really," he confessed. "I talked to Yoko the day after he was killed and the first thing she said was, 'John was really fond of you.' The last telephone conversation I had with him we were still the best of mates. He was always a very warm guy, John. His bluff was all on the surface. He used to take his glasses down, those granny glasses, and say, 'It's only me.' They were like a wall, you know? A shield. Those are the moments I treasure."

Starr heard the news while on holiday in the Bahamas with his future wife Barbara and immediately chartered a jet to fly them both to New York, where he went to the Dakota to offer his condolences to Yoko and Sean. A mass of weeping, almost hysterical fans were waiting outside, in an echo of the days of Beatlemania, reaching out to touch him. But Starr wasn't ready for his grief to become public property: "I didn't want to hear people saying how much they loved the Beatles. I was there for a friend, not because he was a member of a pop group."

Harrison was at home asleep when the phone rang in the middle of the night. Before he touched the receiver he felt something must be wrong. It was his sister Louise, still living in the USA. George prepared himself for what he was sure must be bad news.

That afternoon, in London, Derek Taylor wandered over to Apple's last sorry incarnation on St James Street to sit with the company's managing director, Neil Aspinall, and wait for the calls to flood in. After a couple of hours painful reminiscence, they parted and Derek took a cab to George's London office. There, he summoned up the courage to ring Harrison. "George," he said, "maybe you should make some sort of statement, just to get the bastards off your back."

"I can't now," the reclusive guitarist replied. There was a long pause. "Later, maybe."

The line went dead. Taylor hung up and lit a cigarette. He knew that the longer George waited to speak, the worse it would be. Less than an hour later he rang George again. This time Harrison agreed to help him formulate a press statement: "After all we went through together I still have great love and respect for him. I am shocked and stunned. To rob life is the ultimate robbery, to the limit with the use of a gun. It is an outrage that people can take other people's lives when they obviously haven't got their own lives in order."

After phoning the copy through to all of the major London news agencies, Taylor caught the train home to Brudon Mills, his simple country house in Suffolk. He stared out of the window and, like millions of others around the world, asked himself, "Why?"

That morning, in Chester, Julia Baird heard the terrible news: "Around eight o'clock I thought I heard a very slight tapping on the front door and rushed to investigate. It was one of the neighbours, come to tell me that my cousin Leila was on the phone. We had only just bought the house and decided not to rush out and have a telephone installed. Leila? I thought. What on earth does she want at this hour of the morning? I dashed across the street and ran to the phone, but, strangely, stopped just short of actually picking it up. It was just a feeling of dread. 'Hello . . .' I finally stammered. 'Leila, what is it?' 'Then you haven't heard the news yet?' she asked. 'No . . . what is it? Are your kids all right?' 'Julia,' she continued, 'it's John. I'm afraid he's been shot.' I was stunned. Although I hadn't seen him in years, the words cut through me. She had to repeat it several times before I slowly began to pick up the thread. 'Is he all right?' I asked. 'No, Julia, he's dead.' 'Are you coming over then?' I said, trying to hold back the tears. 'Yes, I am. I'm coming straight away. Just sit tight until I get there.' 'All right,' I promised, trailing off into nothing as I placed the receiver back on the cradle.

"Leila and I sat together in my kitchen talking of old times. 'Do you remember that special secret whistle John always had to call for his mate Ivy through the garden? And how he loved fishing for salmon with Uncle Bert when he visited Mater in Scotland?' So many special memories, so much tears and laughter. I had lost my only brother, and I was simply numb.

"None of my children ever really knew their uncle and that was a very great shame. To them, their uncle John was simply one of four smiling faces staring up at them from the cover of a Beatles LP. Now, of course, it was for ever too late. A reality I struggle to accept to this day.

"Many people have asked me how I feel about the fellow who killed my brother. All I can say is that it was a cowardly act obviously carried out by someone with a very, very sick mind. Still, strangely, I don't particularly feel any great hatred for this mixed-up American madman. As the years roll by, I become more and more convinced my brother was truly one of the greatest artists of the twentieth century. Eventually, I could have seen him branching out further as not only a musician but as an author, poet, painter and philosopher."

Several other people close to Lennon were besieged by the press in pursuit of their thoughts and feelings on the tragedy, especially Mimi and Cynthia. Both women were overcome with grief and only reluctantly consented to talk after it became apparent it would be easier to do so than to refuse. "Since his mother died, John always looked upon me as his mum," said Mimi. "There was never any possibility he would be just an ordinary person. He'd have been successful in anything he did. He was always just as happy as the day was long. I will never recover."

Cynthia stated, "Despite the fact that we were divorced, I continue to hold John in the highest regard. I would like to talk to you about John, but I know that if I tried, the words would not come out. It's very, very painful. All I can do is to stay here in England with my washing and ironing to try and keep my mind off it."

By 1980, George was feeling that the time was right for him to record another album. He gathered together an array of old friends, Ringo, Allah Rakha, Ray Cooper, Herbie Flowers, Willie Weeks, Al Kooper,

Jim Keltner and Tom Scott, and began sessions at Friar Park for what would later become *Somewhere In England*. The album he submitted to Warner Brothers Records in Los Angeles some months later consisted of eight new tracks as well as two standards, "Baltimore Oriole" and "Hong Kong Blues". The cover showed Harrison's profile merged with a satellite shot of a cloudy Great Britain.

The executives at Warner Brothers were not impressed with either the music or the art and rejected it. In the end, four tracks were deleted, "Flying Hour", "Lay His Head", "Sat Singing" and "Tears of The World", and in their place, four new songs were added, "Tear Drops", "Blood From a Clone", "That Which I Have Lost", and "All Those Years Ago". Reluctantly, Harrison contacted photographer Caroline Irwin to put together an alternate cover. The album was released in June 1981, and spawned two singles, "Tear Drops" and "All Those Years Ago", George's touching tribute to John.

Recorded at Friar Park Studios, "All Those Years Ago" was originally intended as a vehicle for Ringo. After Lennon's murder, though, Harrison rewrote it to include references to the tragedy. On the spur of the moment, he decided it would be fitting if he were joined on the session by Starr and McCartney, who agreed. It was the one and only Beatles reunion of the new decade. Produced with the help of George Martin, the song included backup vocals by Linda McCartney and Denny Laine – who later claimed he was not paid for his work on the sessions. The song rose to number two in the charts and today remains a popular jukebox choice in North America. Laine remembers the top-secret sessions: "The last time I was at George's, Paul and Linda were also there. Paul has a way of coming in and taking over and making everything a bit edgy. Everyone was uptight. When he and Linda left, the atmosphere suddenly changed and became more relaxed. Everybody seemed to physically go 'Phew' and start enjoying themselves. Paul thinks he's easygoing but he doesn't trust people and it shows."

George, on the other hand, was a nice guy as long as you kept things light, non-invasive, and never brought up the Beatles unless he clearly wanted to talk about them. During his thirty years in Henley he made friends with anyone who was friendly to him, and didn't hesitate to get involved in local issues, such as the closing of a local cinema to make way for a supermarket. He also attended sponsored walks in aid of cancer research and official openings. As a child, his son Dhani played hockey with a local team, went to state schools, and was brought up and behaved like other children of his age, despite his background.

Kirsten Grepne, a family friend of the Harrisons, was a frequent visitor to Friar Park in the early eighties with her two former boyfriends, a roadie named Magnet, and the former Bonzos drummer "Legs" Larry Smith. Speaking in 1984 she said, "George has pretty much always kept himself to himself. He's not seen. It's not that he fears going into a place, but it doesn't happen often. My next meeting with George I was in the company of Magnet. We went up for tea and a boat ride on the lake in 1981. We just popped in briefly for dinner. The Park is absolutely lovely. The buildings are all washed down now. It looks like a fairy castle made of pink and white stone."

The Harrisons' inner circle of friends was somewhat exclusive: they preferred the company of other musicians, no matter what their recent status on the record charts. "There's always 'Legs' Larry Smith, who may or may not do a tap dance," said Kirsten. "Jon and Vicki Lord, Joe Brown and his wife were also favourites. Ian Pace is another chum, as well as his wife, who is the twin sister of Jon Lord's wife. There is a set of people who've been around for the last few years."

Unlike Ringo and Paul, who have actively collected Beatles memorabilia for years, George's home showed little evidence of his celebrated past, although Kirsten recalled: "There is a jukebox in the massive front hall, where we used to have assemblies as schoolgirls. There are several old Beatles records in it. There are also several gold and platinum records in the video room.

"When I go up there, we just talk. It's a laid-back, normal evening. George is into car racing and has numerous videos of rallies. He loves it. George is interesting, very unaffected and genuine. He has a great sense of humour and he's very calm. Occasionally he wears the odd expensive jacket, but in general he could be anybody."

*

In 1981 the late journalist Ray Coleman phoned Yoko Ono at the Dakota to read her a December piece in a British paper entitled, "I'M PENNILESS", SAYS JULIAN. "YOKO ONLY GIVES ME FIFTY POUNDS A WEEK." From the notes Coleman took during the call (which he gave later to the researchers for this book), he suggested to Yoko that the story insinuated the young man had a real axe to grind, even though Julian readily admitted that he was lazy, couldn't hold down a nine-to-five job, and might rightly be accused of trying to cash in on his father's name.

Yoko pointed out that this was why John never really became close to his elder son. She said that he hadn't asked Julian to visit them often because he and his son had so little in common. She then revealed that John viewed Julian as spoilt – a result of having been brought up by Cynthia. She added that John, who had left most of his property to an estate controlled by her, had drawn up his will in a way that he hoped would prevent her being placed in the middle of a family tug-of-war.

Then Julian was quoted as saying that when he first arrived at the Dakota after his father's murder he didn't see Yoko for four days. She hid out in her bedroom, consulting legal advisers about the will. She all but ignored Julian, who was mourning his father, which alienated him even more.

Ono's reaction to the article was anger, denial and outrage. When young Lennon stated, "The papers say I'm heir to twelve million pounds, but Yoko has total control of everything," she exploded that he had no claim to even a penny of his father's estate.

When Julian suggested that his father's murder had left Cynthia "even more upset than Yoko", she gasped, "Oh, God, how can he say that? Do you believe this?" And when he revealed that during his visits to the Dakota he had had to ask permission of the staff to go into his father's bedroom, she retorted, "Not true!"

Julian also aired fears about becoming a target for yet another gunman or kidnapping. "I hope that doesn't ever happen, because Yoko is the only one with any money and she has already told me she will never pay any ransom for me." He also recalled an incident that occurred just after John's death, when he picked up the cassette

Lennon had been carrying when he was shot. Yoko had launched into a hysterical outburst, and Julian learned later that it was a Japanese custom not to touch any item of someone who had died for forty days afterwards. Yoko responded that she'd never heard of such a custom, and that she had not lost her cool.

After Lennon's death, McCartney and Harrison were theoretically free to express their feelings about Ono. When I visited George in the winter of 1983, he told me he had never been invited to meet Sean and that Yoko, in his mind, was "a witch". Neither did the McCartneys really seek out her company: they seemed to put up with her because their business interests were linked and after 8 December 1980 Yoko Ono, to all intents and purposes, was John Lennon. Within the delicate framework of the complex Beatles consortium, it was important that the public sensed unity between the remaining Beatles and Yoko, even if the truth was different.

Paul has always been a very canny player and, in a highly unusual, unexplained move, he and his wife agreed to appear in a video documentary entitled *Yoko Ono: Then And Now*, released in 1984 by Media Home Entertainment. Although they did not disparage her, it was obvious to an informed Beatles watcher that they had no real love for her. But business is business. The film included perhaps the only good thing Paul has ever said about the woman who, in the opinion of many, contributed much to the breakup of the Beatles, both professionally and personally: "The problem in other people's eyes is that she is honest. The honesty is what hurts a lot of people. We didn't know her too well really until quite recently, until the beginning of the eighties. I just thought maybe I misunderstood her, it's my mistake. I telephoned her and started talking about general things. She said, 'Why are you telephoning?' I said, 'Well, you know, I think I've misunderstood you, and I think I've made a big mistake. As you were John's wife, and I was very fond of him I feel he would have liked me to telephone you and kind of say hello and see what's going on.'

"She said, 'Well, don't do me any favours out of pity, out of sympathy. I don't want charity.' I nearly hung up, and then I thought she was right. I'd thought she was a hard woman, but now I don't think she is, it's just the opposite. I think she's a very loving, caring woman. I thought she was pushy, which I think is wrong. I think she is herself. She is determined more than other people to be herself. Some people just give in, but she won't."

By his own admission Ringo Starr's substance abuse stretched back to his early Scotch and Coke days with the Beatles, eventually graduating to legendary boozing escapades with fellow ravers like the late Keith Moon and Harry Nilsson, and then to LSD, cannabis and even cocaine.

When a reporter broached the subject in a 1976 interview, Starr was downright touchy: "I've taken several substances into my body. I never talk about this. It's like religion or politics: it's nothing to do with you or anyone else out there."

His drug habit became a key factor in his 1975 divorce from Maureen, and created a tempestuous relationship with his son Zak, who was ten when his parents split. As a teenager Zak went to live in Ascot at Tittenhurst, with his father and stepmother Barbara Bach, whom Ringo had married in 1981. "We fought a lot," said Starr. "He was a very arrogant teenager and I was an obstinate father. He'd come home drunk and I'd get angry. But when he came home sober I was the one who was drunk."

"I became quite an accomplished drinker at a very early age," says Zak. The father–son discord became so contentious that Ringo sent his son back to Maureen when Zak was fifteen.

Starr later admitted that his worst period started in 1983 and lasted for about four years, coinciding with a string of flop records. "I'd lost the power to have a couple of drinks," he explained. "I didn't understand having one glass of wine. It was a case of bottle after bottle for me. As for drugs, I used to be an advocate of 'Don't Say No.' Then I had a second of clarity through the pain and bewilderment."

Also, he spent all day every day with Barbara, who was drawn into his destructive downward spiral until she, too, became hopelessly co-dependent. Their insistence on always working together meant it was increasingly difficult to find film projects. After minor roles in Paul McCartney's *Give My Regards to Broad Street* and an insipid television adaptation of Judith Krantz's *Princess Daisy*, the offers dwindled. The pair idled away their days hatching plans that evaporated into a stoned fog. "Of course, I'd get so bleeding drunk I couldn't move," Ringo confided. "The result was, nothing happened."

A close friend described how bad things became: "Their biggest problem was alcohol. They'd both been drinking heavily for years. Ringo and Barbara were also cocaine users. Starr was snorting up to a gram a day and Barbara admitted she'd been using about half a gram daily. In addition, Ringo also smoked marijuana." Starr once said that since they'd been married, virtually all they'd done was sit in a room and use drugs. Barbara revealed that at one time it was the number one priority in their lives, more important than family, more important than each other, more important than anything. Both said they were convinced they were going to die unless they got help.

By 1987 Ringo's woeful state was gravely affecting his professional life. In February he hooked up with guitarist Chips Moman at his Three Alarm Studio in Memphis to record a new album. Among the fourteen tracks were covers of early rock standards "Some Kind Of Wonderful", "Ain't That A Shame", and "I Can Help". The sessions were marred, however, by Starr's excessive drinking. "On certain nights," Ringo said, "we were all under the influence of wine, tequila or whatever else we felt like drinking." One of the tracks, "Whiskey and Soda", hit far too close to home. The result was a spectacularly below-par album mired in a drunken haze. Starr went to an Atlanta court to block release of the work, citing inferior production quality. The project, which remains unreleased, is known as the "Lost Ringo Album".

At his worst, Ringo suffered blackouts in which he would trash a room, pass out and, on awakening, remember nothing of what had happened. In the aftermath of one particularly harrowing rage he made a horrifying discovery: "I trashed Barbara so bad I thought she was dead," he said. "They just found her covered in blood. I'd beaten her up and had no idea."

Later a friend said that after the incident "Ringo looked back and realized he'd lost something good in his marriage to Maureen and that he could easily have lost what he had with Barbara too."

In October 1988 the couple checked into the Sierra Tucson rehab clinic, Arizona's answer to Betty Ford. They'd barely got through the door before they were making their own rules. Ringo, paranoid from his coke-bingeing, refused to be separated from Barbara. The pair demanded to share a room, which was forbidden at Sierra. The clinic made an exception and the couple began their five-week stint. After the all-important initial detox phase of the programme, they were eventually assigned separate quarters and began to make real headway. "It doesn't happen in a flash," says Starr. "You have to work it out. We got a great grounding in Tucson. They set you up and tell you, 'It's up to you now.' That was a real support system for us."

Zak observed, "When the state he was in finally dawned on Dad he went to a tough place and cleaned up. I'm very proud of him for that. It took courage and real bottle to face up to it and sort it out."

When he emerged from the clinic, clean and sober, Ringo pulled his life together. In 1989, he formed his popular All-Starr Band with Joe Walsh, Billy Preston and Clarence Clemons, among other pickup superstars. He has continued to tour with them, even bringing Zak, also a drummer, on board. Inspired by his father, Zak has now conquered his own drinking problems. "We used to hang out together and have a beer, and it's no different now except we don't have the beer. We still have a laugh, the drink isn't necessary."

A rejuvenated Ringo revelled in his new-found sobriety: "I work and I play drums. I play with other musicians. I wasted a good number of years. If you look at the last four years it's hard to think of anything constructive I did. It kind of snuck up on me and I suddenly realized I was in the middle of nowhere . . . The only way I was comfortable was with a drink in my hand. That gave me all the confidence in the world."

Paul McCartney was among the first to note the positive change: "Ringo's just a lad. Everybody always loves him. And now that he's all dried out he's just a lovable, interesting, intelligent bloke."

In 1991 Barbara, with Patti Boyd and Lucy Ferry (ex-wife of singer Bryan Ferry), founded the Self-help Addiction Recovery Programme (SHARP) in London. She also went to UCLA to study psychology and was awarded a degree in 1993. For the first time in many years, life had "more meaning" for her. While she devotes many hours to fund-raising for SHARP, she plans to become even more involved as a drug counsellor.

Today, Ringo attends AA meetings regularly. Actor Ed Furlong, himself a recovering alcoholic, recalls encountering Starr at one such gathering: "It was funny. I heard someone say, 'We were all powerless to alcohol and drugs,' and I thought, Hey that sounds like a Beatle. I looked around and it was Ringo."

Starr has criticized the state's methods of dealing with substance abuse. "I don't think the anti-drug campaigns the English and American governments have adopted have served any purpose," he declared. "It's just a waste of money."

Since 1969, Beatles bootlegs have spun their way around the globe. Snapped up by collectors, these unauthorized compilations show how the Beatles worked together – and what they produced that they chose not to share with the world. Over the years, with the advent of digital technology, the quality and content of bootlegs has greatly improved. Now rare CD bootlegs are available online and from under the counters of small record shops on both sides of the Atlantic. But how did this apparently top-secret material ever get out in the first place? Surely the guardians of the Beatles' cultural legacy spent millions on keeping all of the Beatles' priceless tapes secure? Far from it. Two trusted employees of Abbey Road were ultimately responsible for the unauthorized release of part of the Beatles' unpublished catalogue, in the highest digital quality sound.

In the late sixties when radio DJs obtained copies of the early *Get Back* acetate, an entirely new industry in the non-stop demand for Beatles recordings was established: bootleg LPs. Early Beatles bootlegs lacked outtakes. Although one or two leaked out, on an acetate or obscure radio broadcast, the majority of bootlegs surfacing in the 1970s contained concert recordings, the Decca audition, various BBC broadcasts, or the occasional *Get Back* outtake. This, however, changed when EMI decided to dig into its extensive vaults.

In 1976, when the Beatles' nine-year recording contract expired, EMI took a hard look in the archives for material that might be used on new releases or reissues. Several more outtakes were considered, but instead the public were fed reissues (*Rock'n'Roll Music*, *Rarities*, *The Beatles' UK Singles*) and one live Beatles album (*Live At the Hollywood Bowl*). One album of outtakes nearly reached the printing stage, to be titled *Rarities II*, but it shrank first to an EP, then a single, and finally disappeared altogether after John's death in 1980.

The story picked up when one of EMI's young balance engineers, John Barrett, became seriously ill with cancer, and underwent prolonged treatment. As Abbey Road studio manager Ken Townsend recalled, "John asked if there was anything he could do to keep his mind occupied. My suggestion was that he listen through every Beatles tape and log all relevant details. He produced a wonderful catalogue with all the information colour-coded with an attention to detail which was quite incredible." In 1982, Townsend, with Barrett, attended the annual Liverpool Beatles convention to promote the release of Brian Southall's book *Abbey Road*. There, the pair revealed many of the secrets of the Abbey Road archives; Barrett's notes enabled them to answer specific questions about the group's marathon recording sessions.

Coincidentally that year, the control room of Abbey Road studio two was in need of an overhaul, and it was decided to allow the public inside for a tour, between July and September 1983. Visitors were treated to a ninety-minute audio-visual presentation, *The Beatles At Abbey Road*, which featured many previously unheard outtakes and remixes spanning the Beatles' career. Barrett sifted through the archives and selected possible tracks for inclusion; in some cases he even made tape copies of entire sessions. US collectors smuggling in a Sony cassette-recorder captured the show in stereo, and the recording was promptly released as a bootleg double album, *The Beatles Live At Abbey Road Studios*. Barrett kept his tapes until his death, in 1984, when they were sold privately.

Roger Scott, narrator of *The Beatles At Abbey Road*, also acquired a set of tapes from the copying sessions done for the presentation, which included the full reel of outtakes for the *Please Please Me* album, and others for the Beatles' early singles. He featured excerpts from these tapes in his own radio show, a nine-part series that aired in 1984 on Westwood One entitled *Sgt. Pepper's Lonely Hearts Club Band: A History of the Beatles Years, 1962–1970*. Scott subsequently sold his tapes before he died in 1989, and selections from his and the Barrett tapes began to appear on bootleg collections, such as *Ultra Rare Trax* and *Unsurpassed Masters*.

After the success of the Abbey Road tour EMI was eager to release its own collection of studio outtakes, and by August 1984, with the help of former Beatles engineer Geoff Emerick, had come up with a final track-listing:

Side A

1. Christmas Time (Is Here Again!) / Come And Get It
2. Leave My Kitten Alone
3. Not Guilty
4. That Means A Lot
5. I'm Looking Through You (Take 1)
6. What's The New Mary Jane

Side B

7. How Do You Do It
8. Besame Mucho
9. One After 909 (1963 Version)
10. If You've Got Trouble
11. While My Guitar Gently Weeps (Take 1)
12. Mailman, Bring Me No More Blues
13. Ob-la-di, Ob-la-da / Christmas Time (Is Here Again!)

The project was titled *Sessions*, but its release was interrupted by McCartney's *Give My Regards To Broad Street*, which took priority in EMI's scheduling for the Christmas market. Release dates were next confirmed for 25 February 1985 for the album, and a single, "Leave My Kitten Alone" backed with the "Ob-la-di, Ob-la-da/Christmas" medley on 25 January.

The *Sessions* project came to a halt, however, once the former

Beatles had been informed of its existence shortly before the release date. An EMI spokesperson in May 1985 was quoted as saying: "We're now discussing the matter with the remaining Beatles and representatives of John Lennon's estate with an aim to releasing an album some time. The format EMI suggested was not acceptable, but one obviously has to start somewhere. We will move on to other formats now, other suggestions and discussions."

To senior collectors, these announcements meant little, as pristine masters of the album were already circulating in trading circles, and the material found its way on to bootleg in early 1986. A treasure trove of outtakes surfaced with the advent of the bootleg CD in 1988, and the success of the underground releases, using material primarily from the Barrett and Scott tapes, eventually forced EMI/Apple to fashion their own collections, culminating in the release of the *Anthology* CD series, which featured many *Sessions* mixes. It was the first time that the Beatles officially allowed outtakes from their studio years to be heard by the public and, most likely, the last.

Tragedy, never a stranger to the Beatles' inner circle, soon struck again. This time it was Ringo's ex-wife Maureen. Since 1989, she had been married to her long-time companion Isaac Tigrett, who had co-founded the Hard Rock Café. In April 1994 she collapsed at the opening of the Los Angeles branch of House of Blues. It was initially thought she was suffering from anaemia, but two weeks later tests confirmed a rare form of leukaemia, myelodysplasia. Maureen's only hope was an immediate bone-marrow transplant. In October she was admitted to the Fred Hutchinson Cancer Research Center in Seattle. There, the search for a donor began. Of all her family it was discovered that her son Zak was the closest match. In late October he gave bone marrow, blood platelets and white blood cells, and the transplant appeared to be entirely successful. Well-wishers, including Ringo and Paul, visited Maureen in hospital and former-lover George sent flowers.

During her recovery from the operation, however, Maureen contracted a fungal infection that her weakened system could not fight.

Towards the end of December, it became clear that she was not going to make it. On 30 December, Ringo rushed to her bedside, with her husband Isaac, her eighty-two-year-old mother Florence, and the Starkey children, Zak, Jason and Lee. Clutching her hand, Ringo whispered, "I love you," over and over, to his first love.

That evening Maureen died, at the age of just forty-eight. A heartbroken Zak stated, "She used to be so full of life. She was up and joking even though the infection was killing her. She was always a fighter. It was the saddest experience of my life. You've only got one mum and once she's gone life can never be the same."

Ringo took Maureen's death hard. Even though they had been divorced for some two decades, the emotional bond between them remained strong. He recalled that in 1989, when he'd cleaned himself up and begun to tour again, Maureen and their children regularly attended his shows. "We were like that," he affirmed. "We'd go as a family to support the family. Even though we're divorced, me and Maureen share the joy of being part of the same family."

One family friend said of the couple: "Maureen took a part of Ringo with her when she died last week. There was so much of Ringo he's lost over the years which only Maureen held in her heart. She was Ringo's last link with his past. He lost track of who he really was years ago, but Maureen never did. Ringo never lost that place in his heart for Maureen."

McCartney too was touched by her passing and wrote an eloquent lullaby for her. The song, "Little Willow", appeared on his successful 1997 *Flaming Pie* CD. "It's a sad song I wrote after hearing about the death of a close friend," he said.

"I thought it would be nice to do a song with this mood. But also for the kids. So I could convey how much I thought of her. I came up with 'Little Willow'. It's one of my favourites because of that."

Reviewers were almost unanimous in their praise of the simple, wistful tune. One critic said, "'Little Willow' is a sweet, heartfelt song of condolence for Maureen's children, adding a profound personal touch that is often lacking in Paul's songs."

Starr also poured out his own grief with his 1998 composition,

"Sometimes". "I'll remember the good times/I hope you remember too/Remember too, that I loved you . . ."

The possibility of a Beatles reunion had been discussed on and off since shortly after the group had split in April 1970. Apple's managing director Neil Aspinall was asked to sift through archival footage of the band for a planned cinematic documentary entitled *The Long and Winding Road.* Due to legal entanglements, however, the project was set aside, but revived in 1980, as evidenced by a 28 November affidavit signed by John Lennon as part of his legal deposition against the producers of the *Beatlemania* stage show. He stated, "I and the three other Beatles have plans to stage a reunion concert." The performance was to be in support of the film slated for release by the mid-eighties.

With Lennon's death, the project was shelved once again, but in 1989 McCartney stated publicly that he and Harrison might be composing some new music for the film. George accused him of sparking reunion rumours merely to promote his own upcoming tour. He also pointed out that he and Paul hadn't written together in some thirty-five years. Why should they start now?

Interestingly, it was George himself who, in the end, was responsible for getting the project off the ground. When rock legend Roy Orbison died, leaving Harrison's pickup band of pop superstars the Traveling Wilburys one Wilbury short, George proposed recruiting the long-dead Elvis Presley to fill in. They could tap into the King's unreleased demos and add their own material to the mix.

In fact, Presley was never a real option, but George was on to something: how about using John's demos instead and resurrect the Beatles? Perhaps Yoko might part with a few of her husband's many demos. "I knew Yoko had some bits and pieces of tapes because she'd been doing things on her own," Paul later remembered. "So I rang the other guys and said, 'Look, if we could get a hold of a cassette of John's, if there's something interesting around, would you be up for that?' I went over to the Dakota, sat up late, just jawing, drinking tea and having fun and stuff."

Ono played him several tapes, which included "Free As A Bird",

"Real Love" and "Now And Then". "It was really emotional," said Paul. "I warned Ringo to have his hankie ready when he listened to it. So I took the tapes back, got copies made for the guys and they liked it."

Early in 1994 the remaining Beatles confided to a few friends that they were developing a "surprise" multi-media extravaganza, which would chronicle the band's history on record, as a television series and even a tell-all book. The *New York Times* got wind of the plan and broke the story that the Beatles would be adding vocals and instrumentals to a John Lennon tape. In January, at the Rock 'n' Roll Hall of Fame in Cleveland, Ohio, which she was attending because her husband was to be inducted as a solo artist, Yoko passed a pair of cassettes to Paul, not missing the irony of the gesture: "I did not break up the Beatles," she said, "but I was there at the time. Now I'm in a position where I could bring them back together and I would not want to hinder that." She did not, of course, mention the hefty quarter-share of worldwide profits that would be added to her coffers.

The "Threetles" got to work immediately, meeting up at McCartney's Sussex studio in a converted windmill. They quickly discarded a track called "Grow Old With Me", which had already appeared on John's *Milk and Honey* album, and turned their attention instead to his 1977 "Free As A Bird", a haunting yet hopeful ballad, said to have evolved from his frustrating immigration battle. "I fell in love with it," said Paul. "I would have loved to work with John on that. I liked the melody, it's got strong chords, and it really appealed to me." He envisaged the rework as, of all things, a 1940s lushly orchestral George Gershwin tune. Fortunately, the austere Harrison disagreed and they maintained the simplicity of Lennon's original demo.

As it stood, the song was musically incomplete and required additional lyrics, another historic undertaking that marked only the second collaboration of McCartney–Harrison. Not since 1958's "In Spite Of All Danger" had the pair composed together. It proved, at times, a push-and-pull undertaking, Paul admitting to a certain competitiveness between them, which had emerged from Harrison's success as a solo artist. "There were one or two bits of tension," he stated. "George and I were vying for the best lyrics. I don't think that's a bad thing. It was only like a normal Beatles session. You've got to reach a compromise."

John's unfinished composition required both a middle-eight and a couple of new lines to complete a verse. The duo came up with "Can we really live without each other/Where did we lose the touch/It seemed to mean so much/It always makes me feel so . . . free as a bird . . ."

Lennon's sparse piano accompaniment was then layered with several complex chord changes, a new arrangement and further instrumentation. George and Paul added acoustic and slide guitars, a little piano and Paul's subtly understated bass line. Finally, the vocals were laid down. "It was good fun for me to have John in the headphones when I was working," McCartney revealed. "It was like the old days, a privilege."

For Ringo Starr, the experience was bitter-sweet. "It was emotional. He wasn't there and I loved John. We had to imagine he'd just gone for a cup of tea, or that he'd gone on holiday but he's still here. That's the only way I could get through it."

With that in mind, said Paul, they could avoid the temptation to view John as "a sacred martyr. It was John the Beatle, John the crazy guy, we all remember. So we could laugh and say, 'Wouldn't you just know it? It's completely out of time. He's always bloody out of time, that Lennon.' He would have made those jokes if it had been my cassette."

Jeff Lynne, co-founder of ELO, was brought on board to produce, succeeding the venerable George Martin, whose hearing had diminished. Lynne recalled that the process was fascinating to watch: "Paul would strike up the backing vocals and it's the Beatles again. They were having fun with them and reminded each other of old times. I'd be waiting to record but I was too busy laughing and smiling at everything they were talking about. It was a lovely, magical time."

"I was shocked, blown away," exclaimed Starr when he heard the playbacks. "I thought, It sounds just like them. It's the bloody Beatles!"

The trio spent the better part of February honing the song, then took an extended break. It wasn't until 22 June that they assembled again at Paul's studio but the session was aborted after, reportedly, they fooled around with the McCartney classic "Let It Be" and yet another Lennon demo. Due to time restrictions, the Beatles decided they needed a change of scenery. The next day, accompanied by their wives, they arrived at George's Friar Park studios. The afternoon was captured on film for the television series with a two-camera set-up. During a chat in Harrison's prized garden the three reminisced about their 1968 trip to Rishikesh. George picked up a ukelele, played "Dehra Dun" and "I Will". Awash in the sentiment of the good ol' days the trio again toyed with the idea of recording Paul's rock lullaby, "Let It Be", to John's memory, but they agreed that, without him, it would be a hollow gesture.

They retired to the studio where they soon returned to their rock'n'roll roots. In a rousing jam they recorded barebones versions of "Ain't She Sweet", "Thinking Of Linking", "Dehra Dun" and "Blue Moon Of Kentucky". "It was just two acoustic guitars and me on brushes," Ringo remembered.

Jeff Lynne observed, "It was a timewarp kind of thing. We played some old rock'n'roll stuff, a couple of Chuck Berry's, even "I Saw Her Standing There".

Regrettably, only a minute-long segment of "Blue Moon Of Kentucky" was shown to the public, on 6 December 1996, on the ABC Television programme *Good Morning America.* Bob Smeaton, director of *The Beatles Anthology* series, pointed out the bitter-sweet nature of the event: "The more we include of the three guys together the more we realize John isn't there. In years to come people might get the chance to see that footage of the three of them playing together at George's place. Knowing the way Apple works, it'll come out eventually in some shape or form. There's a whole load of that stuff – we were there for a full day and the Beatles started playing songs like 'Thinking Of Linking' and 'Ain't She Sweet'. A little bit of this was used when George sang 'Dehra Dun'. They did a whole load of rock'n'roll songs. We also shot a load of stuff at Abbey Road with the three guys and George Martin, which was fantastic. For Beatles fans it's priceless. I'm sure, somewhere down the line, that stuff will come out."

After the summer sessions, Paul, George and Ringo didn't reconvene until February 1995. "It took us another year to get the steam up to go and do it again," explained McCartney.

On 6 and 7 February the Threetles reassembled at McCartney's studio, this time to focus on "Real Love", slated to be the second single. John had written the tune in 1979 and cut some seven demos of the track. Two versions had been released previously: on the 1988 *Imagine* soundtrack and *The John Lennon Anthology* in 1998.

Lennon's jaunty but rough homemade tape needed a repair that only 1990s technology in the skilled hands of Geoff Emerick and Jon Jacobs could pull off. First the hiss that ran through the song, due to its low-level recording, had to be erased. Fortunately, it did not affect John's vocal, just the phases in between. That alone took an entire week to complete.

Next, the arangement required a complete overhaul. A lot of cut-and-paste had to be done, removing John's weaker piano sections and replacing them with a stronger version. Also Lennon had not sung a proper ending so his vocals were borrowed from a chorus and used to produce a fadeout coda.

McCartney played celeste, harmonium and double bass, while George used several Stratocasters. Paul doubled John's vocals. "It was really cool working with the other guys," he said. "It really was just the Beatles. You couldn't really change it much so the style was set by John. We were more like 'sidemen' to John. We had a great laugh."

Although Paul conceded that he preferred "Free As A Bird", he said "Real Love" was "powerful and catchier". "There was one real nice moment when we were doing 'Real Love'. I was trying to learn the piano bit and Ringo sat down on the drums, jamming along. It was like none of us had ever been away."

Starr noted that it was challenging to turn the demo into a "real Beatles track" but concluded that they had done a stellar job. "I think John will love it when he hears it."

"I hope somebody does this to all my crap demos when I'm dead, and makes them into hit songs," Harrison cracked.

The Threetles tramped into the studio twice more in 1995, on 20–21 March and again on 15–16 May. They reportedly tackled a third track Yoko had passed to them. "It didn't really have a title," Paul explained. "'You know it's true/It's up to you . . .' That beginning bit's great, and then it just goes a bit crummy. We all decided it's not one of John's greatest songs."

Jeff Lynne agreed: "The one we tried was either called 'Now And Then' or 'Miss You'. We had a go at it but there were a lot of words which hadn't been completed. It was one afternoon messing with it . . . It was a very sweet song, a sort of bluesy ballad."

It was suggested, too, there was yet another song the trio worked on called "All For Love". Rumour had it that this was another McCartney–Harrison collaboration, but this time from scratch, and the 1996 issue of *Beatles Monthly* proclaimed that work had been completed on this "new Beatles song". Serious Beatle watchers, however, doubt it: in the first place, no one in the group's camp had mentioned the existence of a new song, and neither did Jeff Lynne, present for all the recording sessions. Also, how could there be a true "Beatles" song without John Lennon?

When asked to clarify, Ringo was cagey: "It's there, the unfinished track," he maintained. "Oh, the myth that will grow around that now. The 'Hidden Track'." But what song was he referring to? Some Beatles experts concluded that "All For Love" is most likely "Now And Then", retitled for the new lyrics provided by Paul and George. Others, however, believe the composition might be a new offering from the past. For now, the material remains locked in the Beatles' vaults.

Meanwhile, with little fanfare the resurrected Beatles débuted on 4 December 1995 with the release of the single "Free As A Bird". Paul was defiant in defence of their accomplishment: "People said we shouldn't do it but that kind of focused us a bit. I thought, We'll fucking show you! We pulled it off, that's the thing. I don't care what anyone says. We work well together, that's the truth of it."

Ringo chimed in, "This project has brought us together. Once we get the bullshit behind us we all end up doing what we do best, making music."

Predictably George had a more philosophical take on the experience. "We've had the opportunity to let all the past turbulent times go down the river and under the bridge, to get together again in a new light. That has been a good thing. It's like going full circle."

Julian Lennon heard "Free As A Bird" for the first time when he was in New York visiting his brother Sean. "It's a great song. I love it. Although I must say I find it hard to hear Dad's vocals."

For all the hype of its release, the song was considered a disappointment by Beatles standards. It failed to enter the BBC charts at number one, ironically kept off by Michael Jackson, who had bought the Beatles' catalogue in 1984. It reached the top briefly and sold 120,000 copies in one week, but critics and fans alike agreed that its dirge-like pace and overblown Jeff Lynne production all but annihilated John's wistful, understated sentiment.

By contrast, the "Free As A Bird" video, débuting on the first instalment of the ABC Television *Beatles Anthology*, on 19 November 1995, was first-rate. A fascinating tour through Beatles history featured myriad clever references to Beatles songs (as many as 150), sparking a fan challenge to see how many they could pick out.

The *Anthology* series itself, though, did not command the expected blockbuster ratings. After the first instalment, they dropped off dramatically. To make matters worse, the release of the band's mediocre second comeback single, "Real Love", all but flopped. Apparently the public was saying, "Let John rest in peace".

But the fans embraced the vintage three-CD *Beatles Anthology*. Volume One sold a million copies in its first week and ruled the top of the charts for three weeks. The compilation went on to garner three Grammy Awards. Then *The Beatles Anthology*, their coffee-table-sized autobiography released in October 2000, notched up millions in advance sales. But the band's promise to show warts and all was not fulfilled: instead the book offered an entertaining but essentially whitewashed and well-worn overview of the band's colourful
history.

McCartney still hoped to do more in the same vein, or even venture into a genuine Threetles project, but George slammed the door on the idea. "We always said the Beatles was us four and if ever one of us wasn't in it then it's not the Beatles, and the idea of having

John as the singer on the record works – it is the Beatles! There was talk about us doing stuff on our own but I have no desire to do a threesome."

Starr agreed: "It felt very natural and was a lot of fun, but emotional, too, at times. But it's the end of the line, really. There's nothing more we can do as the Beatles."

ELEVEN

It Don't Come Easy

Resolution

1996–2003

> "George gave his life to God a long time ago. He wasn't trying to hang on to anything. He was fine with it. Sure, nobody likes to be ill and nobody likes to be uncomfortable. But he went with what was happening."
>
> *Olivia Harrison*

The nineties claimed many within the Beatles' inner circle. On 7 September 1997 the band's charming press officer Derek Taylor died at sixty-five. His lifetime indulgence in cigarettes, drink and drugs contributed to his unsuccessful battle with cancer.

The charismatic Liverpudlian, whose early journalistic flair showed itself in pop music columns and on the ghostwritten pages of Brian Epstein's 1964 memoir, *A Cellarful of Noise*, veered off-course when he resigned from the group in 1965 to become publicist for the Byrds, the Beach Boys and the low profile Captain Beefheart. He returned to the Beatles in 1968, at the newly formed Apple Corps, where his wit, wisdom and generous spirit propelled the late-sixties glory years at 3 Savile Row.

McCartney offered public condolences to Taylor's wife, Joan, and their six children: "He was a beautiful man. It's a time for tears. Words may come later." Taylor had been closer to George than the other Beatles, and the guitarist went out of his way to find work for Taylor in his later years, giving him a large role in the publicity and the promotion of the band's successful retrospectives, *The Beatles: Live From the BBC* and *The Beatles Anthology*. Although he had worked long and hard on behalf of all of the Beatles' personal and professional projects for over three decades, only George attended his funeral.

By the close of 1995 it seemed things couldn't get any better for the McCartneys. Paul was basking in the afterglow of the successful *Beatles Anthology*, while *The Grateful Dead: A Photofilm*, which consisted of Linda's photographs taken during a 1967/8 session with the band, was receiving extensive exposure and rave notices. The McCartney offspring were thriving, too, particularly Stella, who was already a force to be reckoned with in the fashion world with her own label, Eponymous.

Then on 8 December, during a routine medical check, a malignant lump was discovered in Linda's breast. Ten days later she checked into London's Princess Grace Hospital for an operation to remove the growth and some surrounding tissue. Afterwards, Paul gave a cheerful thumbs-up to reporters and deemed the operation, "100 per cent successful, thank God. Doctors told her just to get some rest. We're very optimistic about the future and, for the moment, everything goes on as normal."

However, over the next year Mrs McCartney dropped out of sight. Even a close friend and neighbour observed that she hadn't seen Paul's normally gregarious wife in months.

Meanwhile, spokesman Geoff Baker reiterated, "Linda's had a complete recovery. She's feeling great. She's been horse-riding nearly every day."

Eventually the press uncovered the truth. Linda had been undergoing twice-weekly chemotherapy treatments for nearly a year, double the normal course for breast-cancer patients. The McCartneys responded that the doctors wanted to be sure that "they got it all".

Nearly a year later on 23 November 1996 Baker promised that Linda would be on hand for her photo exhibition entitled "Roadworks" at the National Museum of Photography, Film and Television in Bradford: "It will mark her return to public life," he said. She did not appear. Rumours circulated that she had been receiving an intense form of chemotherapy in Los Angeles, a regimen so potent that some five per cent of recipients died from the toxic chemicals alone.

At last, on 17 December, Linda stepped into the spotlight to accept a lifetime achievement award from the animal-rights organization People For The Ethical Treatment of Animals (PETA). Her once glowing complexion was now waxen and pasty, her golden hair reduced to a few thin, brown wisps. Clearly she had been battling for her life.

On 11 March 1997 Linda was not able to be present at Buckingham Palace when Paul was knighted by the Queen. Ever the polished showman, he smiled broadly to reporters and fans and did not reveal the real reason why his wife could not attend.

Later that year it looked as if Linda had turned the corner. She contributed vocals to several tracks on Paul's well-received *Flaming Pie* CD, and was even well enough to shoot promotional photos for that album and for the CD of his symphony, *Standing Stone,* which drew lukewarm reviews but achieved respectable sales from Paul's loyal fans.

On 14 October, she attended the début of *Standing Stone* at the Royal Albert Hall, and the following day she and Paul were cheering on their daughter Stella, in Paris at the Opera Garnier for her first triumphant fashion show. Afterwards, small details of Linda's ordeal trickled out. She revealed that during her illness her husband had bought a "family ring" for her and each of the children. She had given him a watch inscribed, "To my knight in shining armor".

In the winter of 1998, during an upbeat chat with *OK!* magazine, in the kitchen of the family's rambling Sussex farmhouse, Linda discussed her multiple projects. She was compiling a fifth cookbook, putting out a new line of soya-based yoghurt desserts and working on a meatless bacon that apparently cooked, sizzled and tasted very like the real thing. She talked proudly about rescuing cows from slaughter and saving some sixty beagles destined for cosmetic-industry experimentation.

She also teamed up with renowned stained-glass artist Brian Clarke to mount an exhibition at the thirteenth-century Cistercian abbey in Romont, Switzerland. Clarke had transformed her photos, which included portraits of the artist Willem de Kooning, into spectacular stained-glass windows. "Now that the kids have flown the nest Paul and I have become boyfriend and girlfriend again, doing the little things you do when you're first dating. Going to the theatre or just walking hand in hand through the fields. How many married couples of thirty years do you know who wander about holding hands? In some ways we haven't grown up. I guess it must be love!" She concluded, "Yeah, I'm back!"

It was her last interview. When television writer and close friend Carla Lane visited the McCartneys in Sussex in February, "It was all talk about the future. There was no hint anything was wrong . . . I was absolutely convinced she was going to be okay."

A month later, however, Lane spoke to Linda on the telephone: "I knew something was terribly wrong and there was a feeling of goodbye in her voice. The last thing she said to me was 'Hey, I love you, Carla.'"

In a last-ditch attempt to save Linda's life, doctors at New York's Sloane-Kettering Cancer Center began an aggressive high-dose chemotherapy, administering huge amounts of toxic drugs designed to wipe out the cancer cells. A bone-marrow transplant was scheduled to follow. However, by March 1998 the cancer had spread to Linda's liver and a transplant was no longer an option.

Later Paul McCartney commented, "We knew it was coming but we tried to pretend we didn't. I cried a lot. Sometimes I'd be sitting around people and just burst out crying. And instead of doing the manly thing and saying 'I'm sorry, I shouldn't do that,' I would just go 'Ooohh' and cried a lot."

In early April the doctors gave him the final grim prognosis. "I knew a week or so before she died," he acknowledged. "I was the only one who knew. I didn't tell her because I didn't think she'd want to know."

The McCartneys were reported to be on holiday in Santa Barbara, California, when Linda's condition suddenly took a turn for the worse. On 17 April, the immediate family, including Stella, Mary and James, gathered at her bedside. Paul cradled his dying wife in his arms: "You're up on your beautiful Appaloosa stallion," he whispered, "and it's a fine spring day. We're riding in the woods. The bluebells are all out and the sky is clear blue . . ." Aged fifty-six, Linda slowly drifted away.

Her body was cremated after a simple, family-only ceremony. That night, Carla Lane said, "Paul and the family were terrified of him sleeping on his own after so many years with Linda, so James bunked in with him. I thought that was so touching.

"Paul's being very brave," she continued, "but it will hit him two weeks from now. They were riding two days before her death and had a wonderful time. The next day she didn't want to ride but she was still up and about, laughing and joking with everybody. After riding Linda felt tired but she was well enough to get up and walk around.

"They sat and laughed and joked all day. The next morning she didn't want to get up so she stayed in bed and died later that day. It was very peaceful and the entire family were there at the end. They didn't want to make a fuss and have a huge funeral. They just wanted a quiet ceremony, just the family together."

That weekend the McCartneys flew back to Britain by private jet and Paul scattered Linda's ashes on the family farm.

The extended family was not informed of her death until some thirty-six hours after it had occurred. Even Carla Lane was taken by surprise: "I only found out the cancer had spread to her liver when I spoke to Paul on Sunday. He was surprised Linda hadn't told me. But she really didn't need to say anything to me."

"Linda had no idea things were so bad, nor did anyone else," said Geoff Baker. "I don't know the precise details of where the funeral took place but it was decided by Paul and the kids they just wanted to be alone."

After the official announcement on 19 April, condolences poured in. George Harrison said, "Linda will be missed, not only by Paul, her children and brother John, but by all who knew and loved her. She was a dear person with a passionate love of nature and its creatures, and in her passing she has earned the peace she sought in life. May God bless her."

Ringo and Barbara sent this message: "We were privileged to have known her. Her positive courage through her illness was truly inspiring."

George Martin said, "We will miss her enormously. Everyone is diminished by her passing."

Yoko Ono, a breast-cancer survivor, told the media, "I'm very saddened. I've spoken to Linda over the past year and she seemed to be her usual powerful self. I can't believe it."

As the city of Santa Barbara was holding a vigil for Linda, a news item came in to the press from the local sheriff's department. There was no record of Linda McCartney's death certificate. She had not died in an area hospital, as they had assumed, and apparently hadn't even died in Santa Barbara. The public, the media, even the authorities had been duped. Meanwhile, the *Arizona Daily Star* reported that Linda had died on a 150-acre Tucson ranch that the family had owned since 1978. Moreover, some of her ashes had been scattered there. The resulting police probe confirmed the story. Linda's death certificate had been signed by a cancer specialist at the Arizona Cancer Center in Tucson, where she had been a patient; Arizona state medical examiner Dr Bruce Parks authorized the cremation, which had taken place at Tucson's *Bring Funeral Home*. Under Arizona state law, death certificates are not public record.

Geoff Baker, who later admitted that his white lies had added to the confusion, had a ready answer for the subterfuge: "Everyone always assumed it was Santa Barbara, California. So in an effort to allow the family time to get back to England in peace and private it was stated she died in Santa Barbara."

Carla Lane shed further light on the situation when she spoke of a conversation she had had with Paul just before Linda's death. He had told her, "I just want you to plead with people not to reveal this place because we'll need it more than ever in the future . . . We can't just sell it and move on."

"They have one place in the world which is secret and free from harassment," Lane said. "It was Linda's favourite place. When she got sick they decided to go there. When Linda died, rather than give the name of the place, they said she died in Santa Barbara. It wasn't too much of a lie and that was all it was."

But there was further fallout from the unfortunate episode when a McCartney press release dispelled any notion of assisted suicide: "Any suggestion that her death was assisted is complete and utter rubbish, a total nonsense," declared Paul. This bombshell exploded out of nowhere: no major media source had even hinted at such a possibility. It clouded an already muddy issue: Linda's sudden passing, the death notice delayed by two days.

Adding more fuel to the fire of controversy, Dr Linnea Chap, an oncologist at the UCLA Johnson Center, said that patients with advanced liver cancer became "typically lethargic, maybe even in a coma-like state. This diagnosis doesn't really chime with pictures released by the family of Linda horseback-riding just days before her death."

Was it possible that, knowing the end was near, Paul had stepped in to end his wife's suffering? It certainly brought a new twist to his statement that "The real blessing was that the end came quickly and she didn't suffer." One family insider, however, quickly disputed the innuendo, insisting that Linda fought valiantly: she had wanted to see her daughter married: Mary, a photographer and photo editor in Paul's Soho offices, had announced plans to marry television producer Alistair Donald in a small ceremony in a Peasmarsh Sussex church. "Linda wasn't ready to die just yet," the friend asserted. "When she got the news that Mary and Alistair were getting married she shrieked with joy." Finally, Linda's oncologist, Dr Lawrence Norton, issued a press statement, quashing all of the speculation: "Linda died of natural causes of metastic breast cancer."

Once the controversy had died down, McCartney arranged two major memorial services, the first of which was held at London's St Martin-in-the-Fields in Trafalgar Square on 8 June 1998. Although many rock stars attended, including Elton John, Pete Townshend and Peter Gabriel, the event was billed in the press as a Beatles reunion. As George and Ringo joined Paul for the service, anticipation ran high that the trio would sing together: they were expected to perform "Let It Be" in tribute to Linda.

One ardent Beatles fan, Jean, from Liverpool, was outside the church and reported that each guest received a bouquet of lilies imported from Holland to be planted in their home garden. "Ringo arrived with Barbara and took a moment to wave to the crowds," she said. "When George stepped out of the car with Olivia and Dhani it was obvious he was hooded to annoy the press. Or was he hiding his loss of hair from his own ongoing chemo? He walked straight up the steps [into the church] without turning his head and they didn't realize it was him until he was at the top."

When the McCartney family pulled up in a silver Mercedes, Paul acknowledged the crowds with the peace sign. "He was obviously moved," noted Jean, "overwhelmed and close to tears. His face was stricken and he was clearly finding it hard to keep it together."

The three remaining Beatles sat together in the front row with the McCartney family, as Paul's wistful Scottish ballad of 1977, "Mull Of Kintyre" floated over the congregation. Then he stepped up to address the gathering. "I have lost my girlfriend and that is very sad. I still cannot believe it, but I have to because it is true. As a lover she was the best. We had a whole lot of fun making those babies . . ." Two Shetland ponies, which Paul had given Linda for Christmas, were led down the aisle, a heartbreaking image.

As "Let It Be" rang out, heady anticipation rode over the crowd, but the three Beatles remained in their seats.

Two weeks later on 22 June the second service took place at New York's Riverside church. It was equally, if not more, impressive. The exclusive guest list included Paul Simon, Chrissie Hynde, Neil Young, Twiggy, Diane Sawyer and Ralph Lauren. Yoko Ono was absent, although May Pang, John Lennon's one-time love, was there. "You can see that Paul has the support of his kids," she said. "The family would clap and make sounds of approval as the string quartet played and Harlem Boys' Choir sang. Paul sat next to James and when it was time for him to get up you could see how hard he was trying to hold it together. There wasn't a dry eye in the house."

The two-hour service included childhood stories told by Linda's siblings, Louise, Laura and John, and renditions of Paul's ballads to his wife: "Maybe I'm Amazed", "My Love", "Warm And Beautiful". The highlight of the celebration came when equestrian Pam Fowler rode into the church on a stunning Appaloosa dressage horse, shipped from Texas. The magnificent animal walked up the aisle to the altar and gracefully pirouetted.

Over the next few months McCartney retreated to mourn in private. "There have been moments when nobody could reach him," revealed Geoff Baker. "Paul and Linda were always a team, so close they were one person. Now robbed of the only true love of his life he was in despair . . . He has retraced their favourite walks through the woods . . . the hoofprints made by Linda's favourite horse, Blanket, taking on a sad significance. Those closest to him talk publicly of his bravery. But privately, they fear for him."

But Paul himself admitted that his grief wasn't the emotional wringer he had anticipated, although he wept openly during a Los Angeles award ceremony when he presented the first Linda McCartney Award to Pamela Anderson Lee for her work on behalf of animal causes. "I thought I might be dead by the end of the year, it was so unbearable," he later recalled. "I half prepared for that. The nearest I did get to that was grief and crying. But I thought, That's a slippery path. So I tried to counteract it by just going from day to day."

Surprisingly, McCartney revealed he'd sought professional help to deal with his loss: "I got a counsellor because I knew I would need some help. He was great, particularly in helping me get rid of my guilt. Whenever anyone you care about dies, you wish you'd been perfect all the time, and I wasn't. That made me feel very guilty after Linda died." He added, "It's always good to talk about Linda. If you lose someone there's an ever greater distance between you. So to talk about them lessens the distance even if it's only for a second. If you're lucky enough to love someone and be in a very strong relationship you grow reliant on each other because you're half of each other's life. So when you lose them, I thought, I've lost half of me! That's the real shock."

Paul dedicated himself to putting out much of Linda's unfinished work, including a number of photo exhibitions. He also oversaw the release of her *Wide Prairie*, a six-minute animated film about a woman's fantasy of fleeing her mundane life by riding across the prairie on horseback with her dream lover, based on a country-and-western song she'd written. She had worked on the project with Argentinian animator Oscar Grillo for two years. The accompanying CD, *Wide Prairie*, included sixteen songs, thirteen written by Linda over twenty-five years, plus three covers. A few tracks received positive reviews, especially "The Light Comes From Within", a sharp response to her critics. The work's quality, though, sprang largely from Paul's musical arrangements and recording mastery.

As a further memorial, Paul McCartney made multi-million-dollar donations to Sloane-Kettering and the Arizona Cancer Center in Linda's name. He was particularly honoured that the Royal Liverpool Hospital named its new cancer centre, which opened on 24 November 2000, after his wife. It is dedicated to combating specific cancers in a relaxed, comfortable, friendly environment.

In early April 1996 George Harrison went on a pilgrimage of all of the Vaishnava holy places in India accompanied by Mukunda and Shyamasundara.* He passed through Delhi, then braved the rigours of the accident-strewn Aggra Road and headed for Vrndavana, a two-and-a-half-hour journey.

He checked into the Pritu ashram, run by Pritu Dasa, then performed *parikrama* (ritual devotional circumambulation) of the holy places, including the site of Radha and Krishna's *rasa* dance, the sacred Yamuna river and Prabhupada's private quarters at the ancient Radha Damodar temple, in the heart of Seva Kund, considered by devotees the "spiritual hub of the universe". On entering the temple's modest stone courtyard George took off his shoes, as is customary. They were almost immediately stolen by one of the scores of Vrndavana's bandit monkeys, who lie in wait on rooftops and in trees for unsuspecting pilgrims to put down a pair of sunglasses, a camera or whatever, which they then, remarkably, hold for ransom. Harrison offered them a bottle of mineral water, which was duly accepted. The shoes were then dropped on to the cobblestones below.

"There's no way he's going to be able to get that cap off for a drink," George joked.

"Don't be so sure," said Mukunda. "Some of these monkeys in Vrndavana were great yogis in their last life!"

In 1993 George had attended the twenty-fifth anniversary celebration of the Hare Krishna movement's first trek into Britain at the

* Vaishnavas are followers of Krishna in his many incarnations.

Bhaktivedanta Manor in Radlett, north of London. He sat in a circle, leading the chanting, with his old friends, Guru Dasa, Shyamasundara, Mukunda, Malati Devi Dasi and many others.

The evening of 30 December 1999 was pleasant for the Harrisons. George had been to visit his brother, Peter, and his wife Pauline, who were making plans for the next day's New Year's Eve Millennium party, complete with fireworks and celebrity friends. Around midnight George settled in to watch a movie with Olivia and then locked up. The couple had gone to bed at around two a.m.

At three twenty Olivia was awoken by the sound of breaking glass. She woke George: "Somebody's in here. I heard a window smash!" Thinking that perhaps a chandelier had fallen, George fumbled for his boots, tossed on a jacket over his pyjamas, and began to make his way to the hall. He smelt cigarette smoke, looked down over the banisters and saw a shadowy stranger. "You get down here!" the man bellowed, adding cryptically, "You know what it is!"

The man, around six feet tall, wearing blue jeans and a black leather jacket, had a mass of long blond hair. George called the housekeeper and told her to ring 999, while Olivia alerted the rest of the staff on the intercom. His mother-in-law and Dhani were sleeping in another wing, and Olivia was close by, so Harrison didn't think twice before he went downstairs to confront the intruder. The man was holding what appeared to be a pole, and a knife with a long blade.

He saw the man pace frantically about from room to room, and hoping to "confuse or distract" him, George yelled, "Hare Krishna, Hare Krishna!" This enraged the man, who lunged up the stairs waving the weapons. George took him on and a ten-minute struggle ensued, throughout three rooms on the first floor. Olivia appeared on the scene and hit the intruder in the groin with a brass poker, whereupon he grabbed her by the throat. She twisted free, and the struggle moved into the family's meditation room, then towards the master bedroom. The attacker saw that the much-older Harrison was tiring and plunged the knife deep into his chest.

In desperation Olivia grabbed a leaded Tiffany table lamp, and struck their assailant's head. He grabbed the cable, so she hurled it at him, finally felling him. Dhani appeared in the room, and they managed to hold the man at bay until the police arrived.

When Thames Valley detectives stormed the house at three thirty they found the man slumped on the landing. He had dropped the knife and surrendered. George lay on the floor, holding a towel to his chest, drifting in and out of consciousness as Olivia knelt next to him. After a cursory look at the crime scene, Detective Chief Inspector Euan Read assessed the attack as "vicious". The pole-like object George had seen was a section of a stone sword that the assailant had broken off a Friar Park statue of St George and the Dragon.

Minutes later paramedics arrived, to find Harrison lying on his back, with his son crouched at his side. It was later reported that Dhani kept his father conscious and alert: "Stay with me, Dad!" he pleaded. George, feeling his life ebbing away, told his son, "Dhani, I'm going, I'm going. I love you, Dhani. Hare Krishna," and closed his eyes.

As the ambulance whisked the former Beatle off to the Royal Berkshire Hospital in Reading, the intruder, now in handcuffs, grunted to police, "You should have heard the spooky things he was saying as he was going. The bastard! I should have got the bastard better." He added, "It's all in the Book of Exodus. He got very close tonight."

At the hospital, doctors gave George a tetanus shot, intravenous antibiotics and a host of powerful painkillers. His most serious injury was a punctured right lung, which collapsed: he was fitted with a chest drain. Harrison was found to have at least ten wounds, including three to his chest. The major chest wound required six stitches. The blade had just missed the artery that connects the heart with the brain. Dr Andrew Pengelly, medical director of the Royal Berkshire, stated, "If that had ruptured he would have perished within a matter of minutes from internal bleeding. He was extremely lucky."

Fortunately Olivia had escaped serious injury, but was treated for a skull laceration and minor cuts. Doctors praised her bravery. As one family friend put it, "Olivia gave him a good clocking and probably saved George's life." According to her friend, London fashion designer Elizabeth Emanuel, "She's fit and strong. I imagine she'd be very brave in those circumstances. She's quite tough."

Following emergency treatment, Harrison was transferred to the Royal Harefield Hospital in north-west London, renowned for their first-class thoracic surgery unit. He quipped, "I can see the headlines already: 'Beatle George Has A Hard Day's Night!' On his attacker, he said, "He wasn't a burglar and he certainly wasn't trying out for the Traveling Wilburys."

Public reaction poured in. Paul McCartney said: "Thank God both George and Olivia are all right. I send them my love." Ringo added, "Barbara and I are deeply shocked. We send our love and wishes for a speedy recovery." From George Martin: "I am astonished and appalled. George leads a very quiet life. He's very down to earth. He likes nothing more than doing his garden. George is a very peaceful person who hates violence of any kind."

Rolling Stones drummer Charlie Watts confided to the *Observer* newspaper that Ringo had told him the attack had been far more harrowing than was reported. George was not stabbed ten times, as the media had reported, but closer to forty. "He would have been dead if he'd been lying in bed; he wouldn't have been able to fight," Watts said. "I think George is still going through trauma. He's bound to. He's lived in that house for over thirty years. It's just so shocking it should happen to a guy who's so inoffensive. George has never been nasty to anyone, he's only preached love and peace. He was not like John Lennon. He's never made strong political statements or anything. He's just an average guitar player."

According to a close family friend, the police had arrived in the nick of time. "I don't think Olivia or George could fight much more if he attacked them again. You have to remember this bloke was incredibly pumped up with adrenaline. He was out of control while George was half asleep."

In fact, the break-in had been the second within a week for the Harrison family. On 23 December, Cristin Keleher of New Jersey was arrested for breaking into George's rambling Hawaiian bungalow in Hana, Maui. His sister-in-law, Linda Tuckfield, found the twenty-seven-year-old woman inside the home eating a pizza, drinking root beer and doing her laundry. She had apparently strolled in through an unlocked sliding door. Caretaker Don Carroll told police that Keleher had been stalking the Maui house since October: she had approached him to ask when she might "run into George", claiming to have a "psychic connection" with him. Charged with first-degree burglary and fourth-degree theft, she was held on $10,000 bail. On 25 August 2000 she pleaded guilty to a reduced charge of misdemeanour trespassing. She was released on probation and returned to New Jersey in her parents' custody. "I thank God George didn't press charges against me," she said. "I learned a great lesson."

Back in Henley, Harrison's attacker was treated for minor injuries at Oxford's John Radcliffe Hospital, then held at St Aldate's police station. He appeared at Oxford magistrates' court, charged with breaking and entering, aggravated assault and two counts of attempted murder. Then he was sent to the Scott clinic in Rainhill, Merseyside, a medium-security forensic psychiatric unit, to await a February hearing where he entered a plea of not guilty by reason of insanity.

The police learned that his name was Michael Abram, and he came from Huyton, Merseyside, in Liverpool. The thirty-three-year-old former gardener and television-advertising salesman was an unemployed father of two.

Having decided on robbery as the attacker's motive, police in Oxford and Liverpool began to piece together the events that had led up to the break-in. Abram was well known around his neighbourhood as "Mad Mick". One resident revealed, "He was always shouting day and night. He's the local nutter. Every neighbourhood has one and he's ours." He was frequently spotted at the Bow and Arrow pub in Huyton's Woolfall Heights district. One patron said, "I've seen him sitting on his own for hours with a glass of beer in a trance-like state."

It was also discovered that Abram would frequently stand on the balcony of his tenth-floor flat in the run-down Page Moss area, often naked, shouting and throwing beer-cans at passers-by. On one occasion he had threatened to jump. A month before, he had been arrested and fined three times within ten days for writing graffiti on public property.

As the investigators dug deeper, a more sinister portrait emerged. After the birth of his second child, Abram had begun to smoke cannabis, then graduated to heroin. According to his mother, Lynda

Abram, "Drugs destroyed the family. He thought he could control it, but it was only a matter of time before it controlled him." Abram had sought treatment at various Liverpool drug clinics. His neighbour David Blackburn observed, "I used to see him going over to the chemist's for his dose of methadone every week. He used to muck about with the kids on the estate but you could tell he wasn't normal."

Abram had shown promise at St Columbus Roman Catholic comprehensive school in Huyton, but a ten-year history of paralysing psychological disorders and months spent in psychiatric hospitals had quashed what might have been a bright future. Lynda Abram told the press that her son had become obsessed with the Beatles. He borrowed her old tapes and walked the streets, listening endlessly to them. Then he developed a consuming interest in the Beatles-influenced band Oasis and believed that their 1995 hit "Wonderwall" had been written exclusively for him. "He has been running into pubs shouting about the Beatles," his mother said. "He hates them and believes they are witches and takes their lyrics seriously. He started to wear a Walkman to play music to stop the voices in his head."

Family members confided that Abram thought John Lennon was a prophet and Paul McCartney the devil. "He talked more about Paul than George," Lynda Abram said. "He identified with George Harrison because of 'My Sweet Lord'. He played it over and over." Her son believed he was on a mission from God: "He said it was too late for his generation but not for the children. It was his task to save the children from drugs and witchcraft." Seventeen hours before the event, he'd been picked up on security cameras in Liverpool. Abram was last spotted at around six p.m. in his favourite haunt, the Bow and Arrow. Before leaving he remarked to a patron, "I've got things to do."

The Harrison's million-dollar security system was not in evidence that evening. George had cancelled his contract with Vanguard Security, whose services included trained police dogs roaming the grounds. Security floodlights did not alert the staff and the burglar alarm inexplicably failed.

In London, George was recovering remarkably well. Olivia stayed with him in his private double room, to which home-cooked meals and fresh fruit were sent from Friar Park. Soon George issued a statement: "Olivia and I are overwhelmed by the concern expressed by so many people. We thank everyone for their prayers and kindness."

The aftermath of the incident was predictable. Paul McCartney and Ringo Starr were alerted to the possibility of copycat threats. Oasis members Noel and Liam Gallagher were likewise advised to tighten security. Yoko Ono cancelled plans to make a surprise musical guest appearance at New York's Knitting Factory. An inside source said she was "spooked" by the incident, and that she would not be making any public appearances in the near future.

George was released from hospital in the evening of New Year's Day. He arrived at home to welcome old *Monty Python* friend Eric Idle on an extended visit, and security was stepped up with security guards and dogs. It was reported that George hired two former SAS soldiers to guard his home.

On 6 January, London's *Daily Mirror* received an anonymous call from a man who spoke of bomb threats and claimed to have been at the gates of Friar Park earlier that day. He said a police guard told him George had received a letter from Michael Abram that read, "I'm sorry about the attack on you and your wife. Get well soon. You're always on my mind." It was confirmed later that he had been there, but police dismissed the note as a hoax: no police were posted at the Harrisons' home.

Although in public Harrison shrugged off the near fatal attack, his psyche was badly shaken: "This was a nightmare scenario for them," said a friend. "You try and protect yourself and be as normal as possible, but after John Lennon's death there's always a fear in the back of your mind. There were other people staying in the house and George thought he had to see what was happening."

Another added, "You live with that [fear] every day. Everywhere you go it is somehow there after John's death. George knew that."

Michael Abram's trial for attempted murder began at Oxford Crown Court on 14 November. Olivia and Dhani attended but George was absent due to illness.

The proceedings opened with Harrison's account of the event, which was read aloud to the jury.

Olivia told of how she had watched in horror as Abram bolted up the stairs and stabbed her husband. After she had hit the man with the poker, he had lunged for her and knocked her down: "I reached up and tried to grab his testicles. I just got a lot of fabric in the trousers he was wearing." George had leaped on to Abram's back and the three had fallen together in a heap. "At that point," Olivia said, "I didn't have any weapon in my hands. There was blood on the walls, and the carpet. There was a moment when I realized we were going to be murdered. I realized this man was succeeding in murdering us and there was absolutely nobody there to help . . ."

The second day of the trial focused on Abram's precarious mental state. Three court-appointed psychiatrists concluded that he suffered from a "complex delusional system" and displayed symptoms of paranoid schizophrenia.

According to Dr Phillip Joseph, Abram saw himself as the fifth Beatle: "He remembered John Lennon once said the Beatles were more famous than Jesus. That upset him. He thought the Beatles had gone too far." Abram believed that the four men had entered into a demonic conspiracy with George as its central evil figure. "He could see how all roads were leading to George Harrison who was carefully instructing the others how to possess people," said Joseph.

Things had deteriorated in his life when he had a fight with his girlfriend and moved out of their flat. "His life was falling apart, he was living in squalor," Joseph explained. "He was looking for meaning but was preoccupied by his mental illness." He believed his girlfriend had stolen eighty thousand pounds from a drug dealer, masterminded by George Harrison. The idea had come to him from George's 1987 solo hit "Got My Mind Set On You", with the lyric, "It's gonna take money/a whole lotta spending money." Abram also believed he was the Archangel Michael sent by God to kill the beleaguered ex-Beatle because he was the "phantom menace", an apocalyptic figure alluded to in the writings of sixteenth-century astrologer, Nostradamus. "He thought Harrison was the alien from hell," said Joseph. "He thought the Beatles were flying on broomsticks from hell."

Abram wrote an apology to the Harrison family, which was read aloud in court:

> I'm writing this letter in the hope it might be passed on to Mr and Mrs Harrison. I wish to say how sorry I am for the alarm, distress and injury I have caused when I was ill. I have seen many doctors prior to the attack and I was never told I was suffering with schizophrenia or any mental illness. I thought my delusions were real and everything I was experiencing was some kind of witchcraft. I know that Mr and Mrs Harrison fought for their lives on 30 December 1999 and that they must have been terrified by the lunatic in their house . . . I am deeply embarrassed and ashamed about the terrible thing I did to George Harrison. I feel very guilty about it, but I can't turn back time and all I can say is that I'm very sorry. But I hope people may understand what happened to me and appreciate it was not my fault. Physically I did it, but I was not in control of my own mind at the time.

The jury, instructed by Judge Michael Astill, had reached their verdict within an hour of leaving the courtroom: not guilty by reason of insanity. Michael Abram was remanded to the Scott clinic for an indefinite period. Judge Astill deemed the attack "horrifying" and stated, "He will be held without time restriction," his release contingent on approval by a mental health tribunal.

The Harrison family was far from satisfied. Dhani stood outside the courthouse and read the following statement: "Michael Abram was acquitted by a loophole in the law. We shall never forget he was full of hatred and violence when he came to our home. The prospect of him being released back into society is abhorrent to us. We hope the authorities will act with the utmost responsibility in avoiding it in the near future and allow us to be consulted before reaching a conclusion."

In the wake of the case, media attention focused on comparisons with Lennon's murder in 1980. Both Michael Abram and Mark Chapman were social outcasts and loners who took an extremist view of Bible-based good and evil. Both found "subliminal" messages in Beatles lyrics. The pair also indulged in ritualistic behaviour. Chapman once told a writer, "Alone in my apartment in Honolulu I would strip naked and put on Beatles records and pray to Satan to give me the strength. I prayed for demons to enter my body to give me the power to kill." Likewise, a neighbour of Michael Abram once observed, "He sat naked on an overturned plant pot listening to John Lennon and the Beatles." Both were driven to murder by hearing the commands of demonic voices in their heads.

In early 2001 the Harrisons learned that Abram was allowed half-hour walks in the village near the clinic where he was held, escorted by only one unarmed attendant. George, outraged, lashed out, "We find this absolutely incredible and horrifying. Perhaps only a fatality will awaken the psychiatrists to the dangers of a man like him. We've hardly begun to recover from our ordeal. Is the clinic already preparing him for integration back into the community?"

Still, there was even greater heartache looming in the Harrisons' future. While tending to his beloved garden on 22 July 1997 George had discovered a hard, discoloured lump on his neck. Within a week, under the alias "Sid Smith", he entered Princess Margaret Hospital, in Windsor. In a ten-minute operation a sample of lymph tissue was removed and sent for analysis.

On 2 August, Geoff Baker issued an upbeat statement: "George is absolutely fine! There is no reason he shouldn't be. He had a quick operation for a small lump on the outside of his neck."

Although the nodule was widely reported as benign, Harrison soon checked into Britain's leading cancer hospital, the Royal Marsden, to undergo two courses of intense radiotherapy. "I was very lucky," George said later, "because it didn't go anywhere. All it was was a little red mark on my neck. Maybe I'll record a track called 'Radiation Therapy'."

It wasn't until ten months later that a very different story rumbled through the Thames Valley. On his show, American shock jock Howard Stern probed Ringo about recent newspaper reports that George was battling cancer. "No, he had a problem with cancer," Starr replied. "He's had it removed."

Finally, in June 1998, Harrison responded to the intense media interest in his condition: "I'm not going to die on you folks just yet," he said. "I'm very lucky." He referred to his years of chain smoking, and added, "I gave up ciggies many years ago, but started again for awhile, then stopped in '97. Luckily for me, they found this nodule which was more of a warning than anything else. There are many types of cancerous cells and this was very basic."

Eighteen months later he disclosed that the cancer cells hadn't been limited to his throat: "I had a piece of my lung removed in 1997."

For the moment, though, things looked fairly good. Harrison's follow-up screening, performed at Minnesota's Mayo clinic in January, gave him a clean bill of health. He was riding high on the good news when, on 19 January, he learned that his friend and early musical mentor, Carl Perkins, had died following a series of strokes at the age of sixty-five. He stunned everyone by appearing unannounced at Perkins's funeral, held at Jackson, Tennessee's Lambuth University. Carl's son Stan felt it was a courageous gesture: "It took a lot of love for him to do what he did. He didn't know what he was getting into. But he was focused on one thing. He was determined to pay his final respects to a dear friend."

George did more than merely attend. In the middle of the service, he got up and moved to Perkins's coffin, tapped it lightly three times, then took up Ricky Skaggs's guitar and sang Carl Perkins's 1957 classic, "Your True Love". Throughout the number, George's eyes were riveted on the family to gauge their reaction. "I smiled at him," recalled Stan, "and it seemed like it lifted his spirits and he really wanted to sing."

While Stan excused Paul's absence because of Linda's illness, he took the opportunity to deliver a good-natured jab at the other missing Beatle: "Ringo is Ringo. That's just the way he is. He was probably in Barbados, or something, lying on a beach with someone fanning him and dropping grapes in his mouth. That's his attitude. That's just Ringo, man!"

A couple of months later Harrison met Perkins's three sons and musician Wes Henley at a Los Angeles hotel. "The visit," said Stan, "was really about George wanting to grieve and be close to somebody close to Carl. I knew how much he loved my daddy, and I knew how much I loved him and was already missing him. There was a deep connection there and he just wanted to reminisce."

For Harrison, it was also a fact-finding mission. He pressed the brothers for details about their father's health problems, particularly Perkins's two-year battle in the early nineties with throat cancer, which he had won. Wes Henley had the impression that Harrison felt he was living on borrowed time: "He knew he was much sicker than he was being told," said Henley. "He said they found a spot on his left lung but they said there was nothing to it. George wasn't so sure."

The visit concluded with an exchange of gifts. Stan pulled out Carl's prized custom Peavey guitar from his induction into the Rock'n'Roll Hall of Fame, and gave it to George, who presented everyone with a personally inscribed copy of *Autobiography of a Yogi*, his preferred text on the Vedic yogic ideal.

Over the next three years Harrison's health problems seemed behind him. He was regularly spotted round the globe at Formula One racing events, often with Ringo. He also went to concerts, granted interviews, and attended a party at Christie's in London in honour of Eric Clapton's generous donation of one hundred guitars. He was said to be working on new compositions for an album jokingly entitled, *Your Planet is Doomed*. In September 2000 he was at racing-driver Damon Hill's fortieth birthday party where he and Ringo entertained guests with *ad hoc* Beatles versions of classic Who hits. On 27 November they attended The Who charity gig at the Royal Albert Hall, and both saw the Cirque de Soleil in London, George with camcorder in hand to tape the colourful event.

On 10 January 2001 Harrison celebrated a personal musical milestone by rereleasing *All Things Must Pass* to mark the thirtieth anniversary of the acclaimed 1970 three-album set. It was remastered by producer Jon Astley with a few new songs: the previously unreleased "I Live For You"; two demos, "Beware Of Darkness" and "Let It Down"; a karaoke-like version of "What Is Life", plus a new take on his 1970 smash "My Sweet Lord", which he reworked with Dhani and the sultry singer Sam Brown.*

* The hit was rereleased as a single after his death, and shot immediately to number one on 20 January 2002, with all profits to the Material World Charitable Foundation George had set up in 1973. The proceeds from the trust originally went to myriad projects, from various Hindu charities to funding the advancement of classical Indian

While he was doing the rounds to promote the album, George mentioned that he didn't pay much nattention to the current pop scene. "I don't read the papers, I don't watch TV and I don't go to concerts," he went on to say. "With my music, it doesn't matter if I did it twenty years ago or tomorrow. It doesn't go with trends. My trousers don't get wider and tighter every six months! My music is what it is and that's the way I like it." Later he admitted it was rather nice to be a part of musical history. "In some ways the past is like a previous incarnation that catches up with me every time one of these records comes out. I now have six-year-old kids asking me for autographs."

He even agreed to a global online chat on 15 February. One cyberfan asked if Paul McCartney still got on his nerves. George quoted Sir Frank Crisp: "Scan not a friend with a microscope glass. You know his faults, but let his foibles pass." He then added a twenty-first century caveat, "I'm sure there's enough about me that pisses Paul off but I think we've now grown old enough to realize we're both pretty damn cute."

Asked about his health he replied, "It's a difficult thing to get over. But I feel I've got over it physically. My breathing is a bit less percentage than it used to be. Other than that, I'm pretty cool."

Music was clearly still very important to him, and Dhani remembers that his father always carried a ukelele with him, playing it in cars, airports and even on planes, where he would often stand in the first-class aisle and strum through an impromptu set of vintage Cole Porter classics for the delighted passengers.

It was during this period too that he recommitted himself to his Hare Krishna faith, encouraged by Shyamasundara Dasa, the young man who had first introduced him to Bhaktivedanta Swami at Tittenhurst Park estate on 11 September 1969. "I spent some time with George this summer," the American-born Dasa said in an interview. "George has reached a very high level of spiritual development, I'm happy to say. He chants 'Hare Krishna' every day. He's totally serene

---

music, but at the end of his life George stipulated that only children's charities around the globe should benefit.

and has accepted life as it is. He's actually achieved a much higher level of self-realization than I could ever hope to imagine. He's peaceful and serene to the degree that is very rare – and at such a young age! Bhaktivedanta Swami benefited him so much." Dasa also remarked that George was thinking of buying a small island off the coast of the highly Hindu-populated Fiji, but abandoned the idea when the political situation on the main island became increasingly unstable. His dream of a Utopian Hare Krishna community was dropped.

By the spring of 2001, Harrison's world was rocked when his lung condition erupted into a life-threatening crisis. On 21 March, he checked into St Mary's Hospital in Rochester, Minnesota, affiliated with the Mayo clinic. The following day he underwent a four-hour operation to remove a large cancerous growth from his left lung. "The operation was successful and George made an excellent recovery," said his lawyers. "He's in the best of spirits and on top form, the most relaxed and free since the knife attack on him in 1999. He is now enjoying a holiday in Tuscany. Although all things must pass away, George has no plans right now and is still living in the material world and wishes everyone all the best, God bless, and not to worry." The tongue in cheek statement, however, was in fact authored by the sly Harrison himself.

George was discharged on 2 April but barely had time to recuperate before further tests revealed devastating news: the cancer had spread to his brain. Ironically the same disease had taken the life of his mother on 7 July 1970 in Liverpool. His father had also died from cancer, after years of heavy smoking. Later that month George entered the Oncology Institute of southern Switzerland, known also as the San Giovanni Clinic, in Bellinzona. He and Olivia leased a palatial villa in Luino, Italy, a forty-minute drive from the clinic. There, in the care of the clinic's director, Dr Franco Cavelli, a renowned cancer specialist, George underwent several courses of cobalt radiation therapy to shrink the tumour. It didn't work.

In fact, when Harrison was told by his doctors in Switzerland that the cancer had moved to his brain he was content to forgo any further treatment, withdraw from the world and prepare himself for death by completely giving himself over to Krishna. At the time, the Vedic scholar Steven J. Rosen, a passing friend of George, said, "That's a very mature, spiritual sentiment when you learn death is near and you resign yourself to that. Krishna enables one to face death gracefully. A devotee knows what to do at the time of death, how to focus one's mind and heart on God. I know George is aware of this as we've discussed it."

The Hare Krishna religion sees this life as a karmic bridge to the next. Errant Krishnas return to the material world again and again to perfect themselves, while the best go on to the Krishna heaven, Goloka Vrndavana. As Harrison's life drew towards its close, this lofty ideal inspired him to let go of this world in the hope of a better one to come. "Let's face it," he had said in 1984, "if I'm going to have to stand up and be counted, then I'll be with the devotees rather than the straight people. Krishna consciousness isn't something I do in the road anymore. It's something I do inside myself."

"Bhaktivedanta Swami saw Harrison as a sort of demigod who came from a higher planetary system to assist in revealing true spirituality to the world," said Rosen.

Still, even in his picture-postcard Swiss village, George was hounded by the media. In an attempt to maintain his privacy, he used many different vehicles with alternating British, Swiss and Italian number plates, and moved into a fourteen-room villa, called Collina d'Oro (Golden Hill), close to the clinic, and told villagers in Montinola above Lake Lugano that he planned to make it his permanent home. Sadly, he had agreed to abandon his beloved Friar Park.

"He was looking to the future," said Pietro Balerna, the parish clerk who helped George find the villa. "He seemed peaceful and almost jolly. He was full of hope."

One of the most moving songs from George's rereleased *All Things Must Pass* was the demo for "The Art Of Dying" in which he sang, "There'll come a time when all of us must leave here. Then nothing Sister Mary can do will keep me here with you . . . There'll come a time when most of us return here. Brought back by a desire to be a perfect entity."

Shortly before his death George paid a final visit to the Maharishi

– then well into his eighties – in Vlodrop, Holland. The old master tried to give him courage and hope, comparing his sick body to an old coat with holes in it. He said he was happy that George would soon discard that garment and put on a new one.

It was reported that George was only just strong enough to attend Dhani's graduation from Brown University and cope with a visit from Paul McCartney in May. The July news from the clinic was anything but promising. A hospital spokesman said, on behalf of Dr Cavelli, "George was here in May and June. He has not recovered. But he is not my patient any more."

These grim words forced Harrison to engage once more in off-the-cuff damage control. "I am feeling fine and I am really very sorry for the unnecessary worry which has been caused by the reports appearing in today's press. Please do not worry."

That summer, the now semi-retired George Martin found himself embroiled in an international tabloid controversy: London's *Mail On Sunday* of 22 July quoted him as saying: "He's taking it easy and hoping the thing will go away. He has an indomitable spirit but he knows he is going to die soon and is accepting that. George is very philosophical. He does realize everybody has to die some time. He has been near death many times as well. But he knows he is going to die soon and he's accepting it perfectly happily."

The line, "He knows he is going to die soon" echoed round the world. And the Harrison camp fired back: "The reports are unsubstantiated, untrue, insensitive and uncalled-for, especially as Mr Harrison is active and feeling very well in spite of the health challenges he has had this year."

Immediately, Martin insisted he'd said no such thing to any of the tabloids, although on 18 July he had talked to Christian Koch of the World Entertainment News Network, a prominent London news agency. According to Koch's transcript, this is what Martin actually said about George Harrison: "He's abroad at the moment. He's been having treatment and he's just taking it easy and hoping the thing will go away. He's very philosophical, I mean everybody's got to die some time. I'm nearer to that than most people because I'm so old. George has been near to it many times and he's been rescued many times. So I guess he's hoping he's going to be rescued again. And I think he will. But he knows perfectly well there's a chance he may not be and he's accepting it quite happily."

Starr was said to be "disappointed and disgusted" by the ghoulish media frenzy. He'd seen George in early July and pointed out, "If he had been bad he would have told me. I didn't panic because I'll wait until it becomes a reality. The news is real only when George or Paul tells me! We do that to each other. We say, 'Watch out, something's happened and they will be calling you.' "

Sadly, George's three-month medical treatment had not arrested the cancer. Michael Palin saw him in August and later observed, "I could see all the treatment he'd been through had taken a severe physical toll." By now Harrison had hired security guards to prevent photographers snapping shots of him.

As summer waned, Harrison made a final pilgrimage to India, to the holy city of Varanasi (also known as Banaras, or Kashi), considered sacred to all orthodox Hindus. There, he spent time chanting in local Krishna temples, and bathed in the Ganges, an age-old ritual in preparing for death, ultimate rebirth and, hopefully, final release.

In Banaras he bumped into an old Hare Krishna friend, Sacinandana Dasa Bramachari on the stone steps of an ancient ghat where the old, sick and dying come to make their peace with their preferred image of God. The old American monk instantly recognized George, despite his emaciation and the long grey chudder round his head. After the two men had greeted each other, they sat together for about twenty minutes and talked quietly about the holy art of dying.

A few days after George died, the monk sent this author a long e-mail. He told me that after he and Harrison parted, he hurried back to his small room in one of the Dharamshala pilgrim ashrams that line the river and wrote down what he could remember of what was said and his final impressions of Harrison:

As far as one can reach the goal of true spirituality within the body I'm certain George has found it. I'd last seen him in

Vrndavana in the spring of 1995 and he was pretty much the same cheery image of a man I'd known since the early seventies. But here before me now was another George, his closely cropped white hair framing those deep brown, penetratingly truthful eyes that always struck me upon seeing him. I was shocked at how small and thin he was. I remember noting the bones in his elbows and knees protruding from his taut, slightly scaly skin as he entered the holy waters for the traditional dipping down seven times in submission to our Holy Mother Ganga. At first he didn't recognize me and made only the traditional namaste gesture and answered back, "Hare Krishna," when I approached him. In fact, I had to reintroduce myself twice before he fully understood who I was. George and I were never great friends, but I'd walked with him once on an early-morning japa stroll in Vrndavana and had eaten with him maybe two or three times along with a group of other devotees in Krishna's dusty cow town outside Delhi. To be honest, I hadn't even heard he was sick. I'd known, of course, that he had been stabbed at his home in Henley; I had no clue how bad he really was. Seeing him, of course, I instantly knew both his material body was almost finished and why he was there. "Hare Krishna," he said to me again, placing his small waxy hand on my shoulder.

"How are you, Prabhu?" I asked.

"Fine, fine," he whispered, obviously trying to keep the always fragile peace of the bustling Banaras riverside mornings.

"Let's sit down," I said, steadying him gently as we sat on the slippery steps only two or three feet from the rapidly rushing river. I do not recall seeing either his wife or his son anytime near him at that point. I think he wanted to be alone making his final formal prayers to his God.

"I don't have much time left," he told me. I didn't truly understand whether he was alluding to his own imminent demise or the fact that I might be simply bothering him. He then quickly continued.

"I did it to myself, you know, with the smoking, the boozing, the women. I couldn't even keep a vegetarian diet once I started seriously following Formula One circuit around the world. Everything Prabhupada warned me against, everything he so patiently taught us by example."

Trying to think of something half-way intelligent to say, I stumbled. "Don't you see, George, everything you did has made who you are now? Prabhupada knew how weak we all were. He said many times, even the simplest rules he gave us we would never be able to follow once he left. Prabhupada's gift to us wasn't the rules and regulations of Krishna consciousness, but rather, a deep insight into ourselves. The door to a higher consciousness, the possibility of a life deeper, richer and broader than the one our parents lived. It was never a guarantee."

"I'm not afraid," said George, looking straight and deep into my eyes. "Not even of the pain. I'll tell you something, man. I've never had to rely on faith in my spiritual life because I know, I've always known since I was a kid, that God is real and we are an intimate part of Him. Maybe one of the reasons I wasted so much time was because I was so sure of an afterlife. Now I see it just made me smarmy and preachy. I could have done so much more than I did. Helped so many more people understand, but part of being a Beatle was having the whole world thrown at you and whatever you wanted whenever it came around. For a long time I fell into the trap. I became smug. When I was with Ravi Shankar I was a sort of all-purpose Hindu, thinking Siva, Durga, Krishna, Rama are all One. But when I was with Prabhupada I understood and accepted that Krishna was truly the Supreme. I'd hang out with my muso friends in London and it would all somehow just slip away into whatever party was happening."

Again, I argued, "But it all brought you here, now, to a really good place. 99 per cent of the world thinks they are their bodies, have only one life and need to screw out every last bit of enjoyment they can, but you were too hip for that. I come here every morning, George, and I see a lot of highly advanced souls, a lot of very purified, renounced, almost egolessly invisible beings on these old stone steps. Men and women on the thinnest strings between life and death completely transcendental to their own personal drama. They have achieved the goal. I see you like that," I said, choking a little bit on the pure emotion of the moment.

George immediately raised his hand and rebuffed me. "I see these people too, but believe me, I'm not one of them. Prabhupada once told me, 'Time doesn't make saints, only old men.' I've tried, but mostly, to be honest with you, I feel I've failed. Failed Srila Prabhupada, failed my family, failed the people that looked up to me and failed Krishna as well."

I smiled. "That's exactly the way you should feel. Prabhupada said the moment anyone feels themself spiritually advanced, they're finished. All I can tell you is what I see and I've been a devotee for thirty years now, living here in Banaras for the last four. I see a heart empty of ego and pride, and after everything you've been given and accomplished that seems almost superhuman to me."

"Anything I have," countered Harrison, by his darting eyes seemingly wanting to end the somewhat embarrassing conversation, "is simply grace. It's nothing I've earned, won, even achieved, but whatever spiritual consciousness I do have, or have managed to hang on to is simply a gift. It's the only thing I have and the only thing I'll take with me. But I'm grateful for it. I don't even worry about my family really. I know Krishna will take care of them."

"Just one more thing, George," I said, rising from my kneeling position on the cold, mossy stone steps of the ghat. "There are tens of thousands of souls all over the world who first heard about Krishna and yoga from you and that changed their lives forever. When Prabhupada was alone, without resources, you helped him. There are many, many people out there today who are inspired to spiritual life by your example. What did Prabhupada used to say? 'Whatever a great man does, common men will follow and his actions all the world pursues.' Hare Bol, brother." I squeezed him gently around the neck. He put his hand on my knee and patted me and silently looked out over the rolling Ganges, now strewn with swiftly floating floral offerings with lit camphor wicks stuck in the

> middle of these floating prayers. I walked away, stopped to look back just once. What I saw was what I saw every day. An old yogi saying his prayers, worshipping the river, making peace with himself and God. Understanding who he once was in this world, amongst all the retired Indian civil servants and doddering primary-school headmasters, jarred me a little, but that was just the drama of his life and it was clearly almost over. George then slowly disappeared like so many I'd seen before into the river and into himself.
>
> Some time later I heard he'd died somewhere high in the Hollywood Hills. As far as I could see, death had very little hold over George Harrison. To paraphrase one of the sonnets of William Shakespeare, "For I shall feed on death that feeds on men and death once dead there is more dying then." Clearly Harrison slowly had been killing the death within himself for years. It was the art of dying he sang about on *All Things Must Pass* and he achieved it with my guru Srila Prabhupada being the only other living soul I've known to beat death at its own game.

Buoyed by his inner strength, George kept working. In July he laid down a guitar track for ex-Traffic drummer Jim Capaldi's single, "Anna Julia", released on 2 August. The record went nowhere. He played slide guitar on Bill Wyman's single, "Love Letters", and on two tracks for Jeff Lynne's Electric Light Orchestra revival CD *Zoom*.

Harrison was also hurrying to complete his final solo album, then titled *Portrait of a Leg End*. The twenty-five working tracks were laid down at his Friar Park studios in Henley. With its bluesy, acoustic-driven rock sound it was a blend of old and new, some compositions dating back to the early eighties, and he recruited such heavyweights as Eric Clapton and Bob Dylan, along with Jeff Lynne, Ravi Shankar and Neil Innes, to play with him. Session drummer and long-time friend Jim Keltner, who also contributed to the project, said it was great to be in the studio with George, who insisted on a sparse, minimalist approach, devoid of computer wizardry. "Some of the new songs were very poignant concerning his life over the past few years. It will be obvious when you hear them what they are about." "Rising

Sun" is said to address his devotion to Hindu orthodoxy, and Dhani's emergence as a blossoming musical talent. George and he performed a father–son duet on a cover of Bob Dylan's "Abandoned Love". Other unreleased songs included "Valentine". The problem, however, was neither the thoughtful compositions nor the flawless musicianship, but the weakness and frailty of Harrison's former engaging vocals.

On 2 October at his Swiss villa, George cut what was to be his final song, "Horse To The Water", a catchy pro-yogic tune written for ex-Squeeze keyboardist Jools Holland, to appear on Holland's *Small World, Big Friends* CD. "He was only too pleased to do it for me," said Holland. "I was honoured and grateful." Co-written with Dhani, the sixties-Dylan/seventies-Lennonesque song was a sideswipe at those of his friends whose nihilistic lives, devoid of spirituality, were sputtering out of control. " 'Say, man, this could turn out to be risky,' he said, 'everything's okay,' as he downed another bottle of whiskey." The copyright was filed under RIP Limited, 2001.

Harrison's health declined throughout the autumn, and Olivia was desperate for a way to extend her husband's life or, at least, lessen his severe pain, and hours of internet research led her to Dr Gil Lederman, who performed experimental cancer treatments at Staten Island University Hospital in New York. At the end of October George and his family flew to the USA for him to try Dr Lederman's non-invasive procedure known as fractionated stereo tactic radio surgery. After a frame had been attached to the head focused beams of radiation were aimed directly at the tumour, zapping it with such precise accuracy that the surrounding healthy tissue suffered only minimal damage. The beams were also rotated around the body, enabling the tumour to be attacked from all directions. Although the treatment boasted a ninety per cent cure rate for brain lesions, it could not halt the metastatic spread of the cancer's primary source, the lung. In cases like Harrison's, the treatment served only to relieve the severe pain of final-stage cancers. As one male nurse observed, George appeared "very frail and gaunt" when he entered the hospital in a wheelchair. "It was shocking to see him that way after thinking of him as so young and vital for all those years."

Although a friend told the press George had made a "dramatic turnaround", word from the family indicated otherwise. His sister-in-law, Pauline Harrison, admitted, "We are all very concerned. He is very ill, but putting up a real fight."

Harrison was determined to soldier on for as long as he could. Dr Lederman revealed that his patient played several of his new songs at the clinic. He was even working on several compositions for the album. "They were great songs," said Lederman. "One was called 'Brainwashed', which was about the conflicts between the government and people. Before George left Staten Island he saw my children and brought over a guitar to play some songs and then signed the guitar 'To Ariel from George Harrison'."

Dr Lederman described his patient's final days at the hospital as "quiet and dignified. George was very different from many people in that he didn't have any fear of death. He felt life and death were part of the same process. When he was stabbed in his home two years ago, he got up with the knife having been in his chest and went to the balcony and cried, 'Hare Krishna.' He was always a very religious man. I think he will remain a legend. I believe for generations people will talk about George Harrison and his music."

It was also a time for mending fences. Louise Harrison, George's older sister, then seventy, drove a thousand miles from her home in Illinois to reconcile with her brother, whom she hadn't seen in four years, since she had christened her bed-and-breakfast Hard Day's Night. "He was very clear about what he wanted and what he didn't want," recalled Dr Lederman. "He didn't want to see his sister. But finally, probably because Olivia encouraged him, they spent about half an hour together. They reconciled."

At the beginning of November, the public too realized the end was near when Paul and Ringo gathered at his hospital bed. Afterwards McCartney told the press, "The best thing for me was seeing him for a couple of hours and laughing, joking and holding his hand. Afterwards, I realized I'd never ever held his hand! We'd been to school together and got on buses together and we didn't hold each other's hands. It was a great moral compensation. He was rubbing his thumb up and down my hand and it was very nice."

Certainly Harrison and McCartney had their differences over the years, but these, thankfully, were all settled when George looked up at Paul and said quietly, "None of it matters anymore."

For Ringo, it was an especially wrenching time, laced with bitter ironies. His only daughter, fashion designer Lee Starkey, aged thirty-one, was in Boston's Brigham and Women's Hospital, fighting her own battle with brain cancer for the second time. She was reportedly receiving radical radiation treatment for a secondary tumour.

Just eight months after Maureen's death, another crisis had struck the Starkeys. On 24 August 1995 Ringo had been on the western leg of an American tour with his All-Starr Band when he received an urgent call from home. His daughter Lee had collapsed and been rushed to a London hospital. With images of Maureen's battle still fresh in his mind, Starr cancelled the remaining concert dates and caught the next flight to be with his daughter. "Family is more important," he told the press.

Lee was treated for fluid on the brain, but the cause was not immediately known. However, after a barrage of neuro-scans she was diagnosed with a rare brain tumour known as ependymoma. On the advice of doctors, Lee flew to Boston and entered the Brigham and Women's Hospital, renowned for its first-rate neurological department. On 16 September Dr Peter Black, head of neurosurgery, performed the delicate cranial operation. Afterwards Lee underwent six weeks of daily radiation sessions to knock out any remaining cancer cells. The treatment was deemed, guardedly, a success and Lee went to recuperate at her stepfather Isaac Tigrett's home in California's San Fernando Valley, with her grandmother Florence and stepsister Augusta.

"It's terrifying," said Starr at the time. "You don't want it to happen and you don't believe it. But you just have to stand up and get on with it."

Now, six years later, in November 2001, just when it seemed Lee had beaten her cancer, she was back at the Boston hospital where doctors discovered another tumour. Ringo flew from George's bedside to be with her.

Once again Lee undertook a six-week course of radiation therapy and, by all accounts, the procedure was a success. At the hospital she received a huge bouquet from Julian Lennon: "I hadn't seen him for a long time," she said, "but it was a very nice gesture."

Beatles fans Howie Square and his friend Josh claim they spent half an hour chatting with George Harrison only days before he died. The two men drove to Staten Island University Hospital hoping to meet their idol. They insist that George invited them into his room, and that Paul and Ringo called in after several minutes. Square later said, "George meant so much to our generation, we felt we ought to try to see him." At the hospital's reception desk the two men were told Harrison was receiving visitors and they were sent up. "We knocked at the door, and George said, 'Come in.' He was sitting there in his hospital gown, reading a book on Eastern religion. When we expressed concern about his health, he told us, 'I will transcend this body. I will have a new beginning after I leave this shell. I will watch over Olivia and Dhani. I'll live with them and through them.' He seemed tremendously optimistic."

Square said he and his friend left quietly when the other Beatles arrived. "They looked great," said Howie. "Paul introduced himself as Paul McCartney, as if we might not actually know who he was!"

Discharged from hospital on 10 November, George and his family flew to Los Angeles on the evening of Thursday, 22 November from JFK aboard a private jet owned by actor Jim Carrey. George almost died on the way. He was lying in a hospital bed fitted into the aircraft by the aviation firm after they had removed several rows of seats. Every move he made was excruciatingly painful and at times he even hallucinated. He did not want to return to Friar Park because he knew the media vultures would be lurking outside the gates awaiting news of his death. "His body would have had to be taken out in a hearse or undertaker's van and he didn't want that photograph as his epitaph," explained a friend from his local pub in Henley, the Flower Pot. "Nor did he want a scrum at the church or cremation."

In a last-ditch attempt to buy himself a little more time, Harrison endured a taxing course of chemotherapy at the UCLA Medical

Center. A friend said at the time, "I don't think he'd ever have an unrealistic perception of his grave condition. George Harrison is a very spiritual person. He believes death is an integral part of life. I doubt he'd be inclined to fight death."

During the last week of November drummer Jim Keltner saw George: "It was a great gift to us that he was so beautiful. He looked fantastic, like a prince. He didn't look like a person suffering from cancer. His skin was shining and he was smiling."

On the twenty-ninth, family and a few close friends gathered at his bedside in a private estate in the Hollywood Hills. In addition to Olivia and Dhani, Ravi Shankar, his wife, their daughter Anoushka, and Hare Krishna friends Mukunda and Shyamasundara were there. George drifted in and out of consciousness as he chanted "Hare Krishna." Anoushka later remarked, "We used to say that Uncle George was more Indian than an Indian. He chanted Hare Krishna, he said, because it helped him see God." Ravi noted, "George looked so peaceful, surrounded by love. He was a brave, beautiful soul, full of love, childlike humour and a deep spirituality."

Finally, in the early afternoon, just after the two Hare Krishna monks had left, George stopped chanting and whispered that he was taking his final breath. Paul McCartney later described it as a "golden moment". He died, at 1.30 p.m. on 29 November 2001, as he had lived, in touch with his Higher Power, the Lord Sri Krishna. In the minds of those closest to him he had finally gone "home".

Typically, Harrison had left strict instructions for what was to happen after his death. The first stop was the Hollywood Forever funeral firm. Production director Annette Lloyd recalled: "We received the first call about twenty minutes after Mr Harrison's death. All they told us was that a VIP had died, they didn't give us the name. Two members of our staff at the home proceeded to the address given. It was at that point they found out it was George Harrison. Before the body was taken from the home to the doctor's office, the family, staff and security team joined hands and said a prayer around him. That was the only instance I know of any kind of informal, very brief prayer."

The flower-garlanded body was transported to George's doctor's surgery, Olivia and Dhani following in a separate car. There, the doctor signed the death certificate, the official cause of death being metastatic non-small lung cancer, and the motorcade continued to the crematorium. Lloyd revealed that the Harrisons had opted for a "direct cremation", without ceremony, chapel, or even a coffin. "There was what we call a crematorium [cardboard] casket," said Lloyd, "and that was all. His ashes were then put in an urn."

Afterwards, the family issued this statement: "He left this world as he lived it, conscious of God, fearless of death and at peace surrounded by family and friends. He often said, 'Everything else can wait, but the search for God cannot wait, and love one another.' "

Reaction poured in from around the globe. From Paul McCartney: "I am devastated and very, very sad. We knew he'd been ill for a long time. He was a lovely guy, a very brave man and had a wonderful sense of humour. He is really my baby brother."

George Martin commented: "I've known George for ever and he's a really beautiful guy I love dearly. I remember all the beautiful times we had together and I'd like to remember him like that because I know he would like to be remembered like that. He was a great guy, full of love for humanity, but he didn't suffer fools gladly. He'll be sorely missed by everyone. Olivia and Dhani have borne his illness with enormous courage and devotion. Now I believe, as he did, that he has entered a higher state. God give him peace."

Ringo, on tour in Vancouver, had this to say: "We will miss George for his great sense of love, his sense of music, and his sense of laughter. George is a best friend of mine. I loved him very much and I will miss him greatly. Both Barbara and I send out love and light to Olivia and Dhani." His stepdaughter Francesca Gregorini offered this insight: "Rich was so sad when George died. They had a very deep connection, a soul connection. People think the Beatles were chummy all the time but that's not entirely the case. I knew George only as 'the gardener'. He loved his garden and when we'd visit his house that was what he showed us. He was so proud of it."

Stan Perkins visualized a heavenly music duet between George and his father Carl: "'Everybody's Trying To Be My Baby' is getting played right now," he ventured. "I bet George is teaching my dad the chords to 'Something' right now."

Keith Richards said: "The attack at his home is what did George in. I think he would have beaten the cancer if it wasn't for the blade."

Throughout the world fans flocked to emotional vigils. The family requested one minute of silence on 3 December at one thirty to mark the time of his death. "We are deeply touched by the outpouring of love and compassion from people around the world," read their simple statement. "The profound beauty of the moment of George's passing, of his awakening from his dream, was no surprise to those of us who knew how he longed to be with God. In that pursuit he was relentless."

Controversy, as ever, hounded the Beatles. On 16 December 2001 it was reported that Harrison's death certificate had been deliberately falsified and Los Angeles police were investigating whether his family had knowingly filed inaccurate information. They had to decide whether a crime had been committed before they undertook a full-scale probe.

Initially, Harrison's spokesman Gavin de Becker claimed that the musician had died at his home, but when the death certificate was filed, a non-existent address, 1971 Coldwater Canyon, was given. The district attorney's office said it was believed that Dr Rosen, who had signed the certificate, had only filled in the cause of death. "Who actually filled in the certificate will be investigated," stated the spokeswoman.

In the end it turned out that Hollywood Forever employee Soledad Luera had entered the bogus address. It cost her her job. She was fired – for breaking the Harrisons' confidentiality agreement by sharing details with other employees and failing to notify the company of the false address. Luera sued Olivia, claiming that she had only filled in the information Mrs Harrison had relayed to her.

It took until February 2001 to clear up the confusion. The Los Angeles district attorney's office finally issued a statement that an associate of Gavin de Becker had supplied the incorrect information. The revised address was now given as 9536 Heather Road, near Griffith

Park, a secluded four-million-dollar 1938 French country manor house, recently owned by rock singer and actress Courtney Love, now belonging to Mike Walley, an alleged colleague of Paul McCartney. Several months earlier US media had reported that Paul had taken possession of the property. Despite the ongoing controversy over the exact address, de Becker is adamant that the location of Harrison's death is strictly confidential.

As of 22 May 2002 the Staten Island doctor who treated George was under investigation by the State Health Department for publicly discussing the ex-Beatle's last days. The investigation began after Harrison's estate complained that Dr Gil Lederman had violated confidentiality rules by giving interviews concerning George. Although Lederman had not talked directly about George's specific medical condition, the "revealing of personally identifiable facts, data, or information obtained in a professional capacity without the prior consent of the patient, is defined as gross misconduct". If found guilty, Lederman, who had enjoyed a long, celebrated career, could face anything from censure and reprimand to licence suspension or revocation.

"George actually spoke with Dr Lederman very little. But he mounted a press tour exploiting George in the most shameless way," said de Becker. "They still don't know where George died, and they never will. Which proves that even a very famous man can lead a private life and have a peaceful, private death."

Despite worldwide speculation that Harrison's ashes would be strewn in India, at Friar Park or even in Liverpool, the official export licence for them issued to the family in Los Angeles, listed George's permanent address as his Swiss villa and the final destination of the ashes. Vedic scholar Rosen said, "In the Hare Krishna tradition the body is quickly cremated so there are no subtle aspects of the being hovering by its remains. The living entity is then able to go back to Krishna, because the body is completely finished."

The music on which George was working until he died was finished by Dhani and Jeff Lynne and released on Dark Horse and EMI on Tuesday, 19 November 2002. Entitled *Brainwashed* but recorded under the working titles of *Your Planet Is Doomed!* and *Portrait Of A Leg End* the album featured eleven new compositions.

"We started working on the album in 1999," Jeff Lynne explains. "George would come round my house and he'd always have a new song with him. He would strum them on a guitar or ukelele. The songs just knocked me out."

Lynne adds: "George talked about how he wanted the album to sound. He told Dhani a lot of things he would like to have done to the songs and left us little clues. There was always that spiritual energy that went into the lyrics as well as the music. George told me, 'If you're going to do this record, I don't want it too posh. I want it more like a demo.' I had to make it sound like a George Harrison record. Not like somebody else messed with it."

"My dad knew what this was going to be like," said Dhani. "He didn't want it to be too polished. The majority of the detail came from what he'd imparted to me in the years we'd spent in the studio mucking about.

"You couldn't cram more of my dad's real, true self into one album. The first part of his life was as hectic as anyone's has ever been. He went everywhere and did everything in the most intense way. Then, for the second half of his life, he was in the garden, and he enjoyed nature, planted trees and wrote music. Those two contrasts made up a great balance.

"I've seen a lot of strange things happen to my family in the last few years. Someone broke into our house and tried to murder us, and then, of course, there was my father's illness and the mêlée that ensues when the media intrudes upon your life. But you can experience only as much joy as you have had sorrow. Sorrow is like the hollowing out of a wooden block, and joy is what fills it up. The more sorrow you've had, the deeper the joy you can experience."

After Harrison's death, rumours circulated about his will, drawn up four months earlier. When details were finally revealed on 29 November 2002, it appeared that he had outwitted everyone, including the taxman.

His estate was valued at £99,226,780, but reduced to £98,916,464 after expenses. Although the document listed his address as Montagnola, Switzerland, it stated that he was a British subject and thereby his affairs would be handled under British law. Of his many properties, including his Maui bungalow and the Swiss villa, his beloved Friar Park was said to be worth £15 million. The bulk of his wealth had been accumulated from royalties accruing from his 1970 hit "My Sweet Lord" and the 1979 *Monty Python* classic film *Life of Brian*, which had started his successful career as film producer.

In the final year of his life, however, George's net worth jumped by 25 per cent. The Beatles' greatest-hits compilation CD, released in late 2000 titled *1*, flew off the shelves, thanks largely to the under-thirty crowd. The title became the fastest-selling album of all time, launching the Beatles into the new world order of classical pop artists.

Notably absent from George's will was any bequest to the Hare Krishna movement. For months it had been assumed that he would bequeath a tenth of his fortune to the faith he had embraced. Krishna disciples were quick to point out that he had donated generously during his lifetime to the International Society for Krishna Consciousness. They vowed to create a memorial garden to him in Mayapur, north of Calcutta.

George left his entire fortune to Olivia and Dhani. He placed the estate in trust, and, with the many sizeable charitable donations he had made earlier, he bypassed inheritance tax. Harrison was determined that the taxman would not collect the "one for you, nineteen for me," as his biting lyric ran. The will further granted Olivia and Dhani the power to transfer funds from the trust as they saw fit, and the freedom to purchase homes anywhere in the world.

The revelation of his will coincided with a 29 November memorial concert at London's Royal Albert Hall in his honour. Five thousand fans packed the venue, and profits went to Harrison's Material World Charitable Foundation. Music heavyweights, headed by Paul McCartney, Tom Petty and Ravi Shankar, performed at the concert, and a rendition of "While My Guitar Gently Weeps" featured Paul on piano, Ringo on drums, and Eric Clapton re-created George's haunting guitar solo. At one point Paul brought out a ukelele, telling the audience, "Sometimes we'd go round to George's for dinner and the ukes would come out. The last time I was there I said, 'I've got one for you, George, and it goes like this . . .'" With that, he launched into Harrison's trademark "Something", a heartfelt performance that brought the house down.

Thirteen months after Linda's death, McCartney first saw blonde ex-model Heather Mills presenting an award at London's Dorchester Hotel in May 1999. Heather clearly made an impact on Paul, as did her speech on helping dozens of limbless victims in war zones such as Bosnia and Croatia. He later remarked, "When I saw her at that award show I thought 'Wow she looks great'." McCartney soon donated $240,000 to the Heather Mills Trust, an organization focusing on providing limbs for landmine victims around the world. At the time Paul was still unaware of the fact that Heather herself had lost half of her left leg when she was hit by a speeding police motorcycle in August 1993.

McCartney slowly returned to public life and revisited his roots by releasing the album *Run Devil Run*, hosting his own rock'n'roll radio show, and performing at the new Cavern Club in Liverpool. Paul also acquired Heather's phone number and the two collaborated on the charity single "Voice", released in the UK on 13 December 1999. "I thought it was a joke when I first heard him on the voice mail: 'Hello, Paul McCartney here,'" Heather says. "He said, 'Look, I want to help your charity. I think you do great work.'"

"We had three or four meetings, all very prim and proper," Paul later remembered. "She came to the office to talk about the charity and I realized I fancied her. I did fancy her from the start but I was playing it cool." By the end of the last meeting, Heather was beginning to become aware of the added attention from Sir Paul: "I got into a lift and just felt these eyes on my back. I turned round and saw him peeping round a corner. I said, 'I think you're eyeing up my bum.'"

In the months that followed, the couple were seen together at various media events and by March 2000, Paul confirmed that they were in fact "an item" and he professed his love for her on national television that October. In early 2001 their engagement was rumoured in the press until it was finally confirmed in July. "When I proposed I was a bit nervous but I managed," said Paul, describing how he popped the question on one knee when he took Heather to the Lake District.

"I thought someone had shot him in the back of the kneecaps 'cause he just fell to the ground," remembered Heather. She refuted the charges that she was after the McCartney fortune: "He knows and I know why I'm with him," she said, and added puzzlingly, "If I was going to go out with anybody for their money, it would be with someone a lot richer."

The relationship was hard at first for Paul's children, as he remarked to the *Sunday Telegraph*, "They find it difficult to think of me with another woman. I think a second marriage is hard for the children, but it's how it is and how it must be, and I think that more than anything they want me to be happy – and this is what makes me happy."

The two were wed on 11 June 2002 at Castle Leslie in Glaslough, Ireland. Among the 300 invited guests were Ringo, George Martin, Jools Holland, Chrissie Hynde and of course McCartney's three children: Stella, James, and Mary. Paul's brother, Mike, attended as best man, and Heather's sister, Fiona, was maid of honour. Heather entered the church to a bridal march based on McCartney's song "Heather" from the *Driving Rain* album, and they both exited the church to Paul's wedding march from *The Family Way*. They spent their honeymoon in the Seychelles, on a private island in the Indian Ocean.

Despite the happiness the relationship brought the two of them, Heather deemed 2002 to be "horrendous, publicly. Really, probably the worst year of my life . . . worse than the year I lost my leg." Paul drew comparisons to his first marriage in 1969: "Linda got rubbished in the first year or so. Then she was established and people got over it. It's a bit par for the course. But you know, get over it!" Heather concludes, "When I hear people criticizing us, I feel sorry for them because I think life is short and we're here to do good for others. We live for today. That's all we've got."

As in his relationship with Linda, Paul prefers to be with Heather at every moment of every day, as she confirms. "We are together twenty-four hours a day . . . I learned I am bossy. We fight, we each have our ways. If you love somebody, you have to argue sometimes. They are usually about silly little things. He is no different than any other man. We have learned to communicate, it's give and take . . . I will never become a 'yes' woman . . . He is always communicating to me while he is on stage, always blowing me kisses and looking for me."

Although Linda was musically limited, her girl-next-door backup vocals added a classy American echo to Paul's solo work with Wings. And of course he took a lot of flak for inviting her to join the band. Heather has stated that if it was up to Paul she would be on stage with him too every night: "He is always asking me to play on stage with him on saxophone . . . Watching him work is amazing. Even when he is sick with the flu he can still sing great." To date she has not yet joined him in performance.

"The latest album is mostly about me," she said proudly, "and he wrote a song called 'Heather'* . . . Most of *Driving Rain* is about me."

She told Larry King that she encouraged Paul to write "Freedom" and to play a benefit for the victims of the World Trade Center disaster. "I don't know," he told her, "it might look bad. They might think I am promoting my album." She said it didn't matter what people thought as long as he was using his status to help people in need.

What the future holds for McCartney is anyone's guess; for all his apparent human shortcomings and trials, he is the consummate bass player, an innovative composer, a keen, creative mind, a loving family man, and committed to helping make change for the better in the world as he sees it. Paul McCartney deserves any happiness that comes his way.

Ringo Starr has returned to the pure joy of making music, touring the world with his All-Starr Band. He continues to delight audiences with an eclectic mix of his own greatest hits and those of his musical colleagues. Of course, all of his childhood dreams of stardom were

* His second song with this title. In 1969, he wrote one for his adopted daughter.

fulfilled in the years of Beatlemania, and those who know him say that, apart from his easy-going good nature, he is a deeply spiritual man who harbours no illusions, either about his glorious past or his responsibilities as a concerned citizen of the earth. Liberal in his politics, kind and compassionate by nature, he is quiet about the causes he generously supports.

The loss of John and George weighs heavily on Ringo, but inspires him to live each day in as uplifting a way as possible. It seems somehow fitting that this icon should be one of the last men standing from the magical time that spawned not only the Beatles but also the Rolling Stones, Jimi Hendrix, Bob Dylan, Woodstock and a generation of turned-on, spiritually conscious rock'n'roll seekers. It was not without good reason that one of Ringo's most recent albums was entitled *Vertical Man*.

In the end, when the Beatles and their original fans had all grown up and moved on, there was only the music, a living legacy of the genius of four young men from northern England. There was in them that most elusive and special of all gifts: pure magic. Although it can be marketed, managed, even bought and sold, magic can never be manufactured. It is a gift from God to the artist, and the artist to his audience. Finally, when the songs have all been sung, and the composers silenced by time, it is the magic, within the infinity of musical possibility, that will draw people together. The spark of a fire bigger than we will ever know.

Sources

The author has drawn from the following sources in the production of this work. In no case has the material used exceeded the limitations of the fair use statues.

Unpublished material

Author interviews and conversations with Paul McCartney, George and Olivia Harrison, Pete Best, Yoko Ono, Sean Lennon, Julian Lennon, Mike McCartney, Angela and Ruth McCartney, Harry Nilsson, Peter Brown, Derek Taylor, Alistair Taylor, Maharishi Mahesh Yogi, Gerry Marsden, Julia Baird, Bob Wooler, 'Legs' Larry Smith, Allan Williams, Norman Birch, Lila Harvey, Clive Epstein, George Speerin, Vivian Stanshall, Mary Hopkin, Mukunda Das Gosvami, Dhanajaya Das, Harry Harrison, Jo Jo Laine, Kirsten Grepne and Shambu Das.

The author has also drawn from previously unpublished correspondence from the Beatles, the private diaries of John Lennon, Mal Evans, Brian Epstein, Ravindra Damodara Swami, Kenny McCain as well as rare court documents relevant to the dissolution of the Beatles.

Internet Sites

ABCnews.com: 17 October 1998; 8 November 2001
Abbeyrd's Beatles page: Abbeyrd.best.vwh.net

Acosh.org
Animalrights.net: 12 October 1998
The Beatles Connection: suite101.com, 30 June 2000
Beatles First Wives Club: Shelovesyou.com
Blacklisted Journalist: Bigmagic.com
BBCNews.com: 26 October 1998; 25 July 2001; 23 October 2001; 13, 14 December 2001
Carnival of Light: Rockingvicar.com
Chakra.org
CNN.com: 31 December 1999; 3 January 2000; 26 July 2001
Dotmusic.com: November 2000
Eonlinenews.com: 23 April 1998; 3 May 2001
Evil Beatles: Stargods.org
George Harrison: Hariscruffs.com
Hollywoodunderground.com: 2 December 2001
Iamthebeatles.com
JacksonSun.com
Jam Music: canoe.ca/JamMusic
Maccacentral.com
MayPang.com
Mike Dolan's Transcendental Memories: www.trancenet.org/personal/dolan/midnight.shtml
Naqvi, Saeed: Yoga, Ragas, Holidays . . .: www.indianexpress.com/ie20011202/op2.html
Penny Lane: geocities.com/penneylayne
Peopleonline.com: 17 January 2000
Ringo Starr 1976 interview: geocities.com/~beatleboy1
Rockabillyhall.com: 26 October 1996
RMB: rec.music.beatles
Showbizmusic.com: 23 April 1998
Straitstimes.asia1.com
UK.music.yahoo.com
VHI News Wire: VHI.com: 29 June 1998
Zakstarkey.com

Periodicals

Asian Age: 18 November 2000
Beatles Book Monthly, 1963–1970
Boston Globe: 3 December 2001
Classic Rock News: 21 September 1998
Daily Mirror: 21 April 1998; 6 January 2000; 11 November 2001
Detroit News: May 2002
Entertainment Weekly: 20 April 2002
Fabulous: February 1964
Flip: May 1965
GQ: October 2000
Guardian: 31 December 1999; 31 December 2000
Hit Parader: January 1968
International Times: March 1971
Jam Music: 2 March 2000
Observer, London: 9 July 2000
Mail on Sunday: 22 July 2001
Mojo: April 2002
McCall's: May 1993
New York Daily News: 22 November 2001
New World: 18 June 1998
OK: 6 March 1998
People: 12 March 1998
Pop Art Times (date unknown)
Rolling Stone: 12 February 1976
Salon: 8 December 2000; 3 August 2001
Star Bulletin: 25 August 2002
Sunday: 7 May 1992
Sunday People: 1 April 2001
Time: 30 November 2001
The Times, London: 21 April 1998
USA Today: 25 January 2001

Books

Badman, Keith, *The Beatles: After the Break-up 1970–2000*, Omnibus Press, 1999
—, *The Beatles off the Record*, Omnibus Press, 2002
The Beatles Anthology, Chronicle Books, 2002
Bedford, Carol, *Waiting for the Beatles*, Blandford Press, 1984
Benson, Ross, *Paul McCartney: Behind the Myth*, Gollancz, London, 1992
Brown, Peter and Gaines, Steven, *The Love You Make*, McGraw-Hill, NY, 1983

Clayson, Alan and Sutcliffe, Pauline, *Backbeat*, Trans-Atlantic Publications, 1994
Coleman, Ray, *Lennon: The Definitive Biography*, Perennial, 1992
—, *The Man Who Made the Beatles*, Sidgwick & Jackson Limited, London, 1984

Davies, Hunter, *The Beatles: The Authorized Biography*, McGraw-Hill, NY, 1968
DeWitt, Howard, *The Beatles Untold Tales*, Horizon Books, 1985
Dowlding, William, *Beatlesongs*, Fireside, 1989

Engelhardt, Kristofer, *Beatles Undercover*, Collector's Guide Publishing, 1998

Farrow, Mia, *What Falls Away*, Bantam Doubleday Dell, 1997
Fink, Mitchell, *Off the Record: An Oral History of Popular Music*, Warner Books, NY, 1988

Giuliano, Geoffrey, *The Beatles: A Celebration*, St. Martin's Press, NY, 1986
—, *Blackbird: The Unauthorized Biography of Paul McCartney*, Dutton, NY 1991
—, *Dark Horse: The Life and Art of George Harrison*, Dutton, NY, 1990
—, *The Illustrated John Lennon*, Sunburst Books, London, 1993
—, *John Lennon Forever* (unpublished)
—, *Lennon in America*, Robson Books, London, 2000
—, *The Lost Beatles Interviews*, Penguin Books, NY, 1994
—, *The Lost Lennon Interviews*, Adams Media, Massachusetts, 1996
—, *Two of Us: John Lennon and Paul McCartney Behind the Myth*, Penguin Studio, NY, 1999

—, and Baird, Julia, *John Lennon: My Brother*, Henry Holt & Company, 1988
—, Giuliano, Brenda and Black, Deborah Lynn, *The Illustrated Eric Clapton*, Sunburst Books, London, 1994
—, and Devi, Vrnda, *Glass Onion: The Beatles in Their Own Words*, Da Capo Press, 1999
—, *Things We Said Today: Conversations with the Beatles*, Adams Media, Massachusetts, 1998
Goldman, Albert, *The Lives of John Lennon*, William Morrow & Company, 1988

Harrison, George, *I Me Mine*, Simon & Schuster, 1983
Harry, Bill, *The Beatles Encyclopaedia*, Virgin Publishing, 2001
Hutchins, Chris and Thompson, Peter, *Elvis Meets the Beatles*, Smith Gryphon, 1994

Lewisohn, Mark, *The Beatles Recording Sessions*, Harmony Books, 1988
—, *The Complete Beatles Chronicle*, Hamlyn, 2000
Lennon, Cynthia, *A Twist of Lennon*, Star Books, 1978
Lennon, Pauline, *Daddy, Come Home*, Angus & Robertson, 1990

Miles, Barry, *Paul McCartney: Many Years From Now*, Secker & Warburg, London, 1997

Pritchard, David and Lysaght, Alan, *The Beatles: An Oral History*, Hyperion Books, NY, 1998

Saltzman, Paul, *The Beatles In Rishikesh*, Viking Press, 2000
Sheff, David, *The Playboy Interviews with John Lennon and Yoko Ono*, Putnam, 1981
Shotton, Pete, *John Lennon: In My Life*, Coronet, 1984
Sutcliffe, Pauline and Thomas, Douglas, *The Beatles' Shadow*, Sidgwick & Jackson, 2001

Taylor, Alistair, *Yesterday: My Life with the Beatles*, Pioneer Books, 1991
Taylor, Derek, *As Time Goes By*, Straight Arrow Books, San Francisco, 1973
Turner, Steve, *A Hard Day's Write*, HarperCollins, 1999

Wenner, Jann, *Lennon Remembers*, Verso Books, 2000
Wiener, Allen, *The Beatles: The Ultimate Recording Guide*, Bob Adams Inc, 1994
Williams, Allan, *The Man Who Gave The Beatles Away*, Macmillan, 1975

Broadcast Sources

CNN: *Larry King Live*, 12 June 2001
Francie Schwartz interview, Westwood One
The Frost Programme, BBC: 29 September; 4 October 1967
Grammy Awards, NBC: 18 May 1965
John and Yoko on *How Late It Is*, BBC: 2 May 1969
Kenny Everett interview, BBC: 9 June 1968
Mal Evans interview, KCSN: 25 & 29 November 1975
Paul McCartney interview, Julia Radio
Paul McCartney interview, Radio Luxembourg: 21 November 1968
Paul McCartney Routes of Rock, BBC: 20 & 27 October; 3 & 10 November 1999
Ringo Starr on *Howard Stern*: 1 August 2001
Ringo Starr on *Late Night Line-Up*, BBC: 10 December 1969
Where It's At, BBC: 20 May 1967

Audio (all dates refer to the recording date)

Al Capp/Lennon conversation: 1 June 1969
Beatle speech: 8 November 1965
Get Back sessions: 2–31 January 1969
Harrison, Lennon, Starr interview, Bangor, North Wales: 27 August 1967
Harrison/Lennon interview, KHJ Radio Special: 21 December 1974
I'm The Greatest session tape: 13 March 1973
Kyoko/Lennon tape, Denmark: January 1970
Lennon/McCartney reunion session: 28 March 1974
Lennon/Ono Tape: late May 1968
"Maharishi Song": April 1969–1972
Mike Love Tape, Rishikesh Ashram: 15 March 1968
Rishikesh Tape, TV7: 29 February 1968
Yoko Ono audio diary: 4 June 1968
Yoko Ono primal therapy diary: April–August 1970

The Editorial Team

Geoffrey Giuliano: The world's most lauded and prolific Beatles biographer is the author of over thirty books and eighty spoken word CDs on popular music and culture. Websites: geoffrey-giuliano.com & puripada.com. E-mail: info@geoffrey-giuliano.com.

Deborah Lynn Black: Mr Giuliano's long-time writing and researching partner heads up the editorial team with three years of painstaking detailed research and superlative organizational skills. A celebrated author and journalist in her own right, her work has appeared internationally in many of the world's top periodicals. She is co-author with Geoffrey of several popular titles.

Vrnda Devi: Ms Devi is the co-author of several of Geoffrey Giuliano's books and the author of *Compassionate Cuisine*, a lacto-vegetarian cookbook and philosophical work on the science, history and culture of non-violent eating. Her next book is called *Recipes For A Holy Life / Thai Secrets Of Inner Peace & Beauty*. Website: vrnda.com. E-mail: vrnda@vrnda.com & info@vrnda.com.

Erek Barsczewski: At nineteen years old Mr Barsczewski already possesses an astounding knowledge of the Beatles and an incredible aptitude for research, organization and writing. As executive researcher on this project, Erek uncovered much of the rarest material included in this book. Without his selfless dedication and discipline much of the exclusive information in this work would certainly have been lost forever to time. E-mail: erekbeatles@hotmail.com.

Avalon Giuliano (Ananda Manjari): Avalon is associate researcher on the forth-coming *The Harrison Chronicles / George Harrison In His Own Words*, and several other Giuliano family works including *Carry That Weight*. Avalon is the musically talented middle daughter of Geoffrey and Vrnda. E-mail: manjari108@hotmail.com.

The authors are deeply indebted to the following people for their kind assistance in the production of this work.

The Robert Smith Literary Agency, Robert Allen, Robert Baker, Sriman Symananda Dasa Bramachari, Tiffany Marie Brant, Sriman Bramananda Dasa, Sriman Garagamuni Dasa, Krishna Kanta Devi Dasi, Krishna Kirtan Caju, Seth Spellman Esq., Catrina Marie Angelica Giuliano, Devin Giuliano, Gianna Sky Giuliano, India Skye Giuliano, Sesa Giuliano, Goose Gray, Sri Radhe International Inc., SRI / The Spiritual Realization Institute, Cera & Geneva Johnson, Kashi Nath Narayana Jones, Varsana Nicole Jones, Larry Kahn, Mai Kaidee, Lance Kutchabella, Bhakti Promode Puri Maharaja, Miles Ross, Dr Martin Schiffert, David St Onge and John Barry Sylvano.

Index